ON BREAKING ONE'S PENCIL

And Other Vagrant Thoughts: Essays from a Curious Mind

Robert T. Sorrells

FriesenPress

Suite 300 - 990 Fort St
Victoria, BC, Canada, V8V 3K2
www.friesenpress.com

Copyright © 2016 by Robert T. Sorrells
Photography by Bonita
First Edition — 2016

All rights reserved.

No part of this publication may be reproduced in any form, or by any means, electronic or mechanical, including photocopying, recording, or any information browsing, storage, or retrieval system, without permission in writing from the publisher.

ISBN
978-1-4602-8224-3 (Paperback)
978-1-4602-8225-0 (eBook)

1. Biography & Autobiography, Personal Memoirs

Distributed to the trade by The Ingram Book Company

CONTENTS

Foreword..i

PLACES
   New York...1
   Pelham Manor, New York: A Boy's Idyll..................5
   Nashville: A Love Song..29
   Clemson...74
   TQ95DZ...97

WRITING ADVICE
   Letter to a Student..113

CHURCH MATTERS
   Doris Grumbach and Prayer.................................141
   About Churches..142
   Shape-Note Intro..147
   "Then Take it Seriously": A Shibboleth Made Real.....150
   Creeds and Covenants..153
   Thank You...155
   Forgotten or Ignored?...159
   Previously Published Essays..................................163
   The Gift of Language..165
   What Have We Taught Them?..............................176

The Game: Originally published in *Aethlon: the Journal of Sport Literature* XI:1 Fall 1993 185
You in There, Us Out Here 201
First Meditation 210
Second Meditation 213
Third Meditation 216
Fourth Meditation 220
Fifth Meditation 224

ESSAYS

Hawarya? 233
Rediscovering the Humanities 252
Some Thoughts on the Gee Affair: Revisiting a Recollection
with Hopes For Something Approaching Tranquility 274
Bob Dole and the March of Time 283
A Reflection: "What's Past is Prologue" 283
Once More into the Breech 298

-30-

I Never Heard My Father Sing 311
What Do You Think? 328
You Were Not Too Late, Mr. Truman 331
Bill 334
Dear Moe and Family 347
A Gift of Uncles 351
The Singer 358

-30-

Robert T. Sorrells 369

FOREWORD

I INITIALLY CONCEIVED OF THIS book as a personal and private matter—a sort of sweeping up of essays I had written but which, for the most part, had not been published. I then realized that I wanted it to be a little bit more than that. I realized that what I am most proud of as a writer is the variety of both my writing and the audiences for which I have written, while continuing to be a fiction writer: "serious" fiction in university quarterlies and journals as well as in *Penthouse* and *Playgirl*; and book reviews, personality profiles, features, and news items for Clemson University's tabloid *CU News* and its faculty/staff newsletter, and while living in Rochester, Minnesota, where my wife was the minister of the First Unitarian Universalist Church there, I was a volunteer at the Mayo Clinic leading Art Tours as well as writing articles for their quarterly publication *Mayo News*.

Back in the early sixties I wrote brochures for special projects while working for Vanderbilt University's Development Office during a 30 Million Dollar Capital Gifts campaign, and during the seventies and eighties wrote slide/tape scripts for Clemson University as well as a 30-minute film on land use for the state of South Carolina, plus a number of radio programs for the South Carolina Educational Radio Network (SCERN at the time, now ETV Radio).

Beyond that I have written publicity; papers delivered at scholarly meetings of the South Atlantic Modern Language Association (SAMLA) while I was **not** a member of anybody's English Department; the initial draft of a minor speech for Clemson's then president; and the citation for an honorary degree being presented to a state senator by the University.

While an editor/writer for Clemson's Department of Publications and Graphics Services, I worked on typical copy-writing chores: fliers, recruitment brochures, posters, tent cards, annual budgets, annual reports, etc.

In 1983 I was commissioned to write a history of the Clemson Experimental Forest to mark the fiftieth anniversary of its founding.

...

Otherwise, I have received grants from the National Endowment for the Arts (Individual Grants to Writers, 1978); the South Carolina Committee for the Humanities to create a pilot radio program for the SCERN entitled "Rediscovering the Humanities" (1981), and a PEN/NEA Syndicated Fiction Award (1983).

My book of stories—*The Blacktop Champion of Ickey Honey*—was published by the University of Arkansas Press in 1988, and for a number of years was available through the services of the Authors Guild and *i-universe.com*.

...

I have arranged these pieces into six sections which more or less cohere internally: **Places, Writing Advice, Church Matters, Previously Published Essays, Essays, All in the Family**, and **-30-.**

PLACES

NEW YORK

MY SOUTH WAS A HEARD thing starting first with the Pine Bluff, Arkansas, accents of my mother and father in our apartment in the Tudor City section of New York City. That address was 345 E. 41st Street, and was a double apartment with a hole knocked through to make one place for my parents and their then three children.

I don't remember any of that, naturally—except for the stories that swirled around for a while, drifting at last into nearly still eddies, the silences of time hushed by the imperatives of having to deal with the details of current life.

What I knew or felt I couldn't possibly remember, but I was told that it was my brother, John, who held me in the taxi when my mother took me home from the hospital to our apartment. Again, I can't remember, but I think it's verified in the details of my later life after my father died, and then my mother, too, when it was my oldest brother who became my surrogate father. I expect there were reasons for that.

When I was born, James J. Walker was the mayor of New York City. I have read that he was a fabulist of sorts, probably a crook, always an entertainer. I gather, further, that his main problem was he never made the distinction between his beloved stage and his mayor's office. Still, New Yorkers seemed to love him, and what the hell, New York is New York.

But *my* mayor was Fiorello LaGuardia, the "Little Flower." My main sports hero was Joe Louis, and my main man was Franklin D. Roosevelt. They were the triumvirate I grew up under. Later, there were others: my father; of course; Robert Watson, a black man with a stutter, whom I loved dearly; the Brooklyn Dodgers; Doc Blanchard and Glenn Davis, the "Mr. Inside" and "Mr. Outside" of Army football teams in the forties; John W. Vandercook whose mother, Margaret, gave me an autographed copy of his book *Black Majesty* because of an impassioned defense of FDR I had made—had cadged, actually, from a radio program I had just been listening to—at a cocktail party in my parents' home in Pelham: She had dated her inscription November 5, 1940, election day; and it came with a note that read,

> Dear Bobby,
>
> I don't believe you'll remember me, but
> I wore the red velvet jacket at [your] mother's party last
> Saturday, and you and I both were for Roosevelt. I
> am sending you this book my son wrote with my best
> wishes. Perhaps you'll be a writer some day, or maybe
> President.
>
> Sincerely yours, Margaret W. Vandercook.

Eventually, of course, there were more: Kenneth Grahame's *The Wind in the Willows*; J.R. Williams, the cartoonist of *Out Our Way* and *Born Thirty Years Too Soon*; Holling C. Holling's *The Book of Cowboys*, which I still have and still re-read occasionally. And much later Edmund Rostand, Dylan Thomas…

But I was talking about New York. Though I was well and very comfortably brought up, being born in 1932 did things to a lot of people in this country. It was the heart of the heart of the Depression, a time FDR referred to as "these crushing days of want," and though by 1932 the actual crash of 1929 had come and gone, its effects were by no means over. The causes of the greatest economic failure we've ever endured, apparently, are varied and complex, but well worth recalling—even through my own hazy, layman's understanding—because they brutally marked an entire generation or more, including that "greatest" one which Tom Brokaw spoke of so lovingly and with such admiration, and which at the very least partially accounts for so vast a gap in understanding between generations. The experiences of the folks born between about 1920 to about 1940—the early Depression Babies and the Baby Boomers or Gen Xers of later times—are almost as though talking about two totally different countries. This nation in 1930 bore almost no resemblance to that of 1960—never mind 1990 or 2015, for God's sake!

During the First World War, American farmers became more productive than they had ever been before. There was a need, there was a market, and there was a will to produce…produce…and produce yet some more. We had an increasing population at home to feed, and we had a large portion of Europe to feed because the ravages of that entrenched war were destroying not only Europe's future—more than 10,000,000 of their young men killed—but their ability to produce their own food and fiber crops. If it hadn't been for Herbert Hoover and the Belgian Relief which he organized and headed, millions more civilians in northern France and Belgium would have starved to death during the German occupation. America didn't get into the War until it had been going on for nearly three years, a fact which helps explain some of our towering increase in production: We weren't having to manufacture gunpowder instead of fertilizer, or caissons instead of tractors. And because foreign markets were so desperate, prices were abnormally high. Thus farmers had an incentive to produce as much as they could.

With the end of the War in 1918, the returning veterans came back to work, and in America at the time, jobs, to a very great extent, meant agricultural jobs. As late as 1929 farming constituted 25 percent of total employment in the United States. In 1919-20 there was a world-wide boom when nations were hustling to replace the inventories that had been depleted during the war years. This was followed by a brief recession, which in its turn was followed by one of the most sustained periods of boom we—or any other nation in the world—had ever seen. For about ten years a tidal wave of goods swept across the land, and with the increasing surges of manufacturing magic came parallel waves of buoyant enthusiasm on the part of our citizens, still high from "winning" The War to End All Wars. There was such a feeling of inevitability about the wealth and power and progress associated with our having come of age, that virtually no one bothered to question how long the swell of prosperity could last. The possibility that it might end seemed not only absurd, but downright unpatriotic as well.

But banks started to fail in the first half of 1929. It started off as a regular enough sort of day, but when 20,000 shares of GM stock showed up for sale in one block, people who were already jittery got positively nervous, and those who were already nervous, got absolutely panicky. That was the day the only thing finally to be heard on Wall Street was the increasingly frantic roar of "Sell!" But there was nobody around who could buy. At last we were made to focus our attention on those economic problems which had been building for so long, that collapse which was as predictable as darkness after the sun sets.

Those were the times that clutched *my* soul in a smothering grip to mark me as their own, surrounding my early years with the terrors of their presence just as surely as though I had known all about them. I have sometimes wondered what I might have seen in that infancy, what I might have heard that I will never, ever be able to summon up.

PELHAM MANOR, NEW YORK

A Boy's Idyll

THE HEARTBREAKING ANGUISH OF A return to a place of one's past is the anguish of seeing all the changes all at once. It's like not looking in a mirror for twenty years: there is bound to be a jolt to the mind if not the glass, a shock rippling across the surface and down, deep into the image and past it to the quick-silver. It is all gone; so much gone, past, passed: irretrievably, irreparably done with. Something like that.

I don't know whether I would have liked Pelham if I had stayed through high school or not. I left, is the thing, after grades three through eight. It wasn't precisely a choice of my own. I "chose" to go to Staunton Military Academy in Staunton, Virginia. That was in 1946. (A note here: it was my oldest brother who initially *wanted* to go to SMA because he had wanted to be a soldier since about age three; my older brother was *sent* to SMA because he had what currently would be called "issues," and I—being the youngest and final and most naïve child—went because I more or less assumed that's how we did things in our family.) We moved into an apartment back in New York City then, but in February of that next year (1948) my father died quite unexpectedly and my mother and I moved to Memphis—back to Memphis, for my Mother.

Basically I didn't get back to Pelham until 1956, then a visit in 1958, then 1978, then 1997. If the dates aren't exact, they're close enough to make the point.

But Pelham as I knew it from the summer of 1940 through the summer of 1946 was a boy's idyll. It was a grand place to grow up in because even though it was a suburb of New York City, it was also a place of its own, with its own long history, with a center, or centers, to the life there: Four Corners; the Pelham Theater; Butch, the motorcycle cop; Fourth of July parades and bazaars on the athletic fields at the high school; stink field; the public library in New Rochelle; and the trolley cars (electric, ding-ding-ding). There was a sense of time (World War II), of place (the Three Pelhams), and of security and serenity. That last isn't complete fabrication, either. Boys can have and grow up with a sense of serenity even if their personal lives—their emerging pubescence, for example—are anything but serene.

...

We didn't stay in the Tudor City complex of New York City (across the street from the UN these days) very long after I was born, only about nine months, I think, but maybe as much as a year and a half. Then we moved to Chappaqua, where my memory of the world began, where distinct images stay with me always.

There was Robert, the jack-of-all-trades who worked for us, who—quite accidentally (well more or less)—shot a deer in our front yard. There was also a set of mounted antlers in our basement. I don't know if they were from the deer Robert shot or not. I expect not.

There was a blueberry field, I think, fairly near where we lived, and I see my mother with a bunch of us out there. (But here, as always, memory can play tricks. Are there blueberries in Westchester County? Were they blackberries instead?)

There was the backyard apple tree I loved to climb, with a fairly low branch I draped myself over, like a sated leopard, early one morning—well before breakfast—when I had to admit to my mother with only the embarrassed, silent show of all the fingers on my right hand how many of the green apples I had eaten.

There was a crib in my bedroom (for me), and a bed for my older brother. I think they both left the bedroom before we moved.

There was a stalled commuter train we saw from the car my mother was driving. The train had stopped, for some unknown reason, on the tracks—pretty well below the level of the road we were on. The conductor was outside, periodically tossing switches cut from willows near the tracks under the train which then mysteriously lurched ahead several feet each time. Somehow I am stuck thinking my father was on the train and we were trying to meet him, though that makes no more sense than the actions I remember of the conductor.

There was the nursery school down the road from us, which in my memory will always be redolent with graham crackers and orange juice; and there was the huge plow horse we all got to ride sometimes, our legs sticking out from its massive back like fat rolls of clay from the round, squeezed torso of a child's morning creation, and the grief I felt when I heard the horse had died. I forget its name, but *Jerry* comes to mind.

I don't know where it happened, but I have in my memory a yard like the one in Chappaqua, a deep expanse with a couple of grass terraces breaking up the straight shot down to the hedges and fence that marked us off from the road in front. I remember rolling down the hill, but apparently had a coat hanger with me and fell on the sharp hook of it, hurting myself. But that could have been in Pittsburgh in the back yard of Ed Leech ("Uncle Ed," we called him in the good old Southern way of dealing with close but unrelated friends) editor of the *Pittsburgh Press*.

What I *do* clearly remember is being in my parents' bedroom one day sitting on one of their twin beds. I had one leg crossed over the other and was carrying on a serious conversation with my mother. My father may have been in the room, but I'm not really sure about that.

At one point mother just looked at me and somehow conveyed a certain amazement.

"You're just like your grandfather," she said. "It's uncanny: the way you cross your legs, the way you move your hands when you talk…"

My grandfather—my *father's* father—had died, followed by his wife five minutes later, in May of the year I was born.

In 1936, after three years (or possibly just two) in Chappaqua, we moved to Scarsdale, where I first remember being scared.

Not really scared, probably, but nervous. If I was really scared my older brother, Bill, likely had a hand in it. Like many an older brother, I suspect, he encouraged that sort of thing. What it was, was a shadow in my bedroom, a shadow I took to be Robert in a top hat. Robert himself didn't scare me, unless I had been misbehaving and he threatened to tell my parents. But during the night, the shadow on my ceiling, as it folded down onto the wall where the Venetian blinds were pulled against the dark of the outside, was a strange and sometimes disconcerting phenomenon. My brother tried to find out if Robert had a top hat. As I suppose we expected, he didn't.

As a rule, the night didn't frighten me. Thinking about it now, the dark never seemed actively to protect so much as passively to conceal me from whatever needed to be feared. It wasn't until later, in Pelham, after I had started to read the tabloids' eager stories of the City's violence and unspeakable horrors, that a vision of the world as a force leaning more and more heavily against the pales of my life started to take shape: that the world was a place where there were people who not only didn't love me, but who positively meant me harm. The tabloids and the train rides into Grand Central Station.

That ride from Pelham, where we moved in the summer of 1940, was thirty-two minutes, according to the schedule, and two of the stops were Columbus Avenue and 125th Street. The Columbus Avenue stop was pretty bad, but the 125th Street was the terror for me. On one side of the station was the *125th Street Hotel*. On the other side was, as I recall, the *Naomi*. Both were old, deteriorated places when I was a boy, and populated, I always assumed, by transients. I always wondered who they were. They were very poor, the area was terribly dirty. Well, *dirty* isn't the word, of course. It was filthy in the way blighted city streets are filthy: garbage, blowing papers, piles of trash: a total sense of disorder and threat. The only sign of some kind of community I sensed was the harsh leavening of kids, now and then, playing serious stick ball in the street.

But mainly—Bill and I used to talk about it—I remember the men in the summer dress of their undershirts leaning from the windows of their rooms and staring: some into the streets, some across the street, some at nothing I could see. I don't remember that anyone ever stared at the train or at me.

And I remember one other vivid image. One day in the City I was in our car with my father. Robert was driving—in livery, no less (yes, I was one of Brabantio's "curlèd darlings of the nation")—and we had come to a stoplight. While the cross traffic moved and right before the light changed, a bum—remember, this was the 30's or 40's and "Street People" were called bums, hobos, and panhandlers then—leaped onto the running board and asked Robert for a handout. Or at least it was clear that's what he wanted. I really don't remember a voice so much as a murmur. But in the most practiced air of a New Yorker, Robert waved him away with a snarling, "Nah!

Nah!" It was a tone and a gesture I'd never heard or seen in Robert before, and that unsettled me.

I can't say for sure that I remember what the man looked like. I seem to recall a checked or tweedy jacket: old, dirty, worn. He needed a shave. He was wearing a hat, I think, what's now called a driving cap. When he cupped his hand slightly for the hoped-for bill or change, I could see his nails black against his dirty wrist. The whole thing couldn't have taken more than three seconds. But it terrified me, and the odd thing is that I never felt personally threatened. If anything, I was mortally embarrassed to be in the Cadillac. That seemed wrong to me when people like that man were out there hustling nickels and dimes.

I was just a boy—eight or nine years old, maybe. I don't think the War had started for us yet, because not too many months after Pearl Harbor we donated the Caddy to the government. Who had gas for a Cadillac? But the country had just gotten its nose and mouth up out of the Depression. So it was late 1940 or early 1941 possibly. It doesn't seem likely I would have had any *thoughts* about that, but—coupled with the *125th Street Hotel*—they were *images*, visions of an evil surrounding me, terrible things that could destroy me simply because I was in their way. Like Paricutin, the volcano that came up in some poor Mexican's corn field in 1943 when I was still in grade school, or the 1939 hurricane that tore so brutally through New York, the one I watched from the bay windows of my sister's bedroom in Scarsdale, sensing my mother's own anxiety about the terrible wind, the floods of water whipping down.

Years later, I linked the image of the man who tried to get a handout from us with the pictures of the prisoners at Dachau or Belsen or Buchenwald, the pictures taken as they were freed. They simply stared at the light, at the American soldiers, and at the freedom they didn't recognize at first; or with that photo of the American soldier in Korea—a medic, I think—who was so tired from the combat, the weariness, the death all around, the collapsed emotions of the other soldier he held; and Dorothea Lange's classic "White Angel Breadline," the one taken just a few years before—or possibly after—I was born, of an old man with his back to the others in the soup line, his forearms across a fence, his tin cup sitting empty on the top rail. *Abandon Hope*, concluded the sign over the portal to Dante's Hell. *Abandon Hope All Ye Who Enter Here.*

And astride my life until the beginning of the Second World War, actually, abating only after Pearl Harbor, was the Lindberg kidnapping, an event that seemed to put its special mark on an age and seems, from here, like an eerie prelude to the balance finally shattered by the *Krystal-nacht* when kidnappers and murderers had become the State itself.

Well, the Lindberg business stuck around up East, somehow informing my entire life at the time, and even now the thought of it sets up an unpleasant nervousness in me, an apprehension that whispers of horrors so terrible we can never even guess what they might be.

Aside from the panhandler, though, and the ghost of Lindberg, three things frightened me while I lived in Pelham. The first, a one-legged teenager across from the public library in New Rochelle, the next town north and east of us; second, the tough kids from Mount Vernon, the town bordering us on the other side, who sometimes edged over into "our" territory on Stink Field where a bunch of us played our baseball all summer; and third, an event I saw in the woods right next to our house in the fall during the season of burning leaves.

...

The New Rochelle Public Library was a brick building, as I recall, built, probably, in some Classic mode or other. I got there on the trolley, which was part of the whole scene in that section of New York in those days: straw seats, dinging bell, and all. ("Ding, ding, ding went the trolley/ Clang, clang, clang went the bell/ Zing, zing, zing went my heartstrings/ From the moment I saw you I fell.")

I got on at Four Corners in Pelham, and got off not too far into New Rochelle. The library was on the right hand side of the street—US 1, by the way, the Boston Post Road—and so was easy to get to.

Going up the steps, I would always realize that I was about to enter another world, the center of whatever life of fancy and imagination or even incipient erudition I might have had.

Inside, there was a large round room, as I recall, with the circulation desk at its center. All I remember about the librarians was that they were there, that they marked the books for return dates, that they *did* check my library card, and that on one or two occasions they might have questioned the appropriateness of a book I was checking out. Otherwise, they were nice enough: as friendly and helpful as need be. But I seldom had to deal with them until I was ready to leave.

I would circle the round rooms, usually in the children's section, finding every possible book about horses I could. Books about pony trekking in England. Books about how to ride horseback. Books about black stallions, others about their returns. Books about how to draw horses. It was such magic for me, that library: high ceilings, wonderfully sun-lighted windows, and the aroma of the books that is as lasting as ever the fragrance of the madeleines was to Marcel Proust bolstered and cosseted about in his bed.

Sometimes I would go with one of my friends, and that was all right. The trolley was more fun that way. But when we got into the library, I felt pressured. It seemed that whoever it might happen to have been always said—or looked like they were thinking—"Let's get our book and go." I felt that I was always holding him up and that my attitude about libraries must have been terribly different from most people's, if what they wanted was to get the book and *Go!* I was going to get my books, all right, but the object was to take as much time as I could. To *see* them, to *feel* them. Oh my God, to *SMELL* the gorgeous things.

Sometimes, the object seemed to be to avoid finding a book to take back home. What I needed on those days was simply to *be* there for all the rest of the stuff that was part of the library. To read things right on the spot, for instance, was a good way to go lots of times. Or to look at magazines. Or people, even, as they went through the Stages of their own Ways. Or just to sit with a newspaper across my knees, pretending to read, while really just listening to the whispery quietness.

But one day, a winter day blustery with snow showers, it was finally time to get back home. Dark, early, winter days for young kids from Pelham were best not spent too late on the streets of New Rochelle. It was a Saturday, I expect, about 3:30, mid-December, and my friend and I finally headed out of the warmth from the books and crossed the Post Road to the trolley stop. We must have just missed a car, because we seemed to wait a long time and were getting cold.

What we usually did when that happened, though, was to stare into the window of a doughnut-making shop just right nearby. There was a machine that made the doughnuts, and the owner was canny enough to have put the thing right there where people could see the transformation of dough to doughnut, starting with the circular squirt of goo down into the small vat of hot grease which flowed gently, carrying the cooking batter along until it passed over a comb-like device that flipped the doughnuts over so they would cook on the other side. Then they were lifted off by another comb to fall into a collecting bin until someone in the shop made their periodic rounds to carry the doughnuts somewhere else to be sugared, powdered, glazed, chocolated, or finished off in whatever other wondrous ways there were.

So we were watching all that going on, our ears trained by usage to listen for the *skreeek* of the trolley's wheels or the warning clang of its bell. But I glanced up at one point—no doubt sensing some unpleasant thing about to happen—and saw them coming. There were three of them, and the meanest looking had only one leg.

One real leg and a false one, false like no leg I'd ever seen in my life. It was like a crutch, the bottom half of an aluminum crutch with the rubber piece on the tip and everything. It was, as I recall it, only two or three tubes of metal that came down to a point where it touched the ground. How he attached the thing to his body I couldn't guess.

There was something ferret-like about him, something as thin and hard looking as that leg, his face pinched, drawn in: a Dead End Kid, but real. And twitchy, his eyes looking all around taking everything in, ready for—as well as willing to make—trouble.

And he had two buddies with him, kids who looked as tough as himself, but a little afraid of him, buddies or not.

I poked my friend. He looked at me, then up the street to where I was looking.

"Oh no," I heard him whisper. It was an involuntary little expulsion of breath. Both of us looked past them hoping to see the trolley. They saw us, and the one-legged kid steered them straight our way with a jab of his chin.

Nothing really happened. They intimidated us by their looks, their clear intent to wander the path of threat awhile just to see where it might take them. An adventure. Something to tell the guys about later or, possibly worse, forget altogether. Some primitive form of getting even with our world which so clearly was not anything like theirs, which might even have caused the head guy to have to wear a false leg that looked like a strange, homemade, underbuilt superstructure. They might have tried to shake us down—demand some money for doughnuts, maybe. Maybe even rough us up some. Grab a hat and run. Grab a book and chuck it into the street. Who could tell? Those things happened around there.

But then salvation came. I can't even remember his name now, but he was the Boy Scout who was our Cub Scout pack leader. He was a true Big Guy (the toughs were bigger than we were, but not as big as he was).

We saw him at the same time and yelled to him, waving. He was striding down the sidewalk, cocky and self-assured looking like a race horse prancing to the starting gate, his Navy, three-quarter P-coat (possibly come from a big brother or an uncle in the War?) flapping open in the cold, and he was coming right for the trolley stop, too.

Whether the three toughs were ready to move on anyway, or whether they didn't want to tangle with him I don't know. But he came, they left, and the three of us got on the trolley that came right behind him. It rocked its way south, clanging for Pelham, and those hard, cold, straw seats felt better and better until the two of us got off at Four Corners, safe, while our Savior stayed on until he got to his stop a few blocks on down the line. He waved us goodbye as we got off, without ever saying a thing the whole trip about the kid with the crutch leg, even after we told him how glad we were he'd happened along just then. He'd just nodded and let us talk.

...

The Mount Vernon toughs were a different matter. They never showed. They existed mainly in our imaginations. Mainly, not totally. There were documented cases. People we knew who had been caught down there at Stink Field and been chased off. Or, worse, depanted.

That was the big cruelty then. Let a bunch of guys catch some kid they didn't like, and the result was that they would hold him down and strip him of his pants, though never of his underpants, from anything I'd ever heard. After, any number of things could happen. They'd run away with the pants, which were never to be seen again. Or the trousers ended up in a tree. Or soaked in Stink Creek then tied in knots. Whatever, the Poor De-panted was left to wend his weary way home facing the public humiliation of not having on any trousers. If that happened to me, then what if I met Barbara Henriques, or Oldriska Peniczek, the two most beautiful women in the world? Or *Frances Sommers*, for goodness sake, she with the gorgeous honey-blond hair and the pink sweater with its sleeves rolled up to her elbows, and the plaid skirt; she who had recently moved up from Louisiana, whose Southern way of talking was almost more than a committed anti-Yankee such as myself could stand to hear without laughing so brightly inside that people surely would have to have heard me! What kind of life would be left me then?

They never came, the Mount Vernon toughs. At least not when I was around.

We played baseball down there at Stink Field a lot in the summer, and I never once saw a tough from Mount Vernon come across the thin line that separated Us from Them. But we came automatically to keep a fairly sharp eye out in case. The stories grew. I believed them all. I feared for my safety, but never missed a game unless I was out of town.

Still, the fire was real enough. That was quite real.

...

I had been playing in my yard. It was a big yard, sweeping grandly (though nowhere nearly as deep as the one in Chappaqua) from the front of the house down to the street, with a side yard that had a huge boulder next to the driveway, a rock I loved to sit on and from which I could contemplate my world—both inner and beyond.

The back yard wasn't especially large, but plenty ample, and the area to one side and part of the rear were the back and side yards of other houses, and for the most part were stands of trees, certainly not forested by any means, but wonderful play areas for children, cats, and dogs.

There were sufficient trees and storm-downed branches so that in the summer we could skulk like Indians or, more likely in those days, like sneaky Germans readying a cowardly ambush for the unsuspecting American patrol, or brave Americans planning to ambush a squad of cowardly Krauts. I played back there a lot by myself, with my German helmet (sent me by my paratrooper brother from Europe), and my model rifle.

In the fall there were leaves enough to keep owners or yardmen busy raking for weeks. The earth around through there was rich, smelling of deep-down things. Refreshingly cool to the touch in summer, it started to feel crisp, as September days fell away like snapping skim ice lifted from a pond, a crispness that watered our mouths with thoughts about the apples coming down the Hudson Valley to us, and with *them* the promise of great pumpkins soon to be carved into the ghouls of Halloween, the pumpkins reminding us of the frosts to come, and pumpkin pies that would announce Thanksgiving, and when *that* blessed day arrived, why Christmas was practically there.

I think Autumn in that section of New York is as beautiful as anyplace I have ever lived. Other places are also beautiful—Fayetteville, Arkansas; Clemson, South Carolina; Rochester, Minnesota. But to me they're Falls, not the Autumns of my New York youth, misplaced Southerner or no.

Still, there is a dead time in there when every year I would sense the sweet unrest of the world's bounty, a time near late October or early November when the magic of the fall had finally run down, and the world was in stasis before the special treats of winter had begun. It was in that trough between seasons when I was frightened for the third time in Pelham, that idyllic home of my youth.

There wasn't all that much to it, not to *see*, in any event. What happened probably didn't take more than half a minute.

I was playing around in the front yard and up past the big rock on the side of the drive. Playing what, I don't begin to remember. I could have been chewing up my baseball bat by hitting small rocks out of Dodger Stadium like Duke Snyder. More likely at that time of year I was just lollygagging around waiting for Thanksgiving or simply letting the internal fires of a boy stir and roil me as they would.

But I saw the fellow raking leaves among the trees, and I saw the younger boy—older than I was, and possibly fourteen, maybe fifteen—over there near him. I don't know what had been going on between the two, but it looked to me like the youngster was ragging the fellow doing the raking, a *young* man, but certainly no longer a boy at all. Looking at them, no one would have figured a fight between them to be even.

I don't know what had caught my attention—a sudden shift in his movement, maybe. There had been a constant, smooth flow of motion, the raker steadily reaching and pulling, reaching and pulling, moving his small piles of leaves toward the fire, then deftly flipping them onto it.

But suddenly the steady movements of his work turned erratic, spastic, and the two of them were no more than three feet apart facing each other, the boy with the fire at his back. And then the raker's arm shot out and his hand or his fist caught the lad square in the chest. He fell back, his feet awkwardly trying to keep balance but failing, and just like that he was sitting down in the middle of the fire.

He leaped up, brushing his backside quickly, not quite frantically, then leaped again from the low, softly burning ring of fire and ran off.

The raker looked after him for no more than a second, then went back to his work: reaching, pulling, reaching, pulling, gathering up the detritus of the season into small piles, pulling the piles neatly, efficiently toward the fire, flicking them in without any apparent concern.

I kept still, staring at the scene, scared to move a finger. Nothing else happened. The boy didn't come back, the raker kept on with his raking, the fire burned on still under control. No one came around to yell or threaten or ask what in the world had happened that a fourteen-year-old had been violently shoved into a fire—no matter how small and controlled it may have been.

I piddled around a little, then went on in the house. The day was chilly, the dark was coming, and I wanted to talk to someone about what I had just seen. But there wasn't anyone there to talk to. The kitchen was dusky, still, but I knew people were in the house. My brother was probably up in his room doing some egg-headed thing that would push people to another kind of modest limit with him. Mother was probably just about ready to come down—from her sewing room, likely—to see about starting dinner. Dad wasn't home yet.

I got a jar of apple cider out of the icebox and thought about heating up a mugful. That's what I really wanted to do. I was about to look for some cinnamon sticks, but gave up on it and drank the juice cold. It was good, so I poured another glass and sat down at the long, plank breakfast table off the kitchen to eat some graham crackers with the cider. But I still felt chilled.

Later, there didn't seem much point in saying anything to anybody. What was there to say? What could they tell me? What did they know I didn't? *I* was the one who had seen it, after all. *I* was the one who already knew about it. *I* was the one that haunting image had locked on to by chance, that desperate symbol of something I have never yet understood.

The rest of the day and evening wore down as usual. Supper, then the radio, then some lessons, a bath, and bedtime. After a few minutes under the cool covers I was warm, and realized how nice that was. But as I turned the radio down low so Mother wouldn't know it was on—or at least couldn't hear it—I wondered again what had caused that terrible thing, that impulse on the part of the boy to bully or shame or whatever it had been, that frighteningly cool loss of control by the young man, and that chance vision of mine that bound the three of us into this violent, wordless, unholy, and inexplicable union, one which, in addition, only I knew about.

...

But Pelham was more than that. The years I lived there made it the home of my youth. Life is always a leavening of sorts, and when I think about Pelham, I think about freedom as well as fear, incredible freedom to wander and roam, nipping through the neighborhood backyards, wearing paths across the empty lots—the High Ways of my childhood.

There was Mr. Daily, for instance. He generally managed five double steps on the crutches before a rest on his way to Four Corners, three or maybe even just two on the way back. That depended on how many bottles of Ballentine's ale he'd had. His name was actually spelled *Daley*, of course, but we thought of him as Mr. *Daily*, mainly, I think, because we saw him nearly every day, saw him leaning into those crutches then swinging his body from the armpits down. It was *Creak* on the crutches and a solid *Thock!* as both heels of his wood-stuffed shoes hit the concrete sidewalks of home. *Creak, Thock!* five times, then a rest.

We knew nothing about him except that he lived in the third house from the corner on my street, the Esplanade, lived (obviously) with someone whose house looked out on a neatly trimmed front yard largely hidden by a hedge tall enough for most of us children not to be able to see over without really straining on tip-toes or leaping up jackrabbit style as we passed.

He often needed a shave, and lots of times his eyes were red-rimmed. In summer, he wore a white shirt and, often, a straw hat with a bashed-about look to it. Most of the time he sweat a good bit. But on his rests, he would wipe his face—an Irish face, I always thought—and if he saw any of us, he'd wave or nod his head with a glint in his eyes and a half grin on his fair but always ruddy face. He was probably at least forty-five, very likely much closer to sixty. It was hard to tell. But we all loved him.

At least, no one was afraid of him, and none of us ever talked ugly about him or thought up ingenious ways we could trip him or do him harm. He never did anything *for* any of us. Quite. He was pleasant in a slightly standoffish way. But pleasant in a way we understood: Mr. Daily liked to see us on his way to get his ale. He liked to talk to us a little if he had stopped. But we also knew he didn't want much in the way of company on his way home. Clearly he wasn't the least bit interested in being the neighborhood grandfather, any more than we wanted him to be.

Creak, Thock! Creak, Thock! He was Mr. Daily, a part of the scene. A pleasant part. And when it finally seeped into our heads that he must have died, because one day one of us remarked that he hadn't been around in months and months, there were many kids stunned into a silent and monstrous realization for the first time in their lives of what it means to say someone has died: They are gone and you never see them again.

Mr. Daily was gone, and with him the sounds of his coming and going; the musty smell of his too many years of drinking too many bottles of ale too many afternoons; the corners of his mouth spreading as he talked to us; his eyes looking like he'd like to get us into some slight devilment. Gone. All gone.

...

I was an ice-cream addict as a child—I like to think I got it from my father—and possibly still am, though it's under control by now. It was down at the ice cream-and-whatever store at Four Corners where I usually got my quarts, and I remember seeing Mr. Daily in there many a hot summer afternoon, or even on cold winter afternoons. We had our separate tastes and needs.

Four Corners was the crossroads of Pelham Manor in those days, and possibly still is. (There were Pelham, North Pelham, and Pelham Manor—the Three Pelhams, some often called them when they didn't choose to single out any particular one). It was the junction of U.S. 1 (the Boston Post Road) and Pelhamdale Avenue, which ran through most of the town. Four Corners was one of the major trolley stops in the area with a brown stucco police box on the southwest corner, catty-corner from a small shopping center where there was the drug store, and just around the corner a place where all of us kids got our major supplies of comic books, cheap toys (balsa wood gliders made for people like me: All you had to do was slide the wing and tail through the slots in the fuselage, take aim, and throw. It dipsy-doodled pretty well without any tinkering, but the engineering [or the merely fastidious] types would always fuss to improve, adding a paperclip here or cleverly devised weights of some other sort somewhere else to get more lift, more drag, greater distance, or whatever), strange and wonderfully ugly little stuffed animals that we assumed the girls liked, peculiar puzzles I never understood the point of, and so forth. The aisle in that store hardly existed, crammed as it was with the racks and shelves of purchasables.

Other stores stayed in business around there, too, perhaps a small grocery, possibly a dry cleaners, but I can't remember them. The toy store and the drug store are the only ones that stick out clearly. There in the drug store Mr. Daily sat at a small round table in the rear, his bottles leaving their rings on the top, almost like his way of counting how many he'd had—like the stiff cardboard coasters waiters in Austria would set out—a reasonable enough, reusable tally sheet.

Hand-packed ice cream in those days was the way you got ice cream. Pre-packaged stuff was usually the bland, individually wrapped portions mothers bought in cartons of ten or twelve for birthday parties, thinking more about product cost and weekly food budgets than taste: the vanilla that surely gave vanilla its bad name, and the chocolate or strawberry that you ate because, well, if you liked ice cream, then your taste measured quality only among the varieties of Good: OK, Not Bad, Good, Pretty Good, Real Good, Great!, and whatever might in any year express the idea of Superior. (We had to wait some while before we got into those potables that were described as Rare, Very Superior Old something or other, Aged-in-the-Wood, etc.).

At the drug store there was a large man who worked behind the soda fountain. I don't remember his name—probably never knew it (or even wanted to)—but I do remember clearly what he looked like. Think of Tony Galento, and that's about as close as you need. "Two Ton" Tony Galento was a bouncer at a bar, as I recall, who managed to wangle a heavyweight championship fight with Joe Louis during Louis's Bum-a-Month campaign. At the opening bell, Galento rushed out and walloped Louis with a powerful right haymaker of a hook, I expect. He nearly knocked out one of the greatest heavyweight champions EVER. But *nearly* with Louis was a dangerous thing to bet on, and Galento, who allegedly trained on beer and cigars, didn't even finish the round, I don't think.

He looked like his name: a round head, a round and hairy body with round and hairy arms and legs. There wasn't the Mr. Michelin look about him at all, just the kind of fellow you hated to play football against if you were a lineman because he was set so close to the ground you couldn't ever get under him for a good block.

The fellow who dished up the cartons of ice cream was built pretty much like that, only with a bald head and without the look of being someone who ought to have a cigar in his mouth. His arms were huge, and I always wondered if they got that way jabbing the flat scoop into the ten gallon cartons down in the freezer, pulling the big globs out, then stuffing them down into the quart or pint containers, tamping it down until it was packed solid as a brick.

Once, I was up on a stool at the fountain thinking about the best combinations to get that afternoon. When he asked me what I wanted I told him half a quart of chocolate and half a quart of orange sherbet.

"Half a quart?" he said with a sort of *Huh! Huh!* snicker some adults always seem to affect around children. "That's what I call free use of the King's English. How about a pint of each?"

It was still half a quart to me, but when he got the right sized containers out and started his digging and packing, I relaxed. So that's what a pint is, I mused. It seemed to add a certain legitimacy to the whole venture of getting that fattening sweet stuff in the first place.

...

We never walked beside Mr. Daily more than a short way because he took too long to get anywhere. In the summers, though, when he was on canes rather than the crutches, and when he found a wall just the right height to sit on (there weren't all that many), I might sometimes sit with him a short spell. I always wanted to ask him about the crutches and the canes; ask him who he was; ask him what happened to his legs; ask him lots of things that weren't any of my business, or at least things I was raised not to ask strangers.

Mostly, though, we just talked a kind of inane chatter at each other: the weather some, a little baseball (not really a major concern of mine in those days), whether muzzles on dogs did any good or not (I allowed as how our dog could get hers off in about ten minutes if she was really unhappy with it): the mere sailing ships and sealing wax, the cabbages and kings of old men and boys who haven't really much to *say* to each other but who manage, still, to have some kind of *stake* in each other. He was there and so was I, and it was the Home of My Youth, a paradisal place where the Mr. Dailys *Creaked* and *Thocked* around the sidewalks to get their ale; where the blind brother of my dear classmate, Emily, quick-stepped his way around that end of town; where I saw the old mother of the maiden ladies in the house that reeked of their seemingly dozens of yipping Pekinese fall in an empty lot across from their house while she was gathering sticks; where Butch the motorcycle cop knew probably every kid in town; where there were still Fourth of July parades and trolley cars and neighborhoods where people knew each other (well, usually); where life—even that close to New York City—was lived at a reasonably human pace, where kids could ride their bikes most places they needed to get to and parents didn't need to fear over-much about their safety.

...

One of the things that takes some getting used to is that *our* homes aren't necessarily the homes of our children. *My* childhood home remains Pelham Manor, New York, locked almost forever safe in the glass-fronted cabinet of grade and junior high school remembrances: the days before Pearl Harbor through the days shortly after Hiroshima and Nagasaki; the days of Stink Field and cheaply priced school matinees at the Metropolitan Opera; the days when my mother and father felt mostly all right about turning me, age ten, and my older brother, age 13, loose in Manhattan to take a bus from near the Roosevelt Hotel up to the Museum of Natural History where we haunted the Egyptian room, the wonderful glassed display of tigers, water buffalos with the most real looking mixture of water/drool spilling from their mouths as they looked back through the glass, held forever in surprise at the noise of our even quietest approaches; then lunch in the museum restaurant followed by the show at the Hayden Planetarium; then back to Grand Central Station and home—just 32 minutes away—on the Stamford Local; from the station we could walk home.

My home was Siwanoy Elementary School and Split Rock Riding Academy, piano lessons every Wednesday afternoon during the school year, and—would you believe it?—ballroom dancing lessons once a week, lessons replete with blue suits, black shoes, neckties, and white gloves. It was wonderful in the most awful kind of way.

We knew just about every toe-stubbing tree root and grass-stubble mound through the empty lots, but there was always a discovery to make, something to mark in the mind to come back to and explore more fully later: after school, maybe, or next week. *Surely* before summer was done. Or, if we were too late with the getting back, if way had led on too quickly to way, and we didn't return before the lot was gone—not to mention the people we would have shared the discovery with—and houses or condos had taken over, or, if we had simply forgotten, we might have to hold whatever it was in our memories until it or we were ripe enough to recollect it in tranquility. One of those finds I've stumbled on was going to the Met with Bill.

Those were wonderful trips to me. The Old Metropolitan Opera House, of course, was down near Madison Square Garden. Siwanoy (I gather) would arrange to have someone from the Met out there to talk to us at an assembly to prepare us for the Matinee. We could buy tickets at a fairly cheap student rate, and there would be a lecture about the performance we were going to see that week, a lecture deliberately humorous so as to catch our attention, pique our curiosity, make *Grand Opera* less intimidating, I assume. I have to admit that even with such condescension they were still instructive.

But going to the Met was one of those commonplace pieces of magic. It was common-place because of Frederick Jaegle, for instance, who lived right there in Pelham. Once when my brother and I were at the Pelham Country Club to swim, Bill all of a sudden looked over and said, "That's Frederick Jaegle."

"Ah," I said. "Who's he?"

Bill looked at me with the utter contempt expected from an older brother, knowing perfectly well I didn't have a clue who Frederick Jaegle was. Jaegle was a Met tenor—not a Jussi Björling, maybe, but what the hell. And he lived out there in Pelham. As a matter of fact, there was a story about him that had him unexpectedly called up one Saturday morning because the tenor who was *supposed* to sing that afternoon had been taken ill and couldn't, therefore…

Bill got a pencil and scrap of paper from somewhere, and, with me in tow, went over to the chair where Mr. Jaegle was seated, sweating and tanning. With only a trace of nervousness in his voice, Bill said, "Mr. Jaegle, may I have your autograph, please?" The man laughed gently.

I thought my brother had finally blown it: made a mistake with me right there to see him make it. But Jaegle took the tatter of paper and wrote his name for us, for Bill. I don't have any idea how long he kept it. He wasn't generally the sort who bothered with that kind of thing.

On Breaking One's Pencil

So what else could you call it, but commonplace? People like Jaegle lived in our town. Because we lived where we did, we could get in to the Met often. But because it was *The Met*, and because it was Helen Traubel and Lauritz Melchoir and Lawrence Tibbett and Leonard Warren and Jan Peerce; and because it was *Aida*, and *Lohengrin*, and *La Bohème* and who knows what else, it was magic.

Bill and I would take the train in to Grand Central, then hoof it to the Met. We'd walk through the lobby, past the bars, under the chandeliers and glitter, find our way to our seats, and sit. There we stared.

Actually, we liked to get there before the fire curtain was raised, a huge, ugly, gray thing that protected either the stage from a fire on the audience side, or the audience from a fire on the stage side. In any event, when it was raised, it went up slowly—God knows how much the thing must have weighed—and with a very un-operatic noise, more a utilitarian, groaning grind. But behind it, being revealed bit by bit, was the stunning stage curtain—the very one Tonio would come from behind to announce the tragedy of what was to follow when poor Canio realized he couldn't compete with the handsome Silvio.

Though the fire curtain may have groaned and creaked, that glorious stage curtain could open with such a sudden whoosh and roar of energy, it was like nothing else in the world. If you'd had any doubts about why you'd come, they disappeared as surely as the inconsequential world out on 37th Street or wherever. The magic was simply beginning.

I think my favorite opera was the one I was watching at the time, but my brother liked the double bill of *I Pagliacci* and *Cavalleria Rusticana* because he loved the way the conductor (in those days) got to lean against the podium, his baton hanging casually from his hand, between the two performances. Usually there was no intermission between them, simply a delay to change the sets.

After the opera, we walked back to Grand Central Station. It was generally pretty dark by then, and we picked our route carefully, hoping to avoid the smaller, murkier-seeming cross streets, but if we wanted to get to the entrance that was really the most convenient one for us, we'd have to nip down 43rd. Otherwise, we'd make the grand entrance from 42nd so we could stand up at the top of the stairs and look down at the whole Grand Concourse. There was never such a sight. Never.

Then we'd make our way down those broad, curving stairs and go, most times, on down to the lower level to wait for the next Stamford Local. On the ride back we'd often be quiet, trading no more than a few comments about the opera we'd just seen, each of us wrapped in our own little whorls of ecstasy, listening again in our own ways to the applause at the curtain calls, the *Bravo*s, taking our bows along with the singers, throwing kisses to the cheering masses. At least that's what I was doing. I never knew what Bill might be reliving.

...

When I was a truly little boy—this must have been in Scarsdale, I imagine, though possibly in Chappaqua, even—I made my own first appearance on stage. I was dressed in a cunning cowboy costume calmly awaiting my gig, when—without any notice beforehand—I was told to make an announcement to the audience—proud, if edgy, parents and other family members. The production was a dancing hodgepodge, as I recall, with the children attired in a variety of ways to do dances that matched their getups: little sailor hornpipes, flower waltzes, sweet wedding marches, and so forth. I eventually did mine, whatever kind of dance little cowboys are supposed to do. But the *true* moment was after I had been asked at the last minute to go before the curtain to make the announcement about not smoking or applause or whatever.

It never occurred to me that I should be nervous. Rather—if anything at all occurred to me—it was that they had made the right choice. On the appropriate cue, the curtain was parted, I stepped out on the stage all by myself, made the announcement, bowed, and returned to the ranks, awaiting my time: a born repertoire theater man—and possibly why I felt so close to Tonio in later years.

But something had happened out there. Out there by myself I heard the hum and buzz of the people in the vast hall (as it seemed) drop to silence waiting for me to speak; beyond the spotlights that were focused on me, I could make out individual faces watching my every move; and when I was through, I heard the deep breath of approval ripple through the applause, saccharine though it may have been and larded with relief that I hadn't bobbled the announcement. In short, I felt the power of being the center of attention at a time when I was supposed to be that center, when I had something to say that all of them were supposed to hear.

Small as the event may have been in the context of history—or of anything else, for that matter—it was a feeling that comes seldom in most people's lives, I think: a concatenation of events experienced by few—much less so early—being the right person at the right place at the right time, and knowing it.

But I was a fifth or sixth grader at Siwanoy School before I got my first taste of the professional theater. So much was done for children in schools—at least in Westchester County—that it's really quite remarkable. Oskar Homolka, for example, was in a show in town—that is, in New York City—and one afternoon representatives of the local School Presses, or whatever, were invited to hear Mr. Homolka talk about the play he was in, theater in general, and whatever else we chose and he agreed to respond to within the time allowed.

Mrs. Lacy took me and another student to the affair. Mrs. Lacy, by the way, was a woman I loved with a profound passion. She was thin, beautiful, gentle, and kind. It was love at first sight with me, though I'm not sure how much she reciprocated.

Nonetheless, the "deal" was that whoever went to the lecture had to write a piece about the adventure for their school newspaper. I had no problem agreeing to that, so off we went.

I don't remember the trip in, I don't remember how we got to the theater, what theater it was, what the play was, or anything else. I do remember spending time later half reclining in my bed, sitting up, scrunching around, sucking the eraser end of my pencil as I tried valiantly to write the article.

But in the theater, we sat out as an audience. Mr. Homolka came on, did his thing, talked about the play, etc., etc., etc. The house lights were fairly dim, because I recall the glow of the place. And Oh! it was magic.

We even got to ask a question. I like to think that I thought it up—surely it wouldn't have been whoever the other person was: a girl, no doubt—but I can't honestly say it was me. I suspect that Mrs. Lacy—wonderful, dear, beautiful Mrs. Lacy—asked us if we might like to ask that question.

We obviously concurred, having no particular thoughts on the matter ourselves. She asked Mr. Homolka how long they rehearsed a play before it opened.

About six weeks, he replied.

She thanked him, then as she sat back down, she looked to us, her eyes bright, as I recall, and whispered, "That's about how long we do, too."

I was in heaven. There we were, in a real theater, talking to a real actor, and not only that, but knowing we were in the same business in the same way: We both took about six weeks to get our productions on the boards. *Wow!* Was life worth the candle or what?

That wasn't the only theater experience I had in New York. One night—it was a special night, I think, though I can't remember who it was special for—I went to a production of one of the *Charley's Aunt* plays. Ray Bolger was Charley, and to see the real Scarecrow of *The Wizard of Oz* was a treat all in itself. The play was the usual hanky-panky of Charley and his Aunt, and the only thing I really remember, other than enjoying it all immensely, was the bit where Bolger took a flying leap starting from the left rear of the stage up to center stage front. He must have run about four quick strides, before diving—high and head first, arms forward and trailing down—into the jacket being held for him. It was one of the innumerable quick-changes called for in the play.

The whole audience gasped then cheered with that kind of spontaneous, quick outburst coming from amazement coupled with relief when the potential danger of the stunt blew in on us across our delight at the whole thing.

And there was the night I saw the Jimmy Durante-Gary Moore radio show. I remember that it was funny. I remember being surprised by the pre-air warmup so we would be laughing when the broadcast started. I was fascinated at the characters walking on and off the stage to get to their mike positions. I don't remember anything about the content of the show itself—mainly it was the usual Durante tomfoolery, I suppose—but I *think* I remember the closing, "Goodnight, Mrs. Calabash, wherever you are." And I *do* remember Gary Moore watching the sound engineer very closely, holding tightly to the script as he looked off stage, and then as soon as he got the signal that they were off the air—the finger slicing across the throat, I assume—he threw the script out toward the audience and yelled, "To hell with it!" Not in a mean or nasty way, but with great high good spirits, a sort of, "There, we've gotten a good one, you've been a great audience, and here's your reward: a piece of the action."

Magic. Oh! such magic.

But in the spring of my sixth grade year, when our school put on its annual production with Colonial Elementary School (the Colonial-Siwanoian), I did not get the lead. I should have: I wanted it, I was graduating, and I was the best actor available.

That put my stage career on hold for about sixteen years, not to be picked up again until Nashville, Tennessee, when I played Mr. Miller in Terence Rattigan's *The Deep Blue Sea*, and, later—with Zazu Pitts, no less—Jeffrey, in John Patrick's *The Curious Savage*, and many years after that in Clemson, South Carolina, Harry, in Brian Friel's *The Loves of Cass McGuire*.

...

Pelham, unlike the Harding Place kind of "residential area" where, as an adult, I later lived in Nashville, Tennessee, was a town in its own right, lived in by the Siwanoy Indians way back when NYC was mostly good farmland, not, that is, just a residential suburban area. At various times I have reminisced about the place on two counts: 1) that it was a kind of perfect place for me to have been in for those six years and, 2) that I might not have liked it had I had stayed through high school.

On occasion—idle times of idle thoughts—I have "wished" that Pelham had been even farther from NYC, enough farther so that it could not have been considered a suburb at all, but a town all its own, all in its own right... and that my father had been editor of the *Pelham Sun*. Then I realized that his brother, my Uncle Walter, editor of the Pine Bluff, Arkansas, *Commercial*, had led the life my spindrift ruminations had devised for my father. Sort of.

Other moonglow inventions summoned up Dad's having stayed in Fort Worth as editor of the *Fort Worth Press* instead of moving to New York City and Chappaqua and Scarsdale and Pelham, from which I then went to Staunton, Virginia, home of the Staunton Military Academy. I went there because my older brother Bill had gone. He went there because he was a mess of sorts, and because my oldest brother John had gone there, and *he* went there because he wanted to go to West Point so he could become a professional soldier, and rightly enough assumed he'd have a better chance to get into West Point after four years at a good military academy.

About that he was probably right enough. But the problem was that his math wasn't as good as his military background, so he didn't get admitted to the Point, settling instead for Washington and Lee University, our father's alma mater. Too, the Second World War pretty much killed his interest in professional soldiering, I think, not to mention a woman who told him he could have her or the Army, but not both.

"Then that's simple," he had replied.

...

I went back to Pelham once some thirty-two years after we had moved. I had been there since, but that was the first time for twenty years. The platform at the New York New Haven and Hartford (by then called the New Haven Line, I think) was all different, and the place had a guarded look to it, like it could defend itself if it suddenly came under attack. I started to walk to my sister's—a pretty hefty piece, actually—and had just gotten down on the sidewalk under the railroad overpass when I realized that two early teeners were up on the rails. One of them was pissing over the side onto the sidewalk—not at me especially, just any target of opportunity, I assumed—while the other looked on and giggled.

The shops along the way in the Village were familiar, though usually with different owners and often with different purposes. Up Wolf's Lane I went, turned left onto Esplanade where we had lived, soon walked past our old house, closer over toward the Post Road where there is a traffic light now.

On the way, I had looked around. There weren't any vacant lots that I could see, and there had been some additional building, but the main thing I noticed was that the trees were bigger. They weren't especially taller, but they were bigger around, the way trees usually grow—getting their height quickly, then filling out. Otherwise, the place looked pretty much as though I might see John Jim or Bobby or Richie or Herbie or Marion or Frances or Oldriska come biking or roller skating around some quick corner of time, waving to me to come on and let's go.

I listened for Mr. Daily, too, feeling almost like I should turn to see if by some peculiar warp of time he could be behind me, resting on a low wall or swinging his body in his slow, determined exertion to fend for himself at least enough to get his by-God ale every day. But of course he was as gone as the vacant lots, the bikers, the skaters, and all the rest: alive only in the keening ache of my memory.

NASHVILLE

A Love Song

I'M SINGING BALLADS HERE. DIRECTLY and unashamedly I'm singing ballads of love and youth, of love and age. Not singing just of the love that saddens and hurts, merely, but also of the love that breaks hearts. I'm singing here of lovers who come at each other so hard and on tangents so contrary they bump and scrape hides as they pass. I'm singing of love that was nearly always out of phase, of two lovers—like circus aerialists in different but parallel acts—reaching for each other from orbits of ineffable desperation as they spin and tumble themselves dangerously high above the upturned faces of curious crowds, the band's sounding brass, the always tired-looking and disinterested elephants, the clowns sweeping spotlights down until they disappear and the world turns to dusk.

Which is to say I'm singing a love ballad of Nashville, Tennessee, mainly of the 1950s and a little into the 1960s: its springs of greens and blues; its winters of rain, rain, and more rain; its boulevards and pikes; its moil of people stepping sometimes easily from the tonks of town to the Clubs of suburbs, people straddling the trenches that separate the University from the Ryman Auditorium; the whole mad ruck of intellectual and moral ferment that possesses a young man who truly believes that life is worth the candle and the gamble, who trusts that life is too valuable and worthy to be snickered at.

And I am singing here of memory, prayerfully hoping my songs will help nudge me toward the redemption that only the laying on of love's hands can grant, will help reconcile verses' ancient pains and joys with the shy wonder of what would have happened if my refrain had been turned into another verse.

...

So to start I will tell you this about Nashville: *It is* the capital of the state of Tennessee; *It is* the principal city of Middle Tennessee; *It hunkers* in the Nashville Basin, a geological scoop out of the earth that once upon a time, in winters, held the coal smoke from a million chimneys as close to the earth as dew; *It is* the home of the Grand Ole Opry, which was very different when it played in the Ryman Auditorium downtown and before it took on the "theme park" aura it now wears, out off Briley Parkway, an Interstate connector; *Its nickname* used to be "The Athens of the South," because of all the colleges and universities there, though now it's probably better known as "Music City" or even "Music City USA"; *It has* the world's only full-scale replica of the Parthenon; Centennial Park, where that replica now sits, is still—visually—one of the loveliest of city parks; Edwin and Percy Warner Parks—still near the western edge of town—used to be the places where many a young swain realized in the evenings of the deepening spring nights (after walks, games of chase, a picnic, and before the police swept through about eleven p.m. to close the places up), that he was hopelessly in love; *It is* where I first saw a basketball play unfold: previously, I had never seen anything but ten people in two different-colored uniforms running up and down the court taking shots and so on, but that night I actually saw the *form* of the thing, saw order and intention. *It was* the first Vanderbilt University basketball game I had ever seen. I was a graduate student. I saw it with a young lady I was immensely fond of—Helen, I'll call her, because I love that name—a young lady I loved, it would seem, "not wisely but too well," as Othello said of himself before he died upon his kiss.

Thus, even as Pelham Manor, New York, was the home of my youth, Nashville, Tennessee, was the home of my young manhood: my intellectual coming of age, some of my heart's most grievous joys, my mind's broodings, and my spirit's anxieties. One way or another, in short, I still live there every day of my life.

...

Many who consider themselves Nashvillians didn't like the movie named for the city, mainly, I sensed, because they felt the movie didn't show the city in a totally complimentary way, no "uplift," no reassuring pat on the head to confirm the virtue of their biases about themselves, their often smug insistence that all was fine, just fine: not an especially odd reason to dislike a movie, it seems to me. But I mention that because Nashville, the city, was, in that flick, probably a symbol more than anything else, and it may be that I responded to it as positively as I did because the city is a symbol for me, too—which is what happens when you don't live in a place on a regular basis: It's hard to *live* in a symbol.

In any event I recall the place in images, very sensate images, the kinds of images that do what poetry is always supposed to do: appeal to our sight and smell and touch and all the rest—to make corporeal that which otherwise would remain abstract. So Nashville to me is a series of images, or less a series than a dense and complex matrix of them, both woven and mashed into a material which—though often at odds with itself in the fibers of its details—always manages, finally, to be at one with itself. And when I say that, I'm remembering the place in the profoundest of ways. Those who think of symbols and images as *merely* symbols, or *only* images, won't get the full import of what I'm saying, probably. They will be the ones, for instance, who feel compelled to take the Bible literally because they don't understand the power of metaphor, the uses of parable, the overwhelming strength and staying power of memory when it is compounded and nourished by imagination.

As a gentle suggestion, though, please try to accept this as less an autobiography than *A Sweet Unrest*.

...

Nashville, for me (during the time-frame I'm dealing with here), is divided into three principal kingdoms: the city itself, Vanderbilt University, and the young lady I spoke of earlier. Like discussing the elements of a story (the plot, theme, characterization, whatever else any given person may choose to discuss) the three can be separated—perhaps *have* to be—but that can be misleading, because then the unity of the whole scene can be misunderstood, the point of the whole story missed, the forest go unperceived behind the showy trees.

For instance, in the summer of 1981 I went back to Nashville for a short week to attend an Alumni College seminar that dealt with the Humanities. I was still interested in the topic as a topic because the South Carolina Committee for the Humanities had funded a project of mine to write a pilot radio program I had entitled *Rediscovering the Humanities* for the South Carolina Educational Radio Network (now called ETV-RADIO.)

But after the seminar was over I stayed another day to visit with some Nashville people, and even attended a Sunday afternoon concert in Centennial Park with one of the ghosts from my past, or at least with a person whose former relationship with me was a ghost of my memory.

Concerts in the park (I don't know if Nashville still has them) were among the most wonderful of cheap pleasures: It's not just that they were free, but they came with such serendipitous extras. That afternoon there were the young mothers who, having stumbled in on the concert because *it* was there and so were *they* (and besides there were some benches and chairs around to take a blow on), couldn't possibly have paid much heed to the gorgeous music, because they were too busy chasing their little children who couldn't have cared less about Quantz, Mozart, or any of the rest. And there were what appeared to be intense interns, haggard in their green scrub-up trousers, who seemed to be letting go of something festering in them. And, naturally, there was the music, once you managed to close out all the fascinating distractions.

Nearly everybody seemed to be enjoying something: a little child discovering a rain drain; a slightly older one seeing someone she knew who was listening intently to the music; and still others watching yet others taking notes.

A mixed crowd, then: brown T shirts and red, bushy beards; neatly jacketed academicians; mothers desperate to get out—anywhere. Seeing the youngish mothers with their small children, I didn't recall or think, quite, but somehow finally sensed, finally perceived through everything the tiny wins, those balming prolongations of the implied and tenuous commitments parents and children usually manage to develop, those constantly new starts that emanate from the random, pudgy-handed squeezes by a tot, the spontaneous burst of hugs that keep the young parents going one more hour when they are already exhausted: just one more hour—and at the same time it was precisely that, that gave rise to the sadness in this older man whose own children were no longer little. So much gone, it seemed.

On Breaking One's Pencil

Nashville sounds and sights, and of course the memories, the *deja vu*: I was sitting, as it happened, with the old girlfriend—long since happily married—nothing untoward: an old friendship by now, by now more or less familiar with each other, comfortable after a fashion, still very much in love, probably. But we don't *choose* love, do we? We experience it. And besides, I lived a long way off. What the hey!

...yet the musicians played on, giving us their Telemann, their Dowland, and through that, their love...

Such a wondrous circus.

...

So there are the three of them, you see, come together as always: the University, the city, and the old love. I simply can't separate them.

But there is more.

...

While I'm already there, there's Centennial Park, a beautiful expanse of grass and flower beds, of picnic tables and playground areas, an old fighter plane, a steam engine, a creek running through, and, by now, the usual alcoholics, junkies, and sad searchers for all the varieties of sexual experiences the imagination can possibly summon up. Plus, no doubt, muggers and worse.

Amidst all that, there's a wonderful sculpture. Well, I say sculpture. I'm not sure what it ought to be called, really. What it is, is a huge concrete ball on top of a plinth. The thing was donated by a group of Nashville ladies (as I remember the story) and the explanatory plaque states the theme of the statue, in case it had escaped the casual viewer: "That which is round can be no rounder."

I love it. When I look at it I think of myself as Humpty Dumpty, because it's one of those sayings that can mean pretty much whatever I want it to mean. Is there a round, rounder, and roundest? Or is *Round* one of those absolute terms like *unique*? That makes it a concept, possibly, even more than an adjective or a noun. Heavy going, those concepts. I have tried to avoid them whenever possible.

But dominating the entire park, and visible from most places in it, is the Parthenon, set on a mound so it's slightly higher than anything else around, and surrounded, for the most part, by nothing but space. If you can see it at all, you can see it pretty well. And what a thing it is to look at: The balance and proportions truly are stunning, and the mathematics not only of the columns, but of the proportions from any angle of vision, the relationships of all the parts to each other from *any*where you want to look. Well, others have talked about all that far more knowledgeably than I can. I tend to approach such things the way Thomas Mann approached Schopenhauer: Read as much as you can absorb and use for your own purposes. Then move on, move right on.

There is an art gallery in the basement of the Parthenon, and shows are mounted there periodically, and there is a permanent collection—not as notable as the Athens of the South ought to have, it always seemed to me, but "Athens" never sought my opinion on the matter, either.

The main floor used to be interesting, but now-a-days if you try to wander around in there, Athena-the-Monstress—all gold and white and horribly out of scale to everything around her—stares from huge but unseeing eyes, making me feel like one of Swift's Lilliputians hiding from a fast-striding Gulliver on his way back from a pub of his own devising, not hostile toward me at all, but as though wrapped up in his own thoughts—about the nature of roundness, per-haps?—and therefore unaware that he might accidentally squash me into a stain—or, worse, think me a little fire and try to put me out, too. I'm intimidated, in short. More, she makes me feel claustrophobic.

I know that Athena—of that size—apparently really *was* in the original Parthenon, and I *do* appreciate the years of effort devoted to restoring, or in this case placing, her image in her rightful spot for the sake of authenticity and all that, and, priding myself on being somewhat of a craftsman, too, I certainly admire the labor and skill that went into her making. But her resurrection here in Nashville strikes me as being somewhat akin to bringing back button hook shoes, flat tops and duck tails, or some other fashion long since fortunately perished.

Nonetheless, it was in that huge, deep sward of parkland stretching from West End Avenue up to the Parthenon that I first knowingly fell in love with Nashville and with everything that might imply or subsume: my education, my friends, my dearly beloveds; that Eden of Middle Tennessee; that Christminster of crushed hopes and loves; that bounteous refuge of things possible; that stifling fen of things past; that attracting field of so many top-notch teachers and scholars and writers and admirable (if unlovable) university presidents . . .

...all came together right there during a Fair of some sort, and it changed me forever, apparently. It was an event, for sure, but it was also one of those symbols. Maybe it was an epiphany. People used to have epiphanies back then.

...

The Nashville Arts Festival used to be an annual affair, and the year of my Nashville Epiphany it was held in Centennial Park (possibly in conjunction with the Italian Street Fair) where tents were set up all over the area. There were speeches, crafts for sale, old books; plays at night (*Tartuffe* was selected to be the theatrical presentation that year, 1960, the first time I'd ever seen a Molière); God knows what else. I went to it because it was going on and because the weather was fine. I didn't buy anything, but the epiphany I experienced must have been the eruption of things that had been going on in me for a long time.

I had been wandering through the Fair for an hour or so, watching the people, talking to some I knew, even chatting with strangers. It was one of those kinds of events. Everybody seemed to be in a smiling mood. Even little children were happy, their romping a joy rather than a trial. People seemed trusting, willing to look straight into your eyes, to talk to you, to smile at you without having to fret over how that smile might be interpreted. There was simply an openness and an acceptance of the rest of the people there. Like a huge family reunion, there was a sense that everybody belonged, and there must have been three-to-four hundred at any one time.

I finally found myself toward the edge, nearer West End Avenue than not, looking on at the crowd, when it started. It was a kind of out-of-body sensation: I was there in myself, yet just a little bit above, watching myself as I looked at the scene. Then I felt a slight rushing in my ears, the sort of feeling that can come when you get up too fast from the bed in the morning after a strident alarm clock has thrown you into the day. My eyes were puffy, bulging. Blood pressure, maybe, but the rushing in my ears turned into something solider, heavier, almost corporeal.

And then it was more than that. What had been noise was transformed into sound, the sound then transported into a choir rising in a crescendo of chords stacked on chords, both the harmonies and rhythms running into, looping through, then pouring out of other harmonies and tempos, joining them, building on them, transforming them…

I didn't know that I was in such turmoil. It had been ages since I had known my heart to suffer those "plunging waterfalls," "lightning strikes," or any of the rest of the *Sturm und Drang* Goethe could summon up as well as any. But clearly whatever I had thought of as former aches of the heart were still pretty current, for whatever was happening to me that morning seemed like an answer to the prayer in the closing line of the "Pater Profundis" of the *Faustus* in Mahler's Eighth Symphony: *Erleuchte mein bedürftig Herz*—"Illumine my needy heart." It literally took my breath, probably because I hadn't known how needy my heart was, hadn't known how out of touch with myself I had become in some terribly important way.

Eventually it faded. Calm, then, I was back in the Park with the comfortably quotidian sights and sounds of the carnival, except that everything was sharper, clearer, brighter: the light, the colors, individual blades of grass, shoe laces, women's make-up, brands of cigarettes showing through men's shirt pockets. Everything.

It was then that a sense of community quietly was within me, like seeing the face of a dear friend appearing in a crowd, smiling, waving. All so perfectly natural. Nothing forced or strained, nothing complicated, nothing odd. But so moving, so powerful, so sure in its simplicity.

Community had always been a concept I understood in my head. Donald Davidson—teacher, poet, historian, archtraditionalist—had talked about it a lot. But it had been, largely, a head trip for me until after the angels had quieted themselves or moved on to mystify, to bless, to feed the souls of others. Then, I *felt* it. I *knew* it. I understood it in my heart and blood and body and soul and consciousness. It was *mine*. I owned it as totally as any human being can possibly own anything. It was part of me, and I was part of it. Forever.

Then the world slowly became the world again. The ecstasy subsided. The thrumming grew fainter. The voices receded. But everything was now in me. It might have been there all along and had just come out, had just been released because I was ready to experience it. I don't know, but I do know that for the rest of the day—for the *rest of the entire day*—I felt joy. The day was quiet, serene, even beatific because I now *was* the song that choir had sung. And, as with love, I had not asked for it to be.

…

That was one bit of the Nashville matrix. Another was an evening spent with a friend teaching at Murray State College, at the time, a colleague I had taught with up there. He had written a novel with his brother after World War II—*Thy Men Shall Fall*—a good book, possibly swamped and out-shouted by Norman Mailer's *The Naked and the Dead*. Whatever, after I moved back to Nashville I kept up with him and his family—Murray, Kentucky, was only about a two-hour drive—and one summer he was down for a short week to do some research at the Joint University Libraries on the Vanderbilt campus for a scholarly book on Poe he was writing.

One Thursday early evening, probably, before he headed back to Kentucky for the weekend, he appeared at my digs with a bottle of Black Jack—Jack Daniels, Black Label—the finest grade sour mash whiskey the Jack Daniels' distillery put out at the time.

I was delighted at the sight of the bottle, but Sidney, my friend, seemed on edge, clearly not inclined to open it for a shared tipple. He chatted me up for a little while, then asked if I knew someone there in Nashville. I didn't know the name. Actually it was in Belle Meade, he said. Right, I said, explaining that by then Belle Meade was a mostly posh west end section of the city.

Sticking to the point, he asked if I could get him to a certain address out in Belle Meade. I looked at it, and said, Sure, why not?

I got out one of my maps of the city, figured out where the place had to be, and we got in my car. On the way, he explained his mission. Characters in his novel were thinly disguised members of his outfit in Europe. After the War, after the book was out, he sent a copy of it to an army buddy of sorts, "A very Southern guy," he said. "Very much a gentleman, and also a bloody damned good officer." The man had been his battalion commander, a major with an address in Belle Meade, Tennessee. Later, Sidney got a lovely note from him—especially lovely because he enclosed a handsome check and a request for additional copies of the book to give to friends. They were sent. Later, still others were requested—and paid for, as I recall the story. There was no sense that The Major was looking for a freebie.

So now, Sidney and I were on the search for the man's Belle Meade home, which we found with no trouble, except that it wasn't The Major's house, as it turned out. It was his father's. After almost pushing the doorbell a second time, we were met by a quite elderly lady with a cane, her mouth set slightly in a pleasant, public face as she opened the door. Sidney, staring at her and wondering, no doubt, if I had deliberately brought him someplace we shouldn't be, introduced himself and explained who he was looking for. She looked slightly puzzled, but invited us in and led us to the living room.

There were two men sitting there, and she addressed the younger one. "A Mr. Moss is here looking for you, and a Mr. ah . . ." She looked at me.

But the younger man leaped to his feet before I could answer.

"Moss!" He shouted. "Good Lord, man. Come in, come in. Where in the world have you been? How in the world did you find me here?"

The Major seemed pleased like a man in the unexpected company of the diminishing squad of truly worthy friends, so pleased that I thought Sidney must have been less than candid with me about his knowing The Major only as an enlisted man and not as a personal friend. Then I looked at Sidney and saw the bemused surprise on his face, too.

"Lucky you caught me," The Major said after Sidney explained how he had found him. "I'm only here a week and I'm leaving in a few days. Mother, Father," he turned to the older couple still standing, waiting patiently for the introduction, pleased that the strangers at the door were friends. "I've told you about Moss. The fellow who wrote the book with me in it. Come in, sit down."

I've forgotten over these years the name of The Major and his family, so I'll simply call him Clay. Clay Grady, to round it out. It seems to fit, though I don't think that was his real name.

There were also two others in the living room. Clay introduced us to his sisters.

"Moss!" Clay exploded again. "I was thinking about you just a few months ago. I ran across a copy of that book and re-read it. My God, man, if you'd gotten a reputable publisher
instead of that quickie outfit you'd have made Mailer look sick."

Sidney shrugged—his Yankee trademark—smiling in slight embarrassment at not knowing how the old folks—much less the sisters—would take to having a bottle of raw whiskey waved around in their living room like that. (Like so many northerners, Sidney operated on his own mythos about Southern propriety.) But Clay's mother smiled as she took the bottle from him, as though relieving a dear neighbor of some bulky nuisance, and carried it herself to the kitchen to be prepared: the bottle itself, its seal cracked and the cap off, a sign to help yourself, with cut glass tumblers in a row before it; a silver pitcher filled with ice and cold water poured over; an ice bucket with the tongs where you could reach them; all brought in on a silver tray: an extraordinary display of what we mean in the South by *manners*, I suppose, of making a stranger feel at home without ever letting him have cause to think he's being *made* to feel at home. A mostly lost art.

What I remember about that night was not that the house was so old—it certainly wasn't one of the very few "old" old houses that still existed here and there around Nashville—but it seemed old because of the furnishings, for one thing, and because of the people in it for another. The rug in the living room, for instance, was worn from years of traffic, but I could tell where coffee tables and chairs had once been placed from the sections of the rug where the nap was thickest. I could also tell there had been a time when the rug was turned regularly to keep the depth of the pattern and the nap as even as possible. But staring down deeply into it, its colors faded by then into a general bluish-gray with washed-out reds here and there, I could also tell it hadn't been turned in a long time.

It was a very fine rug once, but looking more closely at the old man and his old wife and at their three children—one in his mid-fifties, a teacher-artist, a bachelor; one in her early fifties, still living in Nashville but no longer in her parents' home, a spinster; the last married with two daughters, on her way somewhere to meet her husband and rarely any longer in Nashville—I understood why no one bothered about the rug any more or cared whether it was turned or not.

Across the room from me, the old man sat as straight as he could in his overstuffed chair, one hand gripping a cane, the other fidgeting over the armrest. Pinned to the headrest was an antimacassar. I noticed it when he leaned forward so he could better hear what his married daughter was saying to his bachelor son. I could see the tidy was yellowed, but I wasn't ready to see the dark spot on one side of it where the elder Grady must have leaned his head back year after year during afternoon naps. It didn't seem dirty. From where I was sitting it seemed to have been washed often and ironed with care. But there it was: yellowed, shaped to the contours of the chair's back, the dark stain off to one side as though defying any soap or detergent to lave even that much of the old man from existence.

What a strange place to have been dropped, I remember thinking, sipping Black Jack, watching Clay Grady—thin so he appeared taller than he was, his hair still reddish on top but whitening around his ears, his mouth working like the rest of his body, in twitches. He spoke with a long, straight smile accentuated by his eyes and the rest of his face. He smiled while he spoke, speaking always directly to us. Then, while listening to our replies, his eyes—blue and pale like the no-longer-deep colors of his red hair—would continue to look at us as he listened to our words, absorbing them, storing them up. I felt compelled to pay attention to what I was saying so it wouldn't sound as trivial as it might at first have started out to be. Then he would speak again to our remarks, and again his straight lips would spread, his face twinkle into the warmth of the good host, the good friend, the good man: knowledgeable, perceptive, keen, personal, informed: very Southern, very gentlemanly.

Comfortably seated, drinks in our hands, and the glow of good fellowship and warmth on our faces, we settled into general conversation for a while, the catching up on where's and when's. Then the talk turned to war. The two old soldiers—Sidney and Clay—were reuniting, for one thing. Then, too, Major Grady's father was a retired colonel. Along with a slew of other older officers, he had been retired at the beginning of the Second World War because he was already sixty-five, and because the need, as he so graciously admitted, was for young men.

But before we eased into the conversation, there was a casual tour of the downstairs of the house. Not a tour, quite, for Grady—a painter in fact and by inclination, but a teacher of mechanical drawing at Virginia Polytechnic Institute as the next best thing to earning a living—wanted mainly to show Sidney (and his friend, of course) some of his paintings in a back room.

I took in as much of the house as I could without actually staring. There wasn't anything unusual about it. It was filled with musty-seeming Victorian furniture, and on the wall of the staircase were the family portraits glaring down at the banister of dark, no-longer-quite-properly-cared-for oak. The fixity of the gazes from those kinds of portraits always startled me. They were so grim looking, those people. So unsmiling and harsh looking. Maybe they didn't have anything to smile about because they were pioneers. Or, it

On Breaking One's Pencil

occurred to me, maybe they hurt most of the time: hemorrhoids and rotten teeth. Two of the pictures were oils, the other five tintypes.

I wasn't surprised at the presence of the portraits, but had wanted out of curiosity as well as courtesy to go back with Sidney and The Major to see the paintings. Still, something held me at the bottom of the staircase, something about those people whom I neither knew nor cared about, really. The arrangement of family in that way was nothing peculiar to Nashville houses, but I kept on staring at them, fascinated.

"My great aunt Ella there at the bottom," Mrs. Grady was saying near me. I turned my head and smiled, then turned back as she continued, pointing with her cane.

"That first one. And then right above her, my blessed father. One up," she let the cane touch the floor again, "my beloved mother."

Her voice was silken in my ear, old but touched, still, with a sense of herself as a woman. She let her left hand rest gently on my arm.

"And then up, my uncle 'Spring' Wheeler," she chuckled. "They called him 'Spring' because in his day he was always going down to the spring to bring up a fresh jug of whiskey—much against the wishes and rearing of his mother and sisters. But that was when we lived out in Franklin. You know Franklin, Mr. Sorrells?"

I nodded and smiled. Franklin is now a small city southwest of Nashville, the place where the South really lost *The War*, as far as some of us are concerned.

"And then a cousin on my Aunt Sarah's side, and then Aunt Sarah herself. At the top is my own first cousin, son of his father's second wife…"

The explanations trailed off and the two of us were back in the living room with the others, seated, glasses refilled and sweating.

They talked…

As she fingered her cameo brooch, I watched the old lady study Sidney's face intently, enough to make me look at him too: his nose with its broad nares, its slightly olive color, its aristocratic arch; she studied the nose and seemed aware of the thick glasses over the dark eyes, aware of the sensuousness of his lips; she even seemed aware of the mind obviously edged behind the eyes.

"From Chicago," she said politely, still tracing the tips of her fingers around the smooth edge of her brooch. Then to me, "And New York. How nice."

They talked of war.

…but not about the Kaiser or Hitler, not about the power politics of the Allies or the Central Powers. Sidney told a story about standing by his truck while the convoy he was in was halted for some reason on a provincial road in Southern France. About a hundred yards back from the road was a beautiful old farmhouse, its downstairs mostly stone, its upper story mostly wood. Sidney speculated that it had probably gotten fired on because someone in the convoy was bored—there weren't any Germans within eighty kilometers of them. It was a white phosphorous shell from a bazooka. It struck up on the eave and of course started a fire.

Sidney and all his buddies saw it, saw the fire burning bigger and bigger until the corner of the house was blazing. Then it became apparent that the house would burn to the ground, because there wasn't any way to put the fire out. There was a lot of smoke. A fair amount of the shell must have gone into the house through the wall. All of a sudden a head showed in a win-dow, then ducked quickly back inside.

Then two or three heads were sticking out. Then they ducked back inside. It was like an old movie cartoon, Sidney said. A speeded up, herky-jerky action comical to see. Directly, stuff began flying out the windows: a mattress, a bunch of quilts and sheets, a chiffonnier, a chair or two. Then out came the headboard to a bed. Soon everything was being tossed toward the mattress. An old man outside bounced around among the flying objects like he was going to catch the stuff as it was tossed from the upper story, but at the last second each time, he skittered away, jumping aside so that nothing landed on his head.

The fire had gotten bigger by that time, and there wasn't a thing in the world the people outside could do. Their home was burning up. Then the convoy geared itself into motion again. Sidney piled back on his truck and watched the house until he couldn't see it because of a dip and a turn in the road. He said they could see the smoke from it for the next two hours. He wasn't sure where in France they were.

Then old Colonel Grady told of being commissioned a second lieutenant in 1899 and that when he was in Mexico, his company commander, a captain, had an arrow wound from one of the Indian actions of the 1870s. He also had the arrowhead itself and he carried it around with him all the time. Colonel Grady's company had made contact with a scraggly bunch of Pancho Villa's friends, and he and the captain ended up taking cover behind the same dead mule waiting to see what their tactical options might be. All the time, the captain kept that arrowhead between his teeth, grinding and grinding and grinding on it.

The conversations spun around, then, with the third double whiskey until I didn't know what they were talking about any more—that is, didn't know where in history they were—until I finally had the impression—because that's all that was left since I could barely keep up with the campaigns and dates after a while—that all that's left of a war after it's over is ghosty little wisps of remembrances. There was the old colonel in his white duck trousers, white shirt, and white, blue-piped cotton sweater, his white shoes and socks, holding on to his cane and talking about one war—not even the First World War, the biggie of his career as a professional military man—while his son went on and on about Thermopylae, Alexander, Napoleon, Agincourt—the classical wars of our epoch—and how they were like what he had been going through as an officer himself in the campaigns he had seen action in.

And during all of this, the Colonel's lady politely offered comments at appropriate places, so that eventually a complete narrative about the Civil War emerged from her conversational interstices, just as surely as though she had been there herself, which, just as surely, she had not. But she might as well have been, because her mother had told her all about it, and what her mother couldn't remember, because she had been just a child, *her* mother could.

The old lady there in the living room that night was telling us how her mother remembered playing with cannon balls on the road from Chattanooga to Nashville. They had left their home and everything but what they could load on a wagon and were going to the comparative safety of Nashville which had been captured early in the war and was under a basically stable if often brutal civilian government. Though they had relatives there, they figured they could also put up with others in Franklin. So they decided their children would be safer and life for all of them would be more settled in Middle Tennessee than in their own home.

But the old lady played in the dust or the mud or whatever it was with those expended cannon balls. That is, her *mother* did. But to sit there in that living room listening to her tell the story, I would have sworn that she was the one who had been wagon-toted to Nashville instead of her mother, and that it had been her mother instead of her grandmother who had secreted the family's pearls in her bodice.

At several points during the evening I could have contributed tales of my own, had once nearly started to tell the story of the fellow in my outfit in Austria soon after the Korean War cease fire—a young man we all called Elmer because in size and voice he was the spitting image of the cartoon character Elmer Fudd—who got gonorrhea after dropping a radio on his foot. It didn't seem appropriate, though, so I demurred. But it's still a good story.

...

That night I had experienced so much of what I thought of as "old" Nashville that I kept thinking of my dear friend, and for a long time I couldn't understand why. Then I knew: familiarity. It wasn't just the house and its furnishings, its people, its conversations, its sense of his-tory, its portraits lining the walls, its graciousness, its on and on and on. Rather, I felt cradled by its total aura. It was the old shoes you can barely feel, the old sweater that's molded itself to your shape, the old friends you know so well that there have come to be things you simply don't have to *explain* to them.

The image of that night—I still see the entire evening as a single image—was so powerful to me that I needed to talk about it so I could get another reading on what it had all meant. But the one person I *needed* to talk to was the one person I *couldn't* talk to, her husband, by then, being, still, a bit touchy about such things.

But there was that trio again: The Clay Gradys were Nashville; Sidney was in Nashville because of Vanderbilt; and the *Gemütlichkeit* of the whole evening summoned up in me how intensely I had become a part of my former love. Things simply *fit*.

Still, in spite of the tales—about Pancho Villa, the Second World War, Henry the Second's campaigns against the French, or the depredations practiced on each other by the Athenians and the Spartans—the slightly fetid aftertaste of the ghosty South's old lost causes was never far beneath the surface of things. There was a sense that the wars had been mere points

On Breaking One's Pencil

of reference, and only Sidney seemed to be the one who saw it in all its grim realities, realities that might be turned to great art, but not to great life. Sidney, though, wasn't anywhere near being from a military tradition, having been born in England and carted over here by his mother when he was an infant, and growing up in a po' boy's Chicago without a father. No officers or gentlemen in *his* background.

But I had long shared a grief of loss that so many Southerners quite genuinely suffered, although our losses weren't the same. Theirs—the Southern Way of Life, the eventually trivialized Lost Cause of the Confederacy—they had nourished well into my own young manhood, nourished and cherished almost to regional madness and personal destruction—certainly to the rest of the nation's bemused boredom and occasional wrath. My own losses were personal ones, however, mainly family deaths, which added another layer to my sadness, a slightly altered form of loss—and it may be this that has most united me with so many of the Lost Causers—the loss of something I had never had. For them—people my own age, I'm talking about, people of the nineteen Fifties—it was a South that had ceased to be, and they had become frozen into a Time most of them had never known. For me, it was the loss of my paternal grandfather. He and my grandmother died within five minutes of each other in May of the year I was born in September. Since then, death seems always to have been a close kin. Too, what I missed was a "Home." I was Southern by parentage, Southern by inclination, but born and raised Northern. I envied so many of the Nashvilleans I knew their having a home, and I came to want Nashville to be my own home.

But Nashville was a strange place, in many ways. I had lived there as a student for five years, as a temporary "nearby" resident in Murray, Kentucky, for two more, as an "Army" resident for two more, and for another nearly two years on my own by the time that evening's visit occurred. Yet I still felt like an outsider in Nashville. It was a city that could do that to people.

Too, I suppose it was that inability to separate the legs of my Nashville stool that hasn't ever left me. At the time, I kept itching with a sense that something was close to surfacing in me—something both *of* me and *not* of me—that everything going on in my head and my heart, everything coming out of my mouth or out of my pen—was an effort by that Whatever-It-Was within me, and that *it* was in me to uncover something deeper, something below the mere names of things, wrestling through me toward some essential though shapeless identity—like Chaos before God created order. And I felt that it was going to do that no matter whether I especially wanted it to or not, because in another very real sense it had nothing to do with me at all. I felt so often during those days that I was just a vehicle for this other Thing, this urge, itch, yen, this force thrusting up through me that would break my heart—or be willing to have me break someone else's—without a qualm.

That evening at the Gradys made me understand things in a strange way. Not even understand, I guess, but perceive, maybe. Intuit. I don't know. But I felt both lost and found all at the same time. The chorus in the *Original Sacred Harp* hymn "Antioch" exults,

> Shout on pray on, we're gaining ground,
> Glory, hallelujah!
> The dead's alive, and the lost is found,
> Glory Hallelujah!

I was the dead come to life; I was the lost come to be found. Yet even with such bursts of joy so intense I could barely stand them, there still hung the pall of a sadness so wrenching I couldn't fail to understand that death and loss were to be the twin themes of my life.

And it wasn't the Black Jack.

It may be as simple as this: There are times—isolated, though never really separated from the main thrust of our lives—when we are so closely attuned to the world we can feel the subtlest tremor of the earth, sense the faintest stir of air, trace the slightest shift of color in a sinking winter sky, marvel in awe at our insights into the most perplexing mysteries of life. At such times, it occurs to us with stunning wonderment, *we* must be the very ones whom Henry James admonished his young neophyte writer to be like, because at such times we seem to be the chosen, the ones "on whom nothing is lost."

...

In October, 1956, while I was a graduate student at Vanderbilt, my mother died of breast cancer at Methodist Hospital in Memphis.

She had first noticed the lump shortly before I came home from the Army in November 1954. She had a mastectomy in January 1955, waiting—as parents will do—until I had gone back to Nashville and gotten more or less settled in school again before even telling me about the pending operation.

She had responded well to both the physical and the radiation therapies until about March of 1956, the year my friend and I were awarded our bachelor's degrees. Soon after, my mother noticed tiny little bumps—like a rash—on her chest where the breast had been removed. She thought it had something to do with the radiation: burns or some such. The doctor had a look and, I assume, blanched. Not a rash, unless you could call it a rash of tiny, tiny little cancer lumps. Mother said it looked—after she had stepped from the shower and was still wet—like someone might have blown a dust of sand over the area where her breast had been. She went back to the hospital for more treatment. Then out. Then back in. Then out. Then in early September—my first fall, my second semester, in graduate school—she was back in for what turned out to be the final days of her life.

Until I went down to Memphis the week before she died, the last time I had seen her was in early August. I couldn't believe the change. It didn't beggar description—because she could easily be described—but it certainly beggared my comprehension.

Vanderbilt was playing Ole Miss in football down in Oxford, Mississippi, that year. Vandy, which had gotten the reputation for being the Homecoming Queen of the Southeastern Conference because it could almost always be counted on to lose—handily so virtually *all* the boys on the host team got to play—was the patsy for another homecoming game.

I knew Mother was in bad shape—my brother who lived in Memphis by then had written me that much—so I decided to go see her, and the trip to Mississippi was the perfect excuse. Memphis was only about sixty miles from Oxford, so I got a ride to the game with friends who were going to head on up to Memphis after the slaughter for pleasures of their own.

It was the first time I had ever been on the Ole Miss campus, and I was struck by the gentleness of the place, or as it seemed. People were having picnics under the same trees their families had been having picnics under for generations, I gather, and the usual festiveness seemed also to have a profound aura of true *home* to it, didn't seem to have quite the carnival air usually found at most campuses now where homecomings can be so Disneyworld-ishly *produced*. It was more subdued, more family-like. It touched me greatly, probably because of why I was really there.

We lost the game, of course, playing our usually fine first quarter, our usually all right second quarter, our usually badly slipping third quarter, and our usually disastrous fourth quarter when the other team called on the boys whose numbers seemed barely to have been sewn on their jerseys. After, my friends and I headed north through Holly Springs, then northwest to Memphis.

They dropped me off at the hospital where I met my oldest brother. He warned me that I might not recognize Mother at first. I'm glad he told me, because I couldn't believe how she'd changed in just two months. Her face was yellowed by the jaundice she had developed, the skin around her mouth tight, drawn back into a permanent grimace like it had been removed, tanned, then stretched back over her skull. Her teeth looked huge, her body gaunt, sallow, and wasted.

But she was still alert, trying to introduce me to the nurse on duty. My brother had to do it, though, because Mother couldn't do much more than lie there on the bed and grunt hoarsely. She just about couldn't talk, yet I didn't have that much trouble understanding what she said. At least, I knew what she was telling me.

She wanted to know why I was there.

I told her about the football game.

She wanted to know if I was glad to be back in school.

I told her it was more wonderful than I had ever hoped.

She wanted to know who my friend was.

I didn't know what to say.

"You've written to me about her," she croaked.

"Just a friend," I said.

She let it go at that, tired.

I held her hand for a long while, then just sat by her bed and talked about classes, the weather, my nephews and nieces, how sorry I was I hadn't gotten down there more during the summer, but that graduate school demanded more than undergraduate...

She laughed at that. She said I'd come at the right time. I think she smiled.

Then she slept. I kissed her forehead, touched her cheek, and left with my brother.

He took me to the Peabody Hotel where I'd agreed to meet my friends. We were going to go up to the Penthouse, have a drink, sack out with some other friends, then start back to Nashville early the next morning, Sunday.

On Breaking One's Pencil

...

It was just the very next Tuesday that my brother called me. It was about 6:30 in the morning, and I knew, when I heard the phone on the landing, who it was. It stopped ringing when the fraternity pledge answered it. I listened to him mount the half flight of stairs, heard him turn left to come toward my room, and felt him pause at my door. I was already sitting up looking at him as he eased it open. I just nodded when he said the call was for me.

I told my brother I'd get the *City of Memphis* that noon if he'd meet me at the little suburban stop just over the hill from where mother and I had lived ever since my father's death eight years earlier.

Helen was the first person I told and the first person I needed to be with. I was waiting outside her office on campus when she got there at 8:00 that morning. She looked at me and knew something was wrong. I asked her if she could take me to the station to catch the train.

Later in the morning when we got there we had about half an hour to wait. We strolled through the huge, vaulted, echoing waiting room of the L&N Station to the escalator down to the tracks. We strolled up and down the platform together talking about mothers and cancer and death; fathers and heart attacks and death; wars and soldiers and death. I had left my bag at one end of the platform, so both hands were free.

It wasn't unexpected, I told her.

She said that she was so glad for me—and my mother—that I had gone down there the week before.

I agreed it had been a good idea.

She murmured something about being sorry she had never met her.

"And your brother will meet you?" she asked again.

"At the Buntyn stop, yes. He won't have to go clear in town."

"It's near where you live?"

"Yes. It's a row of two-story apartments right across the street from CBC," Christian Brothers College which was then a small Catholic high school and junior college.

We heard the train coming, so we strolled back to my bag. We stood there watching the train arc around the curve of the approach to the platform. I checked my watch. I thanked her for bringing me to the station. She asked me how long I'd be gone. I told her probably a week. She said for me to be sure to let her know as soon as I got back in town.

I said I would.

"Bob," she said, "I'm so sorry."

It was starting to hit me, I felt. This death in my life. My mother seemed so young, even if she was older than my father had been when he died. He was not quite 52, she was not quite 58. I wondered what that might mean for me. We would all be going back to Arkansas to bury her, and all of a sudden I didn't want to do that. I didn't want any more funerals: my father's parents whom I had never known, my mother's father who died on a visit to our house when we lived in New York, my father, my mother…

I looked at Helen and realized I was squeezing her hand so tightly she was having to bite her lip not to cry out, and looking at her, it suddenly occurred to me that if I ever had children, they would never know my parents, even as I had never known my father's, and it struck me that that was unfair, just plain, goddamned rotten, dirty, stinking, bloody unfair.

"Helen," I said. She looked at me, holding my hand in both hers. When I held hers in mine, I saw the deep red grooves on either side of her ring finger where I had squeezed so hard. "I'm sorry, Helen," I said. "I'm sorry."

We gave each other a quick, awkward hug. Our cheeks touched for just a second. My lips may have brushed her face. Then I was on the train. As it jerked into motion, I saw Helen on the platform staring after me. I gave a quick wave she may not have seen. The train jerked again and started its slow, grinding way through the city's yards. It jerked once more and I nearly got sick to my stomach at the thought of not being able to see her for a week. The tears were in my eyes, but I wouldn't let myself go as I lurched into the stark knowledge of what it was I was already missing.

I snuffled, inhaled deeply, and stared out the window to watch, for the five-hour trip, as Middle Tennessee flattened slowly westward to the bluffs of Memphis and the River that rolled on through the rich delta land of Mississippi and Louisiana, down to the Gulf of Mexico.

…

When I got back it was clear to me I had to talk to someone, and that was Helen. It wasn't a good situation. Let's just say we shouldn't have been seeing each other—and, well, they eventually got married anyway. Still, when I first saw her again I knew that the spontaneous gesture she made toward me was more than sympathy for a good friend whose mother had died.

I've had to deal with death and loss and grief a good bit in my life. I've had to comfort people as they trembled, stunned by blows to their expectations and desires, those sledgehammer jolts that sometimes knock us so far off the tracks of our habits we think there's no way we can ever be the same again—and often we're right. I've had to survive them myself—more than many people, as best I can tell.

There *is* that formal feeling Emily Dickinson wrote of when the mind retires a part of it-self, rejects what it doesn't want to be, yet keeps on working in other ways, carrying out the routines that have to be carried out: Death or no death, small children need to be bathed and fed, the cat needs to be put out, the clothes still get dirty, dishes do keep piling up.

With my mother, though, death was one of those odd releases from a kind of physical agony most of us, probably, never have to endure. The cancer, once it reestablished itself, was as fast and merciless as old mortality. The autopsy report told of the cancer spreading from her breast through the lymph system to practically every one of her internal organs, and then to her spinal cord, rising toward her brain like a column of mercury in a thermometer measuring a child's fever.

The doctor said her physical pain had to have been intense. Yet she refused over and over to take more than the usual doses of medicine to still the hurt. According to the nurses she never complained, simply asked for some ice to be put in her mouth or to be turned in the bed, if it wasn't too much trouble. They said she always asked about their children, their husbands, their sick in-laws, whoever.

The end, apparently, was calm: She simply drifted off when it was time, never woke up, never fought one of those rear-guard actions that couldn't ever have saved the main body in any event.

A minister at one of the services for her said that she knew herself and accepted her fate. Perhaps, though I wonder if it wasn't more a matter of being so debilitated by the cancer that she didn't have much choice, simply couldn't fight the stuff anymore.

Knowing my mother the way I did, I finally decided she probably had accepted her death the same way she had accepted her life. It was that kind of assurance she had about things—including herself. She seldom *doubted* life. Hers had ranged from good to very good. But after my father died, I sometimes felt she was mainly just marking time.

I told Helen that she had nearly remarried—a former high school sweetheart. Dad had been dead about two years when she got the first phone call from him. He called her "Ducky," I think. Or she called him that. He was a widower, a dairyman in North Carolina. They came to my high school graduation with each other, as I recall. At home, she would sit on the phone with him for hours. Murmuring sweet nothings, I reckon. I was amazed.

They would have gotten married—the plans were all made, more or less: the children on both sides approving, essentially, and accepting that both of them were pretty good people—but, in a weird concatenation of events, he, too (like my father) died of a sudden heart attack. Then she got the cancer, so it may have been for the best after all.

I talked to Helen for hours about all of this, even ended up talking about my father because of her, telling her things that had been hanging around for all those years that I hadn't ever had the person to talk to about. Or maybe the occasion. Or possibly the opportunity. But all three came together in Helen.

When you're a young person—I was twenty-four—and your last surviving parent dies, you are slammed rudely face to face with the fact not only that you are an adult, and not only that you are mortal, but that you are now really and truly on your own. Maybe what that means is that you start becoming aware that you've got a history and that death is the constantly recurring line of demarcation in so much of your life, aware that things happened before your father died or after; things happened between your father's death and your mother's; other things happened after your mother's death. And so forth.

I got my first car, for instance, because my mother died. That wasn't how boys—young men—were supposed to remember their first cars, according to one of the myths of Life in These United States. They were supposed to be "crates" or "jalopies" or have silly names and all that. Not mine. My siblings, all being older and married, already had cars. So I got the Buick. My oldest brother got everything cleared through the estate business so I could take it back to school with me after Christmas.

A brief digression here. Years and years after that October of 1956, my father-in-law died in a nursing home in Seneca, South Carolina. That was in 1987. I was in Boston, my wife was in Knoxville, Tennessee, my daughter was up in Canada camping out, and our son was wandering around Southeast Asia after a brief stint "teaching English to Japanese yuppies," as he put it. We had been more or less prepared for her mother's death, but not for her father's.

I was on the phone to my wife and various people during the night, and before I went to bed—I was at a weeklong Unitarian Universalist training session for new congregation organizers—a minister who was one of the live-in instructors asked me how *I* was. I said, "Fine," a little surprised at his question. My wife's father and I had been on basically good terms, but were never at all what would be called close. So why should I be having a problem other than making certain my wife was ok and getting the support and help she would be needing?

But that night after I had done a little reading and finally turned out the light, I lay on my back for a few minutes—what I do when I don't really want to go to sleep right away. And then the tears started. I was really surprised. Why was I crying over my father-in-law? The answer? I wasn't. I was crying for my mother, for my father, for my nephew, for my grandparents—for everyone I had ever known and loved who had died. That's what happened back in Nashville. It was my mother who had died, but it was my father I was finally grieving for, and it was Helen who both figuratively and literally held my hands while I was working through a lot of that.

Mom's funeral was what funerals are. Not too many people there—certainly compared to my father's funeral—but a nice crowd. Well, I suppose we all want a good house on closing night. It wasn't that I loved my mother less, but that I missed my father more, and her funeral brought all that out. I was just fifteen when Dad died. And it was so sudden. Boom! Five minutes and it was over. And I was away at school. The last sight I had of him he was bending over to wave at me and my older brother as the train pulled out of Penn Station taking us back down to Washington where we changed from the Pennsy to the C&O for the trek to Virginia. He was smiling.

But with Mother there was that awful cancer, so her death was one of those wretched blessings we talk about. There wasn't any life left for her with that. Too, I had lived with and around her an additional eight years. At fifteen I had still *needed* Dad a lot, but at twenty-four I didn't *need* Mother as much. It was just totally different.

Back in Nashville I didn't feel any pain at all and only a little loss. I think that trip the week before she died, when we both knew she would be dead soon, after I saw her—I think that trip drew off any poison I might have had in me about her death. I felt terrible loss, but mostly I felt sad. And tired. The *pain* was still for my father.

I'd never gone through much with him. Never had a chance to say goodbye. Never was old enough to tell him I loved him. I think we might have been on that slippery verge when he was shifting slowly from being my father the Responsible Authority, to being my father, the mentor, the guide. A friend. Someone I could know as a person as an adult. But when I was told he was dead, it was like being told the movie was over before the last reel had ever finished showing.

With Mother it was different. We'd been through some pretty rough times with each other, but we'd made our peace with all that and come through it ok. No embarrassments. No things left unsaid. We'd seen each other in her death, had held each other. Said goodbye, after a fashion. I don't know. Somehow there had been time enough for things to have gotten settled between us, to have gotten all right. Whatever kind of closure there can be with someone who is dying, I think I had with Mom. I felt her loss, yes, but mainly I was sad because I would miss her terribly.

Going back to Pine Bluff, Arkansas, going back for her funeral, seeing her casket, seeing that wasted body in the casket, hearing a minister she didn't know say the things he was supposed to say didn't affect me especially. I kept waiting to see the coffin actually lowered into the ground, wanted to see the mechanism that would do that, wanted to hear the hollow *Whump!* of dirt on top of the casket.

But what her burial did was to unearth every shred of grief I was still feeling about Dad, and I hadn't even known I was still hauling all that stuff around with me.

It was these things over time I talked so much to Helen about. It was after that, that we admitted how much we loved each other.

...

What I didn't tell her about was how I had acted some six years earlier when my mother first told us she was planning to remarry. I knew about the phone calls, about *him*, Ducky, knew that something was going on, but I hadn't known what to do about it—as though there was something I was *supposed* to do about it. It seemed strange to me, oddly impure, as though she were having some sort of "innocent" affair while Dad was away.

I was a junior in high school when they started up their relationship again, and by my senior year they were pretty well clear on what they intended. By my freshman year at Vanderbilt they were engaged and making plans.

I remember one night talking to my oldest brother, John, about it. I asked him if he liked the man. He said he thought he was an honest and good man. I asked him if he thought Mother would be happy. He said she was mature and because she had known him in high school and had spent a good bit of time with him during the past two years or so she knew him well enough to be able to make a sensible judgment about it.

I asked him where they would live.

He said probably over in North Carolina where his home was.

"Well," I said, sitting on the edge of my bed, winding my watch, getting ready to turn out the light. I set my watch on the night table between us, leaned over, and flipped the switch. "Well, I guess there won't be too much in the way of sex with them, will there?"

My brother was nearly ten years older than I was, and he had his ways that to me were sometimes awfully, well, I'll just say "direct." Not to put too great an edge on it, but he hadn't wanted to be a professional soldier since he was old enough to know the difference between a rifle and a fishing rod for nothing, hadn't spent World War II as a paratrooper in the 82nd Airborne for nothing, hadn't bribed a jump school instructor to be sure he by God! *passed* one of the jump tests for nothing, hadn't deserted from a hospital in Europe to get back to his unit for nothing, hadn't survived a combat jump into France on June 6th of '44 for nothing. In short, in an earlier age, John might have considered the long bow a coward's weapon, himself preferring to stick with the broad sword that let you get in closer to your enemies so you could see the shock in their eyes, could see the luster go out of them when you got in a telling blow.

And yet…

And yet something in him knew about something in me that I didn't know about. Something in him felt the fear in my voice. Or the concern. Or the whatever it was at eighteen that was gnawing at me about all of this.

"Oh, I don't know," he answered, pausing to let me go on if I needed to. Or could. "I expect there'll be sex," he said, his voice gentle in the dark of our room. He was there on business, staying with us for just a few days. That's what he and Mother said, but I doubt that it was quite the whole truth. He hadn't ever had any business in Memphis before. I didn't know why he suddenly had come right then when Mother was making marriage announcements all over the place and I was about to be off to college or was home for Thanksgiving or whatever was happening at the time.

"You do?" I asked, trying to sound as though this was just a matter of little moment, but not to the extent that I wanted him to think I had a prurient or even idle curiosity about it.

He was quiet for a minute. Then he said, "Bob, our mother is a very attractive woman. She's even truly beautiful. When she was in high school she was the 'Belle' of Pine Bluff, Arkansas, which may not have been all that much, but it was where she was. The week Dad asked her to marry him, she was engaged to another man. And now she's planning to remarry. He's not our father, but he's a good man and I think he'll be very good to our mother. I also think he'll be very good *for* our mother. She's not an old woman, Bob. She's just barely fifty-two. I imagine there'll be sex."

I sensed he had other things to think about that night and wanted mainly to get to sleep, but I also felt him turn his head toward me. In the dim light from the street lamp in the garage lane behind our apartment, I saw him looking over at me and I knew his eyes were open, waiting.

"Well sure," I said. "Sure."

"Bob," he said, still gentle with me, "it's all right."

"But do you think they really love each other?"

"Yes. Yes, I do."

"But how can she have loved Dad and now love him, too?"

"People can love more than one person, Bob."

"Have you? Have you ever loved anyone else besides Mary Morris?"

"No."

"Then how can Mom?"

"But I'm still married to Mary Morris, Bob. Mom's not married to Dad anymore."

"Well it's not like they ever got a divorce or anything."

To this day I can still remember the pressure of the gorge from the panic rising through my chest into my throat. Through it all, my brother stayed calm, trying to keep me calm, too.

"Bob, Dad's dead now."

We had been half whispering because Mother's bedroom was just around the corner in the small apartment, and I didn't want her to know what we were talking about.

Dead, I repeated to myself. *Do you really think I don't know Dad's dead? Damn it, do you really think I don't know that? God **knows** I know **that!***

There weren't any tears, just the impulse toward them. But in that regard, I was still a dry socket. I snuffled up a little phlegm, but that was about it.

"I just don't see how she could have loved Dad and love this guy, too," I kept on, in terrible control.

He waited for a minute, until I even thought he'd gone on to sleep instead. But finally, "Bob, don't you remember all those days in the summer in Pelham when you hit the streets about seven in the morning looking for all your buddies? You'd have lunch in one place, play baseball someplace else, go swimming someplace else, and finally drop back home about supper time—if you didn't stay to eat that someplace else too?"

"Of course."

"Do you think Mother ever worried about you when you weren't around?"

"I don't know. Why should she have? Pelham was safe, and besides, I always called from wherever I was to let her know wherever I was going."

"That's what I mean. She trusted you to call her and let her know what was going on. She still trusts you. Why don't you try trusting her?"

We each rolled over on that and went to sleep. I felt a little better. Not a whole lot, because he still hadn't answered my question. But he had tried, and I have always loved him for that.

...

Sometime after Christmas, after three months of Helen's letting herself be the sponge that soaked up the puddles of emotion I had become, I was sitting down late, late into the night to a paper I had convinced myself I was working on. I wrote that night until it was done.

At four in the morning I went to bed and slept like a dead man, but about six, when it was still dark outside in Nashville, Tennessee, and very cold, I woke up: crying because I was in love, because I was in mourning, and because Helen was in love with one man too many. It was a time when my jaws still would clamp against tears, but that night, I remember, my heart was heavied not only for lovers everywhere who had to sleep apart, but also for all sons whose fathers' deaths had betrayed them into ignorance and loss for ever and ever.

...

The Grand Ole Opry is as good a metaphor as any to get another kind of grip on Nashville. Certainly it sits at *a* center of things there. When I was an undergraduate at Vanderbilt, for instance, I can remember that the Opry was pretty much looked down on by the folks out in the West End of town, and not too many years later I recall being told by a friend of mine, as he was driving me somewhere in his father's Mercedes Benz, how embarrassed he had been by an advertisement airing over WSM—presumably during the Opry.

It happened that one weekend he had some friends visiting him from out of town—"from the North" out of town types, I gather—and the car radio was on when the offending ad set his friends off into gales of laughter. It had to do with how to worm your pigs the easy way: just throw the anti-worm pills into their slops and "your pigs will worm themselves."

It sounded like a good idea to me. Anyone who has ever tried to reason a three hundred pound boar into swallowing a pill because it would be good for him ought to have picked up on the idea right away. But my friend, while acknowledging all the practicality of the message, was still embarrassed because it made Nashville look (he thought) like a Hick Town, a Rube Place, a Hillbilly Haven: uncouth, backward, lacking sophistication, and all that—"a dirty little river town," as another friend of mine once put it.

He wanted the message out that Nashville was a center of commerce (which it was), that it was a center of government (which it was), that it was truly the Athens of the South with all its colleges and universities (which it was), that it was *thus* also a center of intellectual and artistic ferment (which it, well, was after its fashion, I suppose, although leaders of business, industry, insurance, sales, banking, politics, and Save Our Traditional Way of Life haven't often been the yeast that raises the most intellectual and artistic of ferments).

On Breaking One's Pencil

As for myself, I got hooked on that Opry stuff years earlier when I was a boy in Pelham, New York, listening to back-to-back-to-back, thirty-minute segments of the Opry, Hayloft Hoedown, and the National Barn Dance on Saturday nights. I had also gotten hooked on "folk" music generally by Burl Ives way back when. So I was in hog heaven (pun intended) by being in Nashville, even though I never went to an Opry performance.

As a matter of fact, when I was in the Army down in Fort Jackson, South Carolina, I remember a wonderful radio station: WCKY, Cincinnati 1, Ohio. The program we usually heard was a C&W affair "brought to you by Hank's Chicks, [Somebody-or-Other's] Tombstones, and [Somebody or Other Else's] Tomatoes." It was a good show, and the interesting thing was that the fellow who usually turned it on to listen was a big black guy from Memphis who was drafted into the Army and who had to wander around that first humiliating day of medical exams with his shirt tied around his waist because he didn't have any underwear. And, by the way, the National Barn Dance started out in Chicago as the WLS Barndance. Folks, not all the hillbillies are from the South or have red necks.

But The Grand Ole Opry was an embarrassment to a lot of the Vanderbilt types, even though Donald Davidson taught his Traditional British and American Ballads course for years. It wasn't until the business types in Nashville realized what a gold mine the Opry was that they decided, in the interest of finances and profits, that it was worth their time to take a look at it without their uplifted noses blocking the view: esthetics phooey! We're not talking D-I-V-O-R-C-E here but M-O-N-E-Y.

Of course, the Opry itself had changed a great deal in the meantime, not at all unwilling to turn a buck in what some older Opry folks considered pretty tacky non-traditional ways.

Even when I was an undergraduate during the fifties, there weren't any electric guitars to sully the purity of the folk sound—at least not when Roy Acuff was on stage and defining that sound (although I remember somebody in a pork-pie hat playing a dobro with someone's outfit, though that may have been sometime later).

Acuff probably was simply following the cue of George Dewey Hay, the originator of the Opry, who himself admitted that the "line of demarcation between the old popular tunes and folk tunes is indeed slight." Still, Hay wouldn't play to horns or drums because he saw those as signifying "popular," not "folk" music. So the acts he signed pretty much stuck with strings. When he started the Opry on WSM, it was called the WSM Barndance, (Hay knew how to tune in Chicago's WLS on the radio dial, too). That was late in 1925, and it was three years before an ad-libbing announcer—Hay himself, apparently—referred to the WSM show as The Grand Ole Opry, after a performance of "real" opera had just aired, at least according to the usually accepted story.

Of course, there weren't all that many electric guitars around then either. But the technology can never be ignored. Besides, to expect Country Music to have been unaffected by such events as the two World Wars with their post-War booms and a Great Depression in between is to expect that which isn't going to happen. "Real" country folk were serving around the world in the Army and Navy as well as were upper Midwesterners including Minnesotans many of whom, doubtless, saw duty in towns where for the first times in their lives, the Lutheran church, if there was one around at all, was not the primary church, and who heard English spoken for the first time without great dollops of Norwegian glottals.

Then too, there was so much more money in the South after the War that lots of folks, who used to live pretty sequestered lives back up in the hollows of the Appalachians and Smokies not to mention the clusters of cabins that marked the homes of tenant farmers as the land gentled down toward the plains and deltas, were able to buy radios pretty easily. Couple that with the development of commercial television and the increasing affordability of the tube, and you didn't have anywhere near the poverty or sequestration of populations as that brought about during the post-Civil War years—which lasted, after all, well into the Thirties.

So people heard the Beetles who had learned an awful lot about how to sing by listening to Elvis. Well, that may be unfair, but perhaps not as unfair as some might think.

Now, of course, all a person has to do to see that things have changed is watch an annual Country Music Hall of Fame program (there seems to be one every couple of months) and watch Garth Brooks leap about on the stage doing his version of some rock group or another, and watch so many of them with headsets and microphones attached just like Michael Jackson, and listen to the way they sing. I'm talking about the pronunciation of words *a la* heavy-duty pop music. Many of the women seem to have Judy Garland

and Barbara Streisand as vocal role models now, rather than more traditional country singers like Miss Kitty Wells or Patsy Kline, and clearly the number of crossovers grows steadily.

Much of that is exciting in its own way because somewhere under it all there is still a lot of the sound and "feel" of the traditional stuff, but it is getting harder and harder to come across. Of course, to those Nashvillians who didn't like the original much in the first place, what difference does it make? Count the bucks, boys, 'cause they're more and more of them. It was ever thus, I suppose, but some of us hate to see things changed even faster than they would have changed left to themselves, by people who could not care less what they're changing to.

But as I suggested, the Grand Ole Opry is still a good metaphor for Nashville, an image of the kinds of changes always going on.

...

My time at Vanderbilt fell into two major divisions: pre-Army and post-Army, the post-Army into finishing the BA in history and getting the MA in English. The pre-Army was marked by a steady decline of grades, a steady increase in my consumption of beer, but a beginning of my coming into an understanding of myself as a teacher and as a human being.

The first two-and-a-third years were mainly oriented toward the fraternity, the final year-and-a-third toward school. The fraternity experience was mainly a positive one for me, though all the negatives people can summon up were there as well: the snobbery, the drinking, the card playing, the on and on. Still, I saw my main job as being one of teaching the younger members—the pledges—about the history of the fraternity and all that. My sophomore year I was the assistant pledge trainer, and my junior year I was the main pledge trainer—until I got drafted.

Those were wonder years in a way, because I was expanded through contact with some amazing people. But the upshot, even so, was that I was chafing under the yoke of too many years in a row in classrooms, even though I basically liked school. But enough was enough.

I hadn't wanted to go to college right away in the first place, but when the North Koreans breached the 38th parallel in June of 1950—the month I graduated from high school—college looked like a pretty good place to be, particularly after the Chinese got into the mess and blew south with their bugles of death, sweeping the U.S. forces down into a pocket that way too much resembled the beaches at Dunkerque.

My father had started college at Washington and Lee where—to hear him tell it—about all he had done was play football and sing in barbershop quartets. Then with America's entry into the First World War, he resigned with honor (rather than being dropped, as a letter from the Dean to his father made clear was likely to happen if he didn't straighten up) to accept a commission as a first lieutenant in the Army. He never had to be in combat, but was assigned the duty of helping whip recruits into topnotch physical condition. After the War, he never went back to college. Went to work instead. Got married. Started a family. I didn't want *that*, exactly. But I had wanted to lay out for a year or so and work. Well.

I got the chance. I started my junior year in 1952, but found out I was supposed to get drafted that October. I requested a deferment until after the fall quarter was over so I could get credit for it. The request was approved, and I was inducted on January 28, 1953. I had basic training in Fort Jackson, South Carolina, radio operators school in the same place, then—because the ceasefire had been signed—I was sent to field radio maintenance and repair school in Fort Knox, Kentucky. Then on to Salzburg, Austria, for what the Army called my "most conspicuous duty" as a radioman with the 510th Field Artillery Battalion, Tactical Command Austria.

Separated from active duty the middle of November 1954, I was back in Vanderbilt for the winter quarter of the '54-'55 school year. Even though I had had a pretty good tour of duty during those twenty-one-and-a-half months, I was anxious to get back to Nashville. As to school, I never would have guessed the strength, the pure passion of that return.

It was like being sixteen and so full of the sweet juices of life you almost can't stand it, sixteen when you're little more than a walking erection absolutely attuned and sensitive to everything in the world that glimmers or trembles or has a taste, a smell, a feel, a sound that you need to *know*, that you need to know in the profoundest ways imaginable, that you need absolutely to possess, to make your own for ever and ever.

Everything was so new and fresh and exciting, I felt like Scrooge waking up after the visit from the last of the Spirits of Christmas and finding that he was still alive—*Whoop Holla!*—and that the world was still there and that there was still *time* to learn and know and love and just flat out *Be!*

On Breaking One's Pencil

The books I read, the people I talked to, the movies I saw, the plays that held me rapt, the music I heard; the very smell of the campus, the feel of the bark on its gorgeous trees; the touch of the paper napkins we so carefully folded into quarter squares to catch the drips of coffee spilled during dizzying conversations; the sudden, unexpected praise from a tough but respected teacher; the squirrels fed by the old and probably mad "squirrel lady" who talked to them, knew them all and all their habits, the little old lady who had adopted them as her children; the taste of the chocolate sodas made by Ethel in the Union: There was no end to the high I was on. And so it went the rest of that year, that summer, and on into my senior year. It even lasted mostly through graduate school as well. And of course, Helen was a major part of it all.

...

Two years later I was back in Nashville after a stint at Murray State College up in Kentucky. Teaching English. Three sections of freshmen, two of sophomores. Whew!

I had come back to write, and after a year of it, I got a part time job with the Development Office, then directed by Don Elliott. After a while, I accepted a full-time job. I was going to help raise gobs of money for the University. Why not? I thought. They were engaged in a thirty-million dollar capital gifts campaign. Why not?

Studying up during the next few weeks, I learned more about Vanderbilt University than I had ever thought there was to know: details, facts; figures about payrolls, electric bills, coal costs to heat the place, pension costs for retired people; age of buildings, costs of repairs versus costs of new construction; then percentages: the number of engineers, businessmen, teachers, doctors, lawyers in the Southeast with their degrees from Vanderbilt; then more: cost of living indices, percentage and dollar figures of tuition increases, how tuition increases in the previous ten years had resulted in a smaller and smaller percentage of real dollars from that source to pay the electric and water bills. On and on: the library, the engineering labs, the healthcare benefits packages, the growing costs of campus security, travel costs for people in Admissions, costs, costs, costs. I'd always seen school as a bunch of classrooms with teachers and students, then football games on Saturdays in the fall.

Armed with all that, I started writing general pamphlets to soften people up to the fact that we were going to be asking for big money, while we waited for the professional fund raisers to finish looking up the major prospects so we—the writers— could start writing more directed brochures for them.

Well, not my kind of work, really, but it was helping keep me in books, food, and typing paper, and I was learning and writing, and I had a desk in a building I loved—Alumni Hall—and even though I hated what they were doing to it, I still had a sensate pleasure those hours I worked there.

The offices I worked in were in a large, paneled room on the second floor. It was lined with moose heads and other such trophies that I always assumed had been donated by wealthy alumni whose wives—after thirty years or so— had told them, "Them or Me," dumping *Them* clearly being cheaper (as well, of course, as more chivalrous) than a divorce by *Me*.

But it was a comfortable room, still, and when I had been in it before the Army, I used to wander around and read those little brass plaques under the elk, moose, and other heads. The space had been used as a faculty lounge, as a room where some lesser poets on the reading circuit would read, as a meeting room. It was one of the fewer and fewer places on the campus where a person could get away from other students, could go to be alone, to try to think things through. That's where I had finally decided that a *two*-year mistake in favor of getting drafted and taking my chances with combat in Korea was better than the *four*-year mistake of joining the Air Force.

But even with the partitions the Development Office kept putting up, along with the desks for the increasing staff, I felt comfortable in there, at home, in a strange way. Once, late in the afternoon when it was clearly turning dark and I was getting ready to go home, I looked out a window. It was rainy as usual, the campus gray with the dreary weight of slickers and damp overcoats. I was looking forward to the solace of getting back to my little aerie out on Bowling Avenue, but I kept standing there for a few minutes as people passed on the sidewalk beneath me—singles, couples, a few small groups. They were quiet, for the most part, but I could hear an occasional laugh or shout from somewhere on campus, some kitchen clatter, perhaps: the sounds of the day ending, the evening beginning.

I noticed one man in particular. Late thirtyish, he didn't have on a topcoat of any kind, only gloves, a knit cap, and a bright red scarf, a splash of color against the day, like a cardinal swooping unexpectedly across a vision of a winter copse. He was smoking a pipe and striding along, head slightly bent, otherwise erect with his bulging briefcase, a smile on his face like a man remembering a shared, sweet pleasure with someone he loved.

I felt a slow rush to my head that made me feel like I might black out—shades of my Centennial Park Epiphany. My face was flushed as the message was pounded heavily and steadily into my chest—quite literally "knowledge carried to the heart," to use Alan Tate's phrase: *I am where I ought to be forever*. I didn't ever want to leave there. I was home.

Then the blood drained back down with a tingling that washed me from my scalp to my feet, but I felt the sense of it for weeks and weeks. It puzzled me, because it made me feel totally secure, and that confused me. Nashville was an alien place to lots of us, a very hard town in which to get accepted on our own terms. They had a weird way, many of those Nashvillians, of making you want to get their attention. Not to be *accepted* by them, for God's sake, but simply to make them admit that *Dammit!* you were *there*, that you were as corporeal as they were, that you, too, laughed and cried and did all those other things as well.

Then, even if they did accept something of that in you, they still could look at you funny, a slight tilt of the head up and away like they smelled something just a little off about you, the strange dog. They weren't really interested in fighting you, but they were still going to circle you, sniffing, catching the faint odor of the outsider, the gate crasher, the interloper, some primal secretion of the territorial trespasser eddying around you, making you someone not quite worth their bother—especially if you were interesting.

Well, that was *my* term. They would have said *different*, I think. Or at least that's what they would have felt. They had an odd way, I recall, of looking at you, some of them, if they hadn't seen you in a while, and saying, "Ah, and what brings *you* back to Nashville?" They smiled and pumped your hand up and down, clapped you manfully on the back, nearly always were courteous. Still, they managed to look and sound nervous, somehow, like they really wanted *Someone in Authority* to check your ID card. Or the visa on a proper passport. Or whatever.

...

Robert Penn Warren is supposed to have said once that we're all stuck with our own skins, meaning, I assume, that we are who we are and we have to live as best we can with that. But we're also stuck with our own times, and my times in Nashville were mainly the 1950s, reaching a short way into the 1960s.

What that meant was the Cold War, the Korean War, Sit-ins of the Civil Rights movement, McCarthyism, and a host of related matters. The Quiet Generation. Uninvolved. Neat young men and women. Pre-pill. I reckon it was, alluding to the Chinese curse, a pretty inter-esting time to come of age in.

The phenomenon of Robert Welch was as symptomatic of those days as the apparently less menacing—and certainly more humorous—phenomenon of Ross Perot in the presidential election of 1964.

Welch, a wealthy businessman, founded an organization, a movement, known as The John Birch Society, named for a young man who had been killed in China after the communists had managed to send Chaing Kai Chek and Madame Chaing packing off to Formosa, there to live out their lives as the guests of the United States government which, apparently, allowed them to live in the pink-clouded dream world of Regaining the Mainland. Or perhaps they created their own Disneyworld vision of how life would eventually, if not soon, be fun again.

Whatever, The John Birch Society—marching to the beat of the times of McCarthy and others of that ilk who had their own dreams of a world safe from Kommies, Kooks, and Kikes (never mentioning the "niggers," of course)—drew masses of discontented conservatives to its membership, and the central drawing card was Robert Welch.

In March of 1961, I think it was, Robert Welch came through Nashville delivering his sad talk about Communism. I was desperate to hear him because, like the sit-ins and Joseph McCarthy, he was a piece of the history of those times. His speech was to be presented in the War Memorial Auditorium, a public building in downtown Nashville. Alas, the public was not in general to be allowed to attend.

Tickets were sold, and those mainly through carefully controlled outlets. Others were distributed free of charge. I was working for Vanderbilt's Office of Development at the time, and Bob Bahnsen, one of my co-workers, and I badgered a friend in the Alumni Office to let us have two freebies. He didn't want to do it because he knew we differed basically on things political—as well as things otherwise. Too, Welch wanted friendly audiences, wanted, it seemed to me, the easy job of preaching to the already converted. All rather like "Dubya" in a later time. But our friend let us have the tickets and off we went.

The crowd was huge, and as we walked through the chill of that March night, we had to wait in a heavy line to get past the security people. Tickets were checked at the entrance to the building as well as to the auditorium itself.

"Jesus," Bahnsen whispered. (He was from Connecticut.) Both of us looked around and marveled. We had known that Welch's brand of conservatism had great support in Nashville and where in Nashville it came from, but we were a little shaken at actually seeing it manifested that night. We muttered to each other as our section of the thick wedge of people shuffled toward the doors where the uniformed ticket takers stood.

Inside, we wandered slowly, waiting for the mass to thin out at the various doors to the auditorium itself. We entered, found our seats, left our overcoats in them, and wandered back out slowly to eyeball the crowd.

During the sit-ins a couple of years earlier in Nashville, the people who opposed integrating the lunch counters and restaurants were predictable enough. The people out in the streets who were actually bashing the Vanderbilt divinity students in the head, kicking the picketers, shouting their nigger slogans, spitting—they were predictable and even, God save them, understandable. They lived their lives out under the general rubric of *Redneck*. They were born Neck, reared Neck, courted Neck, married Neck, begat Neck, and died Neck; it was preached to them on Sundays and taught to them weekdays until that red neck was almost as transformed as the Cross and carried with it almost the same power. It became their emblem of pride, of honor, and even of redemption. You could despair at their ignorance, but you could also understand the surface of their fears: Give a nigger a job and there's one less for a Neck, conversations about Luddites being scarcely germane to much of anything. They sometimes lived in neighborhoods back to back, the Necks and the Jigs, and with Brown *v.* Board of Education already about half a decade behind them, and with All Deliberate Speed creeping along though it was, anybody with one eye and half a wit could see who'd be going to school with them, and it wasn't going to be those nice kids who lived out there in the west end of Nashville. Nossir.

Back then it had been easy to get a mad-on at the Redneck idiots and fools, the vicious, the clearly scummy, the illiterate, the hateful, the mean, the brawlers and tonk fighters who taunted the picketers and placard bearers. They were obvious. What you couldn't see were the people who stood behind them, though you could read what they had to say without any trouble—particularly in the afternoon paper. There was no dearth of editorials about Outside Agitators, Breakers of the Peace, Looking for Trouble, Law and Order, the Need for Preserving Domestic Tranquility, and all the rest of the conservative buzzwords of the time.

But you never *saw* any of those people. They never showed themselves on the street, too busy, probably, taking down the latest gems of wisdom from their maids about how all those people were just troublemakers. It amazed me even then how they could bring themselves to believe the words of people desperate to keep their jobs. Believe what your maid said about not wanting to be able to sit down at a counter to buy a cup of coffee in a store where they were allowed to stand up next to white people to spend their money on goods, and you'd be able to believe that no colored person ever cheered for Joe Louis to knock the crap out of another Mister Charley.

But there in War Memorial Auditorium you could see them, finally, as though they waited for special occasions to take on substance. And I remember thinking suddenly that I wished I was a thief, and how that must have been the finest night in at least a century to hit up the wealthy Belle Meade section of Nashville. All those people were right there with *me* waiting to hear Mr. Welch tell us about Captain John Birch, the nation's first victim of communism, and of the society that Mr. Welch had founded and named for the Captain (a graduate of the Fundamentalist Baptist Bible Institute in Fort Worth, Texas), as well as Welch's own reading of the Supreme Court, that pinko president Dwight David Eisenhower, fellow travelers, com-symps, plots, ploys, strategems, collusions, tentacles, traitors, cancers in the body politic, and all the rest of the night-time day-terrors that spilled from his rag-bag of paranoia. *Conspiracy*, always. Conspiracies flew from his mouth like the angry, frustrated quacks of a broken-winged duck flapping piteously on some frozen piece of the Mississippi flyway in Arkansas as the rest of its mates, ignoring him, flew south to warm themselves for the winter.

There was nothing, it seems, that was not a communist plot, a communist-manipulated maneuver, a communist smoke screen, a communist-dominated

On Breaking One's Pencil

institution, a communist-funded-infiltrated-oriented-perverted facet of life in these United States. In more recent times Dubya merely supplanted Communists with Terrorists. And now we have people inviting very special guests to their Tea Party. It was—and still is—depressing.

All this came tumbling from him as he stood behind the large lectern. Welch, in my memory, looked gentle, benign, and very grandfatherly as he stuck his left hand in his jacket pocket, pulled out a set of 3x5 note cards held together with a plain rubber band, and read from the cards. When he finished each note, he flipped that card face down on the lectern.

Then, never ceasing his talk, he gathered those cards, banged them together tightly, snapped the rubber band back on, and shoved them down into his right hand jacket pocket. It was a process that would have made Henry Ford proud of his assembly line: pull, snap, read, flip, read, flip, read, flip, bang, snap, file; pull, snap, read, flip, read, flip, read, flip, bang, snap, file; pull, snap, read, flip, read, flip, read, flip, bang, snap, file…

For an hour and a half. When he stopped (and there was no real sense of his having finished anything, having arrived at a point, or even having outlined a program, a call to action), my friend, Bob, leaned over to me and whispered, "Damn! If the commies are all that smart we might just as well give it all up right now."

When the audience understood him to be through for the night, many of them rose to their feet to applaud, emphasizing their shared fears. And what, I wondered, did these people really fear? I looked around at them: all white, all well off, all well-educated. Or at least, the sad thought shot through me, all with degrees from places like Vanderbilt, which I so profoundly admired and so dearly loved.

I tried to look at individual faces so I'd at least have a chance to get a handle on both who and what they were, what they needed, why they feared so terribly. Because here were the same people, it occurred to me, who had supported—by tacit approval through their inaction—that climate two years earlier that had loosed the Necks on the coffee counter integrationists; these were the same people whose attitudes created a climate that made bombing synagogues seem all right to people born with grease and grit under their fingernails; these were the clean people who always stayed away from where the actionable action was, but who jacked up the street ante, always, then deplored the obvious results editorially.

These were the people who did *not* get their pictures in the paper; who were *never* out on the streets, their faces uglied by crass screams; who *never* chanced the overnight stay in a jail, a spot on their record, a stain, an imperfection—a variation in their lives, in short. They were here, instead, snuggled safely, warmly in the padded seats of a municipal building sitting rapt before one of their most treasured prophets of doom. They were like children at a horror show, nearly spastic with glee from their own terror.

Four rows and an aisle almost directly in front of us were the two people I least wanted to see, my former love and her husband with two other couples I knew well from my relatively in-nocent undergraduate days.

He was one of the first to get to his feet. His jaw was clenched, his face filled with righteous intensity as he stood to his fullest height on his strong legs, striking the palms of his hands against each other in what looked to me like an orgy of fury, the kind he must have felt some years earlier about me. So the whole scene very quickly became very personal. These were my dearly beloveds, my friends. Looking around I could see more. These were my *good* friends, many of them, people I loved and admired in countless ways, people I had shared so very much with, people I wanted to embrace literally, figuratively, however.

But there they were, showing themselves firm for everything Right, strong against everything Wrong, and, it seemed, never allowing themselves the frightening leeway to have a doubt in the world about what was which.

Helen stood by his side, clapping a little, mostly gathering up her purse and coat, checking its pockets for gloves, kleenex, scarf. I had seen her right before I came back into the auditorium when I was trying to get a fix on the crowd in the lobby. I had my hands in my pockets and probably was slouching a little against the press, when a space suddenly opened up, and there was Helen walking directly at me. We saw each other at the same time, and, slowing only, not ever stopping, she said, "What are *you* doing here?" her face reddening.

I didn't know what to say. I hadn't seen her since a night a couple of years earlier when they had had me over to their duplex for dinner, a lovely, if slightly strained, evening. But thinking of her then, thinking of her during those years of my personal turmoil—a turmoil of the sort people always seem able to get themselves into—then seeing her suddenly through her dress, her makeup, her presence there with him, seeing her as one of those people who

On Breaking One's Pencil

stay so safe and snug, I wanted to cry out, to grab her, to carry her away with me.

But I've never been much of a cave man sort, so I didn't stop to talk, either. When people marry other people they do pretty much ask you out of their lives in most meaningful ways. Still, I found it hard at the time to reconcile what I had known of her with what I was seeing of her, and I answered her question, which really was reasonable enough, considering, with a venom from the old woes that shocked even me.

"Spying," I said, and spit it out with as much of a sneer as I could, foolish as it was. Hands in pockets, I sauntered on past her and on in to the auditorium to take my seat.

Back inside, I saw where they were sitting. It was then that I heard myself chiding myself. I told myself very calmly—like a wonderfully patient father to his naughty little-boy of a son—that she had made the right choice and that I ought to write her a sweet note to thank her for being wiser than I was.

And with that excellent bit of very sound advice to myself, my stomach turned as purely as though a well-aimed, heavy-booted kick had found my groin during a tonk fight. The second it stomped its way in on me I felt heavied by an ineffable weariness sadder and more depressing than anything Mr. Welch eventually said that entire night.

All politics is local, as the old saw has it. Very, very local.

...

And a final image. Not too many years ago (well, pretty many years ago by now, I guess) I was driving from here to there and passed through Nashville. The rest of the world may have to pass through Atlanta to get someplace from anyplace else in the South, but I have to go through Nashville when I'm driving. Maybe it was when I was going from Knoxville to Pine Bluff, Arkansas, one summer to get some pictures of the Sorrells plots in the old and the new sections of Graceland Cemetery. That sounds like a good time for me to have been in Nashville.

Because I spent the night, I had time to drive around the west end some. On other trips I really hadn't been able to get a feel for the place again. Things would slip by me. At one time they would look almost familiar, then they'd dissolve into the nebulous world of half dream: Was it ever here? Was I ever here? Did it ever happen? Was it really true?

But during that visit I started getting the old feel of that part of town, even though streets were gone, whole blocks and blocks and blocks of residences gone for the Interstates, malls, housing complexes, and all the rest of the matter that "disappears" our pasts as surely as any Argentinean government "disappeared" so many of their own young people. It just took a willingness to drive around some.

I had been doing that down in Memphis on that same trip, and discovered the same thing: It was still there, the city I had known as a boy. And Nashville was still there, too. It just took some rooting around to find it, a little metaphorical squinching of the memory's eyes, and there it was: the back streets from the Vanderbilt area out to Green Hills; Franklin Pike (and out from Franklin, by the way, the metal bas-relief map of the Battle of Franklin is still in its little park); the area behind Peabody College where The Little Sisters of the Poor Home for the Aged used to be. Across the street from it, on Horton and 17th Avenue, had been an old house many of us who had lived there used to call "The Catacombs" because it had been divided into so many apartments, the dark caves of our lives...

Much abides, and, as the old saying has it, what goes around comes around—only different.

Some time or other during that stay I was sitting in a McDonald's eating lunch. At one point, while I was chewing comfortably on my sandwich and sipping quietly on my coffee, I felt terribly comfortable. On the drive over from (or back to) Knoxville, or wherever, I had been discussing Nashville with myself, thinking about the people, thinking about the place, thinking about thinking about it: recounting to myself the major events of my life that had been so much a part of the place: school, friends, a job which I did *not* take that probably would have changed my entire life in many important ways if I had, my marriage while I lived there, the birth of our son while we lived there.

From where I was sitting under the Golden Arches (which had not been there in my time), the Holiday Inn (also a relative newcomer) was directly across West End Avenue in front of me. But the Parthenon grounds were to my left, and the Firestone tire store was still on that sharp spit of a corner of West End and Elliston Place. My stomach usually churns when I drive into Nashville, when I think of hurts from old woes, lost chances, unrecoverable opportunities: the whole arthritic gout of age, I suppose.

But there, sitting in that burger joint surrounded by enough of the visual past to leave no doubt as to where in the world I really was, I discovered myself feeling so oddly, so achingly bereft that I knew I must be home. Still, I also felt such an overwhelming serenity, I wondered why I had ever left.

Now, I doubt that whoever may have blessed me in my life (and there have been a few) has ever been blessed in turn by God because of it, as he promised Abraham; certainly I doubt that whoever may have cursed me in my life (and there have been those too) has ever been cursed by God because of it; I don't see any evidence that I've been made into a great nation; and certainly—as a writer—my name has not been made great, as God also promised Abraham his would be.

Still, in what we Unitarian Universalists used to call the "Blue Hymnal," one we used several issues before our present one, there is a hymn called "When Abraham Went Out of Ur," a hymn with haunting music written by Michael Wise in 1684, joined to a 1935 poem by Nancy Byrd Turner. It starts off with the generalization that men leave home going "They know not why or whither," being both "called and compelled." The second verse speaks of these men from the ages stopping as they leave to take another last, troubled look at home, "Their birthright bartered for a nameless dream," as Turner puts it. Finally, she zeroes in on Abraham as he leaves Ur, and tells us how, as he turned in the cold dawn to catch his last glimpse of the place which had nurtured him, the place he had loved, the place which he knew always would be his home, he "bowed himself to his loved earth, and rent/ His garments, cried he could not go…and went."

CLEMSON

ONE MAY, MY WIFE GAVE a sermon honoring the members of the congregation who had been or were about to be graduated. That was mostly the high school students, but actually was intended to include anyone who had graduated or had completed a course of study. Her topic was "Crossing the Threshold," and dealt with the changes—the milestone changes—that mark our lives: graduations, driving licenses, getting to vote, leaving home, serving in the military, bar-and-bas mitzvahs, confirmations, and all.

Good sermons can do lots of things, but one of the more important is to give congregants something to ponder while the rest of the sermon works its way along to wherever it's presumably going. Like a bus—or a merry-go-round—you can always get on or off at different places.

Listening to the idea of milestones (and how in our country there isn't any one such thing that unites us all), I thought about my own graduations, tour of duty in the Army, marriage, birth of children, death of parents, siblings, and other family members. But I didn't get especially involved emotionally until I thought about Clemson. What triggered that was a reading in the service from Herakleitos of Ephesos.

> Whosoever wishes to know about the world must know about it in its particular details. Knowledge is not intelligence. In searching for the truth be ready for the unexpected; change alone is unchanging. The same road goes both up and down. The beginning of a circle is also its end. Not I, but the world says it: all is one. And yet everything comes in season.

Dillman also said something about finding out *who you were* and not confusing that with *what you did*. That scratched an itchy spot with me, because I think we not only *define* ourselves by what we do, but that to a large extent we *are* what we do—something along the lines of Yeats's "How do we tell the dancer from the dance?" perhaps. Still, her idea really had to do with discovering ourselves. My life in Clemson, South Carolina, has been divided into three parts: the first from 1965-70, the second from 1972-1987, the third from 2011 to the present. **Clemson I**, as I think of it, was probably the least interesting; **Clemson II** the most traumatic in certain ways—and the most instructive; **Clemson III**…Well, as an old teacher of German in my high school used to say, "Wait and see. Wait and see."

In the first go-around I was an Assistant Professor at Clemson University in the English Department. I taught the usual Freshman Composition and Sophomore Surveys, plus Introduction to Creative Writing, and, eventually something I called Form and Theory of Fiction.

I even spent time developing a curriculum for a minor in Creative Writing—just in case the University was serious about that sort of thing, which, it turned out, they weren't. For a time there, it seemed that under the leadership of the College of Architecture—where all the visual arts resided—there might be some sort of fine-arts major or minor getting developed, something that would broadly and bravely have crossed the paths of the visual, written, and musical arts. It didn't happen, though, in spite of there being many good artists, writers, and musicians on staff.

Whatever, I also managed to help stack the library with books in my field (those were the glory days: If faculty members wanted books for the library's permanent collection, all we need ed to do was to fill out the forms and in about six months we'd get notices that the books were on the shelves.) And I was active in the local American Association of University Professors (AAUP) chapter (even president one year); was elected to be the College of Liberal Arts' representative to the faculty senate; wrote stories, got three of them published and another accepted in that five years; and was even called upon to make a speech one fine Spring at a meeting of the South Carolina Association of Women Deans and Counselors.

None of which got me promoted, and being a firm believer that most of us live by gestures as well as by more tangible evidence of our worth or value to someone or something else, I made plans to leave.

So we packed up again and went to the University of Arkansas for a year where I was a Visiting Fireman in their program in creative writing. It was a fine year, but because no jobs were forthcoming and because I had been teaching for six years in a row, I decided to give myself a sabbatical.

Actually, that all started when, in a moment of levity while we had money and were living in a lovely house we had built and our future looked pretty much like forever, I told my wife that if she learned Italian I'd take her to Italy. As with so much in my life it didn't turn out quite that way. She never learned Italian, so we never lived in Italy.

Still, because both of us spoke pretty good English, we moved to South Devon, England, for the better part of a year. And what a glorious year that turned out to be. It changed the lives of us all: me, my wife, and both our children.

But there were ominous events floating around, omens most surely, drifting into and then out of sight like floaters in our eyeballs. The day before we deposited the check we were going to live on for the year, President Nixon (of "I am not a crook" fame) devalued the dollar. I should have known something was up then, but I was still young enough (well, at least foolish enough) so that even though I knew the Great Wheel of Fortune rolled on, grinding down those who had been on top, I was not wise enough to understand that I was not to be an exception, certainly not prescient enough to foresee that I wouldn't be able to get a job after that year was over and we were safely back in the States after being broadened by foreign travel. I'd always been able to get jobs before if I wanted—even had a really good one offered once when I didn't want it.

But by the time we got back to the States in July 1972 the academic marketplace had disappeared pretty much from the face of the earth. Basically, there weren't any jobs. Not for me. I was like a teenager: too old and too big to be considered a child, but too young and inexperienced to be considered an adult. I was too old, experienced, and well-published to be seriously considered for an entry level job; too insufficiently published to be considered for a senior position anywhere.

During that time, the East Jesus Techs were always hiring instructors, but we weren't that desperate, quite. Nervous, yes; developing tics, yes; but not frightened. Not yet depressed.

So we ended up back in Clemson. Our two children were ecstatic, my pragmatic wife got a job in the CU Library, and I dove pretty deeply into an emotional slough of despond that lasted far too long. That return was not easy.

As a matter of fact, it almost didn't happen at all. If I had stood up and walked out at one point, or if my wife had, we would have managed some way to get ourselves back onto a ship or into an airplane and head back to South Devon as fast as possible.

That was when we were waiting in the living room of the man who was managing the apartments we lived in, the place we spent our first year back in Clemson. We had looked at one of the apartments, liked it well enough, immediately saw the possibilities of the swimming pool—especially for the children after school—and needed only to drop by the manager's house to pick up the forms to fill out. He wasn't there that Saturday morning, and his wife—a lovely lady—was there tending to her small children, one of whom was sitting on the couch decked out in a mix of morning pajamas and western cowboy garb—the hat, boots, and toy six shooter—to help him watch the westerns flickering through his life of a weekend morning.

The house was a nice tract house in a nice little subdivision, the sort of house that when you walk into it you pretty much know where everything is: The bathroom's down this way, the bedrooms are that-a-way, the kitchen's through there with not enough storage, but the dish-washer's nice and the fridge works just fine and holds plenty for a young and rising family of four.

In the living room, there was darkish wood paneling, no books to be seen, and a big gun case chock-a-block with shotguns, rifles, and a few pistols, as I recall. Topping it was a metal American Eagle in full scream, its wings half spread in threat, its beak parted ready to rend the flesh of any prey it might happen upon. It reminded me a little of my brother's gun cabinet in Memphis.

Here I have to say this about guns. I was raised in a house that had guns in it. I remember a Colt .44, a .38, possibly a .45 service revolver, though I'm not sure, and various shotguns (12 and 14 gauge, I think), a .22 rifle and what I always thought of as my own 25/20 (if there is such a thing. If not, it was a 30/30.) My father was a south-central Arkansan raised by a hunting father; my oldest brother wanted to be a professional soldier for many years starting when he was a little boy; and I spent four years in a military prep school (as did both my older brothers) first with the old Springfield rifle, I think it was, then with the M-1 the rest of the time, plus the two years in the Army hauling around the M-1 (the basic weapon for the Army at the time), and I did qualify with a possible on the Carbine. I am not unacquainted with such weapons. Neither am I intimidated by their presence. Neither do I think they are a curse or whatever. In short, my wife and I disagree about some things.

Nonetheless, when we were sitting in that house where the TV blared away with a program featuring death by gunshot, where that little boy scrunched around firing his toy pistol at the TV owlhoots (I assume), in a bookless living room the centerpiece of which was a gun cabinet, and after nearly a year in England, I was as appalled as my wife.

We didn't have enough money to go back to England, my wife was sick, this was all home to our children, and shock really can paralyze the muscles so they don't function. So we sat there until the lady came back in with the papers for us to sign, her little girl clutching her momma with both knees, riding her hip in the age-old way.

We signed, then left to start our second tour of duty in Clemson, South Carolina.

...

It seems that we all have to keep learning some lessons. I'm thinking of assumptions we shouldn't assume. Specifically, I had never thought of myself as particularly privileged to have a job. Teaching was something I had loved to do, but it had been wearing at least a bit thin. Most of us not only want to do what we like to do (follow our own bliss, I suppose), but most of us also want to do it for people who want us to do it, too.

Increasingly I had started to sense that students weren't all that interested in learning how to be better writers of even mundane prose (a specific and accomplishable task), but also didn't want to lean on the boundaries of their ideas and visions and possibilities (the kind of thing that can happen through reading). Also, they were starting to watch more TV, and reading was clearly starting to move away from the hot center of education toward the periphery of things. And the Humanities? Well, while I was there the best students at a place like Clemson generally were in the math or physics departments, say, rather than in the English or history departments. Clemson had been founded as Clemson Agricultural College, after all, was the state's land grant college, and until recently had been a corps of cadets with, for all practical purposes, no female students. So it was to be likened more to the Citadel, VPI, or Texas A & M, than to Furman, Wake Forest, or the Universities of Virginia and North Carolina.

Given that mix, then, and given the nature of the 1960s—the continuing push from the 1950s of the Civil Rights movement, the assassination of our president, the riotous 1968 Democratic convention in Chicago, the murders of Bobby Kennedy and Martin Luther King Jr., the increasing disgust with the Viet Nam war as the count of returning plastic body bags rose and the only thing clear about the war's aims seemed to be the lack of them, student rebelliousness generally, the increasing use of illegal narcotics (for those who didn't close their eyes to it all), Hippyphobia—any campus in the country was proof against the tired whines of non-academic people about White Tower-ism, "educated idiots," wasting the tax money of *really* hard working people on "merely" theoretical studies—the whole dreary litany from people who either had never set foot on a campus or, if they had, had never had a clue as to what education was all about.

But I was saying something about assumptions. When you *have* something, you assume that you of *course* have it, and you tend to wander around accepting the perquisites that go with it—with a job, for instance—without even being aware that there are any perquisites, that the perquisite was having a job.

But to go back just a little: I have been lucky in my life, being able, for instance, to spend a year in England. That was in 1971-72, and before we returned to America we spent three weeks on the Continent. Even though we crossed the Channel on a Brit-Rail ferry powered by diesel engines and were taking only about two hours or so for the crossing, I was aware that we were plying a route far more than old, older than ancient, even: It was ancient back before the memory of collective civilization, nearly.

We left Dover bound for Calais, where—before the Hotel de Ville, the Town Hall—Rodin's statue *The Burghers of Calais* stands, that cluster of six figures still awaiting their fate as they sacrifice themselves to the English King Edward III in hopes that he will lift the devastating siege that has wasted them for eleven months.

England to France, France to England and back again. The English Channel is a feisty link between England and Europe, and it can bitterly and cruelly separate as well.

In so many ways, that year had been the most wonderful year of our lives. We found that life in our little village was lived on a manageable, a walking, a human scale—not unlike our neighborhood in Rochester, Minnesota, where we lived the better part of nineteen years. But the British have been around for a long time, and they know that the sun never shines for but just so long. So in our little village if you greeted a native on a Fine Day and remarked on what a fine day it was, "Lovely day, idn't it?" you almost always were met with the response, "Yaaaah, but we'll pay for it tomorrow."

After our three weeks in Europe we would be back in England—in Southampton—only long enough to board the P&O ship that would take us back to the States. It was a sad thing for me to think about.

But there on the Brit-Rail ferry, chugging its way from Dover to Calais, I went up on deck to stand at the rail. The channel was behaving pretty decently, our ferry *ka-rumphing* sturdily on. I leaned against the railing and—as though by chance, but actually knowing and anticipating what I would see—I glanced to my left. There was England. I looked very slowly to my right, trying to pretend it was a casual motion, and there was France—and beyond it, if you circled basically east and a little north, was all of Europe clear through what used to be the USSR coming, finally, to within spitting distance of Alaska.

So much in our personal lives had happened and was still happening—travel, after all, is supposed to broaden one's vision—that this, a terminal point in my life in so many ways, was a moment when all kinds of things were coming at me: my own life; my wife and her life; our children and their young lives; what lay behind us; what lay ahead—all the tomorrows that pay for all the todays...

It seemed to me, balancing to the dip and yaw of the ferry, that more good was by me than was before me. I was going back to America without a job, certainly with no career, and, I often felt, without a calling either. It was a kind of limbo I'd never been in before, and I was very frightened.

But ships creak and groan on, flop and puddle their ways through the water; the water itself comes and goes in tides that race or wait, that measure time for us in their accountably natural ways. Standing there on that deck

On Breaking One's Pencil

with England receding on my left and France rising on my right, I became eerily aware of the whole of North America hunkering somewhere behind me tides and waves and unknown tempests away: America—whatever and wherever it was—stretching back across the stunning and awesome depth of a continent—and an imagination: shifting, twitching, squatting, its mere mass an attracting field of energy—like salvation, or a curse.

I was going back to the United States, but in going to England in the first place I had been going back to some form of my past. And in a strange way I had found it there—but it was in the form of my present. In going "back" to England, had I in fact been going forward in life? If so, was I now—by returning to America—going backwards?

As these and so many other questions, emotions, and impulses came bearing down on me at that moment—travel can also be exhausting—I heard the ship's PA system. It had been broadcasting whatever happened to turn up on the jukebox down in the canteen, but then it sent out another tune. It was a tune played by the Pipes and Drums and Military Band of the Royal Scots Dragoon Guards. It was very popular in England that year. The English often called it "The Trans-Atlantic Hymn," but it was our own—as I thought of it then—"Amazing Grace."

There I was midway between England and France in the middle of History, and midway between my own past and future. And when this rendition by a military band of what I had always considered an American hymn of spiritual and redemptive salvation hit me, it charged every one of my confusions: the forwards and backwards, the callings and jobs, the futures and lack of them, the goings to and leavings from—charged them all with a jolt that stunned me. I was supposed to be going home, but our little village in South Devon was more home to me than almost any other place I had ever lived in my life. And as the ferry dipped and rolled in almost perfect rhythm to the music, I was so totally overwhelmed I did the only thing that seemed left to do. My emotional ropes were stretched so taut, I simply stood there and, like a little child abandoned, I wept.

...

When we got back from England we spent seven tense weeks with my wife's parents in Florida before moving back up to Clemson.

...

We had rented a place in a complex called, quaintly enough, The Village Green Apart-ments, nestled on the down side of a hill behind a Kentucky Fried Chicken. Looking through the sliding glass doors at the back of our apartment and out across the fifty-square-feet of our con-crete patio, we had a view not only of the garbage end of the KFC, but, a little nearer, of an abandoned car as well. Its owner—who, it turned out, managed the Kentucky Fried—occasionally salvaged parts from the thing, but mainly he just let it hunker there rusting while it attracted small children and fearless, well-fed rats. Dillman took a picture of me on my fortieth birthday with all that in the background. I was holding the cake she had made for me. It was still in the pan, partly because it had been overcooked a bit, and seemed to be pretty well bonded to the sides. It had also fallen in on itself. The snapshot was what any critic worth his salt would call highly symbolic.

At the time, we were using borrowed mattresses, crates, and whatever else we had man-aged to scrounge up until we could get more permanent digs to put our stored furniture in. Earlier, my wife had part-time work at the Clemson University Library, and I did what I could. Though Clemson had never managed to become "home" to me, it was to our children, and for a while that had to be good enough.

I was out of work and Dillman had been suffering from something—at the time we didn't know what—which turned out to require major surgery, an especially frightening situation, for a time, because we had no health insurance at all, and when the doctors finally found out what the problem was and Dillman actually had to have the surgery, she had *just* been hired full time at the library, which meant, of course, that she could go on and have the operation because she had medical coverage through her job.

As things turned out over the next fifteen years or so, Clemson became home for me as well as for our children, but for a time there, life was pretty tenuous.

...

Life had changed for me a great deal, but there were still compensations. For instance, I discovered the pecan grove on the front of the Clemson campus. That campus for many years, at least, was like a beautiful town park. The

On Breaking One's Pencil

azaleas, the dogwood trees, the greenswards all made for a kind of picture book loveliness that could just take your breath away some springs. It was also a good place to wander, a good place to try to "take stock" as Hans Castorp and the other characters on Thomas Mann's Magic Mountain used to say.

Once, I was shuffling through the pecan grove again, noting somewhere in my head that I hadn't been out there for a couple of years. Simply hadn't been walking that way. Or, I mused, maybe it was just because we had come to have a little more money and the simple pleasure of bringing in a modest crop of my own was gone.

Shuffling lightly under the trees so I wouldn't crunch the pecans that might be hidden beneath the fallen leaves, sensing the pressure on the soles of my feet that would tell me there might be a nut there, I recalled the embarrassment I had caused when I collected bottles that had been chucked out car windows. I had paid for my morning paper with those bottles, courtesy, I always felt with a certain ambivalent tinge of bitterness, of the exorbitantly wasteful shrug of the town's and University's young people.

When the paper was a dime and the bottles fetched three cents, I'd take three of them and a penny up to the 7-11 behind our apartment and get a paper. The clerks hated me. At first they really didn't understand what I was doing. I'd show the three bottles by raising them over my head then lowering them into the return bin by the door. Then I'd get a paper from the rack, lay a penny on the counter, and start to walk out. They really didn't understand at first.

But once they did they got antagonistic. So then I cashed in the bottles by making them count out the nine cents into my hand. I'd add the penny with an elaborate flourish, and end by slapping the nickel and the five coppers down on the counter, taking a paper, and stalking out. Later, the bottles brought a nickel each, so I only needed two for the paper—until it went up to fifteen cents. By the time it got to twenty cents I wasn't collecting bottles any more. And by then there were only machine sales for the paper anyway.

I embarrassed my friends, too, though. When they saw me on my rounds, they knew what the clanking in the grocery sack was: Ole Bob stooping to pick up pocket change for a beer. Or a candy bar, maybe. Always the paper.

They didn't do that. Not even their kids did that. Not even their kids *had* to do that for a few of life's little extras. And at parties I embarrassed them.

When they started talking about how poor they were, I'd smile ingenuously, and suggest they could always sell one of their two or three cars. Once, not long after we had come back from our year away, a friend even told me about getting a good deal on a Cadillac. Said it was only eight thousand dollars. I had smiled graciously and said, "That's how much we grossed last year." Or near tax time the cocktail conversations got around to how heavy the burden was, how hard it was for them to squeak by on what, it turned out, was often three times as much as we had.

Yet I never felt that any of the family was deprived. Then, I finally started to understand why the 7-11 clerks had hated me and why I embarrassed so many of my friends: I was their conscience. Nobody likes that. Besides, I scared them. My being there reminded them that the Great Wheel of Fortune really can turn, and if it can turn on Ole Bob then it can turn on them, too.

And I was an embarrassment because—with my serious bottle collecting year-round, and my serious pecan gathering in the late fall—I represented people—white people, at least—they didn't very often see around Clemson, and, many of them, people they thought about even less.

And there was something else, something that was sadly, uncomfortably near to the heart of the unmasked hatred of the 7-11 clerks. Them I understood better, or at least sooner: that I went on and stooped to do what they didn't dare allow themselves to do, because they were too close to *having* to do it.

Some of the others, though, I came to perceive as always turning from me just slightly because I dared stoop in their presence, and did it, furthermore, without any seeming embarrassment—my stooping, my scavenging, my ragbagging around town being a constant reminder to them of my freedom. They were the ones who were bound; tied; shackled mortgage, third car, and mind to a system that didn't care whether they were there or not. They all knew they could be replaced within forty-eight hours, as one of our department heads had once smilelessly reminded us, without one student missing a single lecture. And replaced, furthermore, with people who had better degrees, more publications, and greater desperations than our own. They saw me, I think, and tasted fear on the back of their tongues as I strode or meandered through town. They saw me and felt that slightly acrid gorge of envy rising in their throats, but swallowed because *they* wouldn't dare spit it out.

On Breaking One's Pencil

In the pecan grove, I felt the pressure of a hard wad under my foot. Gently rolling it out from under the leaves, I saw it was a pecan still in its green husk. I bent over and picked it up, struck, as always, at how like coconuts they were, growing like them in husks, and at how much better they taste when they ripen on the tree. I liked to imagine there was a sound when the husk burst, splitting at the tip into four sections, like a flower opening. Now and again I did hear the solid *plock* as ripened pecans dropped to the ground.

But most people couldn't wait for the natural aging and fall of the fruit. So they came to the groves armed with sticks, or cast about on the ground for fallen limbs that would do, and threw them as hard as they could up into the tree to knock the nuts down.

I used to love to watch the variations of the basic technique. Some used great long limbs to cut as wide a swath as possible through the leaves. Others would use a three-to-four foot length of lumber with a stout rope tied around the middle. A good throw would catch the lumber in a branch. Then the rope could be yanked over and over, shaking the tree vigorously. When the nuts fell, it was a hail of thuddled bumps. At best there would be three hunters: one to knock the fruit down, the others to watch where they all fell and to gather them up.

Once I saw an enterprising old lady in a black dress, stockings, hat, and a fur wrapabout pay a child to climb up as far as he could and shake the tree for her. Squealing together, he shook while she reaped. It was worth the dollar to the boy to perch twenty feet above the common herd.

Some came in packs with carefully folded grocery bags, aiming to fill them up. I always suspected them of collecting for resale. Others, more casual, kicked about the grass and took what they could find that had already fallen.

I looked at the husk in my hand. It had barely started to split open. I reached into my pocket and took out a pen knife, opened it, and carefully sliced the husk at its seams. My mouth watered in anticipation of the acidic smell of the juice that would come from the husk of a nut still so fresh. The juice would stain my fingers, like nicotine from my cigarettes used to do when I still smoked them.

I got out the pecan and flicked the husk away. The shell was a very light tan unlike the riper fruit whose shells were dark—not like blackstrap molasses, but like deeply tanned leather with a curious trace of gray in it, and even darker streaks running its length. Those were the best ones: heavy from the fruit inside, yet light to the heft, too. And the shells were so smooth…

I put it in my pocket, stood very still for a few minutes scanning the ground carefully. If it had been that green, still, it had probably been knocked down rather than naturally fallen. Likely there would be more nearby. I saw one. I shuffled slowly over to it, picked it up, examined it carefully for worm holes, and slipped it into my pocket.

The hunt went on. But you have to be careful, I cautioned, talking to myself, explaining things to myself as though I were a stranger. You can't just tramp about, because you'd be too likely to crush good nuts into the ground. And you have to make sure there aren't any worms. And you have to make sure—especially if you were tossing a stick—that you kept both it and the falling nuts in view. Best to keep the stick in sight and trust your ears to lead you to the pecans.

I had loved coming out—except for the dogs, sometimes—because it was the only place in town I knew of where things slowed, where people were both intensely concentrating, and totally oblivious; where to hurry was understood to ruin; where speed was unwanted; where everybody sought the same thing; and where—in spite of the occasional efficiency monger or pig—most people were helpful—even generous, if a bit standoffish.

Harvesting pecans in such a place is essentially a solitary venture. But eventually everybody came: blacks, whites, students, faculty, needy, non-needy. Everybody came to the late autumn ritual, slowing themselves to a shuffle for a quarter of an hour, or an hour, or more.

I saw a woman walk past two pecans. She hadn't seen them. I followed, hoping she wouldn't turn around. I got them. One had a worm. The other was all right. Then I saw another. Two. Three. Fourfive. I got them all and more until my khaki pockets and wind-breaker were loaded up.

I started home, feeling that I had been mean to the woman who had not seen the first two nuts. Her attention had gone over to her small children. I could have called to her, but hadn't. Pecan hunting was like that, though. You got along with your fellow hunters, even felt a kinship with them. But it was still a loner's task.

…

Those tenuous days were so traumatic, so weighted with a hand-to-mouth and day-to-day mentality that I marvel now how any of us got by without being scarred far more than we were. It wasn't until some years later that I realized I must have been in a pretty deep depression: I had lost myself a job, and felt for years that I had also lost a calling. The loss of the job resulted in a loss of status: that's external, public. But the apparent loss of my calling was a loss of some essential, internal juice of life. I seemed forever on the outside of virtually everything that I had valued—or taken for granted. As for my writing, I still have the numerous letters that were saying, in effect, My God but you're a fine writer, Sorrells. God's speed—and rotsa ruck—in finding someone to publish your stuff.

The only place I was going, it seems, was mad.

...

There is, presumably, a fact about when "unchurched" people start the process of "churching" themselves. It happens when they have children, and it happens when they find they're cracking apart under stress: losing jobs, moving, going through divorce, having close family members die, etc. In short, Kübler-Ross's old Death, Dying, Loss, and Grief impel people toward whatever might help them stay glued together long enough to start the process of reshaping themselves into a form that will fit somewhere *else*, since they no longer fit where they used to.

Sometimes, too, people follow a personal demiurge questing for something in their lives, one of those great sea changes, perhaps, that will alter us forever, as we rebuild our exteriors to protect the essential fire within—possibly even to find out if there is one, and if so, what it is. And if not, well, how to live with that.

So when the Clemson, South Carolina, Unitarian-Universalist Fellowship met in the early fall of 1972 at an ingathering picnic in the back yard of some good friends from our first life there, I went. More than forty years later, I'm still going.

My wife had been a Unitarian (or, more properly, a Unitarian Universalist, the two groups having merged in the early 1960s) for our five first years, as well as for the year we were in Fayetteville, Arkansas, before we went to England. I had gone so seldom because there didn't seem to be much there for me. At the time, a Fellowship normally was a smallish, ministerless group so there weren't any "services," but lectures, and while I was teaching, I lectured all week myself and didn't want to spend Sunday morning listening to talks that weren't as good. Besides, if I *had* been interested in a church, I would have wanted something other than "programs" on sewage disposal, the politics of the local mayoral race, or some other such topic. As for main-line churches, I had long ago understood, if not quite decided, that if I didn't believe in the Apostles' Creed (and the personal god that implied), or in a virgin birth, or in a physical resurrection, or in a life everlasting as typically preached, then I couldn't say I did, and there wasn't much point in hanging around pretending there was nothing wrong.

In short, I hadn't "needed" anything else before. At least, whatever I had needed along the lines of spiritual renewal or maintenance, or what might even be called, simply, grace, I was getting in other ways and from other places. Teaching had been my own pulpit; the literature I taught had been the historical texts in which I was washed in the blood of the lamb in a way that made sense to me; and my own writing had been my own attempts to add to those glosses on the nature of the human critter.

Because of Dillman I found that Unitarian-Universalist Fellowship, though. It was still in cramped quarters at the YMCA on the Clemson campus in 1972, but that didn't matter. That fellowship was there and it took me in. It was a place that didn't care about my job or my status or my wandering around town gathering up bottles—or if it did, it never turned its face from me because of it. It was a place that opened its doors and hearts to me and let me be. It was a place where I could come without any strings attached. It was a place that let me lick my wounds without making me speak them unless or until I was able or willing to. It was a place that was ready to hold me if that's what I needed, or to let me stand in a corner in silence if that's what I needed. It was a place that let me grow in directions I would never have known about or even possibly have been interested in. It was a place that let me emerge at my own speed and in my own ways. It was a place that was not only able but willing to love me so that I could finally look into my heart and accept that I was worthy of that love—not because I was an especially good or lovable or worthy person—but solely because I showed up on the doorstep and was a desperately needy person, whether I knew it or not.

On Breaking One's Pencil

I know that the Clemson Fellowship is still the same in those important ways. I hope as much that Westside UU Church in Knoxville, Tennessee, is still like that in those important ways, that they all—that WE all—will or will continue naturally and automatically to take in those stumbling oddments of people who need what we have to give. I hope that we will let other people know that we are here and know that they are welcome and know that they can grow at their own paces and know that it is possible, first, to learn to recognize and then, even harder, to accept love. Largely because of that little congregation in Clemson, I at last began to learn something about all that.

...

During that second tour of duty in Clemson I eventually became an active member of the fellowship not just a passive attender of the meetings, as we called them then: sitting back and being amused, or entertained, or edified—serviced, in short. At the time I became active, a number of things happened that I became part of. I started off doing brief readings at the weekly services, as some of us quietly started insisting the "meetings" be called, and eventually was vice president, program chair, worship committee member; then, after a by-laws change, president-elect, and president. There were some other things too along the way, but it was all the usual business people do when they get involved in organizations that are important to them.

Later, I found myself moving outside the snug harbor of the church. It started with my going to a leadership school at The Mountain, our camp and conference center in Highlands, North Carolina, then going back the next four summers as a member of the School's staff. At the same time, I had started going to our district's annual fall meeting, the Leadership Weekend, and the Annual Meeting in the spring. *That* got me interested in our Thomas Jefferson District (as it was named at the time) in another light, with the result that I served several years as a member of the District's nominating committee, and then on the board itself for two years as the District Board's Secretary. And during all of that time, I started getting excited about going to GA, the General Assembly of the continental Unitarian Universalist Association.

All of this came to be something of a shock to my system, after a fashion. Even though I'm not a "joiner," I'm a pretty good team player, but I wasn't particularly an institutional man. I'm generally more at home with solitary work, small groups, and quiet conversations. Being basically introspective, I've also questioned myself as to why: Why have I been interested in helping, or trying to help establish new congregations? Why do I care about whether our denomination grows in numbers or not? Why do I still care about certain problems in the Clemson Fellowship or the Westside Church in Knoxville, that have to do with their growth? Why have I bothered with leadership weekends and annual meetings, GAs and district boards, new congregation training and extension ministries?

Clearly enough to me, it all goes back to 1972 when life for us so radically changed. If the presence of a Unitarian Universalist society had that much influence on me, then I wanted such societies to be available to lots more people. If in some profound way my life was made better or more stable or more complete or more whatever, then I wanted other people to be able to have that experience, too. If one small society opened up so much for me, then there were bound to be other people—thousands and thousands of them—who could profit from such societies.

I'm not suggesting miracle cures or melodramatic transformations here. I suppose it could happen that way for people who chanced to be at a time of life when that's what they needed and were ready for. Instead, I'm thinking of something rather quieter, less spectacular, but no less moving or lasting.

...

Some years back I did a service called "Cotton-Eyed Joe," based on what I guess is a folk song—at least of some sort. The only words I knew were two stanzas, the only two I ever heard.

> "Where do you come from?
> Where do you go?
> Where do you come from,
> Cotton-Eyed Joe?"

> "Well I come for to see you
> Come for to sing,
> Come for to show you
> My diamond ring."

Then I raised some questions about what the whole thing meant: Who were the speakers? Why was the one showing the ring to the other? And so on. But I then took off into what I made to be the central questions: Where Are You Coming From? and Where Are You Going? Together, it seems to me they ask, "Who Am I?" Talk about your dark nights of the soul: Ask yourself that question long enough and you'll start to understand something about F. Scott Fitzgerald as well St. John of the Cross.

In Clemson there was a young man who came to our Fellowship regularly while he was at the university there. Understand: He was a terribly difficult person to get along with. His social skills were not what you would call low so much as negative. He could get people angry simply by walking into a room. He had no sense of tact; he quite literally bumped into things—and people—because he seemed to have no sense that they were there—a sort of teen-aged Chief Inspector Cluseau of Peter Sellers fame. He seemed to be unaware that anyone outside his own skin might have been talking when he started talking about something totally unrelated, or that they were about to sit down when he pulled the chair out for himself—or that they might also be hurting.

But after a service one Sunday, one of those where a question and answer period was appropriate, this young man—apparently a brilliant mathematics student as well as a birthright Unitarian (fourth generation), made a comment I've never forgotten. The service, as I recall, was one of those panel sort of things in which several members of the Fellowship spoke and talked about why they were UUs. As often happens with such topics, there was some fairly confessional stuff about people's problems of one sort or another: what you might call the usual kinds of things, and as is also so often the case with us, very thoughtful, and very articulate.

He had listened with great concentration, and after all the questions seem to have been asked and answered as well as they can be, he spoke.

"I want to thank you," he said.

What was this? many of us thought. Him? Thanking someone for something?

"Being a Unitarian can be so hard," he said, his voice quiet, even pensive. We all had our own remembrances about the world of dormitories and how unspeakable people can be toward anyone who's "different." Then—as though he were paraphrasing the first two lines of e.e. cummings' poem

"Credo"—"I cannot find my way; there is no star/ in all the shrouded heavens anywhere,"—he said, "I always thought I was all alone and had to do everything all by myself. But there are lots of people like me, and I never knew that before."

It may be he had found cummings' "far-sent message of the years," and felt his "coming glory of the Light!"

The room was quiet for just a couple of seconds, and then he said it again, sounding both amazed at his discovery and ineffably moved by its import.

"I'm really not alone."

...

When you've lived somewhere for twenty years, much has happened to you. There are people you came to know and love, people you still keep up with. There are jobs you had: writing projects you got paid for, writing projects you wouldn't have missed even when you knew you weren't going to get paid for them; jobs you'd never have learned anything about if you'd still been teaching; experiences of living other ways; knowledge, as the poet Allen Tate put it, "carried to the heart" because you've had to grapple as best you could with something else again.

Heartbreaks. Frustrations. True fear of the future as you grow older and think about having left a safe job with a good retirement and how very foolish that was, and all that. And all of that and more: not only the suicides of friends and your children's friends, not only the deaths in your own family, but friends and former colleagues who stayed on their own courses to become bitter and unhappy people fed up with teaching generally and with teaching in that school in particular.

I may exaggerate the plight of others, I don't know. But I have never regretted doing what I *did* do: the writing has never dropped off my list of what was important and sustaining to me. And since the fall of 1972, neither has the Unitarian Universalist Association.

Maybe that's why Cotton-Eyed Joe comes to visit. Maybe that's the song he comes to sing. Maybe that's even the diamond ring itself he comes to show.

...

On Breaking One's Pencil

I can't speak of Clemson, of course, without at least mentioning my life as a teacher, a bittersweet recollection, take it all-in-all. In my mind I was a teacher forever. It was somehow in my bones, wrapped around my soul, almost as integral to my *self* as writing has been. That teaching has been with me—still is, after a fashion—since I was a little boy lecturing to my fellow grade school students about the D-Day invasion in an all-school convocation; happily taking on the job of Pledge Trainer my sophomore year in college so I could teach the freshmen about the history of our fraternity; the elation I felt in my first teaching job at Murray State College in Kentucky, teaching for a week or so without a textbook because I understood that I knew—really and truly *knew*—enough not to need the book.

Well, so much of this is caught in two scenes at Clemson, both from our second life there, both while I was working at Publications and Graphics Services during one or more of my three, six-month tours there.

The work of an editor/writer in a place like P&GS is both fascinating and tedious, partaking of the ticky-tacky proof-reading necessary to get really good publications out, knowing that many people's first—or even only—impressions of the school will be drawn from those publications: their look, their "feel," their accuracy. The more exciting part is working on a project starting when it's nothing more than an idea, a hope in someone's mind, and seeing it through the whole print process to the day the finished piece gets plopped on your desk for your final approval. That's crunch time because you look at it so carefully you think your eyeballs will burst, and if you can't find a thing wrong—no "dirt," no broken letters, no thumbprints showing on the photos, no typos (like *pubic* instead of *public*), no misalignments of type from facing pages—then you declare it ready to deliver to your client.

It's a crowded life, working on anywhere from a dozen to three dozen projects at the same time, trying to keep up with where everything is, trying to keep a mechanical engineer from destroying your solid prose by replacing it with his own wooden non-sentences, trying to get your production manager to sweet-talk a printer into slipping your job at least a little bit ahead of where it ought to be, trying to get clients and photographers lined up with your own schedule, trying to keep up with the absolutely essential approval slips signed by your clients at every stage of the production of their piece, working with the graphics people so you know what they're about to do with what you know the client wants done, working as hard as you possibly can at learning not only the office you're in, but the job itself, and how to use a word-processor, as well.

I was useful to Publications and Graphics mainly because I had been around Clemson long enough to know a lot of people—certainly in the English Department, but also in electrical engineering, physics, history, chemical engineering, the College of Architecture, economics, and up at WEPR when it was a production studio for the South Carolina Educational Radio Network (now an anomaly called ETV-Radio.)

Into all this there were the times when I was able to get away, more or less, to do something along the lines of my primary interests. One of those was an assignment to write an article about *The South Carolina Review* celebrating its tenth anniversary at Clemson University. A quarterly begun at nearby Furman University by Alfred S. Reid of their English department in Greenville, it was moved to Clemson, to be edited by Clemson English department faculty when Reid felt he simply couldn't handle the load any longer.

I made an appointment with its managing editor, Carol Johnston. There, we talked about the usual things: details of the magazine's history, the dates, the awards won, the authors published, the details of having to go through some 2,000 manuscripts a year on top of a regular teaching workload, plus the business of seeing each edition through to its on-time publication.

It was a good visit, and I was impressed by her as well as by the magazine (they had published a story of mine once, after all). And it was lovely weather, June or July, maybe. School either was out, or summer school had already started. Carol's desk held the usual academic clutter—manuscripts, papers, page proofs, red-ink ballpoint pens, paperclips, no doubt a grade book somewhere. It was afternoon, I remember, and she was in a corner office of a newish building, beautiful views of a beautiful campus. The Clemson campus really did look like a campus is supposed to look.

Not only was the weather warm, but the day itself in its colors, in its mood, in the ambience of the time and the place and the subject—talk of reading and writing and writers and fiction and poetry, of teaching, and of the history of places and people—every one of my love buttons was getting pushed that afternoon. As I was about to leave, as I was standing at the door to Carol's office, my hand already touching the door knob ready to open it, already saying the usual closing words after an interview—"May I call you back to check on things if I get stuck?"—the business and pleasure of the meeting surely done with, I realized I was prolonging my going, was looking again at her desk, at the view from her windows on the sixth or seventh floor or wherever, at the breezes soughing through the trees below. I was trying to soak up some final essence of that moment, that place, that aura that so spoke to me of where I should have been and what I should have been doing all along.

It was so powerful, I was so overwhelmingly possessed by it that I thought I could almost taste it, feel it as surely as I felt that door knob, as surely as I knew the mellowing glow of the latening sun. It was palpable.

I smiled and left to go back to my office where I hoped I could concentrate on the article, give them a good piece, so people would know that Clemson University could do something besides field championship, semi-pro football teams.

...

The other scene, also while I was working at Publications and Graphics, was in another office with another member—or former member, actually—of the English department, a woman who had become a kind of dean, I think, or director, maybe, of some special program at the university. Again, I might have been visiting her about some project or other, but I sense that I simply decided to drop in on her on my way back to the office from some piece of business, and being in the neighborhood, as it were, decided to stop in for a chat. I was pleased to see her again. It had been a long time, for no particular reason, except that "way leads on to way," as Frost put it. She and our family had been close for a while some years earlier, and we had come to the University the same year, as I recall.

So after a bit of chitchat and some planning about the publication (if that's why I was there) I asked her quite innocently if she missed the classroom. I assumed some answer to the effect that Yes I certainly do, but I also think this job is important, etc. etc. etc.

Instead, I got an earful as well as an eyeful of some of the most intense bitterness I had ever experienced.

"If I *never* step into another classroom as a teacher," she said, "it will be too soon." And the muscles of her face had pulled themselves down into striations I thought might never be able to relax.

It was a shock to me, I who had been eating my heart out for years to get back into that particular harness.

I asked her why, of course, and the amazing thing is I can't remember her answer, only her body's response and the whipsnap suddenness of it, as though I had actually heard a bullwhip cracking right over my head. I was as shocked as though she had spit in my face. Here was this woman—intelligent, sharp, quick, well-degreed, a writer, a scholar, an occasional director of student theater dramas—filled with a bitterness about her profession I had never suspected in her before.

Why? I wondered. What had happened between her and the students? Between her and the classroom? Between her and her years studying Shakespeare in England, teaching the plays, going to Stratford so many summers to watch them? What had turned her so? Apparently not bad experiences with the students, I reflected, because her current position dealt with students exclusively, though not academically. She had just finished telling me how ecstatic she was when one of them excelled or something fine happened to or for them. So that couldn't have been all of it.

I never did find out what had prompted that outburst of a rage that hurt so terribly.

Some years later, though, I did grow to understand what it might have been, because I went through it myself: busting my ass, as I finally came to see it, to be where I didn't particularly want to be, doing what I didn't especially want to do any more, amid people who didn't especially want me to do it in any event.

When it finally happened to me, it was a crushing sadness, devastating because once upon a time teaching and being a teacher had been not only a central piece of my life, but a central joy as well.

TQ95DZ

THERE ARE TWO SOUNDS ABOUT Totnes, South Devon, England, that I shall never forget, and with them the two visual images they carry. One is the constant and haunting squalls of the seagulls as they squatted edgily on the peak of the Civic Hall roof, then, after leaping awkwardly into flight, wheeling and wheeling over the Hall's forecourt, diving occasionally down to the flagstones to snitch up a morsel of food—especially on Wednesdays, Market Day.

The other is the manic screech of the rooks swirling in mass about the tower of St. Mary's, the local parish church, as the day dwindled into evening and the birds began their darkening search for their nesting spots inside the tower. We watched them from the kitchen window of our first rented cottage, *Archway House*.

The gulls wheeled and lit individually, the rooks spun and whirled in an anarchy of ragged togetherness. The gulls were sea birds, of course, and the rooks were land birds, but there they were together. As the bird flies, we were only about seven miles from the sea, and the River Dart, a tidal river, ran down to the English Channel, through the town of Dartmouth, and past the Britannia Royal Naval College, to empty into the Channel.

It was there in Totnes—the highest navigable reach of the Dart—that I lived with my wife and two young children for nearly a year in 1971-72. It changed us all in ways we never would have believed.

...

What we found was that it was a town built to a human scale. From South Street, where we lived, we walked easily to the High Street where the green grocers, bakers, butchers, and other shops were located—the main thoroughfare of the town. If you had a car and wanted to drive it up or down South Street, you could. But it was vastly easier to walk. A longer walk was down to the train station—we had no car that year—and the pub that became our local (or at least *my* local) was just up the way from us a little. It was owned by Phillip Potter, a former tenor with the Doiley Carte opera company, and his wife Gillian, a beautiful woman who knew how to entertain as a publican's wife and who had, on at least one occasion, treated me to a shot of bourbon on a slow afternoon because she thought I might be homesick for such spirits of America. (I never told her I *preferred* scotch.)

Why we arranged to be in that town was probably different from the way most Americans come to a year abroad. Others, I gather, head to a particular city because of a job (if their companies Stateside have an "international" element); or to a university, if they're moving on to graduate or post-graduate studies; or to a major library, if they're serious scholars. With us, it was as deliberate and researched, as it was haphazard.

...

I left Clemson University for a variety of reasons, which, taken together, I managed to reduce to the bumper sticker-like slogan, "People live by gestures as much as by deeds." Something like that. We had been there five years, and by the end of my fourth year I had had three stories published, one more accepted; had served on committees; had upped the library's holdings in my field; had been elected by my College of Liberal Arts colleagues to be a representative to the Faculty Senate; had been president of the local AAUP chapter; had a good reputation as a teacher; and had even been asked—by my department head, no less—to make an out-of-town speech to the South Carolina Association of Women Deans and Counselors at a neighboring college for a symposium they were hosting entitled "Personal Development—Positive Involvement."

All of which is just the usual sort of extracurriculars college faculty are more or less supposed to do, but in my case it was at least somewhat more than most of the people in our department had done, certainly as regards publishing. I could have gotten tenure, with promotion to associate professor after a fourth year, but that wasn't in the cards. Gestures. To me it meant I could stay or leave as I wished. They didn't care; it didn't matter.

On Breaking One's Pencil

So after my fifth year I left for a year as a visiting fireman in the program in writing at the University of Arkansas. I did some of my best ever teaching there, I think. But one-year jobs, visiting stuff, is sort of like being a member of the House of Representatives: as soon as you get elected, you've got to start hustling—in their case for reelection funds, in mine for another job.

Two or three years before that, though, in a moment of giddy optimism and outright silliness, I suppose, I had said to my wife, "If you learn to speak Italian, I'll take you to Italy for a sabbatical year."

Well, she didn't learn Italian, but the idea of giving myself a sabbatical sounded better and better. Neither of us knew any French, either, and our German was, well, not very extensive. But we felt pretty confident about our English. So, early in the 1970-71 academic year in Fayetteville, Arkansas, we started to look up places we might want to stay in England, a land we both had been to earlier, but before we had known each other. A real research job.

One evening, nearing the end of our stay in Fayetteville, after we had gotten in bed, we both started talking. My wife is a dedicated in-bed reader, and I usually have no trouble getting to sleep right away. That night, though, she didn't start to read and I didn't start to sleep. We sat there for a minute then started talking almost in unison.

I told her I had spent a lot of time in the library the morning before, looking up places we might want to spend the coming year.

She told me that had spent a lot of time in the library that afternoon looking up places we might want to spend the coming year.

I had been there again that afternoon. She had been there again that morning.

"You go first," she said.

"Well, ok," I said, "but you can go first if you want."

"We can't both go first," she said, as usual looking at the practical side of things.

"Well," I started again, as a sort of wind up. Then I told her that, first, I had made a list of things that seemed pretty important: more or less near London, though not *too* near, certainly not a subdivision, not like Pelham or Scarsdale to New York City; then the weather: I really wasn't into long, deep winters. Scotland sounded good, but it also sounded remote for a full year. As well as cold. Too, I was thinking about a smallish place. Actually I've always lived in smallish towns. I did not grow up on the sidewalks of New

York City, even though I was born there—New York City, that is. Not on a sidewalk.

With that and a few more ideas, I looked at the usual kinds of travel books, and all of them talked about the Southwest in pretty similar terms: it had the most moderate weather (a relative comparison, to be sure), had some of the most scenic countryside in the Isles, had good train service to London, and was relatively inexpensive—certainly compared to the London area.

Then I started running down some other, more fully developed books about the South-west, and found myself zeroing in on Devon. Chasing down yet more books about Devon specifically, I came across a place called Dartington Hall.

At that, my wife's face was a picture of disbelief, her mouth not really dropping open as mouths do in bad movies or in plays with bad actors, but with that quizzical, "I don't believe this" look we all get when we're hearing something we find hard to believe, but which seems to be true no matter.

"And," she started tentatively, "you read about people named Elmhirst?"

Then it was my face starting to go slack.

"How did you know about *them*?" I asked, my cheeks quivering slightly, my nares feeling twitchy.

"And the Dartington Hall Trust?" she went on.

"Yes. And the German and Jewish refugees during the war?" I joined in.

"Yes-yes-yes!"

"So where did you finally settle on?" I asked, hardly daring to breathe.

She cleared her throat.

"Totnes?" she almost whispered.

When she saw my face we were still shaking our heads at what had happened: Separately we had decided not only on the same region, but the same town: Totnes, South Devon, England. From what we had read, it was everything we wanted.

...

In early 1971 when all these plans were starting to take on real shape, our son was eight, our daughter nearly seven. I would be 39 that fall, and my wife was five years behind me.

As a general rule, my life has been one of liberal tendencies in politics and social matters, conservative in medical, dental, and personal fiscal matters—except, of course, when impulse whipped me into a frenzy, no matter how controlled I might look. Christmas, for instance, was made for *me*.

Maybe what I'm saying is that taking my family off to England for a year was not the sort of thing I would have thought of myself as doing. But, then, leaving a job that most would have considered "good" was not the sort of financial prudence I had come to expect of myself either. I certainly might have dreamed of that sort of trip, would have wished for it, could have hoped it might happen, but would never actually have dared to *do* it. At least, not under these circumstances.

So it was plan-making time. I wanted this to be an exorbitant experience, I suppose, and because I'd taken a cruise once—a high school graduation present—I wanted to go over and return on a ship. P&O was the line. If you're going over to England you might as well go on a British ship. And because it was leaving from Port Everglades, Florida, where my wife's parents were living just across the state on the Gulf coast, much about it was convenient.

We left on the *SS Orsova* and came back the following summer on the *SS Iberia*. The two trips were so very different, and it pained me to realize that the *Orsova* was on the scrap heap the following year when we were back in Plymouth getting ready to come home, and that our trip on the *Iberia* was to be its final voyage (out and back) as well.

That was enough to make me feel a little like a Typhoid Mary, but the near-year in Totnes was one that has stuck with all four of us to this day. My son, for instance, worked for a year or so after graduating from college, then spent about half a year in Japan teaching Japanese Yuppies something about how English (as my son interpreted it) is really spoken in America.

On his way back to the States, he spent some time traveling: Phu Ket, Indonesia, Hong Kong, and a few other Asian places. But a sudden and urgent homesickness grabbed him.

He had already made plans to meet a buddy from high school days in Paris at a certain time, but he hopped a plane, flew through Russia to London, hied himself to Paddington Station, where the trains to the Southwest started, and got himself to Totnes. It was that kind of place. It was that important to us.

...

I had made arrangements in the states for a bed and breakfast that looked to be good, but it was only for a week. What we needed was to rent something for an extended period—a cottage or apartment or whatever—and that seemed best done on the spot. A place we could look at to decide on.

The bed and breakfast we had chosen and had made reservations for was a place called the Mount Plym Hotel, owned and operated by Mr. and Mrs. E. Hill. Mr. and Mrs. E. Hill eventually became Ted and Audry, along with their two children (whose names I have, sadly, forgotten). They became good friends, after a fashion, tending to us in various ways, showing or explaining how the locals did, how the locals lived their lives. But not too close. Always a respectful distance between us. And that was not a forelock pulling sort of thing. It was just the way so many were.

We stayed there about a week as I recall, and by that time we had found a place to rent. That is, my wife had. I had gone into culture shock, and didn't come out for a good while.

...

Sean O'Casey, the Irish dramatist who had been heavily involved with the Irish National Theater group along with W.B. Yeats, and the rest, lived in Totnes from 1938 to 1953. This is what he once wrote about it.

> Apart from the quiet hurry of Market Day, gentleness is the first quality to give it; gentleness in its buildings, and in the coming and going of its people; and in the slow winding, winding of the River Dart from the moor to the sea. Oh, Lord, the natural lie of it is lovely. Except when visitors pour in during the brief summers, the town is so quiet that it looks like a grey-haired lady, with a young face, sitting calm, hands in lap, unmindful of time, in an orchard of aging trees, drowsy with the scent of ripened apples about to fall, but which never do.

The O'Casey reference is an interesting one even aside from his trenchant description of the town. Totnes was a place that was good for writers, as much, at least, as any place is good for writers. While we were there, there

On Breaking One's Pencil

were three others—Dexter Masters, Desmond Bagley, and K. Allen Saddler. Bagley (called Simon by people who knew him), and Saddler (a pen name for Ron Richards) were both English. I was known as the OAW, or Other American Writer.

Dexter Masters, a nephew of our own poet Edgar Lee Masters, was a founder of Consumer News and several times editor of its magazine *Consumer Reports*. He also was a novelist. Amazingly, perhaps, the four of us got along quite well. Richards and Bagley were adventure/thriller novelists—(Bagley the more famous with books such as *The Enemy, Spoilers, Wyatt's Hurricane*, etc. and K. Allen Saddler with *Betty* and many others). But Dexter was a "literary" man, as was I. Ron once described Masters this way: "Words to spare, Dexter has. Words to spare."

And as Fate would have it, Dexter's wife, Joan, became a novelist as well, though that was after we had left and after her husband's sad and untimely death. Previously she had been a ballerina with the San Francisco Ballet, studying later under George Balanchine in New York City's School of Ballet, but left all that for Dexter. Some years later—more or less just for kicks and giggles—she decided to see if she could get in good enough shape at her age to get taken on by a European dance company. She did get taken on, but turned the offer down. She had found out she *could* do it, and that was her point. In 1982 she wrote a book about it.

Dexter's novel, published in 1955, was titled *the Accident,* and the fictionalized subject was the 1946 nuclear accident in Los Alamos and what that might portend.

And there was a local musical group called *Staverton Bridge*, a trio dedicated to English balladry—both ancient and contemporary. There were three at first, but two guys and one gal can often create problems having little to do with music. One of the fellows was the son of Ron Richards, our writer friend three or four doors up the street.

So that was the kind of place Totnes was. But nearby was another place—a smaller town ("hamlet," might be a better word), but home to a significant assemblage of coming and going writers, painters, printers, and others—but especially those who worked to preserve the native arts and crafts—pottery, agriculture, and the like.

The Manor House, Dartington Hall, pretty much sat in the center of Dartington Estate. In the 1920's the place was bought by a wealthy American widow who had married an Englishman who was poor. What they wanted to do was "develop the natural resources of the estate"; secondly, find out in practice "how far the use of improved techniques in farming, forestry, and small-scale industry could raise the standard of living of the natives." And along with that they developed an art center, a school, and on and on…

So we were pretty much in the midst of a lot of folks who could be considered "artsy" by some, but just the day-by-day kind of folks we were used to.

…

Totnes, being an Anglo-Saxon borough, is a pretty ancient place dating from at least the 10th Century when, in 959, a King Edwig died. Being a borough, Totnes even had a mint, which—given the vicissitudes of life—went out of business for many years. It existed in the first place because Totnes was one of four boroughs in the Southwest along with Exeter, Barnstaple, and Halwell.

The town also has a Norman fort—which still exists—of the Motte and Baily variety. It's about the highest place in the town, obviously, and the views from the top are wonderful. Apparently the fortress never got used very much, because when trouble arrived the town usually, it would seem, gave in pretty quickly, which may not have been the greatest way to get their warriors reputations for bravery, or whatever, but it certainly allowed the populace the chance to die of standard causes.

Eventually they won the mint back. And later, in the sixteenth, seventeenth, and eighteenth centuries, Totnes was bought and sold a number of times by various Dukes. In 1947 the castle was put into the care of the ministry of Works.

But interesting as the history is, it came to us rather more slowly, and it came mostly from the locals, as they were all called. From the lumpish but pleasant lady who managed the fruit store—cautioning us about how to handle the pears she was handing over to our care, fearful that we wouldn't treat them with proper caution. From the publican who would finally bless us, sometimes, during a night's tipple, with a beautifully rendered tenor solo from one of the Gilbert and Sullivan operettas he had sung professionally betimes. From the bookstore lady who helped, carefully, to point out and suggest to our children books they might like—and profit from in a literary sense. From a local teacher who—with his two children—would take us out for a drive to an interesting river ford or other historic site. From a local plumber who pulled the beer in the Kingsbridge Inn and whose eyes often could be seen crossing dangerously not long before the 11:00 pm curfew; this same man once took me out to the moors where he had some work to do; a manager/dairyman and his wife who showed such wonderful sympathy for our children as well as ourselves

...and countless others.

...

But first things first.

We had two young children who had to be entered into the local school. That, of course, required a visit to the Headmaster, a more or less older gentleman with the obligatory pipe and the obligatory understanding of American school children who, assuredly, would be quite retarded in terms of learning, and who most certainly wouldn't be able to manage very well with the rudiments of "maths," though they *might* be able to grasp the basics of language—English as *properly* spoken—but certainly would need watchful assistance in anything like more difficult studies.

Our daughter Ruth had a hard time with being different. She needed to get into the uniform as quickly as she could (the children wore standard school-child garb: blue shorts and shirts or sweaters for the boys, and blue frocks for the girls); she needed to talk the way the natives talked as quickly as she could; she needed to be a little English girl, is the point, because she wanted to have as low a profile as possible. Being different terrorized her, so she was speaking two languages: American at home, English at school.

Walter, though—early on, when he was getting the most hazing that "new-boys" assuredly have suffered down through the ages everywhere—was once backed up against a link-chain fence on the playground, being rousted by a lad who insisted he should speak some German for them. "You're from America. Speak some German for us, why don-cha? Speak some German!"

As I recall, Walter finally just laughed in his face when he understood the lad really thought we Americans spoke German as our native tongue.

So much for the vaunted intellectual superiority of English over American public schooling.

...

Barry was the primary beer puller in the pub we frequented. Pubs, usually, were divided into two segments, one for the more gentile clientele, the other for the rest. Separate entrances. In the beginning I was advised to find the gentile door, so that's what I did.

Barry usually showed up probably about six or so and spent his nights serving the various beers and spirits—and, not being a shy fellow, and always willing to adhere to the local custom, would, during the course of the evening, and not wanting to hurt the feelings of any of the guests, having a bit on the side when treated. A popular sort of fellow who knew how to tell a good tale. Knew how to reach the lip of the glass which was always another quarter inch above the Full Mark.

But Barry made his living as a plumber during the day. In any event, he was a man proud of his countryside and the places in it, and over a little time, he understood that we didn't have a car, and that I was interested in the countryside and would love to go see the moors. So one night at the Pub he said he had a job out on the moor the next day and asked if I'd like to go with him.

Of course I said I would, and we arranged a place and time of meeting.

...

We were a perfect pair, Barry and I: he a kind of non-stop talker, and I a kind of non-stop listener. Naturals, so to speak.

We left the town, and Barry wasted little time in getting a move-on.

"You've never been out to the Moors?" he queried, knowing I hadn't. "Well, you'll see them today, and you'll understand why folks get a shiver when they first step on to them. They're quite something," he laughed.

He had a couple of stops to make—small business, nothing to take up a lot of time. Then a somewhat bigger job out on the Moors.

We got finished with his small business, and he started out again chatting me up as he wound around on the back lanes he called roads. He pointed out this and that, and how he came to be a plumber, and why he pulled beer for the pub at night, then he slowed slightly as he came to make a turn off the road we had been on and onto what I thought was just going to be on another road. He drove about two yards then clattered over a space that was constructed of sturdy pipes laid across the entrance for about ten feet. The pipes were about four or five inches apart. Then we were on the moor.

"That's so any loose cattle can't get out," he explained. Back on a road, the world had changed.

Just like that.

...

Thomas Hardy's novel *The Return of the Native*: In that novel, the heath—Egdon Heath, Hardy named it in the novel—becomes a symbol, a presence, a character:

> It was a spot which returned upon the memory of those who loved it with an aspect of peculiar and kindly congruity. Smiling champaigns of flowers and fruit hardly do this, for they are permanently harmonious only with an existence of better reputation as to its issues than the present.

The sea changed, the fields changed, the rivers, the villages, and the people changed, yet Egdon remained.

That's pretty much how I felt when I first saw it. You don't come upon it bit by bit. You're just suddenly *there!*

And there is nothing like it anyplace else.

...

In England, Bookies are regulated. When I was "up pub" one night, I got to talking to a fellow who turned out to be a Bookie. I guess my startled face rather startled him, so our conversation turned to his profession—or at least his basic profession: many in England had several jobs in addition to their primary. The conversation went from this to that, and at one point he asked, "Would you like to come by and have a look some time?"

I suggested that the next day or two would be fine, especially since the children would be in school.

So I found his place and he showed me his "Office." He had several phones and a "Telly," as he referred to a TV set, and he had a bottle of Scotch handy—almost as a part of his racing sheets, the phones, the various races, and so forth.

He kept a notebook—several, probably—with lists of names of his clients. I was impressed with his set-up, and even more impressed with the way he had to manage his work. The phones would be ringing pretty steadily, and he wrote down the customer, the amount of the bet, and anything else he needed. It was a fast-paced deal—several races starting pretty close together—and he also had to keep his phones ready to hang up the very second the bell rang that began each of the races.

Still, he offered me a whiskey while explaining what he was doing, taking the bets, writing them down, and so on. Then—just about the most important thing—he had to have a hand on each phone, as he watched the TV so that he could cut the line the very second the bell for the start of the race went off.

I asked about that! He laughed. "Some blokes, they try to get a bet in in that split second at the start of the bell if they see a particular horse looks to be leaping out to a lead." He laughed. "It can be pretty touchy work in here at times."

His clientele? Someone. Anyone. Everyone.

"Your favorite Publican just called on this last race," he said. "Have another whiskey."

...

Leithley Nightingale was a veteran of both World Wars. His wife, Joy, remembers climbing out of their family's bomb shelter after a German air raid on Plymouth, I think it was, in World War II, but it may have been farther down on the coast. A rather large port city, in any event. When she looked around, she and the others saw absolutely nothing that made any sense. There were virtually no buildings standing. All points of direction, all points of reference were gone. Her home city had been virtually blitzed from the face of the earth.

When we knew them that near-year in Totnes, they were both relatively aged, though she was the younger. Leithly was a musician—piano—and had more or less recently decided to have surgery on one of his fingers—one of his little fingers. He was a teacher, and often had to accompany a student on the piano. That little finger had been bothering him because he couldn't properly span an octave with that one hand. Hence, the surgery. I think he was already at the ninety-year mark. And their five grown children were scattered around the globe.

His wife, Joy, was younger, but still of an age. She kept herself busy as a potter. She couldn't have a kiln in their house, but she drove (usually) to the pottery out at Shinners Bridge, near Dartington Hall.

The kiln she used was a large one, and either she or my wife had to crawl into it in order to place the clay pieces (already shaped and dried, of course) properly for the firing. My wife had become interested in potting back in Clemson University where she took classes, and then again at the University of Arkansas, so they could work together pretty well—especially since Joy wasn't nearly as nimble as my wife, being some forty years older.

So they took us in, and at Christmas time they had us to dinner—replete with "The Pudding."

The pudding is a staple at Christmas time, and apparently (though my memory isn't all that good) it was prepared about a month or so before Christmas. Its contents weren't actually a secret, though Brits often start muttering when they don't feel the need to be quite so bloody explicit about things. Americans, they sense, consider *details* at all points to be a necessity. They regard us as pleasant enough folks in the main, but a bit "off," as they say, about having to know *how* everything works.

...

I remarked earlier about a woman who worked in the local bookstore and how she more or less steered our children into the really good youngsters' area. We talked her up be-times and realized we had found yet another person of interest. Margo and Pat—her husband—could also be categorized as artists. Or readers. Or "intellectuals," a word usually spoken with a sneer. But Pat was a different kind of artist. Over time, we became friends, and Dillman especially was wowed at the artistry of Pat. He dealt with Bonsai trees. He grew them. He cultivated them. He loved them. They were his passion.

They lived, as I recall, out in Dartington where Pat did odd jobs of a sort—looking after and tending to the property in various ways, turning out lights at night, or whatever. He may have done other jobs as well, but he loved, he cherished his Bonsais. Also, he had a pretty vast array of toy soldiers—relics, I think—"collectables," as some would say. But they were cherished.

...

Robert T. Sorrells

After a trip to the Continent—France, the War Memorial graves of our beloved World War II dead, over to Salzburg where I had spent my Army time because of the Korean War, down to Florence, and eventually back to England—we packed our bags to begin our trip home. The children, I think, were anxious to get back, but my wife and I—though looking forward to the trip and to being "home" again—had very mixed emotions about leaving.

Totnes—for those eight or nine months—had taken hold of us, had cherished us, amused us, enlarged us, taught us…

…a very special place. Very special.

Its ZIP code was TQ95DZ.

WRITING ADVICE

LETTER TO A STUDENT

THANKS FOR YOUR NOTE, THOUGH it may reflect a pessimism that's way ahead of its time. Writing is so very hard, and requires such an awesome, bulldog tenacity that I never know quite what to say to someone who asks me the question you have. I've said for years that I don't *write* stories, I *re*write them. I think that's true for most writers.

Obviously you have some serious problems with the basic tools of writing—spelling, punctuation, mechanics of that sort. But good writing is not limited to those mechanics. They are important, finally—perhaps as important as anything else—but they are not *all* that's important. Or, they may not be as important as other things right at first. A cabinet maker's cabinets finally determine his worth as a cabinet maker, not the cost or quantity of his tools. Still, eventually he does need to learn how to use the *tools* of his craft—the saws and awls and miter boxes—as well as the *techniques*—mortise and tenon joints, veneered surfaces, beveled edges, or whatever.

In my experience, if it's in a person to write, she is going to write without regard to publication or any of the other forms of "success." She is a writer, and writers write. So it may be that rather than ask me whether you should "give up the idea of becoming a writer," you should ask yourself, "What do I expect for being a writer?" Katherine Anne Porter said, "Practice an art for love and the happiness of your life—you will find it outlasts practically everything but breath."

Still, it's certainly reasonable that if we put all that "blood, toil, tears, and sweat" (to quote Winston Churchill) into our writing, then we want some recognition more or less commensurate with our labor. Alas, we don't always get it. Then the question that has to be answered by one's self is whether or not we should or can continue if the rewards—whether artistic and internal or monetary and external—don't seem to be worth the trouble.

You must also understand that the format of this course may not be especially suitable to your way of doing things. That's not unlikely. At the end of a work day William Styron may have only a page or two written. But those one or two pages are "keepers": They are *done*, they are finished. He re-writes as he goes. John Fowles, on the other hand, writes a novel in six months—then spends five years revising. It's the old business of there not being any "right" approach. It may be simply that—for you—the step-by-step method hinders rather than helps.

As for Mark Costello's story: You don't need to apologize to me, him, or yourself if you find it "boring." Shelby Foote, a good novelist and a top-notch writer—once said that he was willing to grant that Thomas Hardy was a great writer in all kinds of ways, but that he couldn't read the man. Put him to sleep. I understand what he means, but I love Hardy's stuff. I wrote my master's thesis on *The Return of the Native*. As for me, I don't think I've ever been able to finish but one novel by Bernard Malamud. Ho hum! That's no crime. *But* . . .

Not only are we all "stuck with our own skins," as Robert Penn Warren said, but we also live in a particular *time*, and it seems to me that as a writer in the 1980s you're cutting yourself off from the craft you say you aspire to if you don't study some of the contemporary people. I don't know who L. Saunders is, but the good stuff written by George Garrett—*The Succession* (a novel of Queen Elizabeth I's death and the succession of James I to the throne) and *The Fox* (the story of Sir Walter Raleigh and his death by beheading)—are not "at a fast clip" at all. Too, if George Sand had a character with blond hair at the beginning of a story and it had become dark by the end, then maybe she was guilty of sloppy writing, sort of like one of those humorous little *New Yorker* paragraphs that come under the general rubric "Our Forgetful Authors." In any event, we all have to be careful not to praise people for their mistakes.

Another thing you might need to talk to yourself about is what kind of fiction you want to write. If you are stuck on 19th century literature—especially the romantic sort—then are you interested in romance novels (candlelight and moors, etc.)? Or how about historical novels? Or perhaps biographical novels (of the Irving Stone variety—*Lust for Life*, for example)? There are so many genres.

You also mentioned Flaubert. Plus, a great contemporary writer to read, and one of the finest short story writers of our time is Peter Taylor, who once said that he learned to write by reading Chekhov. And Ernest Hemingway was greatly influenced by Sherwood Anderson who was *also* influenced by Chekhov. Yes, we have a great deal to learn by reading—and re-reading—de-Maupassant, Chekhov, Flaubert. But we also have a great deal to learn about writing by reading Updike, Cassill, Coover, and many other contemporary writers who learned their craft from previous writers, but who also "translated" what they read into their own time and their own places and their own voices. Goodness knows I would never give up Shakespeare, Dante, Chaucer, Mann, Hardy, Tolstoy, Thoreau, Forster, Hawthorne, and all the rest. At the same time, I could never give up Fitzgerald, Calvino, Weesner, Dylan Thomas, Gilchrist, Mason, John Irving, Fowles, Gardner, and on and on and on, either.

Well, I'm not trying to argue you into or out of anything, just trying to make up for the obvious problems I have with a correspondence course, I suppose. Writing is hard, the results almost always are personal, the rewards are usually few and far between, and very few really good fiction writers (you talked twice about wanting to write "quality" fiction) make a living at it.

I think you should stay with the writing for a while, anyway. But ask yourself if you should try to shift your angle of vision just a bump. When you talk about Sand being a "personification of success," I'm not sure what you mean. I guess I don't think in those terms, particularly. Perhaps we're talking about the same thing, but I don't know.

To me, being "successful" is being able to finish a story in which all the elements come together—plot, theme, characterization, whatever—in such a way that I honestly feel I have explored something important about myself and, thus, about all human beings. It may not be *the* most important thing in the world, but it is still *an* important thing. If I have been successful with any given story, not only will I have learned something more about how to write, but I will also understand something more about myself than I knew before I started writing, and I will have done that in such a way that if someone else should have a chance to read that story, they will understand something important about themselves as well.

So all I can say is, Be of Good Cheer. And do remember that even if things don't work out as you had dreamed, it is important to have dreamed in the first place.

On Breaking One's Pencil

529 Fifth Street, SW
Rochester, MN 55902

Vanderbilt University Board of Trust
Committee on Athletics
P.O. Box 52, Station B
Vanderbilt University
Nashville, Tennessee 37235

Dear People,

Clearly I'm writing to all of you, but if this gets to sounding more like a personal letter than a "comment" to a committee of the Board, that's because as I write I'm really thinking of and talking to John Hall, John Rich, and Ken Roberts, all of whom were friends and fraternity brothers of mine in college—unless, of course, I've got the right names but the wrong people. Stuff happens, as we all know.

I'm going to open in a way thoroughly lacking any sense of humility, for which I apologize only a little. I'm a fiction writer, primarily, and part of a *Publishers Weekly* review that was blurbed on my book *The Blacktop Champion of Ickey Honey*, said, "A major motif of many of the entries in this… collection is the world of sports and games—its lessons, philosophies and healing powers." Part of a Kirkus review that was also blurbed said, "… Sorrells is a master of the play-by-play…" Last year I also had an article published in a magazine called *Aethlon: The Journal of Sport Literature*, and this year I had a story reprinted in a book called *Tennis and the Meaning of Life: An Anthology of The Game*.

The point of all that, I reckon, is to suggest that I'm really not an effete snob, especially, but that I do love Sports!

To the point, though, much of this letter comes out of a brief but impassioned correspondence I had with Vince

Davis because of an article of his published in the Winter, 1979 *Vanderbilt Alumnus*. In reviewing that correspondence, I found we both agreed and concurred on much.

The short of my statement to you is: **Get out of the SEC as quickly and as honorably as existing contracts will allow.**

The long of it follows.

It seems to me that nothing has changed significantly in Vanderbilt Athletics since 1979, the year of Davis's article. Then, students who were actually enrolled in Peabody were playing ball for Vanderbilt; now Peabody is a part of Vanderbilt, and what that has done to the academic mix I don't know.

The only significant change may well be that the situation is worse than it was: VU has lost more and more games because of the passage of time and with the additions of Arkansas and South Carolina to the conference; more and more coaches have bit the dust after being ballyhooed as saviors of one sort or another; more athletic directors have had to brush up on their double speak to explain, qualify, or otherwise justify all the gridiron impotence; more and more money is being paid for fewer and fewer results; more and more money has been made by more and more people having less and less to do with Vanderbilt University—all the vendors, promoters, stadium cleanup crews, security folks, or whatever.

But to me, the question, "Can Vanderbilt compete in the SEC?" is still all wrong. The question should be, "Why should Vanderbilt **want** to compete in the SEC anymore?" Why, for that matter, has it wanted to for the past 45 years? I can remember when people figured Vanderbilt and Tulane (being the oddballs of the conference) would be the teams to leave, but Georgia Tech surprised us all.

Way back, Harvie Branscomb said, "If Vanderbilt must participate in intercollegiate athletics, then let it be with schools that have similar academic goals to ours." Basically from 1965-1987 I lived in Clemson, South Carolina, and I kept thinking: With Wake Forest, Virginia, Duke, and North Carolina in the ACC, why don't Clemson and Vandy simply swap leagues? Clemson would have been much more at home with Georgia, Alabama, Ole Miss, UT, and the other SEC schools. However, Harvie Branscomb, as many will recall, was not the most popular man on campus, I'm afraid—he wasn't with me, at the time, but time, I think, has proven him right.

He said another thing shortly after, when Byron White was appointed to the U.S. Supreme Court: "Any school that thinks it can field a team full of Whizzer Whites doesn't know what it's doing." I also have a penchant for Chicago's Robert M. Hutchins's dictum, "If it hasn't got anything to do with academics, get rid of it," though actually I feel closer to and more comfortable with the idea expressed in an Emory University catalogue of some years back that stated, "Participation in competitive sports *that require elaborate facilities for public entertainment* is not within the purposes of Emory." The italics, as you may assume, are mine.

I despair when I see so much time and energy, so much emotional capital wasted, from my perspective, on this business of semi-professional athletics. The Pro teams years ago found they could use our colleges and universities as patsies by making them into the teams' farm clubs—and it didn't cost them a plugged nickel. At least the professional baseball teams were a little more honest about it.

I am very uncomfortable knowing that committees such as yours still are having to be formed for these issues when there are other matters that should be getting greater attention. Our administration needs to concern itself with the number of Danforth fellows (if there still are such folks), Fulbright scholars, Rhodes scholars; with the number and quality of entrants and graduates; with *real* scholarship money; with the thousand and one things the values of which will so far outlast those blank-faced undergraduates who galumph about in front of the TV cameras, their fingers poking holes in the sky, chanting, "We're Number One," and all the rest of the clap-trap and bally-hoo associated with varsity athletics that it beggars the imagination.

I know that Washington and Lee, as one example, deliberately got out of the "business" of football. (My father, by the way, played fullback for their 1916 or 1917 team that either beat or tied a heavily favored Army team.) The last I heard they had joined a Virginia league of some sort whose members didn't have grants-in-aid, don't charge admission to their games, and own their own facilities. I like that because then the school—in paying for the sports programs—is also controlling those programs, unlike Georgia's program, for instance, which for all practical purposes is totally divorced from the University budget, even to the point of renting the stadium from the University which makes the University a holding company for the athletic department.

In any event, the W&L solution is the kind of direction I'd like to see Vanderbilt take.

I know there are people who think I'm an incurable romantic (*not* a compliment) about all this. That doesn't bother me a bit. Frankly, I think those people are the romantics, feasting still on the glory days of the Point-a-Minute teams of Noch Brown or whomever, the All Americanism of Bill Wade and Bucky Curtis, Charley Horton and Phil King. Sure sure. But I think of people like the three of you, John H and John R and Ken, as well as Jim Whitehead and Henry Tyler and Sonny Tatum and others who didn't come to Vanderbilt just because of the athletics, nearly all of whom had offers to go to other SEC schools as athletes, but who came to Vanderbilt because it was more than just a likely ticket to the Pros for maybe one-to-five years and then back to Itta Bena or Marks or Hohenwald to coach at the local high school.

I am not a monied person: Part time teachers and fiction writers who are married to ministers usually aren't. But I have contributed my mite practically every year since I've been out of school, and one year when I had been working for the Development Office on the $30 Million capital campaign back in the sixties, I donated my final month's salary to the Living Endowment. I have continued to contribute in the hope that I am helping not only to protect the integrity of my own degrees, but also that my pittance will help to that extent to keep Vanderbilt from folding—as good schools have done—or from falling away from being a truly fine center of learning. I don't want it to drift into waste, mere gossamer in our memories.

Charley McLendon coached at LSU for 27 years, 17 of them as head coach. In winning something like 70 per cent of his games, he went to two Orange Bowls, two Cotton Bowls, two Sugar Bowls, two Bluebonnet Bowls, two Sun Bowls, a Peach Bowl, and a Liberty Bowl.

Then they fired him. At a football jamboree in Easley, South Carolina, he said that as far as the schools were concerned, "The only thing that matters is the bottom line. When the season's over, they don't care who you played, it's just how many you won." Then he said, "We [football coaches] can just hope the athletic directors and college presidents are strong enough to run their own ship when they see a coach is doing as well as he can…"

If that's what college athletics is all about, then—to paraphrase the cartoon about the kid as he stared down at the glob of spinach on his plate—I say it stinks and I say to hell with it.

An item in the November 3 Minneapolis *Star Tribune* of this year mentions your committee and points out that Vandy's SEC football record since 1960 is 35-182-6. Folks, that isn't sports. The fact is that when two, more-or-less evenly matched teams play each other, you're likely going to have a good game. That it has to be Vandy versus # whatever Alabama or #5 Tennessee or #3 Florida—much less Ole Miss or LSU or the others—is nothing but ego. And somebody's Big Business.

The article went on to quote Chancellor Wyatt as saying, "The real question we're facing is how can we be as good as we can be in athletics and still be Vanderbilt, still have the standards we have, still have the values we have. Athletics are a part of our education program. That's the way we treat it. I think we do pretty well in a conference as difficult as this one." He's probably right: 35-182-6 is probably as well as we can do, I expect.

Now if Wyatt's point is that he wants Vanderbilt athletics to be kept in its appropriate place vis a vis academics, then the won-loss record will remain much as it is—at best. But if he's saying we can be consistently "competitive" in these matters (to go back to an old buzz word from at least the Emmett Fields days) and still retain those standards and values, then pardon me, but we've heard it all before, and it hasn't ever worked.

What you're going to have to decide is either to stay in and expect very little more in the way of athletic accomplishment, or get out.

There is, of course, a third possibility: Get good. The trouble with that, is that the *academic* well of competitive-quality players (those with Vanderbilt's standards and values all neatly intact) is incredibly small compared with the well of athletically competitive players that UT, Ole Miss, Georgia, Clemson, and other such schools are willing to haul up in the buckets of their athletic Programs.

Those of us who live out here in the boondocks of Minnesota or South Carolina or wherever (boondocks being virtually any place outside Nashville), have reason to feel that we don't have a whole lot to say about things, at least not that's going to get listened to particularly. And, as I pointed out, I don't have the kind of money it would take to endow a chair of music at Blair or a scholarship fund for poor students with talent or a top-notch art collection or on and on and on. All I can do is try to be persuasive. All I can do is try to give you pause, try to get you to look truly at matters, to discuss these things openly and fairly and not merely go through motions toward a predetermined end.

I love that durned place down there, folks, and I am reminded of an old recording I heard of Toscanini as he rehearsed the NBC Symphony (or the New York Philharmonic, whichever it was). He tapped the players to silence with his baton, at one point, to let them know why he was unhappy with the way they were proceeding, to instruct them in what he wanted. And then, hoping he could wring something more ineffable from them than just merely greater precision in executing the notes, he said, "It must be *good*." Perfectionist and purist that he was, he elaborated in an almost comically simplistic way by saying, "It must be good, *good*, good."

I'm talking Toscanini, here, not Lawrence Welk; Vanderbilt University, not semi-pro farm clubs.

Thank you.

Yours,
Robert T. Sorrells (A'54, BA'56, MA '57)
(507) 289-0997

On Breaking One's Pencil

529 Fifth Street SW
Rochester, MN 55902

Hon. Sheila Kiscaden
Room 325 Capitol Building
St. Paul, MN 55755

Dear Sheila,

I get very nervous when people propose plans to spend gobs and gobs of money on a project, when the language they use to describe that project strongly suggests they really don't understand what they're talking about.

For some time now, I have been reading a great deal about what has been called a "four year university" to be established here in Rochester. As best I can tell, the term was invented by Governor Pawlenty, and has been repeated by virtually everybody since.

My main question is simple: What in the world is a "four year university"?

I have been associated with colleges and universities since 1950: as an undergraduate student, graduate student, and teacher. I have also served universities in non-academic positions as a fundraiser in a development office (during a major capital gifts campaign) and as an editor/writer in a publications and graphics department. I also was commissioned to write a history of the first fifty years of a university's experimental forest. In all those years I have never ever heard the term Four Year University.

First, a *university* is an umbrella term for an educational institution consisting of numerous schools or colleges (those terms being more or less interchangeable depending upon the institution), for example: the Undergraduate College; the School of Forestry; the Nursing School; the College of Engineering; The College of Arts and Sciences;

the Graduate School (or the Graduate and Professional School); the Law School; the Medical School; the School of Architecture; the Divinity School; etc. In addition, some universities offer degrees in certain disciplines that cross from undergraduate into graduate work.

These various sub-groups of a university have widely differing time frames for granting degrees. Typically, an undergraduate degree (Baccalaureate or Bachelor's degree) will take four years; a law degree, three; a medical degree three, four, or more depending; a master's degree typically in one or two; a Doctorate (Ph.D.) two to four, depending upon whether the student already has a master's degree or not, and on whether it takes another two or three years to complete a dissertation.

Given all this, there can be no such thing as a "four year university."

Secondly, everything I have read about the proposed school makes it sound like it is going to be a four-year technical college, not a university. If that's the case, let's start calling it that. But if it does become a *university*—granting graduate as well as undergraduate degrees in a variety of disciplines—then it still sounds like a technical university, presumably using Cal Tech, Georgia Tech, RPI, MIT, and other such institutions as its models, rather than any of the fine midWestern state universities. I conclude this because I have not heard or read one single word about degrees being offered in the arts, humanities, or social sciences, and it certainly used to be that MIT, etc., usually had very strong liberal arts/social science components.

So, are students going to be able to major or minor in Languages? Literature? Philosophy? Art? Music? Theater? History? Political Science? International Relations? The city of Rochester has a long history with the visual arts and music—much of it because of Mayo Clinic—not forgetting the three or so theaters in the area as well. This city is ready to explode into the arts, and if we are going to spend the time and money to create an entirely new institution of higher education, then we ought to be teaching the arts rather than just teaching people how to earn enough money to support them. Too, the number and variety of non-nativeborn residents now living in Rochester would suggest that language study, political relations, and religious studies curricula also would be naturals at a real university.

Then, within the sciences themselves: are chemistry courses going to be chemistry for chemistry, or chemistry for nurses? Physics for physics, or physics for better IBM circuitry development? Biology for biology, or biology for some immediate return on investment, or whatever, rather than on basic research?

Third, when the names of the people appointed to serve on the organizing committee for this new venture were released, there may have been some whose backgrounds are or were primarily in the liberal arts/social studies, but if so, they remained pretty much disguised. I saw businessmen, a former dean of a medical school, science types, etc., but never a former dean of a college of liberal arts, a musician, theater director, or arts administrator. I may be wrong in that, and if so I hope you'll tell me. In the meantime, though: A "four year university"? What *is* it?

With kindest personal regards, and thanks for all the good work you have done for this community over the years—in whatever political raiment—I remain very truly yours,

Robert T. Sorrells

Copies: The Hon. Tim Pawlenty, Governor
The Hon. Tina Liebling State House of Representatives
Jon Losness, Publisher and Editor, the Rochester *Post-Bulletin*

On Breaking One's Pencil

Dear Terry,

I read your letter and was delighted to find out that you are chairman of the Zumbro Watershed Partnership. That gives you the cachet to speak with some authority about the issues you raised. *My* problem with your piece is not in the issue, but in the tone you've adopted to deal with it.

Just as an overview, it smacked of a playground argument between two twelve-year-olds: "Oh yeah?" sez one.

"Yeah!" sez the other

"Oh yeah?"

"Yeah!"

So lemme suggest two things. First, there's an old law school story about a teacher who's giving his class an example. "Suppose," the professor said, "you find yourself the litigator in a suit. If you have the *law* on your side, pound it into the judge. If you have the *emotion* and sentimental appeal on your side, pound it into the jury."

A student tentatively raised his hand when the teacher had finished and asked, "But, Sir, what if you don't have either one on your side?"

"In that case, young man," the teacher replied, "you pound it into the table."

The second reference goes back to the hugely popular radio (then TV) series *Dragnet*, of the '50s-'60s starring Jack Webb as Detective Sergeant Joe Friday. His mantra was repeated by thousands of people in thousands of situations for many, many years: "Just the facts, Ma'am," he would say, his voice flat, his face locked in a stoic, unsmiling stare that suggested he'd heard it all before. "Just the facts."

...

So, about the kids on the playground. In your fourth paragraph you say, "Or, more politely…" There's a snicker in that phrase.

"King Corn" in that same paragraph is the same sort of thing.

First sentence next paragraph. "There's a law, *you know…*" Same smart-alecky tone.

Very next sentence, "…we do have a *so-called* environmental Commission…" Same thing.

Next paragraph: "…but environmental commissioners… oppose *"enforcement…."* Same thing.

And *"educating"* farmers…Same thing.

And at the beginning of the final paragraph, "Oh, and by the way…" Same thing.

…

What I would hope—if you're interested enough and feel you have the time—is that you would develop a series of articles on the topic. The PB, obviously, might or might not be interested in publishing it, but if you want to pursue it I think you should take a pointer from Detective Sergeant Joe Friday, LAPD. "Just the facts, Ma'am."

Get the number of the law, quote from it, say who introduced it for legislation, and what its background was. What impelled the Legislature to enact it in the first place? Who else has been on the Environmental Commission over the years? Was the educational rather than the enforcement attitude present all along, or was that the work of the current members of the commission?

Et cetera.

Harking back to the Law Professor in the classroom for just a second, I would posit that you have both the "legals" as well as the "emotionals" on your side. It strikes me that you're able to pound your case into both the Judge *and* the Jury. That puts you sitting squarely in the catbird seat for sure.

When you enumerate in your first paragraph all the crud and gunk that's in the river—then state that there are still fish there to be caught (a presumed good)—you really engage the reader in what you're talking about when you ask the rhetorical question, "but do you really want to eat that fish?"

No particular pun intended, but *that's* where you have given yourself the chance to hook your readers into where you're going with all this, because you have made it personal *for the reader*. Then you have given yourself the chance to get into the facts of the case, and then it follows that you can also point to ways the problem can be corrected. It seems to me that something going that way is better than being snide or simply venting your outrage.

I don't know if this is any great help to you or not, Terry, but I wish you well in your enterprise. Just don't allow yourself to lose sight of what you really want to get done.

Cheers

Dear Sylvia,

First, what a pleasure to see you again and to have at least met Blaine. I don't remember that he was with you five years ago.

And secondly, how pleased I am that you have been working so hard on your poetry. Writing is an often dishearteningly difficult task: I'm a writer (mainly fiction but fund-raising, straight news, radio, history, etc.); my father was a writer (a newspaper man with Scripps Howard); my son is a writer (numerous mystery novels); and of course Dillman is also a writer as a minister, with three sermons a week plus untold memorial/-wedding/child-naming/and special services. So I've spent my life surrounded by words.

Too, I hope you'll keep in mind that whatever I say about your work is nothing but one man's opinion, one man's sometime suggestions, and one man's maunderings about the whole mysterious business of filling up blank pages with those amazing words.

I'm not a poet, really, though of course I've written some poems. I often think that all fiction writers are frustrated poets—we simply don't have the ability to distill and compress that poets have. Also, believe me when I tell you how humbled I felt that you would show me your stuff. Letting people read you is a scary leap of faith, and one of the hardest jobs of the writer is to separate (as best she can) one's *Self* from one's *Work*, because the work usually is so much a part of the self.

What I'll be doing here is talking about some specific poems of yours, suggesting other poets/poems you might find useful to read/study, and blathering on (probably too often) about just general kinds of attitudes or insights or ideas about all this.

What I like about "Weeping Willow" is the image of the tree and the person. I had a kind of vision of a Japanese *haiku* with this—the lines of the curves involved, the cascading and stooping. I don't know if you've read many haiku or not but they are really worth looking at because in three lines of 5, 7, and 5 syllables you can get almost inconceivable compression. They're like Japanese ink drawings—just *swoosh swoosh swoosh* and it's done. (The falling flower/I saw drift back to the branch/Was a butterfly.) "Sight-Seeing from a Cadillac" raises some questions with me you might feel like looking at yourself. I like the tension there—the pleasure of having won the First-Class-Prize tugging against the vision of folks with losers' lives. The problem I had with Cadillac I also had with some other of the poems, and that's a problem of the rhythms. Let's look at it. She won a trip (di **dah** di **dah**)/To tour the country (di **dah** di **dah** di)/ To see its many sights (di **dah** di **dah** di **dah**)/ To see the attractions (di **dah** di di **dah** di)/ Its mountains and deserts (di **dah** di di **dah** di)/ "First Class" in an air-conditioned Cadillac (**dah dah** di di **dah** di **dah** di **dah** di di).

The interesting thing about it is its sort of jazzy lilt, but even with a jazzy lilt (whatever that is) the lines are all over the place with stressed and unstressed syllables. All poets who work in regular metrical patterns use substitute feet now and then (putting in a trochee [**dah** di] instead of the expected iamb [di **dah**]), but others who work outside regular patterns still pay attention to the movement of the stresses, building toward something or falling away from something already established. In addition, they usually match that rhythm to what's going on dramatically in the poem. What would be the difference if you said "in an/Air-*cooled* Cadillac" instead of Air-conditioned both in terms of the rhythms as well as the connotative shift of *cooled* vs. *conditioned*?

The same kind of thing comes up in "Mother Hubbard's Cupboard," and in a number of others. What I am NOT saying is that you have to slavishly follow a pattern once you've marked it out, but readers get used to a pattern and when it's broken it ought to be for a discernable reason. "Cool Kids," for example, is a lot of fun to read, but some of the lines sound pretty forced, a bit awkward, I guess. I pretty much am with you until "Are they as Cool/As they would/Want you to think?" That sounds to my ear like a line of prose written in three lines, and thus seems out of character with lots of the rest of the poem.

In "Desert Clouds" you've got a poem that I like mainly because of your ironic insight: We are what we are, so there's only so much that anyone can do for us—or us for ourselves. Robert Penn Warren once said, "We're all stuck with our own skins." And I took great pleasure in some of your epigrams: "Rising to the Occasion," and "Easy as Pie." I don't know, epigrams *should* be fun, simply because they're so pithy, packing so much meat on so few bones. I noticed, though, that you never tried a limerick. They don't have to be bawdy, though most tend to be, but you might want to see what you can do with the form.

And I love "Facing Up, Backing Away." It's a wonderful koan ("what is the sound of one hand clapping?") Also "Speaking Up" is a poem I'd like to use if I get to do a session with our Coming of Age group. My segment (if they let me) has to do with reading— reading aloud. Geez, it perfectly fits so many folks who are called on to do readings in church services or whatever. Mumbling and reading as though they were in a race.

"Face Down" brings me to another whole topic. This poem and some others—"Thank You to the Armed Forces," "You Can't Stop What's Right," "9/11," etc. are what I'm calling Didactic Poems for lack of a better term. What I mean by that is poetry intended to sway or convert the reader in some highly specific way. This gets a little touchy, because obviously the poems we write are parts of our *selves* and so we get our egos all bound up in them in ways we shouldn't. (I'm hedging here, right?)

Usually the problem with didactic poetry is that the poem suffers at the expense of the "message," or, simply to rephrase, the message becomes more important than the poem itself. This is a modestly dicey point, I suppose, but when we're writing poetry we owe something to the form of the poem. We want our poetry to be meaningful, and we want it to have a point or a message or whatever, but we also want that point to be made in as poetic a way as possible. By *poetic* I don't mean fancy-pants, I don't mean frilly lace on the cuff of a $300 silk T-shirt or whatever. Subject matter can often dictate the form of any given poem even as it dictates the diction, the mood, and so on.

So even though we want to write a poem in praise of men sent to war or in praise of God or whatever it might be, we still have to honor the words and the fact that we've decided to put noble sentiments into a poetic (or dramatic or fictional) **work of art**. That is, just because the *subject* is worthy doesn't mean that it's automatically going to move your readers. For that, you gotta have the **poetry** as well.

Now, in "Armed Forces…" how else can you talk about making the world free, waving the flag, being brave, defending us, etc.? (Here's where I wish we were in a quiet room sitting face to face with plenty of time for you to furrow your brow and ask me questions which I had plenty of time to think up answers that you might start to buy in to. But… so I proceed.) Do you get a sense from what I've said right here what you might want to start thinking about, a road you might want to start walking down? Free world, flags, defense, bravery: These are concepts, and as such are sitting on the page kinda nekkid. They're skeletons—and terribly over-used skeletons at that.

In fiction writing classes we were always told, "*Show* us, don't *tell* us." The same can be said in poetry. So, how can you *show* bravery? How can you *show* defense? How can you *show* freedom? How can you *show* the profoundest meanings of the flag as a symbol of all these things you're talking about? In fiction, of course, we can develop scenes and mini-scenes, all dressed out with descriptions making use of sights, sounds, smells, movement of characters across the stage and all that. How does this translate to poetry, however, assuming you're going to deal primarily with lyrical rather than with "dramatic" poems? It falls to images, usually. (Just as a quick aside, there is a whole lot of "dramatic" poetry. Check out some of Robert Browning's dramatic monologues—*Fra Lippo Lippi*, and *My Last Dutchess* are two stunning examples.)

"Face Down in the Street" is another you might want to look at again. It has similar problems, though maybe not quite as deep. My suggestion is to put the *persona* in the picture (the voice, the narrator). Make those choices real, not theoretical: "I saw him face down at the curb,/one foot nearly in the street./I had engagements I had to keep, but/ something slowed my step/at least for the moment…"

"Frozen Tears" I like—very much like. Whether it's a *good* poem or not I can't say, but what it does is along the lines I was talking about above, and the line that really grabs me is "Tears know the season they're in…" That's a startling line, to me, startling because the poem doesn't just say how much the persona loves the beloved—which is pretty much what "Songs for You" does. "Songs" is a *nice* poem, but "Frozen" has more substance, it seems to me. And the reason for that, I think, is that you are working with an image: a real live image—even an extended image, which is even harder to control and maintain.

It's through the images in a poem, I think, that we are able to make even the most mundane ideas take on meat, have an edge, rise above the expected. Say it how you will. Miller Williams wrote a poem about a man who, while driving his car, at one point sees a lovely young lady who is trying to get out of a side street onto the very busy main street. He signals her to come on, she waves her thanks or whatever, pulls out, and is gone. No pun intended, but it is a pedestrian enough setting. Then the poet is talking to himself about the incident—that he remembered it because it was somehow meaningful to him. But he's realistic enough to remind himself that "by the end of the day, you won't even be a wrinkle in her brain," or something like that. But it's that "Not even a wrinkle in her brain" that makes the whole thing come off the page. Suppose Miller had left it standing with something like, "She'll never remember you."

Faulkner once said that he realized he was a good writer when he saw that he could "make his characters stand up and cast shadows." Wow! That's as good a way as there is to say what I've been trying to get at.

...

So that's about it, Sylvia. I don't think I need to try commenting on every one of your poems, but perhaps I've hit on enough of them so you get some idea of what I've seen. I really like a number of them, a few very much; and there are some that prolly need some more work, and sometimes the "work" is not technical so much as a matter of re-thinking them: Are they now doing what you really want them to do, or has the "real" poem kept itself at a distance, kept hiding, kept pretending that it was something else so you couldn't really get a grip on it. Writing can be like that sometimes.

And I don't know what poets you've been reading or what books on writing poetry you may have discovered, but if you'd like, I'll happily work up a little reading list that *might* be useful in some way.

And again, thanks so much for trusting me with these.

With kindest personal regards,

CHURCH MATTERS

Doris Grumbach and Prayer

IN HER BOOK *FIFTY DAYS of Solitude*, Doris Grumbach—a novelist, former literary editor of the *New Republic*, columnist for the New *York Times Book Review*, and author of several other meditative books—wrote of discovering in *The Book of Common Prayer* a prayer that she committed to memory and recited every night while on a personal retreat.

> Oh Lord, support me all the day long,
> Until the shadows lengthen,
> And the evening comes,
> And the busy world is hushed,
> And my work is done.
> Then in thy mercy
> Grant me a safe lodging
> And a holy rest,
> And peace at the last.

I love that prayer, but I also love Grumbach's gloss on the lines. "Those were wonderful words she wrote. "Shadows lengthen, the fever of life over, the world hushed, work done, holy rest. Unlike so many other prayers," she went on, "not hallowed names, kingdoms to come, and grace, righteousness, the power and glory forever and ever the resurrection and the life; but instead safe lodging and peace at the last."

ABOUT CHURCHES

FIRST OF ALL, A CHURCH is an institution of a particular sort, and like any other institution it can get bogged down in its own baggage so that its primary purpose comes to be, **Stay in Existence**. That's when people tend to lose faith in it and in lots of the good stuff it can still do. A confusion with the institution itself and the reasons for its existence in the first place is not hard to understand, but is sometimes hard to explain: There's a difference between the Institutional Church and the Church of the Spirit.

I tend to be an institutionalist myself (up to a point) but our UU churches are filled with people who became disaffected with where they were. Often it's as simple as, "I couldn't keep on saying I believed all that stuff you're supposed to believe if you're going to be able to say—honestly—that you're a Methodist (or whatever). So I got out."

For others, the matter is more complicated. We've also had a lot of people who were brutally wounded by their religions—including lots of Catholics and folks reared in fundamentalist churches that battered them with how evil they were, how worthless, how lowly, how pocked by sin and degradation and-on-and-on-and-on. These are the people who are angry angry angry at their churches and, often, at religion generally. I liken them, sometimes, to people who feel betrayed by politicians and who feel that "they're all thieves and liars and cheats …" etc.

Fact is, they aren't all thieves, liars, and cheats, etc. Fact is, churches have saved people from despairs of the worst and most unimaginable sorts. In both political and religious (or churchly) cases I've come to see people expecting too much, or expecting what wasn't ever possible in the first place. One problem in the political realm, it seems to me, is that "The Public" often doesn't want to hear the truth: (We'll have to raise taxes to lower the national debt, for instance; or, Chaing Kai Chek is going to lose to the Communists because he doesn't have any credibility with the people of China, as the China Specialists in the Forties put it; or, The Viet Nam war was the wrong war in the wrong place at the wrong time being fought by the wrong people for the wrong reasons. And Iraq? Well, what goes around comes around—only different. Name your own refusals to see or hear unpleasant things).

So institutions are like that, too. They're run by people. The USA is a nation governed by law not by men, as the saying goes. Yet it was Charles Evans Hughes who pointed out that the Constitution "is what the judges say it is." People and institutions. Fundamentalists want absolute answers to the questions of life. That's why so many of them turn up in military or para-military organizations where authority can be pretty absolute. They don't understand parable, they don't understand metaphor, they can't deal with ambiguity at all, and they don't believe in paradox. Was Bill Clinton a scuzzball? Prolly so. Was he also a good president? The jury may still be out, I expect, but in all likelihood, prolly so.

But I said that a church is a particular kind of institution. What it's good for depends on what you think it can or should do or be. What *is* a religious institution for? Like so many other institutions there are lots of reasons for it to be and lots of things it exists to do. Many UU churches are very social-action oriented. This comes from a belief (word intentionally used) that if we believe in the dignity of all human beings, then we must act on that belief. That attitude is hardly new, going back to all the debates about Grace, Faith, and Good Works. But of course they all had to do with Salvation, something most UUs dismiss pretty much out of hand.

A vast preponderance of UUs don't believe in heavens and hells and other afterlives; therefore the life of love or faith or good works must be done here where our real lives—our physical lives—are, because when we die we're as dead as any zebra eaten and digested by the nearest pack of hyenas.

But the question of spirituality comes up, churches being, presumably, repositories of spiritual growth. (That's intended to sound silly.) It's here we get into the fun part, sort of. In a paper I once delivered to an audience of teachers and writers, I said that a course in Creative Writing may be the very worst place for a person to learn something about how to write fiction or poetry or drama, because educational institutions are often so stuffy and bound by rules, regulations, procedures, and so on. Still, I dared venture, they can be pretty good places if you know how to deal with the Academic Nay Sayers—and with your own tainted baggage.

By the same token, a church can be the worst place in the world to come to grips with what we call spirituality, something UUs for way too many years pooh-poohed. But it's why I got and have stayed connected.

In Rochester, Minnesota, where my wife and I lived for nineteen years, there's a huge complex called Assisi Heights, a convent that once housed many hundreds of Franciscan nuns, but which now has fewer and fewer, and those are the ancient dears waiting for the end when they can be united in Christ. (In fact, Assisi Heights has essentially ceased to be a convent at all, having been purchased a numbers of years ago by the Mayo Clinic.) Still, in the Lourdes Chapel—a beautiful space where magnificent concerts are held during the year—there is a great, arching inscription that reads, I HAVE LOVED O LORD THE BEAUTY OF THY HOUSE WHERE THY GLORY DWELLETH. In that space, it's a stunning statement of faith and hope. Still, it's what's wrong, in my opinion, with so many people's attitudes about "church." The glory of the Lord (whatever that might mean to any given person) doesn't dwell in that house any more than it dwells in anyone's house—or home or heart or mind. That is, that gorgeous, glorious place is not the only place or kind of place where the "Lord's Glory" can dwell.

It seems to me that one source of the bad raps churches get is from those who don't understand, accept, realize, or whatever, that spirituality is a felt state of being, and that attempts to deal with it rationally will always fail. Reason, Logic, Common Sense, and all those good things simply can't reach the spiritual nature of a religious sensibility.

So a church will always fail if it is seen as a fount of spirituality rather than as a route—one among so many—for a person to get introduced to it, to move nearer where he or she needs to be, that way. A church is really no more than a community of more or less like-minded and similar-hearted people who deal with each other by playing, working, and communing together to move toward (or within) the goal of whatever their religious ambitions might be.

Well, this is all little more than so much blather to many, I imagine—which doesn't "disappoint" me, assuming I'm right, but saddens me after a fashion. One problem many in this country have is that when they talk

On Breaking One's Pencil

about religion or church, they too often automatically think of Christianity. What a shame. There's so much else going on.

Our Unitarian Universalist societies, it seems to me, should have us be highly visible models to demonstrate that religion doesn't *have* to equal Christianity to be valuable; that what works for one religious sensibility doesn't *have* to work for all; that if a particular route of faith held by one doesn't work for another, that doesn't *have* to negate or lessen its value for the one; that a calm for our hearts, a balm for our souls, and a passion for living our beliefs can manifest themselves in many and wondrous ways; and that one must *keep on* finding or looking for ways to approach that calm, that balm, that passion. Or, to reverse the process, we need to keep preparing ourselves so we are able to recognize, be ready to gather up, and be willing to embrace those urgencies of mind and heart to make them our own.

I wish I could say I've done all that for myself. Still, in certain ways, I have. It's just that you really do have to keep finding it, have to keep leaning against the tightening strictures of the mortal coil, I guess. It's like the good ole boy football player who told his coach during a tough game that he just couldn't knock that big fellah in front of him down. "Well then, don't try to knock him down, Bubba," his coach wisely advised. "But you still gotta keep leaning on him."

Anyway, I keep finding things out from William Butler Yeats that I've said in other ways myself. For instance, my wife and I were talking about who knows what some time or other, and within the context of our conversation I responded to something she had said with, "I don't ever have 'fun.' I don't do 'fun.'"

Then she said she knew that and it had always been a sadness to her.

More or less surprised at that, I said, "But I'm really into Joy, so 'fun' isn't something I miss." Later, I happened across some quotes from William Butler Yeats in a book called *Writers on Writing*. He said that a poet's passion "is reality" as opposed to the understanding of sentimentalists—"practical" men "who believe in money" and to whom happiness is to stay busy, so that "all is forgotten but the momentary aim." "And for the awakening," Yeats went on, "for the vision, for the revelation of reality, tradition offers us a different word—ecstasy."

So I've found that I'm concerned about Joy and Ecstasy rather than happiness or fun. Maybe that's why—even coming from a not particularly churchy, much less religious, back-ground—I've gotten hooked on some semblance of religion: what it is, what it isn't; what it can be; *how* it can be; what it's about (after a fashion); the joys and ecstasies it can lead to; about how it can help me develop at least a glimmer of what an epiphanal moment can be. In a long essay on Nashville I even raise the question as to whether people still have epiphanies. When I wrote that, I was thinking of a funny remark once made by a very dear friend: "I majored in philosophy," her patter went, "but that was a long time ago, and they didn't know very much about it then."

I've always loved that.

SHAPE-NOTE INTRO

I WAS ASKED TO SAY a few words about Shape-note singing by way of an introduction to this part of today's service, so let's just start with some categories. Shape-note singing is, obviously, music, and just as obviously it is vocal music. Shape-note music is a form of vocal folk music. Shape-note music also is a form of religious vocal folk music.

Within that last category there is gospel, certainly, and spirituals, and within *that* there are white spirituals, as well as Negro spirituals, and these white spirituals are contained in hymnals with such names as *Christian Harmony*, *Kentucky Harmony*, *Hesperian Harp*, *Southern Harmony*, *Harp of Columbia*, and *The Sacred Harp*, which may be the most well-known, though *Southern Harmony* is probably the least changed since it was first published in 1854.

Largely pioneer-American in origin with many tunes that have been traced back to much older English tunes, it is called Shape-note singing because the notes on the printed page—unlike the music you can easily see if you open your hymnals—are not only round, but are also tri-angular, square, and oval. This is a form of musical notation designed to make reading music easier for people who had never had any "real" musical training.

Shape-note singing is also called Fa-Sol-La singing (even though there is a MI) because each of the shaped notes is known as a FA or a SOL or a LA or a MI (as in do re mi fa sol la ti do—the notes of the scale).

Also, each "lesson"—these are not usually called hymns, at least not in the South—is begun by singing only the *fa-sol-la*'s rather than the words in order for the singers to get the pitch, the melody, and the tempo straight.

If you're ever lucky enough to go to a Shape-note Sing—singing all morning followed by heavy tables groaning with food for dinner on the grounds—and that followed by singing all afternoon, you normally will sit in a square and sing to each other, much the way in which madrigals are best (and traditionally) sung. It creates a blend of sounds you can't otherwise get. Also, if you are ever able to attend a Sing, be prepared: these are not performances; so do not think of yourself as a member of an audience at a concert; you will probably end up in the square, choosing the voice you sing—tenor, bass, "tribble" (treble), or counter, and likely you will also end up leading a lesson, because these are terribly democratic groups. There isn't a choir director conducting all the pieces. Each singer there is likely to lead at least one lesson, standing in the middle of the group, sounding the note that will start the singing much the same way someone who is tuning his dulcimer tunes it to "a good note." With one hand holding the hymnal, which the older folks don't really need, and the other beating through the air to line out the tempo, the lesson begins.

The music can sound really strange and wild, partly because it's a little different from what we're used to musically. Generally, we sing a main melodic line—the tune, if you will. Then the other parts function to support that tune by harmonizing with it or to it. But much shaped note music isn't that way. If you were to sing the bass or the "tribble" or the tenor or the counter lines alone, they would make sense without any of the other parts—usually, and more or less. So it can be like four "tunes" being played at the same time, more or less. They complement each other, but none is especially subservient to the others. The term *polyphony* might help describe what's going on, but even that's a relatively vague and possibly inaccurate term. In any event, to my ear it is a very modern sound—wild and passionate.

When Dillman and I attended such a Sing 42 years ago, at the Second Creek Free Will Baptist Church out from Loretto, Tennessee (which is nearly in Alabama), and south of Frankewing, which is south of Nashville by about ninety miles, one of the older gentlemen there told the story of how he learned shape-note singing. When he was a little boy his mother would trace the shapes of the notes in the ashes on their hearth. He grew up knowing the words to the lessons, because he heard them every Sunday—at the least. But even though there had been singing schools around for many, many years, he had learned the Fa Sol La's at the fireplace. That's about as close to *folk* music as you're ever going to get.

On Breaking One's Pencil

On our drive back to Nashville that afternoon, our throats were raspy and our voices spent, but our hearts were full, and our spirits glowed with a radiance from that day that has never left us.

And just a couple of final points: shape-note singing is always communal—there are **no** solos; it doesn't require—much less even concern itself with—trained voices; there are no swells or *diminuendos*, no *ritardandos*, no *con amores* indicated, though often the key in which the piece was written is noted, and occasionally a suggestion such as "Slow," or "Brisk," is offered. What you do is you belt it out. Every time, you belt it out just like it was the last time you'd ever be allowed to sing that lesson. That's because you aren't performing; you're praising God, or at the least, you're raising up a holy sound in song.

Now my work for this service is done, but the work of our church continues. So as the ushers accept your offerings, which make that work possible, our Shape-note singers will offer up the lesson "Northfield," number 155 in my 1960 edition of *The Sacred Harp*.

"THEN TAKE IT SERIOUSLY"

A Shibboleth Made Real

FRANCES WEST WAS LIKELY ABOUT 10 years or so older than I was, though possibly not that much. She was generally a soft-spoken woman, but when Frances looked at you she clearly spoke with the voice of one who did not suffer fools gladly. She spoke with the intensity of one who is really listening to you, not just with her ears and not just with the learned patience professional listeners like psychiatrists and psychologists need to develop in order to retain and guard their own balances, sanities, and selves.

Frances was a Unitarian Universalist minister who died some years ago, now, but in a metaphorical sort of way, she extended my life, salvaging something of me I didn't even know needed salvaging.

Frances lived over around Atlanta where she served one or more churches, and on several occasions she made her way over to Clemson, South Carolina, where my family and I lived at the time, to do a weekend service and workshop for our small, ministerless congregation.

On one of her visits, I was alone with her for a few minutes upstairs in the house of the couple who were giving her home hospitality for the weekend. We chatted about one thing and another for a short time (I was an officer of some sort in our Fellowship), then she looked at me and asked about my background—how I had come to UUism, and so on. I started in on my joblessness at the time, the other changes in our lives since I had left teaching, and so on—what you can call the usual thing. Then I heard myself going through the whole litany of my experiences with death: my parents, my ten-year old nephew killed by a shotgun fired by another ten-year old down the street, my older brother's death from cancer, being the one to tell a friend her husband had committed suicide…

I was surprised to hear myself going on about all that. But Frances had asked me within the context of what she had observed me doing earlier in our meeting house—talking to people, being "with them," as some might phrase it. What *I* saw of me at the time was simply the chatter of a guy who was active in the Fellowship, someone who had held various offices as needed. What *she* saw was a layman ministering to congregants. That's certainly not how *I* would have put it, but Frances could see into things.

After I had repeated my litany of family deaths, she questioned me more closely about my father's death.

"Well," I said. "I was just fifteen, and he was about five weeks shy of his fifty-second birthday when he got sand-bagged by a massive heart attack. He was dead in five minutes. My older brother and I were off at a military prep school."

"That's young," she said, her voice very quiet.

Then she asked about my mother again.

"She was fifty-eight," I answered. "Nearly. She died about *six* weeks before her fifty-eighth birthday. But that was breast cancer, and all of us had been dealing with her on that for a couple of years. I was twenty-four just three months earlier."

Then she asked how old I was now.

"Oh," I answered, trying to get as close to the year as I could without getting too fussy about precision. "Going on fifty. My next birthday, actually." That would have been 1981.

"Are you concerned about that?" she asked.

Her question took me by surprise. I hadn't ever really thought about it. I was healthy, but clearly aware of death—my paternal grandparents had died within five minutes of each other four months before I was born, for example, and by the time my own children were born, my parents, of course, were dead. All of that had created huge voids in my life.

I admitted that I guessed I was thinking about it, or, more accurately, that it was certainly a major influence in my life.

It was then I realized—not how many times I actually and consciously had thought about all that, or had thought about it in terms of how old I was—there simply had come to be, over many years, a tacit acceptance of the probability that I would never see sixty. After all, my father hadn't, my mother hadn't, my older brother hadn't, my father's brother hadn't—why should I?

"So it's *with* you," Frances murmured.

"Yes," I answered. "Yes, I guess it is. Obviously. Well, yes. Sure it is. Some way or another. Every day, actually," I ended lamely.

What happened next was the magic.

"Then take it seriously," she said.

That turned out to be the end of our conversation. A voice called up the stairwell to her. She had to get ready to eat supper with her hosts. I had to get back home. We parted with the truncated, more or less pro-forma embraces people use with others who are respected, admired, family of a sort.

But even before I left that room, I felt…

Even then I felt the cliché coming on, and if there's anything I try to steer clear of in my writing, it's those wretched clichés. But I couldn't help it then, and I don't apologize for it now, but I felt literally that a "Great Weight had been lifted from me." A truly great burden. I felt physically lighter.

Then take it seriously, she had said.

I did. I took it very seriously, and I have felt blessed these many years now, still marveling at Frances West's salvage job on me, a gift that freed me for an extended life: one that broke the cycle of not knowing paternal grandparents, of not seeing our own children growing into adults, of not knowing the grandchildren who have been unable to know their own grandparents.

How glad I was that I could thank her for that blessing face to face at a GA some years afterward and before she herself died.

CREEDS AND COVENANTS

JOHN C. MORGAN IN HIS book *The Devotional Heart* quotes George de Benneville (1703-1793) "the first preacher of Universalism in America," as saying, "God judges men by their deeds and not their creeds. The language of eternal love is expressed in actions. These speak more than words…"

On page 40, Morgan lists seven points that were central to Pietistic Universalism (the subject of his book), and the first point is, "Creeds and formalisms are secondary to a living, tolerant faith."

We tend to "covenant," he points out, rather than write creeds, a covenant being "the central organizing principle of Unitarianism," (Morgan citing UU historian Conrad Wright.)

On page 88, Morgan lists five "fundamental spiritual themes of Pietism," and the first—again—is, "The Pietists were more concerned with experiencing the Christian faith, with life, than with correct doctrine."

What this covenanting approach involved—and still involves—was and is a portion of a search for community. "Every child of God," he quotes James Luther Adams, the late UU ethicist, "has the guidance of conscience, for the Holy Spirit is available to every child of God. But this conscience and the living presence of the Holy Spirit is found in the mutuality of community."

As I see all this, what's meant is that a creed runs counter to the idea of "the guidance of conscience" because it can be seen as assuming a minor distrust of individual conscience. So the **community** is held together by its members' freely accepted (and democratically derived) covenant with each other, a covenant which can be revisited as often as any given community feels or senses the need. Some of this, at least, goes clear back to Phillip Jacob Spener, a Lutheran reformist of the 18th Century, one of whose suggested reforms was that, as Morgan puts it, "Church members need to move from correct doctrine to right living," and the covenant helped define the "right living" of the various church members.

There's also the influence of the idea of the spiritual priesthood of all believers, an anti-ministerial position, mainly, (as I see it) which developed from the corruption of the church with a priesthood exercising dictatorial powers to serve its own ends rather than the welfare of the parishioners. Still, this represents a fairly accurate picture of the creed business as Morgan presents it.

THANK YOU

I have three things I would like to say to you today.
This is the first thing:

WHEN DILLMAN AND I WERE here for Dillman's Candidating Week in May 1992, Jean Hansen's father, Bob Bezoier, died.

The death of one's father, I can tell you from my own many experiences with family deaths, is traumatic to say the least. Even if that death comes in old age after years of work and accomplishment and all the rest, comes after a long period of decline and thus is not unexpected, it still leaves a huge hole in one's life, a loss that most of us never really get over no matter how well we may be able to handle getting past it.

So here we were in the middle of a highly important, highly compressed time period: Two Sundays with two services sandwiching a week of meetings with the Board, meetings with virtually every committee in the church, meetings with any individuals who wanted to see her privately. It was a week important for the future of the individual who was on display, important for the church that was anxious about change, anxious about the new person they had to pass judgment on, anxious about wanting to look good themselves, anxious about their own future based on such a short-term decision…

On Tuesday of that week, Jean's father died. And what did Jean do? She almost immediately asked Dillman to do the memorial service that Saturday.

Think about that for just a moment.

I was awed, stunned, and profoundly moved by Jean's trust in Dillman.

That was my personal response, but that response to Jean personally carried over into a similar trust for the entire Search Committee and the entire institution of this congregation.

Three years ago at about this time, there just happened to be a concatenation of events in our lives having to do with years: we had been here for ten years, I was soon to turn 70, Dillman was going to turn 65, our son was going to turn 40. It was just one of those odd things.

So I made that modest and trivial announcement during Joys and Concerns. But at that time I also made another statement in which I said that I considered this church—First Unitarian Universalist Church, Rochester—to be my Mother Church. My Home Church.

Even at the time, I felt I wasn't making myself clear about the importance of that to me. Likely it just wasn't the right venue, and likely I simply hadn't thought it through enough. So I'll try again. One's Home Church is the place where one starts putting himself together as a spiritual person; starts coming into an understanding of himself in that way, however that understanding may eventually manifest itself. The Home Church is where those kinds of roots start to grow. With me, that was in our Clemson, South Carolina, Fellowship. But it was here in Rochester that those roots were able to spread, deepen, and mature in a more deliberate kind of way.

However, as *Ecclesiastes* tells us "To everything there is a season...[including] A time to get, and a time to lose." That can also be read as, "A time to arrive, and a time to leave."

It is now our time to leave.

...

This is the second thing:

In a piece about Nashville, Tennessee—a place also hugely important in my life—I wrote about finding myself sitting in a McDonald's one time on some journey of mine from wherever to wherever else, years after Dillman and I had moved from Nashville. I was surrounded by enough of my visual past to leave no doubt as to where in the world I really was, and at one point I discovered myself feeling so oddly, so achingly bereft that I knew I must once again have been home, because at the same time, I also felt such an overwhelming serenity at being there, I wondered why I had ever left.

Now, I doubt that whoever may have blessed me in my life (and there have been a few) has ever been blessed by God in turn because of it, as he promised Abraham; certainly I doubt that whoever may have cursed me in my life (and there have been those too) has ever been cursed by God because of it; I don't see any evidence that I've been made into a great nation; and certainly as a writer—or anything else, for that matter—my name has not been made great, as God also promised Abraham his name would be.

Still, in what we used to call the Blue Hymnal, the one we used most immediately before our present one, there is a hymn called "When Abraham Went Out of Ur," a hymn with haunting music written by Michael Wise in 1684, joined to a 1935 poem by Nancy Byrd Turner. It starts off with the generalization that men leave home going "They know not why or whither," being both "called and compelled." The second verse speaks of these men from the ages stopping as they leave to take another last, troubled look at home, "Their birthright bartered for a nameless dream," as Turner puts it. Finally, she zeroes in on Abraham as he leaves Ur, and tells us how, as he turned in the cold dawn to catch his last glimpse of the place which had nurtured him, the place he had loved, the place which he knew always would be his home, he "bowed himself to his loved earth, and rent/ His garments, cried he could not go…and went."

...

And this is the final thing:

In her book *Fifty Days of Solitude*, Doris Grumbach—a novelist, former literary editor of the *New Republic*, columnist for the *New York Times Book Review*, and author of several other meditative books—wrote of discovering in *The Book of Common Prayer* a prayer that she committed to memory and recited every night while on a personal retreat much like the one Dillman took several years ago up at Clare's Well.

> Oh Lord, support me all the day long,
> until the shadows lengthen,
> and the evening comes,
> and the busy world is hushed,
> and the fever of life is over,
> and my work is done.

> Then in thy mercy
> grant me a safe lodging
> and a holy rest,
> and peace at the last.

I love that prayer, but I also love Grumbach's gloss on the lines. "Those were wonderful phrases," she wrote. "Shadows lengthen, the fever of life over, the world hushed, work done, holy rest. Unlike so many other prayers," she went on, "not hallowed names, kingdoms to come, and grace, righteousness, the power and glory forever and ever, the resurrection and the life; but instead safe lodging and peace at the last."

So the wish or hope or maybe even prayer I leave for you is this: may each of you always be blessed with "a safe lodging, and a holy rest, and peace at the last."

Thank you.

FORGOTTEN OR IGNORED?

*The Universalist Pietists
And Yet Another UU Tension*

A MAJOR PURPOSE OF JOHN Morgan's book *The Devotional Heart: Pietism and the Renewal of American Unitarian Universalism* is to make us aware not only of the Universalists, as many have been doing for some time now, but also to bring two other matters to our attention: First, to remind us that though Boston may have become the center of Unitarianism, it did so at the expense of our knowledge about the importance of Philadelphia in our history; Second, to teach us about the Pietist roots within the Universalist faith.

For the most part these days, *piety* usually has a negative connotation that suggests a holier-than-thou attitude, a certain sanctified upturning of the nose at others who haven't managed, well, to come as far as we have. But to Morgan Pietism is simply "a religion of the heart," and is a religious sensibility that exists in many denominations.

So for the most part I'm presenting you with an elaborated book review (though a fairly brief one), of *The Devotional Heart,* and virtually everything I tell you about the Pietist movement is straight out of that book, much of it actually quoted, though I don't try to keep up with all the quotation marks. I have done no original research of my own. But while stressing Morgan's reading of Universalist Pietism, I'll be trying to make a couple of connections of my own during my time today: One is to Harvey Cox's book *Many Mansions,* and the other is to the UUA Commission on Appraisal's publication *Interdependence: Renewing Congregational Polity.*

The subtitles of all three let you see where at least some of this is going. Morgan's is *the Renewal of American Unitarian Universalism*; the Commission on Appraisal's is, *Renewing Congregational Polity*; and Cox's is *A Christian's Encounter with Other Faiths*.

Much of Morgan's intent in his book is also summed up in a quotation from Helmut Lehmann, who says, "The tension between the head and heart, reason and experience, the individual and community needs to be kept alive…"

Morgan traces Universalist Pietism from Phillip Jacob Spener, a Seventeenth Century Lutheran pastor whose book *Pious Desire* (*Pia Desideria*) in 1675 apparently was an identifiable catalyst for much Pietist thought, even though Pietist attitudes and beliefs can be traced back at least another hundred years.

Central to Spener's vision as a reformer was his sense that people simply weren't living Christian lives, and he came down especially hard on the clergy who judge, he said, not according "to who is good and who is evil, but according to their doctrinal agreement or disagreement with us."

Spener offered several ideas for reform including, first, every household's having a Bible so it could be read; second, hearing ALL the scriptures in church, not just some, and they to be read without comment or interpretation; third, believing that small group meetings ought to be re-introduced so the Bible could be read aloud and people could ask questions about matters they didn't understand.

In all this, Spener was an early believer in the priesthood of all believers; and of particular interest to me were his beliefs that we needed to move from "correct doctrine" to "right living"; and finally, that we should be as loving and "right living" toward those outside our faith as well as to those within it.

The Pietistic reforms went in two primary directions: Churchly and Separatist or Radical. From the latter, you can correctly assume that the Pietist movement was a reform movement. Both the Churchly and the Separatists felt that Christians had strayed grievously far from the intent of the New Testament, but the Churchly segment wanted to reform the existing church by pushing on with the business Luther had begun, while the Radicals, obviously enough, wanted to pull out of the church to form new communities which were closer to the way they read the scriptures as intending us to live.

Much of the core of this Pietist debate and thought came through or out of the University of Halle in Germany, which sent many of the earliest missionaries to America where they settled in Pennsylvania, especially around Philadelphia.

Morgan's picture of Pennsylvania during the 18th century shows considerably more heterogeneity than Boston, with English immigrants followed by Dutch, followed by Scots-Irish all between 1680 and the Revolutionary War.

Morgan then recounts a tale about Ben Franklin's asking a Pietist why his group had never published their confession of faith, to which the gentleman replied, "We are not sure that we have arrived at the end of this progression … and we fear that if we should once print our confession of faith, we should feel ourselves as if bound and confined to it, and perhaps be unwilling to receive further improvement…"

Then Morgan talks at length about George de Benneville, an 18th Century Englishman who came to America in 1741, a man of great spiritual influence in his community, but one who never started a church or organized a denomination because he believed in the unity of religious faith and did not want to fragment his beloved Christianity. Professionally, he was a doctor and later an apothecary. A telling statement from him is the following:

> The spirit of love will be intensified to Godly proportions when reciprocal love exists between the entire human race and each of the individual members. That love must be based on mutual respect for the differences in color, language, and worship, even as we appreciate and accept with gratitude the differences that tend to unite the male and female of all species. We do not find those differences to be obstacles to love.

Eventually this voice became stilled, that is what informed that voice became stilled. Morgan suggests about three reasons the Pietists lost what influence they had—all of which, to me, seem to be the normal attrition of time: times change, situations change, other imperatives take over.
- First, the Unitarians, though largely theistic, lashed themselves to the mast of Enlightenment Reason rather than to the "faith of the heart."
- Next, both Unitarians and Universalists became headquartered in Boston, so the Philadelphia folks simply got lost in the shuffle.

- Finally, Hosea Ballou got "Unitarianized," to use Morgan's word, when he began to stress the here and now rather than concerns for an afterlife.

The result, then, was the new trinity of pluralism, humanism, and secularism. From the Philadelphia Convention of 1790 through the Winchester Profession of 1803, and the Chicago Declaration of 1897, the Universalists were in the process of turning away from Pietism toward plurality so that the 1935 "Avowal of Faith" was no longer a doctrinal statement, and the 1959 "Principles of a Free Faith" was no longer even a covenant, covenants originally having been central to Universalist churches.

And when Morgan speaks of spirituality, he is not sliding by on the buzzword it has become in some circles. I read him as being much closer to Gordon McKeeman's religious life that *does* make demands and *does* exact disciplines, much closer to Harvey Cox's statement in his book *Many Mansions* that "Jesus was not a model of vacuous tolerance," but a person who was "terribly concerned about the practical outcome of people's spiritual commitments," and to the Commission on Appraisal's statement, "Being part of a religious community is a personal commitment that reflects a theological vision."

What Morgan wants is for us to know ourselves. "Ironically," he says, "we often turn everywhere else but our own heritage for guidance—do the East, to psychological remedies, to creation spirituality, to feminist theology—all of which are important, but without reference to our history incomplete. Within our tradition," he continues, "two forms of spirituality are uniquely part of our collective identity. One is Transcendentalism, the other is Pietism. Before leaving for India or therapy," he concludes at that point, "we might consult our own religion for guidance."

PREVIOUSLY PUBLISHED ESSAYS

THE GIFT OF LANGUAGE

*The following was originally delivered at the SAMLA
(South Atlantic Modern Language Association)*
ADVANCED WRITING SECTION
Atlanta, Georgia, 1985

IN E. M. FORSTER'S SHORT story "Other Kingdom," Mr. Inskip, in response to the question, "What good has Latin done us?" thinks, *the arguments for the study of Latin are perfectly sound, but they are difficult to remember.* Alas, much the same can be said of the study of what generally is known as creative writing. The arguments for its inclusion in a university curriculum are perfectly sound, but for reasons that to some of us border on the truly strange, they seem to need repeating—a lot.

Two images come to my mind. The first is of Eudora Welty after Andrew Lytle had been going on and on as usual about Southern Writing: the Southern Renascence—or is it the Southern Renaissance?—the Importance of Place, the Sense of the Past—the Golden Apples, in any event—and all the rest. The image is of Miss Eudora looking up with that disarmingly sweet smile of innocent confusion she was capable of right before she zapped your argument into oblivion—not by disproving it, necessarily, but by suggesting that even if true, it's irrelevant. She said, "I guess I just go along with Henry James: 'There's good writing and there's bad writing.'"

The second image is of Peter Taylor on a panel with some bright scholarly types in-cluding Cleanth Brooks, I believe it was. The scholarly types had all had their say about things, so it was Peter's turn. He had been sitting there with his head propped up on one hand. Finally he said something like,

"I don't know why I'm here, because I haven't the slightest idea what these people are talking about."

In each case, the writers were the ones who seemed at a loss about things, at least to the extent that they felt compelled to root the ideas and arguments going around into more concrete and less abstract terms that might be better understood by both themselves and those listening in the audience.

Certainly Miss Welty was as aware of golden apples, myth, and herself as a Southern writer as Andrew Lytle was—also a novelist, after all. And Peter Taylor, I'm sure, was as able to keep up with the theoretical arguments going around the panel he was on as anyone else there.

Then I remember this. I was once eating lunch when a friend, of sorts, remarked—I assume for my edification—"The only difference between a course in creative writing and a course in freshman composition is that in creative writing they don't take off for punctuation."

I smiled faintly, partially writing off the remark as something typical of a sociologist or educationist, whichever he was. After all, neither breed has a reputation resting on the clarity of their prose styles. Too, a little paranoia in the right places never did a writer anything but good.

What did rankle, though, was the implication that the study of English—composition, rhetoric, literature—involved little more than being able to recall the four rules of the comma, say, or (echoing the Medieval logicians and their much talked about arguments concerning angels and pin heads) how long a short introductory phrase could be to be considered short. Involved, that is, no more than being able to summon up more or less arbitrary rules of grammar or punctuation that could be plugged in at the proper time.

What bothered me in a more serious way, though, was that the little scene seemed to typify an attitude on the part of uninformed people about what teachers try to do in a course in creative writing, and what goes on in the classroom itself.

My sharp shooting acquaintance in a more serious mood might have asked, "But you can't *really* teach a person how to write, can you?" And by *write* he would have meant create art in the form of fiction, poetry, or drama.

Next we get bashed with a list of authors from Chaucer to Faulkner, and we're asked what good a course in creative writing would have done *them!* And that always seems to be that.

Conveniently enough, such people invariably mouthed the names of some of the world's literary geniuses: Chaucer, Shakespeare, Mann, Proust, Hemingway, Faulkner. But they miss a most salient point—the teaching and learning that went on in its wondrously informal ways. Faulkner had Phil Stone to talk to, to give him lists of books to read so he could educate himself (Ole Miss didn't seem to be of much account in that regard); God knows how many times Shakespeare had to cross and uncross his legs from the cups of coffee he drank while he listened to Ben Jonson educate an entire generation of writers and thinkers; John Crowe Ransom spent untold hours talking to Allen Tate, Donald Davidson, Robert Penn Warren, and others of the Fugitive Group in Nashville during the 1920s; and what about the relationship between Thomas Wolfe and Maxwell Perkins—not completely ignoring, either, that Wolfe had been a member of a creative writing class at the University of North Carolina and a play writing class at Harvard; and Hemingway? Just think of Paris in the 1920s: Pound, Stein, Joyce—an incredible group of people Hemingway knew and talked to; and Wordsworth, surely, didn't spend *all* his time with Coleridge counseling him about the evils of dope.

Even though writing is a damned solitary business, the writer must occasionally come up for air and converse with his own breed. He may pop up to New York from Durham, or wobble out to Iowa City from Memphis, or simply write letters to other writers, run up bodacious phone bills so he can hear his writer friends' voices, or just send off copies of his work to friends whose critical acumen he has come to trust.

Writers have always found other writers, shown their stuff, looked at the other fellow's stuff, and sat around to talk shop. In short, writers have learned how to write by talking to other writers who are grappling with all the old problems, by talking to or reading other writers who have learned how to cope with a great many of the problems of creating a piece of fiction. And most of all, naturally, writers learn to write by writing a very great deal.

Too, they read. But when writers read, they often read from a pretty technical point of view, one not necessarily relevant to the literary biographer, bibliographer, historiographer, textual critic, or general reader. While a writer may think, along with many another reader, that Emma Bovary is one hell of a woman, something in him is watching how Flaubert kept Homais hooked into the theme of Emma's failure; or a writer may feel, along with many a captive student, that the problems of Lambert Strether are pretty alien to anything he's concerned with, but he can still learn volumes from James about how to handle point of view. Or how Richard Yates dealt with chaptering in *Revolutionary Road*. Or how James Gould Cozzens redeemed old time in *By Love Possessed*.

But to return to the charge that one can't really teach another person how to write, one honest response is, *True*. But it is true in this way: There is no way a teacher can teach a student to have something to say; there is no way a teacher can teach a student how to perceive the world; there is no way a teacher can teach a student to have imagination. But having said this of teachers of creative writing, what has been said that can't also be said about teachers of sculpture, quantum theory, organic chemistry, esthetics, semiotics, or forest management?

The most any teacher can do is offer up a few lighted candles. After that, it is the stu-dents who must stare at the light until they can't see anything at all, or start walking where the light shows a way, or blow the light out altogether. I suppose it is even the prerogative of stu-dents, as they turn to curse, embrace, or be indifferent to the darkness, to stare at the candle in the teacher's hand and remark that his light isn't really very bright.

Earlier, though, I raised two questions: "What is a writing course for?" and, "What goes on in the class?"

To answer the second question first: In a creative writing class students write. Then they re-write. When they have done everything they know to do, they hand in pieces as finished as possible, given obvious restraints of time. As for the rest, I always used the basic workshop technique: Student stuff is copied and handed out to the entire class—preferably earlier in the week—so everyone can read what will be discussed and can have a copy of the thing in front of them. The entire class then joins in the discussion of their peers' work. Writers generally know when something is good, but in their early learner stages they seldom know why something is bad, much less what to do to help make it better.

After the class discussion, the student is faced with the necessary horror of revision: of re-writing again, and again, and again. It's such a simple and effective technique—when the students are willing to play the game—it does make one wonder why teachers of freshman composition didn't pick up on it years and years earlier. Things in one place *are* relevant to things in another if we will but connect. Forster makes more sense every year.

More specifically, I found that a series of exercises can work wonders. First of all, my most complete experience involved teaching both poetry and fiction. (I'm talking about undergraduates, by the way, and usually lower division ones at that. Graduate courses are another matter altogether.) I divided the semester into halves and spent one half on each, poetry first. I am not a poet, so what I went through might give the rigors to those who are, but I found that it worked—again, though, you have to have students willing to play.

The exercises were to write a sonnet, brace stanzas, a haiku, a poem of 10 lines in iambic tetrameter about a tree without using the words *green* or *trunk* or whatever. I required a love poem, also without using certain specified words. I required a series of heroic couplets; I refused to let students even mention the words *free verse*—God, for three or four solid weeks they hated me.

Then a funny thing happened: They started writing very interesting poems. Because they had been required to hand in a specific assignment every Friday (in addition to doing a considerable amount of reading and class discussion in preparation for each assignment), they were doing a lot of writing. They finally understood something about how to control lines, rhythms, images, meters. And once they found they could play with those things, make them work—once those technical details started to become building blocks rather than stumbling blocks—the students quit hating me. And the interesting thing is that I saw it happening to the entire class at just about the same time.

The required midterm project was a group of poems that included certain verse forms, a certain number of poems that had been revised (with the originals), and so on. Then we went to fiction where things were harder, but proceeded in essentially the same way.

To people who see "Creative Writing" (I admit when I see the term, I always hear it spoken with a breathy, awed catch in the throat) as inspiration rather than perspiration (wasn't it Hawthorne who said you write by applying the seat of your pants to the seat of a chair?) this exercise routine must sound truly awful. But I strongly recommend it for a number of reasons. First, it makes the students write. Too many times previously students had come to me pulling long faces, looking terribly distraught, muttering gloomy imprecations about Writer's Block. I was sympathetic—I know what writer's block is, too—but oddly unimpressed. With the fiction, it occurred to me that to tell a 19- or 20-year old to go write a finished story in two weeks is to tell most young people to do something they simply cannot do. Some would call it programming them for failure. I couldn't do it, I don't think. I'm a terribly slow writer. Flannery O'Connor said she didn't see how anyone could write more than one good story a year. Even so august an eminence as the late Walter Clyde Curry had suggested that he mistrusted the quality of work by scholars who wrote more than one article a year. So the pointed, specific, limited exercise kept them writing something they could deal with and finish.

Second, such exercises do lead to completed stories. The kinds of things I required were exercises in description, narration, dialogue, point of view: Write a portion of a scene in standard third person, then re-write it into first person. What happens? Lots more than a simple change of pronouns, usually—at least more than that happens if the student really gets into the spirit of the thing.

Third, teachers do have to give grades eventually, after all, and a series of exercises constitutes a relatively extensive basis for a final grade. My students would end up with something like 12-14 weekly assignments plus two major projects—the poetry and a finished story. It seemed to give them a sense of security to know that an entire semester's grade wasn't going to hang on my perception of one story or half a dozen short poems. It also lets the teacher have the flexibility of recognizing students who, though they may not have been good writers, nonetheless did the work every week and stuck with the stuff through the course.

Fourth, it is a course for which the students are getting academic credit, and I always felt it wasn't a totally bad idea for them to understand that drawn there in the dust were some very real lines they would have to toe.

But the question remains, "What is such a course for?" After all, if students are going to write, they are going to write whether there is such a course or not. Again, *True*.

That question, though, can also be raised for practically every course offered in the humanities. If students are interested in reading—which is to say in learning—they will read and learn on their own. They will find the libraries, they will find the books, and they will find someone who knows more than they do about the things they are interested in. But doesn't that lead us right back to Faulkner and Stone? Ransom and Tate? Hemingway and Joyce? Socrates and Plato? And doesn't that lead us right back to institutions of higher learning: reading on a formal, highly organized basis?

Let me approach the question negatively for a bit. To me, the purpose of a creative writing course is *not* to turn out a bunch of published, publishing, prize-and-award-winning alumni-authors from whom prestige accrues to the university that "produced" them. No-no. A creative writing course is intended basically to help students become better readers. By *better* readers, I do not mean people who read faster and with improved vocabularies. I mean better readers of literature because they have *done* something. They have participated in the joys and horrors of personally engaging themselves in the act of trying to wrestle raw material into the form of fiction or poetry or drama. They are better readers of literature, because having participated in the craft—no matter how awkwardly—they also have participated in the end results of that craft. Even though students may never be able competently to transform an experience from life or imagination into an accomplished work of art, they nevertheless are better prepared to understand the accomplishments of those who *have* managed such transformations.

It is much the same as the fellow who went out for high school football only to face the embarrassment of trotting back to the locker room game after game with a clean uniform on. Such a boy can better appreciate the task of the starters on his team, for though he may never have shared in the Friday night heroics, the dents on his shins and the swollen knuckles from countless scrimmages are no less real for all that, and they have earned him his knowledge of the game.

What won't turn me loose about why so many students leave their final required course in English with whoops of glee and scalding tears of joy coursing down smile-creased faces that never again will have to stare in misery at another grim-visaged teacher of English is that such students have never been required to engage themselves in an act that allows—or even, by Glory, *requires*—them to synthesize within a literary form what they see and do every day of their lives. In simple fact, they haven't ever been given the chance to connect their lives with the life inherent in literature.

I am not naive enough to think that a captive who wrote a story or a poem would go forthwith to pound on the door of the English department and demand entrance into the very *sanctum sanctorum* itself, but I have a hunch that such a person would, somehow, be a better builder of bridges or spinner of threads.

I have asserted that writing fiction or poetry or drama helps make a person a better reader of literature. The value of that certainly might be questioned, and today, from what I can tell, even English departments question it. There are many people who honestly doubt the value of anything that doesn't have pretty specific application, like the mechanical transfer of energy: Turn the crank here, and you get an immediate, predictable result there. It's the old argument concerning the efficacy of a humanistic education as opposed to pragmatic, goal-oriented training.

I assert that literature at its finest intent always is involved with human beings. The students in a typical creative writing class don't intend to be writers. They are going to earn their bread and spend their lives selling insurance, managing mills, raising children, running farms, surveying forests, and being good people generally. Then what does the writing of a story, poem, or play have to do with that?

A very great deal, actually. In composing a story, a writer must discriminate, select, choose, pick, make decisions, organize, think—then have the courage to re-think and start all over again. And because literature at its best, I would say, deals always with people, the writer, in order to come up with something approximating "Truth," must spend a considerable amount of time actively engaged with other people, then spend even more time twiddling his thumbs or scratching in an effort to understand what all the involvements amounted to.

The result is that writers deal with reality of a very high order. They always deal with people, not charts, graphs, or statistical abstracts: "Mere data," as Lord Peter Wimsey might have put it, "ain't enough." Important as facts may be, we can be too tempted to let them take the place of the people they are supposed to represent. Relying solely on quantification to make life's most important decisions is the Old Adam, easy to do because we don't have to expose ourselves to the agony of being responsible for our personal and subjective choices.

Such quantification finally dehumanizes us, makes us like the generals, politicians, and technicians during the Viet Nam war who talked about "overkill," or having to destroy a hamlet to "save" it. But the writer must talk about the death of a human being, must make that human being as full of flesh and blood and bile and the sweet juices of life as words allow. The writer must make that death meaningful. Not celebrated, necessarily, but meaningful.

In the same way, statistics concerning the number of misspellings or whatever in Twain's *Huck Finn* finally tell us nothing we need to know about the relationships between Huck and Jim, Huck and Tom, Huck and the River, Huck and his father, Huck and the rest of society, or any of the other human, ethical, and moral relationships that literature purports to be principally concerned with. They also tell us little about the vaunted "creative process." The writing of fiction, though, helps keep us from mistaking the footnote for the text.

Certainly a course in creative writing in a college or university is not necessary for a person to be a writer. Just as surely, it may not even be good for one to be in college or university at all. There are many writers who simply could not exist in the often stuffy atmosphere of a campus. Even though there are writers who have thrived on the academic fare, a student who is seriously interested in writing must understand that an academic community might be the very worst place in the world, and that a course in creative writing might be totally useless or even harmful.

But for those who can exist with the academic regimen, for those who honestly want to stretch their imaginations and find out what they've got, a creative writing class isn't a bad place to spend some time. And for writers who want criticism so they can learn rather than back scratching or head patting to further inflate already obese egos, for people who want to learn something not only about the craft of writing but about themselves as well, and for people who want to expand their vision rather than merely have their existing views confirmed, it can even be a pretty good place.

...

Trying to pull together some forty or fifty-odd years as a writer of one thing and another can be an exercise in patience as well as frustration. But it strikes me that there are considerations having less to do with making a living as a writer or getting good grades as a student writer or getting well published. There is always something else, always an intangible that actually makes what we do worth the effort.

It came to me finally, that as a writer of fiction—even of history—I am charged in some vital way with two things: first, trying to give voice to and for people who haven't a voice. I am not talking about the politically powerless, but about those who have great feelings, who in their own ways are passionate people even though they can't articulate things as well as I or even most of you can.

We *can* speak for others, oddly. And because we can—no matter how hard it is, no matter how battered emotionally we may get doing it or how we may batter ourselves physically with drink or wild women or whatever other jolly, romantic image some may fashion for us, still we *can* articulate feelings and ideas; we *can* say what is on our minds and in our hearts. That doesn't mean that we alone have those feelings and ideas and impulses. We have no corner on that market even if—as I *do* believe—those who don't have our power of speech are stunted because they don't.

Thus, there is all the more reason to understand, with some considerable humility, that we speak for them, that we write, as Dylan Thomas had it, "Not for the proud man apart/ From the raging moon . . ./ But for the lovers, their arms/ Round the griefs of the ages,/ Who pay no praise or wages/ Nor heed [our] craft or art." We are subbing for them in some terribly important way. *That* is why the teaching of writing—whether freshman composition or novels or poetry or whatever—is so important.

Secondly, like Frost's idea of poetry, education—including the highly charged language and dimensions of creative writing—is the essential stuff that sticks with you after you have forgotten the details. Great singers (usually tenors, no doubt) have said that when there is nothing further they can say about their voices that can't be attributed to study, technique, or style, when everything but the greatness has been explained, all they can say is, "It's a gift of God."

I feel that way about writing, about being a writer, about having been a teacher of writing. Naturally, students considered me daft, if basically harmless. But what we teach we never quite know. I've long suspected it was mostly attitudes toward our work and the work we ask students to do in our classes. Certainly teaching is a form of sharing as well as a form of drawing out, or, in my opinion, should be.

Whatever it is, through language we are trying to help students define their own lives by helping them find their own images and voices. We are trying to help them grow into their voices so that through language they can deepen the ideas, feelings, emotions, and meanings thrumming always close under their surfaces no matter, I suspect, how cool or job-oriented they may consider themselves. I have seen them. They fall in love the way young people—hell, the way all people, middle-aged or old—have always fallen in love. When the beloved says *Yes, Oh Yes Yes,* they are ecstatic. But when it's *No, I'm sorry, No,* they are wounded sometimes forever—again, as we all are.

Those of us who use creative writing use it because we are writers, obviously, looking to our own turf. But more than that, the intensity of fiction, poetry, and drama requires, in its writing, the exercise of that part of ourselves that is most closely guarded, most immediate, most likely to make us vulnerable, if exposed, both to ourselves and to everyone else. It is, therefore, most precious. We are proud of that vulnerability, because it opens us up to the world of humanity. And *that*, finally, is what the world of literature is all about: connecting us, letting us see and understand how or where we share a common humanity—even with those we might most despise, including ourselves.

"Love the words," Dylan Thomas admonished the cast as he was rehearsing them for his play *Under Milk Wood.* "*Love* the words."

It *is* a gift, this union of idea, event, and imagination, this business of story and play, of metaphor, of expanding life through imitation and exaggeration. It is a gift like no other.

WHAT HAVE WE TAUGHT THEM?

*A speech delivered to the South Carolina
Association of Women Deans and Counselors
Converse College, October 18, 1969.*

WHEN I ACCEPTED THE INVITATION to come here today, I did not realize that I was to prepare a thirty-minute speech. However, I finally decided that this might be as good a soapbox as any to stand on in order to get a number of things off my chest—things that might or might not have anything to do with the topic at hand. Further, as a teacher, my *modus operandi* is not the lecture so much as the dialogue. So I am out of my element on several counts: I should be talking *with* you, not *at* you; I should be reading you one of my short stories rather than a speech; and, I think, my wife is the one who really should be standing here, because she is the one who has done yeoman service toward establishing and organizing Clemson's Child Care Center. Too, I am not a woman or a dean or a counselor.

I'm not certain that I can handle the topic that presumably has brought us together today. It sounds like a topic that can mean, as Humpty Dumpty said to Alice about words, "anything you want them to mean." But as I read the title *Personal Development—Positive Involvement*, I read it to mean, "What can adults do to help kids become creators rather than destroyers?" Fielding that question is a tough chance in anybody's league. It is a question that concerned people have been fielding or fumbling or putting off or ignoring for as far back as you want to go.

Youth, to make an obvious sort of observation, has always been going to the dogs. Young people today are often long on hair and high on drugs;

On Breaking One's Pencil

they talk back (sass, we used to call it); they drink too much too soon; they know too much too soon; they have too much money too soon; they have access to too much too soon and to too many too soon—too much and too many of just about everything you want to name. They are "cool," a word that is becoming more and more pejorative to my mind every day; they are cynical; they are brash, arrogant, disre-spectful, disorderly, obscene vulgarians proud, for the most part, of their incredible ignorance about the world, about people, about life, about everything, in short, which happens not to cause some *immediate* sensation from the skin out. And with it all, they are frighteningly naive, incredibly altruistic, and capable of profound strengths, those very strengths becoming so often their most miserable weaknesses.

But having said all those ugly things about young people today, I must hastily add that I'm all for them. In a real sense the hippies, yippies, bippies, and God only knows what all else are the new waves of barbarians crashing at the gates of our culture with their battering rams of energy and restlessness and idealism. They see the future rushing in on us; they are here, and we are not prepared for either them or it.

Now in my little image I mentioned a battering ram and a gate. Two questions ought to surface in our minds: 1) Have we constructed a solid, well-crafted gate that will protect us from the howls of execration from without? and, 2) Why are those people—flesh of our flesh, fruit of our loins—our own sons and daughters—why are they out there attempting to smash down our gate to enter our structure and rend us, send us flying into oblivion? How did that stupid phrase, "Don't trust anyone over thirty" ever come into existence? Have we, like Dr. Frankenstein, created a monster? Apparently so. Why?

RANDOM ITEM # 1: The average college sophomore will be nineteen this year. That means he was born in 1950, the year the Korean War started. His life has absorbed—I won't say he has assimilated, won't say he grew up *knowing* these things, because as I have already suggested, he is incredibly ignorant—but his life has absorbed the Korean War, some three Middle East wars, the American presence in Lebanon, the American presence in the Dominican Republic, the American war in Vietnam; they have absorbed revolt in East Germany, Poland, Hungary (what might be termed a notable American absence), and Czechoslovakia. They have lived through the murders of John F. Kennedy, Martin Luther King, Jr., and Robert Kennedy.

They have absorbed Watts, Detroit, Selma, Montgomery, Chicago; war, riot, murder, threat of war (brinkmanship), more riots, billyclub morality, pocketbook morality. And through it all they have remained largely ignorant, yet beautifully sensitive to the hypocrisy of a nation that sings about the land of the free while vast numbers of Negroes, Indians, and Chicanos are in economic bondage; while senators and congressmen are in emotional bondage to the Pentagon; while thirteen years of their lives the White House was in intellectual bondage to men with little real imagination—one a Johnny-come-lately Republican, the other a Johnny-come-professionally Democrat. (I play no political favorites.) They certainly have had to be aware of crooked generals who sell confiscated guns for personal profit; of drug industries which habitually make use of 400% markups; of doctors who pad their Medicare bills (even after fighting passage of such programs tooth and well-pared toenail); of price fixing among men engaged in really big business who blatt all the livelong day about free enterprise; of all the poisoning of our air, our water, and our soil by rugged individualists who feel indebted far more to corporate profits than to public health and safety; of toy manufacturers who are concerned more with profit and loss than with the well-being of innocents who play with their products; of…of…of…Where does it all end?

They have sensed the immorality of behaving *so that* they can reap the financial rewards doled out to all good little boys and girls. They have come to understand that education is not a matter of sitting down and shutting up, as they have been taught. They have come to understand that education involves risks, including the risk of being wrong. They are learning that "Yes'm" and "No'm" may be good manners (and I am all for good manners), but that *Yes'm* and *No'm,* alone constitute a pretty second-rate education.

RANDOM ITEM # 2: This summer in Florida I read an account of a young man who was going to be denied his place at graduation exercises because his hair was too long—at least as far as his principal was concerned. The ironic thing was that the boy was the class valedictorian. There he was: the most academically "successful" student in that year's graduating class being denied the public presentation of his diploma. According to the standards *we* established, he was the best; according to the system *we* devised and promulgated, he was the finest; according to our own institutional grade-baiting standards of fulfillment, he was tops. But his hair was too long to suit his principal. The article did not say whether his principal also had been valedic-torian at his own high school graduation exercises.

Another extraordinarily similar case happened at the same time—also in Florida. Another valedictorian had his valedictory censored by his principal. The student refused to read a gutted speech, so he was not allowed to stand graduation with his classmates. What peculiar logic have we here? A young man—by virtue of grades—is considered the smartest student graduating, but he is not considered smart enough to write his own valedictory at his own commencement. "We are rewarding you," the system seems to be saying to him, "with a public display for doing better than anyone else what we have told you to do: Make good grades. But," the system says as it wags its finger under his nose, "we draw the line at grades. Learn facts, young man," it seems to say, echoing Dickens' Mr. Gradgrind, "but don't draw conclusions; make excellent grades, young man, but don't permit them accurately to reflect an enquiring mind, or an inquisitive nature."

What else can the system be saying to such a lad other than that he should be acquisitive rather than inquisitive?

RANDOM ITEM # 3: A CBS television poll was taken among high school students in Webster Groves, Missouri. (This was in 1966.) The students were non-rebellious sixteen-year olds. Webster Groves, for those of you who don't know of the place, is an extremely affluent and high class sort of suburb of St. Louis. Seventy-eight percent of those polled had bank accounts of their own. Ninety-nine percent knew who Dick Van Dyke was, but only twenty percent knew who Ho Chi Minh was. Yet more than half of those 688 sixteen-year olds considered it likely that they would live to see a nuclear war.

RANDOM ITEM # 4: A parable by your speaker. At age four, a child asked his father where babies came from. "The cabbage patch," he was told. At age eight, the child asked his mother where babies came from. "From God," she answered. At age twelve the child asked them both where babies came from. They mumbled something about birds and bees. At age sixteen he asked them both again. "We will arrange for you to talk to our kindly family physician," they answered in tight-throated unison. At age eighteen he wanted to know why he shouldn't sleep (or, if you prefer the euphemism, live with) his girlfriend at college. "Because it is immoral!" they answered him indignantly. "Bull!" he responded, his face finally showing anger, for being of the TV generation he had known where babies came from all along.

Young people have always wanted to do right, I think. Observe children who have always been surrounded with good toys: blocks, crayons, paper, pencils, more paper, clay, more paper, empty boxes, more blocks. Observe them building. Observe them drawing. Observe them constructing. Observe them tearing down or ripping up when their little projects haven't turned out right. Observe them creating, out of their own fantastical minds and imaginations, things we'd probably never think of. Observe the moments of infinite patience of which they are capable, as well as the violence of frustration, the pure destructiveness of which they are also capable when interrupted for such mundane chores as washing hands or setting the table for dinner. Which *is* more important: eating at precisely six o'clock, or finishing an amazingly intricate tower or bridge or picture or statue? Which is more important?

Which is more important, having a beautifully manicured front lawn that is a thing of beauty and a joy forever—for the public to see—while the back yard is thick with weeds and rocks, or having a yard which is sort of the way *you* want it to be, even though it may look pretty bare compared to the pride-tended lawns of everyone else on the block? What does a child learn when he sees his father (and hears him, too) attack the hateful yard: the bushes, flowers, grass, shrubs, and all simply so his public face will look like his neighbors'? (No need to worry about daddy's minor cursing. The lad will learn those words soon enough no matter what.) But in all likelihood he will learn something about deceit. What is more important?

What do young people want? Paul Goodman, author of *Growing Up Absurd*, would probably say that what they need is models, adult models who are worth emulating. Paul Goodman does say they don't have them. They grow up in a *Brave New World* atmosphere in which it is important to keep up appearances, this being called pride. They learn to be con-sumers of constantly "new" or "improved" or both "new *and* improved" products which exist primarily so manufacturers will be able to make profits. They learn that buildings are built to last about forty years, so there need be no pride of workmanship there. They learn that trades unions are extremely reluctant, many of them, to hire and train blacks, so there's no real chance to observe brotherhood there. They learn that you don't really much fix cars anymore; you simply yank parts and replace them, so there's no pride in craftsmanship

On Breaking One's Pencil

there, either—especially when the auto repair industry is one of the biggest rackets in the country. They learn that doctors and mill executives, who are forty pounds overweight, who have one very late model large car, one moderately aged "family" car, and one compact for whomever might need it, who live in $60,000 houses, who send their children off to private prep schools and then to expensive colleges—these, they learn, are the ones who slam their pudgy fists hardest onto the solid mahogany or cherry table and desk tops at the private country clubs and complain about being taxed to death. At the same time they complain, the moderately poor man of moderate intelligence pays more for food, more for clothing, and more for housing (on a square foot basis) than does his wealthy counterpart. And of the extremely poor, they can summon up no more than, "He's a lazy bum or he'd go out and get rich."

The young often learn that honesty is taken for impoliteness, that political expedience is palmed off as profound policy, that pointing out flaws or asking questions about "embarrassing" matters is taken for ingratitude, and that using their minds to think their way through problems—personal and public, moral and social, political and ethical and aesthetic—and then ACTING, of all things, ACTING on their beliefs or conclusions is radical. They find that they can, more or less, think what they want, but to determine to *do* something real and so to put their theories to the test is not really desirable because they will be boat rockers or Young Turks or malcontents. People won't invite them to their fraternity or sorority rushes or introduce them to their sisters or brothers. In short, they will very quickly be branded Kooks and perhaps more, if not worse, because they will be different. Oh unholy word: Different.

So he rebels. As often as not he over-reacts, as we old people might say. Why do you wear such funny looking clothes, Bruce? we might ask. So you will notice me, maybe? he replies, and once you notice me you might—just might—talk to me. But why do you wear your hair all—*Ugh!*—long like that? Because I know you can't stand it, he very likely wants to say back. Well, why don't you just behave like all the other *nice* kids at school? Because I don't *want* to be like all the other kids. Well, why not? Because I am trying to make some sense of nonsense, and I can't; because I am trying to make compatible the difference between our absurdly high ideals (as Walter Lippman pointed out more than thirty years ago) and our actual practices, and I can't; because I feel myself slipping away into a *Brave New World* sameness and vacuity of life, and *I am scared*.

In 1967 Robert Kennedy said:

> And let us be clear at the outset that we will find neither national purpose nor personal satisfaction in mere continuation of technical progress, in an endless amassing of worldly goods. We cannot measure national spirit by the Dow-Jones average or national achievement by the gross national product. For the gross national product includes our pollution and advertising for cigarettes, and our ambulances to clear our highways of carnage. It counts special locks for our doors and jails for people who break them. The gross national product includes the destruction of the redwoods, and the death of Lake Erie. It grows with the production of napalm and missiles and nuclear warheads, and it even includes research on the improved dissemination of bubonic plague. The gross national product swells with equipment for the police to put down riots in our cities; and though it is not diminished by the damage those riots do, still it goes up as slums are rebuilt on their ashes. It includes Whitman's rifle and Speck's knife, and the broadcasting of programs which glorify violence to sell goods to our children.

Doubtless it will strike all of you that what I have said has been pretty much a matter of accenting and underscoring the negative. We are a positive nation; we are a positive people; we are an optimistic people; we are a people who have always believed in dreams, then rolled up our sleeves to accomplish them. We are a people who have always believed—as the motto of the Sea-bees during World War II had it—that the impossible only takes a little longer. And yet we have crises in education, crises in the cities, crises in transportation, crises in the pollution of our environment, crises in government, crises in the form of credibility gaps—a euphemism meaning we think our leaders have a habit of telling us blatant lies; we have crises in race relations.

On Breaking One's Pencil

None of these crises started yesterday; they did not begin last week; they were not nonexistent twenty, eighty, a hundred years ago. Every problem we have today has been growing for years and years. Why a problem with Youth, then? Why are we meeting here today wondering what can be done so that our young people will become creators rather than destroyers? Possibly one answer is that it has fallen to many of today's young people to question what has been done, what has been said, what has been preached and politicked to them for most of their lives. We know that eventually *they* will learn there is no perfection in an imperfect world, that many things must suffer the hard, slow crunch of time before they can be made right, that America, really, is no more corrupt than any other nation that has ever been.

But in the meantime *we* must learn to see the world as they see it. This is not the same thing as agreeing with their conclusions about it; this is not the same thing as always accepting their point of view; this is not the same thing as turning everything over to them. But it is a matter of understanding *why* they feel as they do—and, of course, before that, even, under-standing *what* it is they feel and what it is they want. You cannot possibly counsel people if you do not understand them, and you cannot possibly understand people if you are not willing to accept them as they are, if you are constantly looking or talking down to them.

I think most young people want to communicate with us, want to talk with us. I also think that most young people are terribly inarticulate—both verbally and emotionally. That's why *we* have to be less childish, less immature, less likely to react from the skin out as they do. That is why in our own lives we must be the models, the examples available to them, the patterns of life that they find worth following. It is by no means necessary for us to coddle them. It is necessary only that we talk straight. We do not have to be permissive in the pejorative use of that much-maligned word. It is necessary only that we be adults, that we show them worthwhile things to spend their time doing. Watching TV after all finally doesn't do very much but deaden the senses.

I am a fiction writer, and in fiction there is an awfully good rule of thumb—a sort of necessary standard, as it were—and it is: *Don't tell us, show us.* In fiction this means to drama-tize a scene, fill it out with people on stage doing things, talking to each other, letting characters reveal themselves by their actions and their words rather than sitting back and telling the reader what he is supposed to think about a certain situation or what kind of person a character is. In life, too, the admonition *Show us, don't tell us* is equally as valid.

My wife helped establish a day care center in Clemson. Such a center is a school with a structured program of learning for preschoolers—especially those from economically deprived families. The purpose is to expose the children to as much as possible before they get into the rigidly structured grade school system. Its purpose is to get them prepared to see, prepared to hear, prepared to listen; prepared to learn to read, to write, to cipher. It is a project which—if it ends up being well run and well supported—will be worth more to Clemson a hundred years from now than all the Tigeramas, all the Homecoming ballyhoo, all the high school marching bands, all the Sophomore Class Queen elections, all the clap-trap associated with varsity athletics that have ruined our schools for so many years. It will be worth more than all the Phi Beta Kappa keys, all the Deans Lists, all the folderol connected with honors and awards that we now have, because if it is successful, it will instill in those children a sense of wanting to learn for the sake of wanting to learn, a situation in which the rewards are personal and private. Make no mistake, most young people have a built-in nonsense detector (to "clean up" a statement by Ernest Hemingway). And our responsibility as adults is to sharpen their awareness of this in them-selves, to talk straight, to be honest, and to demonstrate in our own actions what a pleasure it is to be over thirty. But if *we* don't talk straight, if *we* can't be honest, if *we* can't accept the responsibilities of being adults, then who will counsel us?

THE GAME

Originally published in *Aethlon:*
the Journal of Sport Literature
XI:1 Fall 1993

RED PARKER, A MAN NEITHER more nor less inarticulate than most professional football coaches, once said, "I want people with heart for the future." He said that in 1975 after Clemson University's Fighting Tigers football team had been squashed 43-7 by a Florida State University team in a game presumed, before kick-off, to be even. It followed exactly one week after the sixth loss of the season, a no-contest rout by the North Carolina State University Wolfpack. At the time, anyone interested in Clemson University football could have said nothing much more optimistic than, "The remainder of the season would appear to be without spectacular promise."

People with heart for the future.

A beautiful phrase, that. One having currency for all sorts of people in all sorts of times.

Mr. Parker said, in those days so sad for him, that he would awake at three in the morning trying to think of what he could do to turn the team around. He said he couldn't sleep. He said he accepted full blame for it all.

I know something about waking at three in the morning, too. I've been there myself. But I don't really mean to talk about the ups and downs of long-gone Clemson football. In Sherwood Anderson's story "The Egg," the narrator said, "If I tell my story right, it will not center on the egg." Well, in the sometimes tiered, multi-dimensional way fiction can have, it both did and it didn't.

Which is to say, simply, that *"Sports!"* can be made useful as a metaphor through which so many of our disparate images, signals, impulses, and quirky snippets of memory and vision and desire and loss can be patted or urged or whipped, if need be, into a perception which, like love—or hate or fear or worry or emptiness or silence—expands and grows the more it is conditioned.

For instance, a football play exists first as mere gossamer in the mind. It can be made "real" only with twenty-two players on a field. But once seen, it can be reconverted to an idea—only changed, as though a magician had flailed his magic wand over the top hat of a blank playbook from which will come…what? Rabbits? A deck of cards? A trick? A mere trick?

Eventually I will tell you why Clemson's 1975 football season was such a disaster and why its soccer team was so beautiful, but be forewarned: Real events, real things are often supra-events and things. They may appear to be perfectly innocent with mundane surfaces and all. But do not be deceived. They tell us things we need to know. Sometimes they merely inform, but they can also warn. They can also foretell. Whatever they do, we must let them connect with us. We ignore them at our peril.

...

Let me announce that I consider myself a Fan of the Game. Just about any game. I like sports. I like athletics, although I disapprove of their professional nature in our institutions that are supposed to exist primarily for education—book learning of a high and noble order. But that's what is known as ambivalence. I make this announcement in these terms—a Fan of the Game—to keep myself separate from local fans who tend to remind me of Mr. Nixon in that they don't see other teams as opponents to be out-played or out-witted, or even out-muscled or out-hearted, all within the formal structure of *The Game*. Rather, they always see enemies to be destroyed. The sad result is that the Local Fan—wherever he may live and whomever he may root for—seldom prepared to behold *The Game* on those rare occasions when it emerges in whatever glory it may have. They always look to the score and hope for at least a little of someone else's blood. But it is *The Game* I keep wanting to see. That's why I went to the soccer matches when I lived in Clemson.

On Breaking One's Pencil

Soccer, for those who have never bothered or had reason to find out, is a game requiring tremendously sophisticated physical dexterity, skill, and endurance. A kissing cousin both to ice hockey and basketball, it is a game played largely by thugs and brutes as opposed, say, to rugby, a game of frightening physical contact—without pads—played largely by gentlemen—at least, so a British Gentleman once told me. Be that as it may, Camus probably was right about Man being at his most natural at the theater or at the arena.

So I used to go to the soccer matches and cheer.

I cheered for Ralston Moore racing across the field. He ran with his knees high. Yet, amazingly, his long legs seemed to pivot only from the hips. He used to run like a champion trotter pulling away from the common herd as it heads into the stretch.

I cheered Clyde Watson whose legs, contrariwise, seemed to flap about in all directions as he dribbled the ball, passed it with such grace and cunning it was done almost before you knew what he was about.

I cheered Papoola and Ogunsuyi and Ogbueze and Ogunjobi as they chipped and passed and fed—*Bip! Bap! Bam!*—toward the opponent's goal: chipped and passed and fed like it was no more than a warm-up weave on a basketball court.

I cheered Clyde Browne who always managed to be where he had to be when he had to be.

I cheered Denis Carrington—or any other goalie—who bolted from the comparative safety of the goal, bolted toward the fringes of the penalty area to dive at a ball, to break up a play be-fore it got properly set up, to break it up before having to save a goal. Carrington would dive head first toward those cleated feet striking at the ball—or whatever was near to foot. He dove hoping that if he could get his hands around the ball, control it, pull it into his gut, protect it…hoped, I say, that if he could do that, then his opponents would honor the game enough yet once more by not kicking him senseless as he lay curled around the ball, exposed.

I didn't know any of those boys personally. I had never met a one of them, but I came to know them through a certain weight of exposure to them. Partly, they came through to me from the field. But something more was needed than just watching them. Cheering helped some, because it put us on the same side of the fence, so to speak. Yet something beyond that still was needed. Until I did something more, they remained limp, like the hand of the Sistine Adam, before God—his stretching finger charged with the current of life—touched him into motion and a corporeality, a dimension, a potential for good and evil he had previously lacked. I named them.

On, Gordon! Go, Clyde! Come, Damian! Pass it, Benedict! Into Godwin! Back to Denis! Clear it out, Mark!

I called their names aloud, and though they had long since been named, had for long been growing up into those names, been increasing the circles of people for whom those names had become flesh, I now touched those names myself, and in speaking them, created them, made them mine even if in the process I felt a bit like Santa Claus whistling his swift corsairs through the cold, black glory of Christmas Eve.

I named them and gave them the life I needed from them. I created them whole. I invented them over and over, and in the process invented myself. Over and over.

I played them in soccer matches. I was the greatest, including Pele. I beat them. I showed them how good—really and truly *good*—good can be. I demonstrated to their amazement the difference between simply very good (which of course they were) and great (which of course I was). None of which, I have discovered, is totally useless or escapist. I find it helps give me a vocabulary that pushes me to examine my world from yet another point of view, which in turn helps open me up to insights that often hook in in the most curious ways to matters totally unrelated to each other. Or seemingly so.

One of William Faulkner's stylistic techniques, for instance, was to examine a thing negatively. He would say that a hand—or a wheel or a look on someone's face—was *not* like…*not* like…*not* like…nor was it like…, but instead *was* like…whatever his image might be. But in his negative assertions he made the connections nonetheless, and the hand or wheel or look *did* then become like all the things he had said it was not like. That is, he had set up the mirrors and echoes for us, so that we saw and heard more than there was to begin with.

So if the goalie is hoping the rules of the game will be preserved yet one more time, I am hoping that perhaps I will be able to see The Game itself. It doesn't come often. It doesn't always last very long when it does come. I think you have to have read Dante, or been the head football coach of a team that has just lost its seventh game and which ended up with two wins and nine losses in a season that was supposed to have brought a conference championship with it.

I'd be willing to bet that Mr. Parker never in his life intentionally picked up a copy of Dante's *Comedy*. But I have a hunch he probably would understand something of the Inferno section. I also have a hunch that Mr. Parker was able to go to bed the nights after the last three games of the season and sleep the sleep of a freshly nursed baby because he had seen The Game.

He said a strange thing back in those days that must have been so dark for him. He said, "I have never been a loser before." Well, that strikes *me* as strange. Never a loser? Never? He clearly did not mean that he had never lost a game, but that he had never been a "loser." But had he never in his life loved a woman who did not love him back? Had he never taken a course in college, regretting later that the lure of the field, the siren call of Success in the Arena had made him squash an intense curiosity about something, squash it into a stain instead of loosing it to grow and mature? Had he never withheld himself from a friend, from a brother who sorely needed him? Had he never—like Lord Jim—jumped ship in some crucial way?

I suppose it's all a matter of how you look at it, of your attitude toward Loserism. Still, it strikes me that the book of *Job* must have been gibberish to Mr. Parker. If he had never read Dante, surely he had read *Job*. But what—before the 1975 football ball season—could he possibly have made of that poor man? Maybe he simply identified more closely with Joseph, a born winner if ever there was one. Even then, though, before that 1975 season what could he have understood about the need to be envied, hated, "whupped up on," and sold into slavery before the mere dream could prove itself, could be transformed into vision, and thus be fulfilled?

Consider Muhammad Ali: the draft, being stripped of his title, the years of idleness, the broken marriage. And then the comeback. Picasso is supposed to have said, "Whenever I paint a pretty scene, I rub it out and it comes back beautiful."

The Game is witnessed by very few people, mainly because it emerges so seldom. But it has done so twice in more or less recent times. Once was in the 1974 heavyweight fight between Ali and George Foreman in Zaire. The other was the 1975 World Series in Boston and Cincinnati. More recently—perhaps—was the '91 Series between the Braves and the Twins.

The Fight: I didn't see it. I saw *Sports Illustrated* photos of it. If the *SI* account was true, it was one of the Great Fights. Each combatant gave to the other. I intend no jest here: I am not talking about giving swollen eyes, or cut mouths, or split lips. Rather, each gave to the other the cruel chance to submerge himself in his brutal craft. Each did what he did best, and each did so well what he did best that *Boxing* emerged.

The sports writers and announcers kept saying the same kinds of things about the '75 Series: "Baseball was the winner"; "This year's Series has been great for baseball." True, at least from the two games I saw on TV and the others I listened to on the radio. I wondered at the time, though, if the sportswriters (who have to write to deadlines) and the sportscasters (who feel compelled to shatter golden silence with mind-deadening cliches) knew what they were saying. Perhaps they did, perhaps they did.

Ask yourselves, for instance: Who was the best player in that Series? Who was the best on either team? Tiant? Rose? Fiske? Morgan? Who? Good Lord, it would be easier just to read the rosters. The reason is that each did best what each could best do. Because that was the case, because all were stars, none starred. They were all up. They were all baseballers. So even while keeping personal identities, they nevertheless were absorbed into the team, and the teams, in turn, were caught, were overwhelmed, were sucked under the surface to become little more than ciphers in *The Game*.

I keep thinking about Rodin's *Burghers of Calais*, a sculpture with six individual figures, each burdened with his own thoughts—and second thoughts?—about why he had accepted the sackcloth and ashes, the ropes of enslavement to give himself over to Edward III. It was to save Calais, of course, to end Edward's siege of their city.

But *The Burghers* is a sculpture that bears some looking at. One of the figures is a beautiful young man who seems to be stunned at what they have decided to do; the old man leans his weight well forward on his front foot as though understanding it is he who must lead the others to their doom, the irony of which is that the doom is imposed from outside as well as being self-elected; another holds the massive key to the city, his face grim; yet another covers his head with his hands—in shame? fear? guilt? They all have their separate stories, yet they all share the same fate.

Sculpturally, they are separate, with space between. Yet they share the same base. Two seem to face the same direction; two appear to be in line, one behind the other; the remaining two face each other, and in facing each other they are naturally facing in opposite directions. But circle the thing, and rather than six figures, there is a single group—which from one particular angle could have been done as a bas relief. The young Burgher then looks like a boy shooing his flock of geese down a lane.

The combinations of these six figures come and go. The relationships among the six shift and alter. But if you keep circling, if you climb up with them like the little boy scouts playing there do—and as Rodin *wanted* them to do—to become a part of them, if you feel their hands, touch their feet, grip the heavy folds of their robes, then bit by bit the entire thing merges into a coherent whole. It won't always do that for you. But if you give yourself to it enough, it can. It *can* become a whole.

Virgil led Dante into Hell, down and down and down until they came to the very bottom. There, Satan was clutched forever in the Lake of Ice, fanning his great wings that kept Cocytus frozen and thus himself locked in place.

Then Dante and Virgil did a strange thing. It confused Dante so much he felt compelled to explain it. With his arms, Dante grasped Virgil firmly around the neck much like a child would hold to its father. Then Virgil, waiting for the proper moment, waiting until Satan's great wings were spread wide, rushed at him, gripped his hairy coat, and began to let himself down the hide of the Great Worm of Evil. Then at the exact spot where the thigh and haunch were joined, Virgil, as John Ciardi has Dante relate, "turned his head to where his feet had been/ and began to grip the hair as if he were climbing;/ so that I thought we moved toward Hell again."

But of course they had simply passed the center of the earth. You can only go down half way, then you're coming up. They had gone beyond Hell.

"Hold fast," Virgil called out to Dante as they clung to the Gross Fiend and Image of all Evil. "There is no way but by such stairs to rise above such evil."

And so the game emerged in Zaire, in Boston and Cincinnati. And in Clemson, South Carolina. That's why the '75 Series was so phenomenal: The players were moved beyond being players, the teams beyond being teams. As we move around Rodin's *Burghers*, we see that the relationships among the figures constantly shift. Yet we are aware that it is we who are moving, not the figures. They remain stationary. It is our eyes that have played tricks on us. It is as if we could see scrape of dust after scrape of dust, chip after chip, hunk after hunk going back to that great wedge of flawed marble in which Michelangelo first saw his *David*. But having seen *David*, we now can also see that slab of marble with the dangerous cantle out of the side, that gross chunk missing that forced Michelangelo to turn his David...*so!* But *David* is more than the solution to the technical problem of how to make a single statue out of a huge piece of badly cracked marble. And even if it is *we* whose point of view alters while we circle the *Burghers*, it alters because *they*, mysteriously enough, also alter.

The teams disappeared and baseball emerged. The Game. An idea of what it can be, made real.

It comes that way in literature and art, too, and perhaps as rarely, though whether that is due to its seldom happening or to our ability to perceive it but rarely, I don't know. I do know that Hemingway surely understood Dante, understood something about going beyond Hell. I'm sure Faulkner did. And Tolstoy. And that R.V. Cassill does. And John Fowles. And that Will Shakespeare most likely awoke often enough at three in the morning, a skinful of visions sweating through his dreams, as D.H. Lawrence once phrased it, frightened because he saw what had to happen to Lear before that old man could die wise instead of silly; angry because he knew Glouscester had to go blind before he could see; both amazed and lump-throated before his own images and visions, spooked by where his own inventiveness and imagination might lead him.

In his novel *Field of Vision*, Wright Morris keeps talking about his characters having to "touch bottom" before they can surface to their rebirth, and surely *I've Been Down So Long It Looks Like Up to Me* is one of the great titles of our time.

And while the football boys kept getting beat up on, there in Clemson in 1975, the soccer boys kept on winning, with only one lapse against Howard University during the regular season and the same snake-bit lapse against them that ended their post-season play, those momentary shudders of failure that proved them human after all. They kept on winning, and I think I know why.

I promised earlier I would tell you why 1975 was such a dismal season for Mr. Parker. It may not matter to him now, because he hasn't been associated with Clemson for years, but I will still tell you.

On Breaking One's Pencil

I used to be a walker. During the football team's pre-season drills, workouts, and scrimmages I was taking my usual four-mile hike from the post office, through town, around the campus, and back home. Walking up Williamson Road I saw something that made me so mad I jabbered to myself the remainder of my walk. I talk to myself a great deal anyway, but what I saw gave focus to my discourse. What I saw was not prophecy so much, but later events proved it to be an omen at the least. As far as I know I was the only person in Clemson who—in seeing it—understood its meaning. I saw the football boys *driving* from their dormitory to the practice field.

Driving, for God's sake. All that gasoline, I thought, as car after car with one or two or occasionally as many as three footballers in it drove past me to practice. All that gas, I thought. Surely, I thought, they could have climbed aboard one of the school's buses and been driven over—if they *had* to ride, that is. Surely that would have saved a good bit of gas. Such waste. Such selfish, dull-witted, weak-willed, unconscionable waste at a time when people like state governors were asking for cuts in expenditures, at a time when the reserves of natural resources were falling lower and lower. Driving to practice!

Then I thought: By God! Not if *I* was head coach, they wouldn't. Not if *I* was head coach. By God if *I* was head coach I'd have the captains or co-captains of the team line up all those specially dieted protein burners in a column of fours and by God jog them over to the field. I know it's a long way (who planned that?). I know it's durned hot in August. But (as I gasped and sputtered and fumed in my new-found righteous indignation) by God any player of mine who got anywhere near a car during the season would be made to wish Henry Ford had never been invented. (Further indignant gasps and red-eared fuming.)

That was before the first game that year.

Some eight weeks later I was walking the same route. It was the Saturday morning of the Florida State game. I was near Williamson Road once more when I heard what sounded like some very early-morning roistering, something like drunken singing. Well, I thought, why not, given the circumstances of the season.

As I got nearly to Williamson Road, I was looking at the state patrolmen who had already set up their road blocks to smooth the way for those Clemson fans who had paid their at *least* one hundred dollars, or however much it was at the time, for Gold Card Stickers. Those stickers allow the bearers to park cars closer to the stadium than the hoi-polloi so they wouldn't have to walk as far in order to watch games played by the boys who drive to practice.

The drunken singing behind me kept getting closer, and as it did, it seemed slightly less riotous and at least a little bit more organized. And as it got closer yet, it started sounding not only far less drunken, but very familiar. The singing—it was more music than not by that time—was being lined out with the steady *slap*-a-*slap*-a-*slap* of many feet striking the pavement, basically in step with each other.

I turned, and what to my wondering eyes should appear but the soccer boys decked out in their warmups, jogging in a column down Highway 93 past the tennis courts, past the old Newman House, and singing that wonderful hymn or song or whatever sound of praise it may be, *Amen*; singing it to the tempo of their trotting, Gordon Alphonso taking the role of leader by calling out the verses, answered then by the other members of the squad—a perfect example of caller-response typical of so much folk hymn singing and, I suppose, related to antiphonal singing, and to our own responsive readings in church.

Even with the more or less formal nature of the column, the boys' song struck a joshing note, a sense of their having a good time both because of as well as in spite of the fact they were exercising. And they stayed mostly in a pretty tight formation—except toward the rear where some of the boys looked a bit worried about the early morning traffic coming up from behind. I turned on up Williamson Road and they trotted on down the highway.

I know where they were going. They had to wait until 1985 to make it, but I think they were on their way to St. Louis where the NCAA soccer finals were to be played that year. I wouldn't have put it past that bunch to have *A-menned* themselves up there at the trot all the way.

I don't know if any of those boys had gone beyond Hell or not. Some, considering where they were from, and guessing possible if not actual backgrounds, had: That year eight were from Nigeria and eight from Guyana. But watching them play, I saw them come so close so often to releasing The Game from under their feet. And once, even, they did it. That was in 1973 when they beat the University of South Florida in four overtimes. What a game! They were conditioned and patient. They played a very smart game, and they helped South Florida play a game beyond themselves, helped them push beyond their own limits of competence.

I had an old history teacher in High school who once told us about the time in college when he set a track record in the 440. He came in second, he told us. Then how...? we naturally asked. I ran so fast, he answered perfectly straight-faced, that anybody who beat me would have to break a record to do it.

And Mr. Parker? The Game surely emerged for him that year, even if negatively. We often let ourselves get fixed into thinking that we really ought to read only literature that is "great" or which has been safely tagged "Masterpiece." Don't worry. I am not a member of one of those anything-is-as-good-as-anything-else schools that suggests that Mickey Spillane was as good as William Shakespeare or whatever, and that there should be no distinctions drawn between the prose styles of a Malcolm Lowry and a Pauline Reage, for instance.

But there is much to say for reading stories that fall, to put it kindly, somewhere well below the line our imaginations and experience have drawn to separate good from bad. I often used to read a couple of stories—absolutely awful stories—to my creative writing classes. They were published in a book entitled *Selected Short Stories of 1939*. They were published by the Pyramid Press in New York City.

Almost to a story they were dreadful. But they were *so* shallow, *so* lacking in sophistication of telling and development that they served as highly useful examples not only of what can go wrong in the writing of a story, but also, oddly, of what elements there are that make up a story. So often the very finest examples of the fictive craft don't lend themselves to our generalizations about what is supposed to be going on in the rarefied world of the Academic Ideal. Too, the finest examples of what we want people to understand—especially people who are still very new at reading well or writing out in the form of poetry or fiction their own responses to the world as they have experienced it—are often so finely wrought, their carpentry so finely joined, that we can't find the seams, can't tell where the solid wood stops and the veneer begins. Thus their lessons can remain discouragingly obscure, what students may mean when they talk with such squinch-eyed suspicion about "hidden meanings" in literature.

Teachers ought to be helping students try to understand the difference between "hidden meaning" and *mystery*. But with those terrible stories I read, my students were able to see: characters, actions, transitions, dialogue, and all the other bits and pieces, nuts and bolts, nails and screws that are used to make fiction. Those stories—awful as they may have been—were also all there. They were complete, finished pieces.

Remember, when Virgil put his head where his feet had been, Dante at first thought they were going back to Hell. He did not realize they had already passed through. It is the same way with literature, I think, with virtually any art. One must begin, one must start seeing pattern and form and order someplace, and the easiest place is where it is most obvious.

But at a football game? some might ask. A soccer match?

Well, why not? What's so trivial about a football game that isn't trivial about a hunt in which a bunch of grown men go out into the woods over a period of many years and—largely while drunk—try to kill a hook-toed old bear that never had done them any harm? Or about the ritual slaughter of a bunch of bulls?

In The Game, you have pattern, form, and order. In Art, you have pattern, form, and order. In both, the structures are in greater and lesser degrees. Look at Ben Shahn's stuff. Look at Picasso's. At Leonard Baskin's. Look at Rodin's, at Michelangelo's. Listen to Odetta. Listen to Pavarotti. What do you see? What do you hear? Truly, now: What do *you* see? What do *you* hear?

Look at da Vinci's notebooks, at Michelangelo's sketches, at any artist's sketchpad. There probably will be lots of planes and perspectives, circles and cylinders, lots of "mapping out" of the sheets of paper, a blocking out of forms and shapes that may or may not be recognizable.

Try to find series of paintings by artists. There you can see how ideas are developed—toward greater complexity one time, greater simplicity another. Read the notebooks of writers. Read the many versions or drafts of poems and stories and essays. Look again at the Clemson football season of 1975. One must begin somewhere: a losing season, a lousy story. And after we have laughed at all the incredible omissions in that tale, the strained plotting, the defeated skipping over of those details that would have let the story be believable, the grossly misshapen parts of the thing, why then what?

Go write one yourself. Make it be better. Don't let it be as bad. But whatever you do, do not deceive yourself into thinking that the bad model has no value. Understand it, then use it. But *you* must use it. *You* must let it connect. You must *let* it connect.

I speak only for myself. I never encouraged anyone to go to the soccer matches there in Clemson. I composed dozens of ugly letters to the sports editor of the nearest city's daily paper about the wretched coverage they normally gave the finest athletic team Clemson University ever consistently had, but I never mailed any of them—for possibly perverse, and certainly selfish reasons, in fact.

I actually liked going to the matches some years earlier when there usually were about 250 assorted Arabs and other foreign students, along with me and some more funny folk. But I feared—for good reason as it has since turned out—that because coach Ibrihim's teams stayed so good, there would be plans to build permanent seats made of concrete or something else squatty and immovable, and that they might even get surrounded by a stadium. The seats would be raised too far above the level of the field. Tickets would cost more. The sport would become popular generally. The sports editor of the local daily *would* start paying attention to them, the sport by then having been tamed into respectability by the school's athletic boosters club. That's when I decided I'd quit going and start looking for the lacrosse team. Or get back to Rugby. Wrestling anyone?

In the meantime I stuck to the soccer team whose labors helped stretch me into another way of perceiving Dante. Pete Rose and the late Pete Maravich with their stunning—if simple-headed—devotion to their work helped make something of Auden and Milton seem nearer. And what could be more American than the World Series and *The Great Gatsby*?

In terms of dedication to one's work, in terms of having heart for the future, what is the difference between Muhammad Ali who "went to the well" one more time in his fight with George Foreman, and Count Leo Tolstoy who completely rewrote *War and Peace* some seven times? Ali apparently was just about ready to throw in the towel on one or two occasions toward the end of that fight, and Tolstoy had a baker's dozen of reasons to stop his work, or call it "ready." We must try to make truly ours what they have to teach us. If we can open ourselves to what they are doing, if we can embrace the best of what each is offering, absorb it until it is wholly a part of us, then what I keep calling "The Game" can emerge. We cannot simply "look but to the frontage," as Captain Vere said about War to Billy Budd. We must try like Virgil, like Dante, to push on, to put our heads where our feet have been and get beyond Hell, to get beyond our own limitations.

Do not understand *me* too quickly, either. I am in no way attempting to say that everything everybody does is equally as valuable as everything everybody else does. I think that Moses and Jesus and Schweitzer and Kant and Shakespeare and Mann will long outlive Tiant and Rose and Zaharias and Pele—and affect us all more profoundly than they *ever* will. But if we are to get beyond the Hell of ourselves, we must turn upside down. Mind you, it is a comic position, a distortion and therefore a lie, but recall what Picasso said about lies and art and truth. I think he was right.

...

No doubt I can be accused of making abstract that which is really quite concrete, but let me offer this. I am not trying to justify what interest I have in Sports. I went to the soccer matches because I enjoyed them. I like to yell as much as anybody. And I certainly am not trying to justify the practice of universities and colleges in buying athletes—the new slaves— instead of scholars. (Let our college coaches fill their squads from the luck of the draw the way teachers of freshman composition courses have to do, and then we'll see how "great" those quarter-of-a-million-dollar-a-year coaches really are.)

But I think I am able to step back from both the sport and the athlete because I remember my own involvement in the heave and grunt, the stain and stink of playing.

On my high school football team I played offensive guard and defensive tackle. At 173 pounds I was the second lightest man in the line. Our right end, for example, was six and a half feet tall and weighed 215. Our left end was six feet three and weighed 195. Our starting fullback was six feet and weighed 200. Mind you, this was in 1949. I never played one single game against anybody my own size. The least number of pounds I ever gave away was twelve. Those were the joyous cakewalks: playing nose-on-nose against mere 185 pounders. Usually I had to give away 20-30 pounds, and in at least one case 40 or so. You don't forget those kinds of odds.

In any event, during one bloody Wednesday—our term for the weekly scrimmage—I was part of a post-lead block when a defensive tackle, a clumsy 220-pounder, tripped and fell on my extended leg. The blow knocked my patella its own width off center so that my lower leg was sticking out at an angle not to be confused with reality, a most odd and unpleasant-looking mis-arrangement, take it all in all.

At the same time, I simply Praised Be that the thing was still attached. It was painful enough already without one's teammates standing around looking at it as though they were going to throw up. I wasn't a scholarship boy, so the knee never got fixed, with the result that I have walked funny on it ever since. And that has caused the other knee to go wacky, too. So every time I stand or sit or walk, I remember the kind of reality we usually think of when we talk about *reality*.

I also remember my left shoulder going out on a freaky accident while I was a hard-charging defensive end in an intramural football game two years later in college. Seventeen years after that I nearly drowned because of it. The shoulder popped out on me while I was swimming with my two young children. I managed to make them get out of the water before I did. Ten feet from the edge of the lake the shock put me down. I'd always been able to get the shoulder back in place, but not that time.

I carry a scar there now. It's all fixed—after a fashion. But I remember it. I still can't swim properly anymore because of it. Or play tennis or softball or touch football or jog. I couldn't even pass the soccer ball with my son for more than a few minutes at a time. Shoulders and knees. And I still have dents on my shins and probably scars on my knuckles (if I looked for them hard enough) from getting down in the lineman's old three-point stance on frozen turf on crisp November days. And my spine curves off slightly somewhere from walking on bad knees and flat feet and weak ankles.

I think I'm a physical wreck.

No, I like my theory because it is well grounded in blocks I missed and tackles I even shied away from. So this is not a justification or an apology. Rather, it is an exploration, an attempt to understand what's what and come to grips with it, an attempt to do in life what's always done in Art: to expand awareness, to create or discover an expanded mode of expression, a vocabulary; to take a thing and stand it on its head to see what it climbs up to, to see what it can do next; to push beyond my own limits; to see if there isn't something more to my daily rounds than I think. Remember, Browning has Fra Lippo Lippi say the artist makes us see what we pass a hundred times and never notice.

For five-and-a-half years I have become a teacher again, though I ply the trade only part time. Perhaps that's why I think a paper such as this is supposed to end with some *Wisdom*, a terminal *Word* to wrap everything up neatly, some sort of *Final Statement*.

Unfortunately, I am as mortal as all, as prone to changes of heart and mind, that is, as those freshmen who squirmed on their intellectual tenterhooks before me. Some time ago I was reading John Gardner's biography of Chaucer, and at one point Gardner said, "Medieval thinkers assumed that the way to truth was through metaphor, that is, through a search for the essence of the world's relationships."

When I read that I put the book down in my lap, looked up and I said aloud (remember, I do talk to myself a great deal), "But the way to truth *is* through looking for the world's relation-ships." I gather that makes me medieval. If so, then so, because, echoing E.M. Forster, I *do* say: Try to connect; always keep trying to connect. It is only through the connections that Art can emerge to transcend the limits of any single story or poem or play or piece of sculpture to become a model, an ideal before us, showing us that we can be better than we are, that there is a *Best* to us, and that that Best is greater than the sum of its individual parts.

YOU IN THERE, US OUT HERE

*The following was originally presented at the SAMLA
(South Atlantic Modern Language Association)
HUMANITIES DISCUSSION CIRCLE:
"The Humanities in American Life," Louisville, KY, 1981.*

IN HIS WONDERFUL BOOK *THE Seduction of the Spirit*, Harvey Cox speaks of the need for people to tell their own stories. So these remarks constitute relevant bits and pieces of my own story.

I spent a number of years in school, taught, raised money for Vanderbilt University through its development office, went back to school, got married, wrote constantly throughout all that time, then taught again at Clemson University for five years. I left there for reasons not especially germane to this paper, to accept a one-year appointment in the Program in Writing at the University of Arkansas.

At the end of that appointment I gave myself a sabbatical, and our family packed up for England for a year. The day *before* we could deposit our funds into a bank in the little town where we were to live, President Nixon devalued the dollar. Life for us, in certain ways, has been downhill ever since.

Meanwhile, back in America, things were starting to get rough—that was 1971—and by the time we got back, in the summer of 1972, the job market for teachers, as many of you may recall, was for all practical purposes gone. It wasn't that there were *no* jobs—East Jesus Tech is always hiring instructors for a year at a time—but the number of jobs that most of us here would like to think of as being at the least OK were just not there. In some respects things may be better today than they were in 1972, but I was ten years in my self-granted sabbatical before I was able to teach again—even as a part-time instructor. I cannot honestly say that it has been all bad. Far from it. The Highs have been wonderfully high, but the Lows, conversely, have been real sloughs of despond.

Nonetheless, life goes on, and a Humanist likes to believe that it can go on pretty well if allowed to.

What I ended up doing—in addition to writing my fiction—was to get involved with WEPR, one of the six stations of the South Carolina Public Radio Network, and, prejudiced though I might be, most likely the best production studio in the state system.

My first experience was as a member of a panel of writers who lived in Clemson. That included Barry Hannah, Mark Steadman, and several others. The program was called "Writers' Roundtable," and Bob Hill, himself a poet, was the moderator. We sat around gabbing for a while, then each of us read a short piece from something he had written.

A good while later, I was teaching a six-week class in Creative Writing through the local adult continuing education course, and one of my students—interestingly enough a Clemson University student—was a fellow who had heard that program and took my course because he had been touched by my reading. Like other kinds of teaching, you never know right away the results of what you do.

Still later, I got a grant from the National Endowment for the Arts—one of two in South Carolina that year—and I thought people ought to know that something happened in Clemson other than football games in which "How 'bout them Dawgs" became, "How 'bout *dem* Tigers?" So I suggested to a friend who was a producer at WEPR that she might want to do a program in which she interviewed me and let me read snippets from some of my published stories.

It turned out that I put the whole program together: choosing the scenes I would read, timing them, getting the musical interstices I wanted to match the stuff I was reading, timing *them*, and then actually doing the readings on mike.

Even later, I put together a half-hour program in which I read Dylan Thomas's *A Child's Christmas in Wales* with musical bridges from Benjamin Britten's *A Ceremony of Carols*.

Warming at last to the possibilities of radio—at least of Public Radio—and at the same time realizing that I had found an outlet for this apparently redundant teacher—By God! I had a bigger classroom than anyone I knew—I wrote a series of four, one-hour record shows called *Gifts of Music*. It was a good set and one I found very instructive.

Then late in 1980 I got a bright idea and applied to the South Carolina Committee for the Humanities for a grant to do what was intended to be a pilot program I called *Rediscovering the Humanities: an Overview*.

To do that, I went to Charleston and taped every paper delivered at the Southern Humanities Conference. Based on those papers, plus tapes of other talks already available to me, plus tapes of the luncheon meeting of the Federation of Public Programs in the Humanities which was meeting in Charleston at the same time as the SHC, I wrote a program that was aired over all six of the SCERN stations. Some of you here very possibly heard that program, or certainly could have.

It was very well received both by the Humanists I had asked to submit written critiques of it as well as the general listening public "out there." It gave me great hope for my future chances of earning a living again for a few years (I had some other programs in mind) as well as for the future of the Arts and Humanities in a working relationship with Public Radio.

I then applied to the SCCH for a major grant to do a series of thirteen half-hour programs based on that pilot. Alas, the Great Wheel of Fortune—as all sensible folks in the Middle Ages knew it did and as Americans now are finding out it still does—proceeded in its inexorable way. My application was turned down—even though it was strongly recommended for approval at staff level—for two official reasons. First, the Committee thought the total funding was too large for a single project. Second, they really didn't think that radio was the best way to reach people with the Humanities. Nevertheless, they had previously funded a project, through the history department at Clemson University, that involved twice as much money and twice as many programs—twenty-six, and of a much more limited scope.

Too, the Committee seemed to be unimpressed by the fact that probably 100,000-150,000 people heard my one-hour pilot. They could not accept that Educational radio probably was the cheapest way in the world for the best of the Humanities to reach a great *great* many people. It was, I think—biased though I am—a massive failure of imagination, if not nerve.

Immediately after that personal blow, Clemson University—in a patriotic frenzy of budget cutting—completely cut its annual $100,000 share of funding for the station. That meant WEPR would no longer have a production staff and would no longer be able to produce its thirteen hours of weekly local programming. That local production, which made such extensive use of the faculty and staff of Clemson University—especially its people in the Humanities—was what gave WEPR its very real signature.

Further, though I am talking about Educational Radio, the fact is that in South Carolina, at least, and I would be willing to bet this is the case in many states, there is more "education" going on through the programs aired during adult hours than during the 8:30-3:30 week-day Instructional Radio slots, programs aimed at the students actually in the schools during those hours. In South Carolina, such programs are seldom used by teachers and schools.

...

In that section of *Humanities in American Life* dealing with radio and television, the heavy emphasis was, I suppose understandably, on television. Being a person who does not own a TV set and being a person whose personal interests and work has been much more oriented toward radio, I found that to be an imbalance that ought to be changed. Realistically, it won't be. TV has the built-in mesmerism of motion. On the other hand, radio is starting to become a medium that does more than hold its own with TV, especially with "talk" shows, news programs, features, and certainly top-notch musical programs. I notice that commercial television now wants *more* news programs built into its daily programming. Whether more will equal better or not no one can say until there is a product to judge, but given its past history, I would not put my money on TV.

I can recall those dim, distant days when we did in fact have a television, and I recall how much my wife and I looked forward to something like the NBC White Papers. They were worthless. They were rehashings of the nightly news with a leader that introduced and a trailer that attempted to wrap up some relatively last-minute results. They consistently disappointed. I strongly suspect the reasons had to do with the medium itself.

Radio, because it cannot capture attention with a moving, a visual image, must of necessity probe deeper into substantive matters. When Anwar Sadat was assassinated, I don't know what was on TV, but from John F. Kennedy's assassination I can guess: lots of people in-ing and outing of offices, crawling into or out of autos with big official seals; film clips of people shooting guns, cursing, waving hands, pointing.

The nature of television is similar to the nature of film: The visual image must tell the story or it won't get told. Anyone who has written a film script understands that. Radio, on the other hand, is perfectly suited to conversation, because the attention is on the word, and I submit that finally we have to get back to the word if we are going to deal effectively with ideas. To me, that makes radio a perfect medium for the Humanities which to such a large extent deal with ideas.

It also seems to me that much more imagination has gone into radio lately than into TV. This is a subjective response, no doubt, but it appears that the best of TV—I am talking about "educational" TV—the best seems to have been bought wholesale from the BBC, whereas the best of the radio programming has come out of the work and maunderings of American writers and programmers. I cannot think of a single TV show that can begin to touch "All Things Considered," for example, and "All Things" has so far surpassed *PM*, the British model on which I assume it was based, as to defy further comment.

But I am not trying to start wars. My concern gets to be a little more covert than that. In *The Humanities in American Life*, again the section on radio and television, is this statement: "Media artists need to know more about the subjects and methods of humanistic disciplines; conversely, humanists need to understand how materials for the media are put together."

In an effort to help me bring things together a little more *here*, I would add a third clause to that and say, "and humanists who earn their bread by teaching in the classrooms of America's colleges and universities should become much more sensitive to and aware of the fact that there are a great many of their own kind on the outside of the Academy looking in than there used to be, and they are there for a variety of reasons from getting caught in schools which closed their doors in total financial collapse, to making right personal and professional decisions—but at exactly the wrong time."

My point is that there is a great deal of work "out there" to be done by humanists.

Now when you are in the eleventh year of a sabbatical, you have earned the right—like an octogenarian—to be a bit of a curmudgeon. So when I say there is a great deal of work out there for humanists to do, I am not talking all that generally. I am not talking about journalists, businessmen, engineers, doctors, or whatever plying their professions with their intellectual roots set firmly in the humanities. That's another paper. I *am* talking about people out there who are professional humanists just as you are: students of literature, of languages, of history; readers of philosophy, of religion; practitioners of the various arts.

I started off by saying that I was going to be telling you my own story. The biggest problem with that, of course, is it puts the storyteller in the embarrassing and highly vulnerable position of appearing to be totally self-serving. But the poet Marvin Bell has said that part of growing as a poet is to "become less and less embarrassed by more and more." So I will tell you of an incident—one of several I could mention—that I hope will serve as an example of what I am trying to suggest to you.

I was *not* invited to be a participant at the 1981 Southern Literary Festival. I can think of a baker's dozen reasons for that myself, among them being that not even by stretching my own desire could anyone claim that I have a national—or even much of a local—Literary Reputation of Note. However, in one of the festival's flyers I noticed a kind of general invitation to writers who might wish to appear as panelists of one sort or another.

Because I always enjoy train trips (this Festival was in Mississippi somewhere) and because I always enjoy the prospect of being somewhere else, I wrote a letter of enquiry which included my vita.

I got a very courteous reply that suggested I might do as a member of a panel, but that the Festival Association did not have the funds to pay expenses for uninvited people, but that if I were on a panel, then perhaps my department might be willing to help defray expenses.

Their assumption, clearly, was that because I was a writer in Clemson, and because there was a college in Clemson, I was part of that college. Reasonable and logical, I suppose. But, Alas! wrong.

That assumption is the nub of what concerns me. There tends to be the assumption that people who *do* things in the humanities as humanists are of course members of someone-or-another's faculty somewhere. Again, it is a reasonable assumption. But again it is often enough wrong.

I wrote back hoping simply to raise the consciousness of my correspondent—God knows mine has been raised enough lately—and informed her that I was not a member of a faculty; that there was no department to support me with travel funds, no matter how curtailed they might still be; that I was just a writer wobbling along by myself as best I could—"I stand not tall it may be, but alone," as Cyrano put it, though I did *not* say that in my letter—and that I had simply written to ask, hoping for the best.

I then suggested rather gently, I thought, and with proper grace and courtesy, I certainly hoped and intended, that the Southern Literary Festival Association and other such organizations should start making themselves much more aware of the fact that William Styron and John Updike are not the only writers in America who don't teach for a living. There are lots of others in that boat, too. And far from being first class passengers in it, we may be more like barnacles clinging desperately to it. I suggested that there probably were quite a few people—like myself—who were qualified to perform, but who got overlooked time and time again because without the cachet of an institutional affiliation, we were required to have the reputations of a Fowles or a Gardner or a Vonnegut. And given the number of good writers around, a virtually non-computable percentage of us have such reputations.

She wrote back, thanked me for my letter, and said she didn't blame me for being bitter, but that they still didn't have any money. I was going to write her yet again to say, "Honey, I am not *bitter*. Please understand that. What I am is *concerned*…"

But I decided to let it go. She had other things to do, and so did I.

But *that* is what I am trying to get across to you. "I am concerned." I am concerned that you understand, as Ronald Gross pointed out in an article in the June 1981 *Chronicle of Higher Education*, that—among others—I.F. Stone, Lewis Mumford, Barbara Tuchman, Francis Fitzgerald, Mortimer Adler, Edmund Wilson, and—going rather farther back—Freud, Marx, and Darwin all were scholars whose work was not done in the Academy.

Certainly my correspondence with the Southern Literary Festival Association is a minor episode to you. However, I could relate several others. But picayunish as they all might be, they are syndromic. Admit, now: Academic people can be among the most intellectually timid and imaginatively backward of people. But academicians must understand—*you* must understand that there are more and more of you—well-schooled, well trained, even well-educated—who are now on the outside of the academy looking in. These are times when there is no longer room for them—for us—in the academy. At considerable intellectual waste, many are quite literally driving trucks, operating electrical companies, working as plumbers, and so on.

It is always easy to accept that one's *self* is ok—that is, employed or tenured—because one's self is deserving of that employment and tenure. But I dare say that many *many* faculty members will admit to their mirrors each morning that they are at the least as lucky as they are deserving. From what I hear, members of search committees country wide are having to turn down appointments and/or tenure to people who, judged by virtually any criteria at all, are at the least as "deserving" as their judges.

What I am saying is simply in support of what a number of people *in* the academy have already started to do: to recognize us, to acknowledge us, to accept that a humanist with the Georgia State Legislature or with a state's humanities committee or an unemployed independent radio producer without a radio station hyphen unemployed teacher hyphen unemployed fiction writer hyphen speech giver—that is, one who doesn't have a department to lay the hands of legitimacy on him—to accept that we are all Family.

We are here and we need to be used. It seems to me that you in there and we out here ought to be working up ways for you to use us. We academicians without academies, we humanists without colleges, we writers without departments *still* have a great deal to offer in our fields. And it may well be that *we* are the best interpreters *you* will ever have for getting the people out there to be graced by your work, your scholarship, the best of the humanities so they can be better builders of bridges and spinners of thread and sellers of insurance and managers of plants and deans of colleges by allowing them the means of being more aware of and sensitive to this world and the rest of us who live in it, too.

After that recognition, my plug—simply as a single specific—is for greater and greater use of the radio (I'll even throw in the boob tube) as a means of teaching. So much more can be done on the outside. Because of a number of reasons—economic, demographic, and Lord only knows what else—we need—perhaps more desperately than we know—to expand our vision, to be in the best sense *in*clusive rather than *ex*clusive; to "look shining," as Auden ended his poem "Petition," "to look shining at/ New styles of architecture, a change of heart."

Perhaps my plea to you is as foolhardy as the brashness of Phaeton when he demanded that his father let him drive the sun across the heavens so he could have some "bragging rights" with his friends; perhaps my disparate ideas are as unwise as that lad's wish, as unrooted in specifics and tangibles as that doomed boy's dream.

But if you believe in Marvin Bell's maturing poet, believe that you are less and less embarrassed by more and more, then you look not to the death of Phaeton, but to the inscription on his grave: *Here lies Phaeton, driver of his father's chariot;/ Greatly he had failed, but greatly had he dared.*

We all still need to dare greatly. But I think—now more than ever—we need to dare greatly *with* each other.

*The Following five pieces are glosses
on an unpublished novel of mine,
but which are relevent at this point.*

FIRST MEDITATION

MY UNCLE GORDON WAS THE first human being I'd ever seen die. The death itself was calm, and when I told my mother-in-law about it, she nodded her head and said that was good. "So many people fight it at the end," she said, thinking back to a lot of hands she had held in her life.

My mother-in-law herself was the second person I was actually with when she died. My wife wasn't there because she was doing a pulpit swap between our church in Knoxville, Tennessee, and the one in Oak Ridge. My son was with me at the nursing home bedside, though, while his wife had gone with mine to be with her at that service. My mother-in-law died just before it started, a hard message for me to deliver by phone. My mother-in-law also died quietly, her breaths simply coming farther and farther apart.

What took her a long time was not the actual dying, but the months and years leading up to it, her body being wasted in series after series of small strokes. What also happened was that after every time she got even a relatively minor illness, the plateau of her general health was always lower than it had been. Her body was strong, and she took a lot of killing, as the saying goes.

I saw my own mother a week before her death, when it was clear she couldn't hang on very much longer. I saw my father a month or so before his sudden heart attack, but he looked hale and hearty to me, no beds or medical paraphernalia. And I probably saw my maternal grandfather the night before he died. But I'm not sure.

On Breaking One's Pencil

I was still in school and likely didn't actually see him before I left that morning. At the time, we lived in Pelham Manor, New York, in a house that had a four-car garage with a lovely apartment over it out back. It was late March, 1946, and I was finishing junior high school, the eighth grade. My older brother, Bill, must have been home from Staunton Military Academy in Virginia, and our grandparents—Big Momma and Dan—must have been up for an Easter visit.

I got home and went out back to the apartment, walked up the stairs from the garage, and saw Bill on the steps. He made a strange motion with his hands, circling his face from his jaws to his pate. I didn't know what it signified, looked puzzled, but finished getting up the stairs.

"Dan's dead," he said, his face calm. Dan was a corruption and truncation, apparently, by my oldest brother, John, when he was a small child trying to say *Grand Dad*.

I remember that my mouth cracked into a quick smile and that I felt a slight rush of excitement pulse into my face and head while something fluttered through my chest and stomach. I followed Bill to the bedroom Big Momma and Dan were staying in, and there he was in bed, his eyes closed, looking for all the world like he was asleep, a handkerchief or napkin tied around his head to keep his jaw from freezing open, I was later told. His glasses were off, the sheet neatly pulled up across his chest as my mother stood beside the bed.

I stared at him for a while, realizing only then what Bill's hand gestures had signified, but the slight rush of excitement I had felt when he first told me my grandfather was dead had gone, and there was only a calmness, a modest confusion, a realization that some Great Thing had happened, but not knowing quite what it was. Ever since, I have felt ashamed of myself because of that initial spurt of excitement, sensing it to be an unseemly response at best, a sadistic one at worst. I expect, though, I'm hardly the only person ever to have felt that way. No other death has affected me like that, and that has made me wonder about the nature of grief. Is it "natural," or does it have to be learned?

I easily understood the absence death caused, the actuality of death, but I couldn't put a name to the sense of loss. By the time Dan died, I had felt the absence of my father's parents, be-cause I knew there was an imbalance in my life: I had a mother here, and I had a father there; I had grandparents here... but there were no grandparents there.

As I got older, I also began to feel the *loss* involved, and when I was even older, when both my parents were dead, I felt it keenly, because I realized that any children I might ever have would never know my parents even as I had never known my father's.

When my mother led me from Dan's deathbed to the front bedroom, I remember Big Momma sitting in a chair with her bodice partially undone so the doctor could listen to her heart. She was looking away from him slightly, looking toward the front windows, her arms draped across the arms of the chair. I had never seen so much of her chest before and was struck with the fact that it was what we used to call pigeon breasted, the sternum tending to stick out slightly. But more than that I was struck by how passive she was, her body settled into a stasis as though waiting for something to touch or breathe her into motion again. Her hair was still rolled up around the back and sides of her head the way she always wore it, her eyes seemed to be staring off through the front windows at things I couldn't see. It would be another twenty years before she herself died.

When the doctor finished, she buttoned her dress slowly and without any apparent embarrassment, while he nodded or spoke or in some way informed us that she was all right, just in moderate shock.

I don't remember a service. I don't remember going to the funeral or the interment in Pine Bluff. I was still in school, but it's inconceivable that Mother didn't go if not Dad. I simply don't remember how all that happened. My aunt, Zuzu, and her husband, Charles, lived in that apartment at the time, yet surely she would have gone down to Arkansas with Mother, but in that case, who would have stayed with me? If I went, it made no impression on me at all.

What I seem not to have remembered so much as understood is that someone in my family—someone I had actually known and seen myself, someone on whose lap I had sat, someone to whose deep basso profundo voice I had listened, someone against whose great girth of chest and waist I once upon a time had snuggled—was now dead. I had looked on it and had intuited that this was the way the world was and would be. Always. It was my first significant understanding that there was an end to things, that life really was not for ever and ever.

SECOND MEDITATION

I'VE BEEN TO ENOUGH FUNERALS to wonder what they're really supposed to do and who they're really for. They're the same question, I think. In nearly any religion a funeral marks a passage from one condition to another. In its simplest sense, it moves us from life to death. In his book *Theater Through the Ages*, Cesare Molinari points out that Pygmies in Gabon use theater to "evoke the memory of the deceased." They aren't trying to commemorate the lives of the dead so much as to remember them, trying, literally, to keep them in mind so the fact of their former physical presence will forestall their complete loss. The Arandas, Molinari says, use theater to make contact with "the elusive…ever-present dimension of dream." So tell me, what is a religious service if not theater?

Traditional Christian church services, for instance, have form and structure: a beginning (often a processional or a prelude); a middle (a sermon the centerpiece, usually, with readings from scriptures, hymns, and responsive readings that lead up to the sermon); and an end (often a recessional, a benediction, a postlude, or a statement such as *Ite, Missa est*). They also have audience participation (the singing of hymns, responsive readings, standing, sitting, kneeling, crossing oneself); a visual focal point: often the minister or the pulpit (with or without the minister), the crucifix, a stained glass window; an intellectual/emotional focal point (the sermon); a context or subtext within which the sermon makes or illustrates or expands on the point made by the reading (usually from scripture).

All of this can be as simple or complex as any other work of art. Within a formalized religious funeral service, there usually are certain readings or forms which are often used: the Lord's Prayer, the 23rd Psalm; in the case of weddings, "Dearly Beloved, we are gathered here today…"

But there is a significant difference between those two rites of passage: people are specifically invited to weddings, which makes them closed occasions; whereas—except in unusual circumstances—anyone is allowed to attend funerals, which makes them open. Why is this so? Why is a funeral so much more a community affair than a wedding? Why is the rite marking the end of a life so much more public than the rite that signifies the creation of a new grouping (a family), with the likely creation of new life? Why is the grief of a survivor subjected to the stares of strangers, when the joy of a marital union is for select eyes only?

It seems to be the nature of people that there is always something we don't know about them. They have lives we know nothing about because they know people even their families often have no idea of. I'm not talking about shameful (or even *not* shameful) assignations—the shady pasts that grip so many imaginations—or the spies of a Le Carre who have had several "Colds" they have had to come in from. I'm talking about simple folk like most of us. Ask yourselves who has touched your life. Ask yourselves whose lives you have touched. Count them. Make some lists. Counting items on lists—mundane though it is—can be amazingly instructive. For instance, list the names of every child you can remember in your first grade class. In your sixth grade class. In your high school graduating class. In your wing of the dorm your freshman year in college. In your Shakespeare, Medieval History, Greek Literature in Translation, organic chemistry, strength of materials classes. And so on through co-workers in all the offices you've ever worked in.

Now make a list of all the people who have influenced you in your life—the third grade art teachers, eighth grade homeroom teachers, freshman English teachers, mothers, fathers, aunts. Favorite uncles.

Now make a third list. I suspect it will be the hardest one of all, and most likely the smallest. Write down the names of all the people from the first two you *know* you have profoundly influenced. Too hard? All right, just those you know you have positively influenced. But you must *know* that you have done it.

Teachers, certainly, know that what their students learn is not always what the teachers thought they were teaching, and they also know that they move people in ways they may almost never find out about. That's why anyone can come to a funeral or memorial service: so anyone in an entire community—no matter how local or how scattered—can bear witness to the existence of the deceased. It is a time, as well as a place, when showing grief is all right, even though the grief may be indirect. I wept the night my father-in-law died, which took me by surprise because though we got along well enough, we were never close. Then, I realized I was not crying for my wife's father, but for my own and for God knows how many other losses of whatever sorts.

So who are funerals for? In some religions they are for the dead, although other rites (supreme unction, for example, used to be a case in point) may be more important. But in practical terms, funerals clearly are for the survivors, and it seems to me that the minister's job (or the job of whomever is officiating) is to help the true grievers come together into a com-munity—no matter for how short a time—of memory, of loss, of love, of sharing our knowledge of our common end, and, as with the case of my father-in-law, to spread those losses out at least just a little so that the weight of no one of them will bear too heavy an onus.

Finally, a note about the Old Dears—those butts of so many jokes and snickers—who seem to go to every funeral in town: Keep in mind, while laughing at what may appear to be their cronish ghoulishness, that funerals are also times and places where we can grieve Grief itself, where we can get used to the idea that we all someday will cease to be, and where we may even tap into some strength from seeing others who have made—and will be making—that passage too. It may help many keep from feeling quite so alone, at least a little less terrified before so fierce a final mystery.

THIRD MEDITATION

I WAS LISTENING TO A recording of Marian Anderson singing "He Shall Feed His Flock" from Handel's *Messiah*. It is so elegantly beautiful it can wash away mere happiness and raise it to the tearful ecstasy of joy. There is such a simple yet exquisite purity about it that in trying to explain it, we realize why music is music and words are not.

But that isn't all there is to say about the music itself. There's that gorgeous voice. And besides that, how can we listen to Marian Anderson and not summon up her life: the strength of it, the discipline of it, the simple pluck of it? That is, we always bring more to these things than we know at first.

My curiosity about my father has grown over the years. Initially, the fact of his sudden death dominated everything, as though it were the only matter of interest, the only matter of importance. What am I saying? I wanted to *know* my father. But what does that mean? Partly, it means I wanted to be able to talk to him while I was an adult. I wanted to ask him why he didn't like college, why he didn't seem to have much of a social conscience. I've wanted to ask him if he went to New York because he knew he'd get bored stiff with the daily routine of editing one newspaper for the rest of his life. How much of that move was really ego and ambition as well as a sense of duty to his profession?

And what else do we want to know at such times? What else do we really want to know about our families? At fifteen most boys are pretty much centered on themselves. There's a lot going on, and when the world intrudes, the disruptions can be pretty rough, because, in one sense, we can't pay attention to ourselves any more. There is now a widowed mother; there is now some concern about the future: What and where will it be? Paradoxically, being forced to accept something unacceptable also makes us concentrate on ourselves even more, makes us take hold of death, for instance, and if not clutch it to our bosoms exactly, still its unacceptability makes us understand that it is a reality and a finality in our lives.

So many people are so uncomfortable with that, I think, because they get conflicted with how they feel as opposed to how they figure they're supposed to feel, with the messages "society" seems to send them about such matters. Further, I suspect that many people never seem to get at all straight about themselves.

Well, this is sufficiently vague, I think. So I'll get back to events.

After my father died I went with my family down to Pine Bluff, Arkansas, for the funeral, an affair that only Mark Twain could have done justice to. It was an elaborate scene, and I put it that way because there's no way to talk simply about the service itself, because the service was only a part of several days' worth of events.

My father was the executive editor of the Scripps Howard Newspaper chain, so at his death there were journalists clear across the country—both in and out of Scripps Howard—who had known him well. During the Second World War, for instance, he had been called to Washington, D.C., to organize the division of press censorship within the Office of Censorship, and soon was also Deputy Director of the entire Office.

Then, not only was he an Arkansas boy, but had been editor of the *Fort Worth* (Texas) *Press* for three years, and before that had helped manage the merger of two papers in Memphis, Tennessee. He also had a newspaper sister in Oklahoma City and another sister married to a businessman there. At the time, Scripps Howard's chain included papers in Knoxville, Tennessee, two in Memphis, and the one in Fort Worth among others across the country.

In addition, Dad's maternal grandfather had founded a paper in Pine Bluff, Dad had worked on it for a number of years and even had become its editor at one time, and his brother had been editor of it until *his* death just two years before Dad's own. Also, his father had been a lawyer in Pine Bluff and a circuit judge—as had *his* father. So Dad was well remembered and still well known.

Finally, my mother was also a native of Pine Bluff. In short, there were a lot of people at the funeral, locals as well as out-of-towners.

I saw this: When the train pulled in with Dad's coffin in the baggage car, there was a substantial crowd at the station. Men stood around holding their hats in their hands, and for a crowd, there was a great silence.

Before and after the service, I was around editors of newspapers in Pittsburgh, Cleveland, Memphis, wherever. The editor of the *Cleveland Press* said to me, "Bobby, your father died young, but he accomplished more than most of us who may live far longer."

I remember the editor of the *Pittsburgh Press* crying softly as he knelt by the casket. I remember Mother being concerned for him. He died within the next two years.

I remember some one of the married in-laws pontificating to my brother Bill and me, "The eyes of the whole Southwest will be on you boys." It struck me even then that the eyes of the whole Southwest didn't have a clue who I was, and even if they had, I wasn't sure I wanted them to be looking that hard at me.

I remember on the train trip back to Memphis after it was all over how gentle my oldest brother was with me and how much I needed that gentleness as I stood in the vestibule between cars staring out the window of the door, trying to keep my balance as the train jounced and swayed, trying to see into the night, trying to figure what had been lost, trying to get a grip on what was gone, trying to understand what had happened to us all, trying to grab onto something and not knowing what or how, knowing only that something of monstrous import had suddenly fallen from the center of things deep within me and that the palpable *Whoosh* of its going would echo throughout my life forever, resonating, still, twenty-nine years later when I was back in Pine Bluff with my Aunt Monica, wanting to find out something more about my father, but without an idea in the world of what.

It gets to be like the image of press photographers as they surround Figures of Importance who're on their way to Somewhere Else. "Just one more," they cry. "Just one more shot," as though with just one more shot, with just one more print to choose from back in the news room, with just one more bit or piece or chance they will be able to capture the essence of the Subject, will be able to know what it is they need or want or think they must have. . .

. . .just one more story, one more image, one more tale, one more remembrance and I will be able to effect the closure that seems so necessary for me to wrap around myself, or maybe to stuff into that still-Whooshing void.

It isn't to be had, though. At least, it isn't to be had in the way I had thought about it for so long. There aren't ever enough *Just One More*'s. And now, maybe, there don't need to be. In South Devon, England, there's a saying: "Enough is as good as a feast." I think about that a lot.

FOURTH MEDITATION

AN AMERICAN DILEMMA. I CAN'T imagine that phrase is original with me, and I know the topic has been discussed for years, but every time another child has to face the possibility or probability, the desire, need, or necessity to put a parent into a nursing home, the question reappears full bore, and no amount of attention paid the fetching articles and sensible books quite prepares us for the terrifying reality of that first research into what to do.

The "sandwich generation" is what people were called those days when they had to raise their children as well as tend to their aged and ailing parents. There have always been sandwich generations, of course—it used to be the norm—but because family structures have changed so much no one saw any particular need to invent a name for what was happening until recently. Children always took care of their parents, often without much grace, style, or wit about it, but that's just the way things were. Now families are scattered, houses have fewer rooms, and people live significantly longer.

Both my parents died before they were sixty, so I never knew them as old people, never had to take care of them. And when my mother was dying of cancer, I was in college in Nashville, Tennessee, which left my oldest brother in Memphis to tend to her—in or out of the hospital.

So when I went to Pine Bluff to look after my uncle and aunt, the duties of family had simply caught up with me. Typically, I didn't live anywhere near them, Clemson, South Carolina, being almost as far from Pine Bluff, Arkansas as Atlanta, Georgia, is from South Bend, Indiana, and even if we had lived closer, I wouldn't have been able to take Monica into our house: It was too small, she was too frail, and we didn't have the money.

What is one supposed to do? What *can* one do?

The first question's not too hard to answer—for many of us, at least. What we're supposed to do is take them in no matter, or at least see to it that they are cared for in as decent a way as possible.

But the second question lingers like the tenacious remnants of a nightmare: What can be done? The Devil, as always, is in the details. In the case of my aunt the matter got settled by itself. She died. But my wife's mother didn't die, and she finally got so poorly and her husband was so unable to cope with her that something else had to happen. My wife moved them up from Florida to Clemson after a small tornado hit their house one year. For each of the five or six years before that, though, there had been a couple of frantic trips from Clemson or from Boston, where she was in divinity school, down to Florida to deal with heart attacks, strokes, or whatever.

But after the tornado, my wife realized she simply couldn't keep that up—and neither could they. That move from the lovely little house they had built to an apartment was hard enough on them, but they were also moving from independence to dependence, from the known to the unknown, and of course, moving slowly through the terrible realities toward the ultimate inevitabilities. One of the steps along that Way was the nursing home.

We looked at several, and the process was essentially what I have just described [in another manuscript], though that was largely a fictional composite of experiences. The one we finally settled on was a "good" nursing home about ten miles from where we were living. Some may say that "good nursing home" is an oxymoron, but again: What is one to do?

The thing about nursing homes is the same as with the thing about hospitals: The closer you are, the more often you *can* visit; the more often you *do* visit, the better care your people will probably get. If the attendants and nurses in the homes know you come over to visit three or so times a week—but don't always know when that will be—the more likely they are to keep things spruced up.

Too, you get to *see* what your folks look like. I told my wife once on the phone that Mom was addled, that she was semi-hallucinating, that she asked me if we were on a train or a ship because the room seemed to be moving. She also told me that she couldn't find me, once, that she looked all over but couldn't find me.

The long and short of it was that when my wife got home from divinity school for Thanksgiving, but before we had to get up to Knoxville for a weekend involving her getting a pulpit, she took one look at her mother, then went out to the nurses' station and said she wanted to know what medicines her mother was on. Bingo! She was still taking stuff that had been prescribed months earlier. She *had* been hallucinating.

So why hadn't the nurses realized my mother-in-law was hallucinating? Why hadn't the nurses questioned the doctor about continuing that drug? Why had the doctor kept her on that drug in the first place? To top it all, my wife had to stand there at the nurses' station while they called the doctor right then. She said he needed to be called. They said, all right. She saw that no one picked up the phone. She said, "Now." They asked, "Now?" She said, "I mean right now while I'm standing here and can talk to him if I need to."

So they did. "Oh yes," he said to the nurse, "I was going to call today and tell you to take her off that medicine."

And what about people who don't know what the PDR is (the *Physician's Desk Reference*) which lists every known prescription drug in the galaxy? Or people who haven't a clue about what the contraindications of various common drugs might be? What about people who live 2,000 miles away and haven't enough money to visit more than once a year? What about. . . ?

Squeaky wheels *do* get the grease.

Remember, my mother-in-law was in a *good* nursing home.

And yet, I think most of those people really do the best they can. But it's hard. In Knox-ville, Tennessee, she was in another good home, and many of the staff had been there for years and were terribly proud of their work and of the place itself.

Nothing is simple. It's terribly depressing. All we can do is the best we can do, recognizing all the while the seas of guilt, the oceans of concern, the seemingly endless days as our folks grow older and poorer, sicker and weaker.

I have long mourned the family losses I have survived, but I have never regretted the suddenness of my father's death, the joint deaths of his parents, the relatively quick deaths of my uncle and his wife. They brought their own kinds of blessings.

And yet, the death of my mother-in-law did too. I got to know her because she was slow to yield up the ghost. I got to know her wonderful, earthy sense of humor. Once (before we put her in the nursing home), she had soiled herself pretty badly. My father-in-law simply couldn't deal physically—or, I suspect emotionally, either—with the situation, so when he called me on the phone, I came over to their apartment and cleaned her up.

It wasn't that I had never done that before, but it had been with my own infant children. My mother-in-law was a horse of another color. Still, with her wisecracks and my own peculiar brand of gallows humor we got it done. From that day, I think we loved each other very much.

FIFTH MEDITATION

IN THE FRONT OF THIS book [referenced earlier] I have a quotation from *Hamlet*. It is spoken by Hamlet, but for years, I had hooked it to another quotation, a famous one by himself. What I remembered Hamlet saying, when he was ruminating about the play within a play, was, "The play's the thing/ wherein I'll catch the conscience of the King, and thus by indirections find directions out."

It made sense to me. The play within the play was indeed an indirection. In certain senses all art is indirection, maybe what Picasso was getting at in that quotation so often attributed to him, "Art is a lie that tells the truth." What I did was add seven more words to Shakespeare's closing of that long soliloquy which ends Act II of *Hamlet*.

The events of the narrative sections of this book [see above] are true. Whether they are factually accurate or not is another matter. In most instances they are factually accurate as far as I can remember them. But in some others, I backslid into a fiction writer's reality. Both reality and invention are equally real, after all. They simply go after the same thing in different ways. A minister, for example, once told me that to him religion was essentially one *materia* spoken in different languages.

From another angle, happiness is often a matter of expectations: the more we expect of ourselves in life, the less successful we feel ourselves to be if we fall short even just a little of those expectations. Similarly, intent makes a difference regarding a piece of writing. I wanted to tell the story of my uncle and aunt's deaths because they resonated with so much in my life. But my intent was less to depict those deaths in rigorous factual detail than to convey something of what Gordon and Monica's passing meant to me. I wasn't interested in reportage so much as in interpretation, in putting things together that belonged together in Truth, if not in Fact.

For instance, the character I call Harry Corn never talked to me about my grandfather's concrete house, but that conversation, more or less, did take place. It took place as I suggested in the narrative: one summer when I was a boy, some of us in the family were down in Pine Bluff visiting for a few days. Mother was driving around the town, with Dad sitting in the back seat pointing out this and that and whatever. We passed his old home (as I recall the episode) and he talked about the concrete house, but he couldn't remember exactly when his father had built it or why or what it was for. As I say, that's how I remember that scene.

Even more peculiar, though, was finding out, while rummaging through one of my bookcases looking for something completely else, that I had merged two people in my head: Albert Alexander—the realtor I call Harry Corn, who *did* give me a copy of the 1914 *Zebra* which *does* contain the photos of my father in the standard football player's positions I've described, and who did know my father in high school—and another Pine Bluff resident, Dolf Kastor, who *had* been in Vaudeville and with whom, according to my aunt, my uncle used to spend hours on the phone. Whether I deliberately combined the two men at some time as a fictional decision or whether it was one of those slips of memory like the Hamlet quote, I don't know.

I do know that I never visited Graceland Cemetery with Albert Alexander or Dolf Kastor, never had a conversation about Dad's funeral song with either of the gentlemen, and was never told that Dad said the other had to sing for the two of them, and so on. That's a completely made-up piece.

Nonetheless, Dad *did* tell me that story about singing at the funeral, as I relate in the narrative. My mother, who probably didn't embellish the matter too terribly, said that years earlier Dad would sing along when he heard Bing Crosby on the radio (before Crosby deepened into a real baritone) and, according to Mother, you couldn't tell the two voices apart. Why shouldn't I believe that?

Historians earn their bread trying to sort out various accounts of what happened so they might come close to the "truth" of a time or an event. But all they can do is deal with the discernable facts. There will always be seas of data that are unrecoverable. Even trained eyewitnesses looking at the same event often can't agree as to what happened. Think of John Kennedy's assassination—or even the mundane instant replays during professional football games.

Even brilliant people, closeted in the same room for months as they pounded out a document that would launch a nation into one of the most incredible experiments of governance the world had ever seen, couldn't agree, within fewer than twenty years, about what the intent of the wording was in specific instances. Obviously I'm referring to the United States Constitution. And in that vein, what is the job of the Supreme Court? To interpret, of course. Judges interpret the law, and—as Charles Evans Hughes said in a 1907 speech, "the Constitution is what the judges say it is." So much for facts.

There was a story about President Johnson—LBJ—that when he was a boy he asked his mother if a story he had just read in a school text was true. "No," she was supposed to have answered, "It's just a story." "Then," said the boy who would be president, "I don't want to waste my time on it," or words to that effect.

Stories: metaphors, images, imagination, make believe, pretense. Stories: *for instance*'s, *for example*'s, *think-of-it-this-a-way*'s. Stories: concrete cases illustrating abstract conceptions. How do we explain what we mean by *neighbors* to somebody who doesn't want to understand? Jesus talked about the Good Samaritan, which made things clear enough even to the lawyer caviling over the tenth part of a hair in his search for a loophole. How do we explain Love? Fidelity? Truth? Duty? Honor? Falstaff has a word or two to say about honor, and in his negatives about its not being able to set a leg or that it was insensible, mere air, a mere scutcheon and so on, he demonstrates both the problems and the solutions of "thingness," of those essences, quintessences, Platonic stuff.

So how am I to write about Loss, knowing that I'm dealing with ineffable matter? One way is by trying to tell the story of my favorite uncle's death and the death of his wife within two weeks, not only because it reminds me so very much of the deaths of my own paternal grandparents, but because it was the first time I ever watched the life go from a human being.

And where, then, should the center of that story be? In the facts? Maybe so. For some occasions and for many people that's exactly where it *must* be. But for me on this occasion, though the facts certainly aren't *un*important, the center of the story's "Truth" is best manifested through the telling.

Consider this: In any situation where people are dealing with each other as best they can—particularly in emotional extremes—much is considered that isn't done; much is thought that isn't said; much is felt that isn't expressed; much is known that hasn't connected; much is stored that must wait to be retrieved.

And all the while, some Demiurge in us is taking notes—and revising.

ESSAYS

Hawarya?

A Reflection on a Question Put to Me by

A Friend Who Is a Minister

Robert T. Sorrells

What is the sound of one hand clapping?
> *Zen Buddhist Koan*

How old would you be
if you didn't know how old you was?
> *Satchel Paige*

And how are *you*?
> *The friend one night at dinner in Spokane, Washington*

HAWARYA?

SO. YOU STARED RIGHT AT me and asked how *I* was.

Being pretty adept, figuratively, at the old soft shoe routines, I managed to slide around some, bounce my cane pretty niftily against the floor, catch it without much of a bobble, tip my straw boater, and do an *Off to Buffalo* step while singing my song—all without having to deal very vigorously with the question.

But I felt trapped, even so. Not *bad* trapped, because I was enjoying the company. Maybe hedged in would be more accurate. Or flushed out of hiding, possibly. I'm not used to that kind of attention, for one thing. For instance, when people I don't know all that well ask me, "What do you do?" I reply, probably with a sickly smile on my face, "I'm a writer," and hope they'll think either that's too bizarre to pursue any further, or even that it's an outright lie (after all, Shakespeare and all them are dead, aren't they? Well, there's Danielle Steele and people like that, of course) and won't ask any more questions in that direction.

But no such luck, usually: "And what do you write?" they ask, nonetheless. "Fiction, mainly," I answer, the silly smile still refusing to fall away, hanging there like dripping playdoh. "Ah," they *will* continue. "And what kind of fiction do you write?" Feeling serious tics skit-tering around my face by then, I manage to come up with something. It never ends the inter-rogation, though. I suppose I shouldn't feel this way, that it's somehow ungenerous of me, but Lordy! What kind of question is that? What would you answer if someone asked you what kind of sermons you preached? Brilliant? New Age? Sci-Fi? Traditional? Academic? Humanistic? Christian? Dull? Motivational? *Collage*-ish? Epiphanous? Ephemeral?

In any event, I have been considering your **And How Are *You*?** question a lot—perhaps, even, way before you asked it—because it's one of those frustrating delights of our language: The question means what it asks at the same time that it doesn't mean that at all. It means, "Hey, howryadoin'?" and it means, "Are you all right?" The first can be no more than a mindless code-word covering the lack of anything really to talk about—like that lonely and lovely scene in the movie *Marty* where the two characters keep asking each other, "Whaddaya wanna do tonight?" and the other always answers, "I dunno. Whaddya *you* wanna do tonight?" The second can run the gauntlet from a nosy intrusion, to a seriously intended and profoundly needed inquiry into the root well-being of one's very life.

Given the nature of the question, then, the answers are just as various, partly because they shift a good bit: Catch me today, I'm down; catch me tomorrow, I'm up. There isn't a final answer, in other words. And yet…

Yet there are threads, usually, that hold, or tend to hold, things together, wobbly lines veering, surfacing erratically through the matrix of our lives, that give a certain structure to them. Sort of.

It strikes me, in short, that I've been thrown a kind of koan here, an unanswerable question, but one that can lead to insights through pondering the possibilities.

I've long thought that one mark of maturity was the ability to deal with ambivalence, ambiguity, and paradox. So my answers to your question might seem circuitous, circling, flopping, finally, like an old hound on a hot August afternoon; not especially direct; possibly sounding like I'm just *tell*ing you things; likely, even, the conclusions I draw not seeming to be inferable from what I say. If so, remember what Polonius said in *Hamlet* about using indirection to find direction out.

Still, I have to admit some things.

I am tired:

> Of moving
> Of being the new kid on the block
> Of not having a real home
> Of doing the kind of teaching I have had to do
> Of growing continually older
> Of getting so little of what I write published.

These lists can go on for way too long, and usually end in some puling, breast beating *Ah, je suis perdu!* while the fact is that a lot of it is wrapped up in the aging business. For some years now I've been having what I call "old man dreams." Typically, they involve dreams about me—usually with one of my old friends when we were both young and virile—in a state of energetic enthusiasm about some project or other: getting it started, planning the whole thing for as far down the line as possible. In one dream, for example, I was holding my son in my hands (he was an infant) and thinking I'm not sure what about him and me and us. But it was fun, it was just plain, old-fashioned excitement.

But then I wake up from these dreams. I'm not quite in a panic when I do. Rather, it's more like those dreams I had when I was a little boy: dreams of going to The Rodeo or The Circus; reaching for the Treasure Buried in the Cave; finding myself starting on some Great Adventure, some dream of profoundly soul-satisfying glory....

Then—literally—comes the crying sense of loss as I move slowly, first, then faster and faster out of and away from the dream: the frantic, fading clanks of the cow bell as the bull kicks and twists to buck its rider into oblivion; the pungent but dissipating aromas of all the lions and horses, elephants and gorillas, mixing with the sawdust at the circus; my hand scratching the wall by my bed rather than scooping up the precious pearls and diamonds, rubies and sapphires, jade and ivory from the pirates' trunk—moving back into the quotidian reality of daily school and Saturday chores, neighborhood bullies and mean dogs—freshman themes and fleeting time.

*I'm at the **end** of everything*, I think as I wake. *Not the beginning, anymore.* On other occasions, that isn't an altogether bad thought, but when it rises out of these Old Man Dreams, it's absolutely crushing.

I can talk more specifically. Not all that long ago I spent the better part of a year going through a lot of my father's stuff. He was a newspaperman for the Scripps Howard newspapers, yet managed to do a tremendous amount of writing even though he spent his final eighteen years as Executive Editor of the entire chain, an executive/management, not an editorial, role.

But sometimes I wonder what life would have been like if he'd decided back in 1930 that he'd rather be the editor of the *Fort Worth* (Texas) *Press* than move to New York City to be the chain's Executive Editor. Who knows! For one thing he'd probably have lived ten to fifteen years longer, wouldn't have died five weeks before his fifty-second birthday. In my own terms, though, I'd have had a hometown. What a strange thought: a real *place* to connect to, someplace to really *be* from, some *place* that I could consider really mine.

Instead, I've had New York City for nine months, then to the suburbs: Chappaqua for three years, Scarsdale for four, Pelham Manor for six; back to the City for two—my first two years in a military prep school in Virginia; then down to Memphis with a legal address, mainly, for the next ten years because I was finishing prep school, doing two and a third years in Nashville at college, then two years in the Army, then back to Vanderbilt for the BA and the MA; then to Murray, Kentucky, teaching for two years; back to Nashville (two places, four years); then to Iowa City (two years); then Clemson, South Carolina (two places, five years); then to Fayetteville, Arkansas (one year); then a year in England (two places); then back to Clemson for the next fifteen years (three places); then Knoxville, Tennessee (five and a half years) Rochester, Minnesota (nineteen years), and now back to Clemson…

What madness has impelled this? I have often wondered.

Yet it's not been all bad, by any means, just tiring after a while.

Then: My father's parents died within five minutes of each other in May of the year I was born in September, so I never knew them; my own parents were long dead by the time I got married, so my children never knew *them*; I had hoped that pattern would be broken with me, and it has been, now that we have been blessed with a grandchild.

Lately, too, the "search" for my father has come to demand that I pay more and more attention to the vacuum his death left me with. Still, it's been a delight, actually, because it's resulted in some wonderful projects and some wonderful writing. But I feel the loss of my boyhood more and more, especially now that I am the last of the four of us Sorrells kids still alive.

…

About teaching, though: No doubt my concern there hooks into the age thing again. I finally saw my students mainly under-prepared for my vision of college-level English courses, and freshman composition, for a variety of reasons, is probably one of the most demanding courses in any curriculum to teach. I had hoped that when we got up to Minnesota I wouldn't have to teach at all, but Rochester is a two-horse town: Mayo Clinic and IBM.

On Breaking One's Pencil

Sleek steeds though they may be, none-the-less that's all there is. Someone immersed in the Humanities doesn't have many options when it comes to alternative work possibilities here. So the question devolved to, "How do I want to spend these later years?" My answer was, "Not in a community college classroom teaching freshman composition."

But maybe there's more to be said about that.

All my life I've been a teacher. I always liked going to school, and in fact in kindergarten when I was supposed to go only in the mornings, I would tell Mother I had to go back that afternoon. There wasn't any reason for her to doubt me at first, but she knew it was odd. One day, though, she called my teacher and asked what gave. "He asked to come back after lunch," she said. "I thought it was all right with you." (Apparently she didn't say that Bobby lied to her.)

Then seven or eight years later when we found out about D-Day, I was one of two students at Siwanoy Elementary in Pelham who was asked to stand up before the whole school and give a report on everything known about the invasion at the time. I loved it!

But I wasn't through. In the fraternity at college, I was the assistant pledge trainer my sophomore year and the head pledge trainer the next year—until I got drafted out of college because of the Korean War. In short, it was always a natural thing to me: Teaching, after all, is a lot like preaching; being a teacher is a lot like being a minister; and both share a whale of a lot with actors: You're on stage and performing.

But so much has changed. Once, I knew what I was doing in a classroom: knew there was a wondrous and growing body of material, stuff, whatever, that I was learning more and more about; and that I was learning more and more about how to present that stuff. Then during all those years off when I was writing everything—my stories, news, copy writing/editing, public relations, history, radio programs, a script for a thirty-minute film on land use for the state of South Carolina, a history of Clemson University's experimental forest, scripts for slide/tape shows; doing voice-overs for slide/tapes, and (God save me) voice-overs for Clemson's ten-second half-time ads during televised football games—it seemed to me that I was amassing an increasingly dense matrix of material and experience and variety of writing and on and on and on…My God there were times I felt like I knew so much

I'd just flat out bust with it all if I couldn't get somewhere to share it or teach it or whatever.

But now it seems that students, sweet and kindly points of light though they may be, really have lost it: their history, their sense of who they are or, worse, who they might still be. When I think these things, I do feel curmudgeony, like I'm telling stories to rightly bored grandchildren about having to walk ninety miles each way through blizzards or tornadoes to get to and from school most days.

This sort of thing really hit home when I thought about some of the reports on stories that were being presented in the junior-level fiction writing class I was able to teach my last semester at the University of Tennessee. I had assigned six people to give presentations about the stories in a text I used. They were right pitiful, those reports. With one or two exceptions, the students didn't have a clue about how to start getting inside a story. I asked one of my best guys to do "Us He Devours," by James B. Hall. The story made absolutely no sense to him: goats? Pan? Satan? myths? appearance/reality? He just really didn't dig it. And I had thought he would be the one in there who would. Silly me.

Well, I guess I wish I could have gotten out of it all, is what I'm saying. I wish that I could have felt that what I was doing—even at the freshman level—was worthwhile. I love to teach, is the thing, and I guess I don't understand why people in college—even junior or, as they're now called, community colleges—aren't especially interested in learning.

A good bit of my problem now, of course, is that so much has changed. Probably a lot of it is for the better, but when certain kinds of pushes come up against certain kinds of shoves, I'm not really convinced of it. I still make a distinction between education and training, but I find it's a distinction not many seem willing to insist on any more. An old bromide has it that if you give a man a fish, you feed him for a day, but if you teach him *how* to fish, you've fed him for life. By extension that's the difference to me: A trained person can perform certain set acts, has specific skills, which, though often vast are even more often limited. But an educated person has learned how to learn forever, has learned how to develop those "inner resources" that sound so mysterious but which amount, for the most part, to simply being able to amuse one's self.

More and more these days, though, (I sensed a lot of the same thing when I was a part-time instructor at the University of Tennessee) "education" has come to mean technical training. Not only that, but the new absolutes in attitudes keep yammering and hammering away to say that lectures by nature are boring; that team teaching by nature is more instructive; that groupie activities by nature are pedagogically sounder; that bashing away at details—because it can be "boring"—is to be avoided; that if learning isn't "fun" (or worse yet "a fun thing"), then the teacher's job is to make it "fun."

The idea that you have to **know** certain things here (now) before you can **do** certain things there (later), and that everything will be a chaos of mystery until you get to that point is a concept now apparently lost to educational pedagogy. In my field, what that means is language will always be a stumbling block to most young people, but never a building block.

Students would come to me and ask how they can, you know, like, they mean, quit getting those clumsy Cs and start making the beloved Bs and the admirable As on their papers. The trouble is that when I tell them exactly how to do it, their eyes go glassy, their jaws slacken, and, I could often swear, some even start to drool.

"Yeah," they finally manage to get out. "Yeah, well, like um, un-hun. I see. Well, like, you know, thanks for your time. I mean, you know?"

What have I told them? The short of it is they'll have to expend a lot of energy in my presence concentrating while I explain and elaborate on the comments and corrections I've already written on their papers; then they'll have to spend many more hours alone comparing the phrases, clauses, and sentences of their own papers with the examples I've referred them to in their text books; besides that, either they'll simply have to memorize the differences, just as one kind of example, among homophones (to, too, and two), homographs (*con*duct and con*duct*), and homonyms (the noun and verb *quail*), or else devise clever little rubrics to remember them; and then they'll have to use up reams of clean paper on lots and lots of revisions; all of which requires *many* hours of labor. **Many**. None of that, of course, deals at all with learning to read effectively enough to really understand the ideas presented in their assigned essays.

"Boys," my high school football coach used to tell us when we were sucking wind in the middle of a particularly grueling workout or scrimmage, "if they had pills to get you in shape, I swear to God we'd get them for you, but they don't." So for us it was back to the wind sprints, nip-ups, squat jumps, duck waddles, push-ups, and all the rest—not only if you wanted to be a starter, not only if you wanted to play pretty regularly, but also if you simply wanted to stay on the team or even make it in the first place.

I tell my students they need to demand as much of their minds as athletes do of their bodies; I tell them you don't get a point in basketball because the ball hits the rim of the basket instead of going through it; I tell them you don't get half a touchdown in football because the ball comes pretty close to but never actually *touches* the goal line. I suggest to them that not many successful coaches will let you stay on their teams if you don't show up for practice, or if you come late day after day, or if you never bother to learn what's in the playbook. In short, "Pretty near ain't quite half," as an old saw has it.

But I began to see so many more students who apparently were raised academically on the proposition that there shouldn't be any grunt work to learning: Memorizing is out; doing work on your own is out; formal lectures are out (I wasn't a lecturer)—never mind really studying—simply reading the assignments seems to be no more than a suggested option; demanding rigor is out; even asking students to expect something more of themselves is out. Bless their hearts, they usually didn't even know what I meant by that.

What seemed to be *in* was gift grades so students wouldn't be made to feel bad about themselves. Calvin, in one of the "Calvin and Hobbes" comic strips, now alas no longer with us, is staring at a returned paper. "This bad grade is lowering my self-esteem," he complains to his teacher. "Then you should work harder so you don't get bad grades," the grumpy-looking old thing retorts. Calvin looks blank for a second, but quickly collects himself and, staring back at his paper, presses on nonplussed with, "Your denial of my victimhood is lowering my self-esteem!"

Or, "Image," as Andre Agassi's camera ads on TV used to have it, "is everything." But what happened to gaining a good self-image by accomplishing something damned hard? Or, to rephrase that old song Pete Seeger used to sing, "Where has all the substance gone?"

Well, team teaching can be good; working together in small groups can be good; dialogue, which is nothing more than formalized conversation, can be good, too. I don't have any axe to grind with doing things differently: Lordy! If this doesn't seem to be working in a class, try that. But formal lectures can be wonderfully instructive in helping students organize material *if* they've bothered to learn something about it already; and groups don't work if only one or maybe two people of the five or six in the group have prepared the lesson; and if neither of the two teachers in a team is very bright, then what's the good of that? In short, there is no salvation in methods alone.

What happened to me was that I lost patience with the students. Oddly enough it didn't show up in the classroom nearly as much as it did some years earlier. In class, by and large, I was usually the soul of patience. I nudged, I cajoled, I gave strokes and helped lead discussions with students until they could start to see a point—maybe not understand it, but at least get a glimmer that there was one there. The problem was in myself: I was still a teacher, but I didn't like to teach any more. It may be that I was uncomfortable with the attitude I saw so much, this sense so many students imparted that they *deserved* something simply because it was there. I saw it as TV issue, I think: They'd been raised on ads that said they *deserved* that fancy car; they *deserved* that trip to Hawaii; they *deserved* that six-pack of beer. So they *deserved* an A or a B because they'd bothered to sign up for the class.

Once administrators started seeing students as merely another kind of consumer and education as just another product to be consumed, the students disappeared, and because they became customer/consumers and because they had the price of admission, then it wasn't unnatural for them to think they *deserved* the good grade: After all, if you go to most movie houses and pay your five bucks admission, you get to sit wherever you can find a vacant seat: down front, on the side, in the middle, at the back. Similarly, students *do* understand there's no dollar difference between the price of an A and an F, so why not assume you deserve the A?

Some of this came about during the '70s when colleges had to start hustling to get students: Severe economic downturns forced many parents to start looking at Duke instead of Harvard, Furman instead of Duke, Clemson instead of Furman, the University of Iowa instead of Coe, Rochester Community College instead of Winona State, etc. The result was that colleges with huge bills (faculty retirements as well as salaries, mortgages, and dangerously long-deferred maintenance and upkeep on vast physical plants—not to mention skyrocketing line item costs for campus security—etc.) called in market people who began their standard processes of research which included targeting potential markets (formerly called students), "selling" the college, and all the rest. Much of that resulted in college administrators who forgot what the academic missions of their schools were, forgot that "selling" education was not a business in the same way that selling cars, RVs, PCs, and municipal bonds was. The marketing terms seemed to fit, but administrators then confused the metaphors *consumer* and *product* with the real thing, students and education—the seekers and the knowledge they were seeking.

My in-class patience may have been the result of being angry with the system that had been allowed to develop, more than with the people filling the chairs in the classrooms, because my sympathy was with them, the folks who, in my opinion, had been screwed over by public education. In the entering freshman class at a local community college in 1994-95, for instance, some 35% were taking what's called "developmental" English, a euphemism meaning English for people who can't read or write at anywhere near what used to be a collegiate level. I thought that was pretty awful, until I found out that about 70% of that same class was also taking developmental math, and as I found out later, taking such courses because of test scores was a suggestion, not a requirement. Though quite a few of those students were more-or-less newly arrived from Southeast Asia, I questioned whether the vital work of teaching English as a second language so our new citizens could participate as quickly as possible in our culture should be done in "regular" English classes. I'm not convinced it is—not, at least, the way it was done.

Fussing about student performance makes me at least a little nervous, though, because, as I said earlier, I got drafted out of college during the Korean War. That was not easy to do. You had to burrow down into about the bottom tenth of your class. I didn't seem to have much trouble managing that. So I loved to tell my students, in order to let them know that I understood failure and that I knew what it was like to grapple with material that didn't come easily for me, that I failed the third quarter of a Survey of English Literature course; that I was a graduating senior before I passed the final required freshman math course ("I majored in freshman math," I would say); that my grades, if plotted on a graph, would have made a wonderful, if unimaginative, design for a smooth, straight ski slope; that I didn't make an A until I was a junior; etc.

There was a difference, though: It never occurred to me that the problem was someone else's; it never occurred to me that I was brilliant and my teachers automatically SOBs or asses for requiring me to come to class and to be

On Breaking One's Pencil

on time about it, too; it never occurred to me that I *deserved* a good grade on a so-so paper; it never occurred to me that I had to argue the preservation of my self-image rather than my knowledge of the material in question; it never occurred to me that I could afford to ignore memorizing *Ich bin; du bist; er, Sie, es ist; wir sind; Sie seid* and other such mundane basics if I ever wanted to be able to read, write, or speak German so it could be understood by an intelligent German.

And then there were the yowling dogs of war loosed upon the effete gentry (people like me, I gather) who failed to understand that this is no longer the age of "elitism," and that such throw-back attitudes are out of step with the "democratization" of standards and blahblahblah. But what is this "elitism" that is so terrible; this "elitism" that attacks self-esteem so viciously; this "elitism" that gets people to thinking they are ignorant simply because they cannot deal in the common currency of ideas, literature, language, philosophy, history, art, science, and other "elitist" pursuits: people who can't, in short, read with understanding?

Novelist Susan Sontag once talked about her concern for what she called the "deterioration of literacy" in America. "People are constantly reducing literacy to communication and information," she said. "As language becomes poorer and as people's ability to use language becomes poorer, we are simply in touch with less and less reality. We become literally less intelligent."

My God! Substitute *competence* or *excellence* for *elitism*, and what have you got? In sports alone you have Michael Jordan, Babe Ruth, Jim Brown, Joe Montana, Brett Favre, Pele, Ty Cobb, Muhammad Ali, Joe Louis, Jackie Robinson, Sugar Ray Robinson, John MacEnroe, Jimmy Connors, Boris Becker, Pete Sampras, Roger Federer, Billy Jean King, Babe Zaharias, Wilma Rudolph, Brian Boitano. Have I missed any? Probably about a thousand or so by now.

Do we really want all our actors to be like John Wayne? Never a Laurence Olivier, a Helen Hayes, an Albert Finney, a Jessica Tandy, an Alex Guinness, a John Gielgud? Nothing but Ronnie Reagans?

Doesn't it bother anyone—black or white—when a university student in this country asks, "Why should I read anything by some dead white man?" I wondered when I read that remark how conversant the young lady was with the work of W.E.B. Du Bois, Marcus Garvey, James Weldon Johnson, Paul Robeson, Langston Hughes, Arna Bontemps, Claude McKay, Countee

Cullen, and on and on and on. Or are dead black men (and women) "boring" and "irrelevant" too—if you have to work hard to garner yet another layer of understanding life from them?

How did it come to be that we expect—and usually get—such excellence in sports, manufacturing, medicine, and space technology, yet have come to demand nothing of our young people in academics? We not only don't demand it but allow it to be ridiculed, demeaned, debased, and trivialized at every turn. As I see it, it's the result of the standardless classroom, a product of the '60s and the "open" universities, which promulgated or at the least pandered to the position that any idea is as good as any other idea no matter how baselessly founded, poorly researched, illogically thought through, or inadequately expressed; that how one "feels" on any given day constitutes a rationale for living one's life or enacting laws. It's the idea that requiring students to know things they aren't already familiar with makes them "victims" of this "elitism"; that wanting to help them discipline themselves is a form of "oppression," growing, probably, out of the '70s, when presumably good wholesome rebellion—like throwing people (deans) out of windows, blowing up classroom buildings, and refusing to take courses because people who didn't know anything about the subject matter found it to be "irrelevant"—was all just hunky-dory.

Once, even, I was semi-"investigated" because when a student failed her research paper for quoting everything in it, I said to her, "We spent three days in class on how and when to use direct quotations. Didn't you even read the textbook on this?"

What she had done was put quotation marks around every paragraph in her paper, which meant that everything in her paper was a direct quotation. On top of that, she showed no sources. When she saw the F grade she came up to my desk and asked why. All the other students were sitting at their own desks working on corrections, so this was a very private conversation. I told her what the problem was. She said something to the effect that she must have misunderstood, that she thought quotation marks meant something else. "Didn't you even read the text book?" I then asked.

So she went to the president of the college and complained that I had "made [her] feel stupid"! The president talked to the dean, the dean talked to my department coordinator (a quasi-democratic, non-elitist place, we didn't have heads or chairs though we did have deans and presidents), and my department coordinator (embarrassed as any honest person would have been) talked to me about the matter. As far as I know, however, the president not only never suggested to the student that she go through already clearly defined channels with her complaint; far worse, to my mind, she never even bothered to find out whether the student *had* read the text or not. What *was* the point here? The point *I* got was that the faculty can kiss off if a student complains.

Not all that many years ago the Chinese destroyed vast numbers of their finest minds in what they called a Cultural Revolution. I look at so many of our schools now and fear the same thing brewing on our own horizon, though perhaps not so bloodily. Elitist? In a country where so vast a wedge of the population goes to college, where there are so many kinds of colleges to go to, and where there are so many ways to pay the piper, how can anyone speak of someone else who has a competent intelligence and a honed intellect; who really wants to be able to make some sense of the world and his relation to it; who wants to know something of his and other people's history; someone, in short, who is educated: How can this desire for knowledge be considered "elitist" unless there has come to be no difference intellectually, ethically, aesthetically, or spiritually between *student* and *consumer*, *learning* and *product*, *sage* and *fool*? We must be very careful about what we really mean, what we really want, when we speak of needing to "level" our playing fields.

I'm afraid it all means that there are those who have conned us into believing this: If *I* don't know about it and it thus sounds "funny"; or if *I* don't know about it and don't want to bother having to learn anything about it; or if it's at all different from what I *do* know about; or if *I* don't happen to see any immediately useful (i.e. income-producing) purpose for it, then it must be bad at worst, unimportant at best. Much more recently, of course, there is the issue of Global Warming. How have people reacted to it? Not with very much open-minded reasonableness.

Clearly this has weighed on me terribly. Much of it, certainly, is the realization that time has passed or is passing me by in certain regards. That's not a happy thought. But it's not only that. Yeats's question from his poem "The Second Coming" haunts me more and more: "And what rough beast, its hour come round at last,/ Slouches towards Bethlehem to be born?" Scarily, I'm afraid that rough beast has already long-since arrived.

...

As for the writing: There's a wonderful cartoon that came to be a classic, or its cutline did. A writer is reading a rejection letter which says, "You write good, but not for us."

That's become the negative ecstasy, the inverted rapture of my writing, I'm afraid: St. Peter on his upside down cross. Once (a kind of synecdoche here), a magazine editor wrote me, "Your stories are lean, hard, and subtle, but [our] readers are looking for stuff that's fat and juicy: hamburgers instead of lean cuts."

"And," as a Vonnegut character used to say: "so it goes."

To earn a living as a writer, you have to write commercially viable stuff. My things aren't really very commercial, and writing for publication means writing to get books sold, because if books don't sell, publishers don't make any money. (*Books*, mind you: Agents have despaired for years over trying to sell individual stories, and to heads of English departments, a hundred published stories carried virtually no weight compared to one book.) A friend of mine told me a long time ago, "Bob, writing may be an art, but publishing is a business, and the sooner you learn that, the better off you'll be."

I learned it, all right, but it was like a defensive lineman learning that Bronko Nagurski (or Jim Brown or Marion Motley: name your favorite BIG, power fullback) was going to run the ball over his position. It was an interesting piece of information, but what was the use of it if you still couldn't stop him?

So I went on writing my usual kinds of things—some of which did fine, and one of which has been a wonderful story for me: "The Blacktop Champion of Ickey Honey" was published first in *American Review # 26*, one of the most prestigious journals of its kind; was the example of my writing I submitted the year I was awarded a grant by the National Endowment for the Arts; was reprinted in Houghton Mifflin's 1978 edition of their *Best American Short Stories* series; was the title story for my collection published by the University of Arkansas Press; and in 1998 was included in a collection entitled *Tennis and the Meaning of Life: a Literary Anthology of the Game*. But all that and fifty cents (depending on where you live) will get you a cup of coffee.

On Breaking One's Pencil

Recently an agent said wonderful things about a novella I'd sent her—but declined to handle it for me. And another agent said the current buzz phrase in the business is a weeping editor telling an agent (or writer), "This is the finest piece of fiction I've ever turned down."

A lot of this is a matter of the state of the business these days. Along with everything else, it has changed. What with mergers, buy-outs, and the like, it has come to pass that nearly the entire book publishing industry is in the hands of about six companies such as TimeWarner. They all have a number of imprints, but over some years the business itself has been restructured as well so that each division—as with IBM, GM, and all the rest—must make its own profits: The profits from one division of NCR, for instance, aren't allowed to pay the freight for another division even though that other division might have made stuff that gave NCR its wonderful Public Image, or whatever. In publishing, that means books that used to get published because they were (or likely would be) "prestige" titles, or because they were considered "important" in some literary way or other, even though there wasn't any hope of their paying for themselves, don't have nearly the chance to get in print they once did. Editors can't take those chances anymore, so they won't go to bat for a manuscript if they can't justify it pretty solely on the basis of its probable sales. Kahlil Gibran's *The Prophet*, for example, apparently used to pay for lots of novels and volumes of poetry every year. No longer, I gather. Of course all I know is what I occasionally read in the trade magazines and such like.

Also, people—even in their most optimistically generous moods—should carry around a fairly hefty bit of skepticism relative to anything we writers may say about our own **un**published material. But give us a little break: agents, editors, and reviewers can give us a hard enough time, so don't expect us to give ourselves the worst of it, too.

Thus, given that this is all *ex parte* business, then, I have to say that often what I see isn't what an editor or a publisher sees. Once, I wrote a letter to an editor at a publishing house in North Carolina—with whom I had had a minor correspondence on another matter—about sending her a group of stories as a possible book.

She said fine, so I sent them, though the upshot was that she turned them down (after some nice praise about the writing, as I recall), her overall problem being something to the effect that I had too many stories with characters who were "victimized by sex and drink," which created an "oppressive" atmosphere.

I got to thinking about that, pondering who my people were and what kind of stories I had been writing. I concluded that I write about the warts and wild hairs that seem to grow so naturally on the souls of the human critter. Much of my stuff seems to be about people who want—and sometimes desperately need—to love other people, but because they are awkward and don't know how, they end up hurting them and themselves instead. And I guess I write about memory, about people who don't want to turn loose of people, or give them up—or give up on them—either. I guess I write about people who try to live their lives with some dignity and some joy, but who *do* stumble, who *do* just keep looking up at the treetops or out somewhere, trying to find a horizon, maybe, but end up tripping instead. My people are precious to me, but they are a bruised, abraded, stub-toed, skinned-nosed lot. Still, they weren't "victimized" by a damned thing. They wore their barked shins, bunged up knees, flattened knuckles, shiners, and the other black-and-blue or green-and-purple marks of a messy world upon them the way an old soldier wore his medals thinking, "What's the big deal? This is what I do."

Beat up on? Prolly so. Scarred souls? For sure. Lordy! If you don't have a scarred soul you haven't been living. But victimized? Naw.

While I partially understood what she was getting at, still, my people usually got through things. As folks often say about boxers and other athletes who win but who look graceless or even silly while they're doing it, "It wasn't pretty to watch, folks, but they won."

More to the point, though, was that she said those stories didn't make into a good book. I wrote back willingly admitting that I likely didn't know how to put a book of stories together; telling her, however, that I had other stories that weren't at all oppressive from characters victimized by sex and drink; and asking her who the editors were who would help a writer like me put a book together.

Unfortunately, she never answered that question, so I didn't learn anything; instead—even more unfortunately—she very badly misread something else I had written in the letter, and thus shut me out completely, which saddened me a great deal, because I don't want to get people needlessly angry at me. I suppose I hit a tender node about the lack of current editors who would—or could—help writers. But all of that may simply have been her way of saying, "You write good, but not for us."

Another way for a writer to make a kind of living—or at least to have time off from a job to write—is to win awards, prizes, grants, and such. The fact is, however, not only are my stories not very "commercial," but I don't write good prize-winning stories, either. For contests and grant applications these days (I've been told by one who has judged a hefty share of them) you need a story that's less than twenty pages (about sixteen-eighteen is best), has no more than two characters a reader has to pay any attention to, jumps immediately into a clearly defined central conflict, and isn't terribly complicated emotionally, philosophically, or thematically, though it's apparently good to have some verbal and rhetorical fireworks or gimcracks. That is, don't let it sound too traditional; try to come up with a literary version of what politicians these days might call a neat "spin."

In re-reading that, I have to admit it's actually pretty good advice—after its fashion—for writing nearly any story. Still, not all good stories are written that way. Some people need more room to maneuver in. Theodore White, for instance, once told Walter Lippmann he'd been thinking about becoming a syndicated columnist. Lippmann pointed out that he'd have to be able to hold his columns right at 800 words, which caused White to remark, "I can't even clear my throat in 800 words."

So what's a writer to do? One thing is to learn how to write to suit current styles. We all live in a certain time and a certain place, after all, and if the norm is sixteen-page stories, there's no point in insisting on writing thirty-two pagers any more than insisting on seriously using mid-nineteenth century diction replete with *'tis, 'twere, ere long*, and *Alas!*

A second thing to learn to do is write novels instead of stories.

And a third thing is to learn how to write the kinds of novels that tickle the popular fancy. For example, there are some wonderful mystery and suspense writers around these days, and have been for years. I mean, they are good writers, good novelists: John LeCarre, P.D. James, Agatha Christie, Graham Greene, my son Walter Sorrells. In addition, we have to remember that during the Nineteenth century Thomas Hardy wrote his novels to make money as much as John Irving or William Styron or Ernest Hemingway in our own time.

Even so, we're all stuck with our own skins, as Robert Penn Warren put it, and you have to deal with the matter of your own soul—"the old verities and truths of the heart," as Faulkner said: "love and honor and pity and pride and compassion and sacrifice, without which any story is ephemeral and doomed." And Hardy, Nineteenth century novelist or not, was just as much on the mark when he said a writer needed to follow the "instinct for expression" that he most naturally responded to.

If this all sounds terribly negative and down, don't be deceived. We grab ahold of whatever silver we can when the clouds roll in, and the silver of the clouds I've been talking about is that a certain freedom keeps bubbling up through all the discouragement and frustration, through the anger and wrath I feel at people who, in my own doubtlessly skewed vision, dismiss me because they haven't found a convenient shelf to set me on. A good friend of many years' standing, for instance, a friend who has tried—and succeeded—to do good things for me on a number of occasions, let slip, after reading my book of stories, something to the effect that he didn't realize I had that kind of breadth of style and subject matter. It took a second for his mind to hear what his mouth had just said, and when it did, he stuttered out that he hadn't meant that—at least not in the way it sounded.

Well, he had too meant it, and meant it just exactly the way he'd said it, *it* being that he hadn't realized I was that good a writer. But I laughed, partly because I've always seemed to have the security of that freedom stirring around giddily in the mix of my various paranoias, fears, cowardices, doubts, famished visions, fallen hopes, errant passions, and all the rest.

I was a cheerful little boy, happy enough to be happy, helpful, and agreeable; willing to do the chores (but profoundly dismayed when others weren't willing to do theirs, too); assuming that people meant what they said; assuming that what people said was true; willing to take the world pretty much on its own terms. Bloody naive, I reckon.

Yet I also had a hefty, fearful sorrow in me, a dark side whose message was always, "Be careful: The world is a dangerous place, not to be approached without caution, not to be completely trusted." I was always frightened by meanness, scared because I didn't understand it, couldn't get a grip on the kind of anger that intentionally hated, deliberately hurt.

Too, as the fourth of four, it seldom occurred to me that there would come the days when *I* would be a senior in high school; when *I* would be a

On Breaking One's Pencil

big guy; that *I* could do all sorts of things that all the big guys could of *course* do because they were, well, BIG guys. Attitude, I reckon.

Nothing much has changed in all that, I don't think.

But that freedom bubbling up through the mix of rancor has let me be my own man in many ways: If I couldn't make a living as a fiction writer, well, then I could write what I wanted to write, too. If my characters were going to get me out of favor, well, then I could report on them honestly. If there was a question of style, well then I could be as galumphy as I wanted or as neat and clean and precise as I could get. In short, I could follow my own vision, no matter how limited it might be. I could be as true to my craft or sullen art, as Dylan Thomas put it, as I was artistically able to be.

So, to return, finally, to your question: Time has ravaged my knees, so I can't dance much anymore (not that I ever did, I have to admit), and that same beggar Time has also stripped my throat of the once pretty-nice voice I used to have, and I miss that, I miss that terribly.

Still, I dance in my heart and I sing in my soul. My dances are as graceful as waltzes, my steps as nimble as Astaire's, my body as beautiful as Baryshnikov's, and when I leap I soar so high and with such amazing power and grace I almost make myself cry.

I'm singing my own songs, too. They're a little sad, I suppose, but they're mine. They speak to me, and I gather they speak to a few others, too. Likely that's as good as it gets for a lot of us, and at that it's probably oceans better than it gets for most of us. In short, "I'm good," as they say up in Minnesota; "tolerable," as they may yet say back home in the South. In any event, I thank you for asking.

REDISCOVERING THE HUMANITIES

*(Originally created and produced for the
South Carolina Educational Radio Network,
and broadcast in June, 1981.)*

MANY YEARS AGO, WALTER LIPPMAN—JOURNALIST, columnist, advisor to and critic of presidents—wrote, "While it takes as much skill to make a sword as a plowshare, it takes a critical understanding of human values to prefer the plowshare."

Mr. Lippman's "critical understanding of human values" is, in a very real sense, what the humanities—at least at their best—are all about.

What I'm doing here is taking a brief overview of the humanities. But for just a minute, think of the humanities as a huge forest covering hundreds and hundreds of square miles. There are going to be many trails through that forest, many overlooks, many waterfalls, a vast array of plant and animal life. It would be impossible for any one person to know all of it fully. So I'm taking just one trail, but one which will afford some awareness of the infinite varieties of experiences available through the humanities, and one which I hope will offer a wider understanding of the many concerns humanists have.

…

Traditionally, we're talking about philosophy, religion, history, language, literature, and art. More recently such subjects as archaeology, jurisprudence, and the social sciences are included **when** archaeologists, jurists, and social scientists emphasize the historical or philosophical aspects and results of their work rather than the more technical methods involved in doing it.

I understand that by using *rediscovering*, I'm suggesting that the humanities have been misplaced or in some way lost. Without belaboring the point it may well be that humanists have lost touch with their roots and have lost sight of their aims in the pursuit of their increasingly single-minded scholarly preoccupations, with the result that our society—our culture—has also lost track of what it is and where it could be going.

To speak of "the humanities" is to speak of so many things. If our particular subject is literature, for instance, we can be talking about the social and intellectual history of the times in which a given writer lived. Or we can be talking about exhaustive critical analyses of a highly technical nature. Or we can be talking about interpretation, the meanings or implications of a given work that rise above the limitations of its own words. If we finally are able to read a poem or story so thoroughly that it has become a part of us rather than something different and outside us, then we have slipped over an edge, a boundary, a dividing line and find that our study of literature has become a study of our Self: of what is good or evil, right or wrong. In short, we are into philosophy—in one way or another. The same holds true for our study of all the areas of the humanities.

In a paper delivered before a symposium at Arizona State University, Frederick Ferre, Professor and Head of the Department of Philosophy and Religion at the University of Georgia, had this to say as he was working toward a definition of the humanities.

"*Quality* and *Value* are two intimately associated strands that run through all the…Humanities. Historians select their topics for research and show thereby their own judgments of significance and value…Philosophers wrestle with values in every corner of their field from logic…to metaphysics… Those who study languages, linguistics, and literature deal directly with the qualitative expressions of mankind…Archaeology…reconstructs the qualitative contexts of pre-historic interactions. Jurisprudence asks the hard value questions about the laws that undergird society itself. History and criticism of the arts are immersed…with the assessing of better and worse, success and failure, in the creative process. Ethics reflects on…good and bad…and the meaning of moral quality in life. And those who pursue studies in religion are dealing with…depths at which the qualitative becomes the sacred."

The Humanities, then, deal with values, and it is this emphasis on values that tends to be a line of demarcation between the humanities and any other discipline that is *not* one of the humanities.

Sadly, we so often live out our lives thinking in clichés and in caricatures—that is, in unexamined assumptions and in exaggerated, thus misleading, images. The humanities, or what we now would consider the humanities, were once central to our culture. It was what we now would call the humanities through which we perceived the world and how we felt about it and how we were to act in it. We understood that values informed all our decisions and all our actions—even as they do today. It's just that today we seem to have stopped recognizing that there can be no significant distinction between values on the one hand and data on the other. How else can this be stated? We *value* data. We *value* objectivity. We *value* quantifiability: The more a thing can be measured by objective, that is by unarguable, standards, the happier we seem to be. But the idea that values are values and facts are facts and never the twain shall meet, is an unexamined assumption.

For comic relief we can easily summon up an image of a philosopher coughing gently from the dust blown off some ancient tome buried deep in the inner sanctum of the library, safe from the eyes of normal people. There, our humanities scholar reads deeply in matters of no particular concern to anyone else, then writes stunning arguments in refutation of what he has just been reading—arguments which no one else will understand. Then he has his paper published in some arcane journal no one else would much choose to read. Until years later some other humanist, his mind sloshing, his brain awash with the trivia of the ages, comes across the paper and, in his own turn, reads on, reads on, deep in thought...

Well, the various subjects of the humanities *are* intellectual disciplines, and the subject matter *is* studied by scholars who, after all, are just people who have come to know a very great deal about subjects that interest them. And these scholars *do* often get quite detailed, *do* tend to spend a great deal of time in libraries, *do* develop a jargon that tends to exclude non-specialists, and *do* write papers in which they try to let others like themselves know what they have found out and what they think. But a danger we face is in confusing the pen-and-ink cartoon with the flesh and blood reality.

In 1981 The Southern Humanities Conference held its annual meeting at The Medical University of South Carolina, in Charleston. There, professional humanists—most of them college and university teachers—met to discuss the humanities through the usual method of reading formal papers.

A number of these papers were quite scholarly—they were being read to other professionals, after all—but what fascinated me was the fact that a *humanities* conference was being hosted by a *medical* university.

That fact set the tone for the entire conference, and it was, of course, quite deliberate, that effort to bring the humanities and at least one of the sciences together physically.

Most of the purpose of that year's meeting was to discuss the role or place or function of the humanities in the daily lives of us all. One of the difficulties faced by humanists is that what could be called their "products" simply are not visible in the same way as the "products" of a scientist or a technologist. For example, how many parents in this country now fear the coming of summer because they know that with the vacations and the picnics and the beach and the tans will also come that awful surge in the number of cases of paralytic polio? In the past twenty to forty years or so we have lost our fear of polio—and of smallpox and whooping cough and malaria and diphtheria—because those dreaded diseases for all practical purposes have disappeared from our land.

How? Basic scientific research including visually dramatic laboratories (long white lab coats, sterile masks, Bunsen burners, and all the rest), plus technical means of producing massive amounts of protective sera (also involving visually dramatic factories, miles of tubing, sterilizers, more people in white coats and masks), plus the technology of a highly sophisticated delivery system (vials full of serum, superb cartons for packaging, plus trucks, planes, hypodermic needles, smiling nurses, crying—but protected—children, etc.).

Or, if a community decides it wants to connect this piece of land to that one, a civil engineer can design and build a bridge to do it. The bridge is—in a highly visible and absolute way—*there*! It exists in fact. You can skin your knuckles on it and watch the blood rise.

But what can we see about the humanities? How does a professional humanist's knowledge of Buddhism or Neitsche or the probable sources of Chaucer's *Canterbury Tales*, or the figuring out of the puzzle of Pope's fragmentary satire *One Thousand Seven Hundred and Forty*, its lacunae, its allusions, and its implications for the political posture of Pope in the final years of his life—what do any of these have to do with us in our daily lives? After all, we drive our cars across the engineer's bridge, and we know well enough that we don't drop dead like flies from various plagues sweeping back and forth across our country.

A problem may well be that we get in the habit of expecting all things to act on us in the same ways. We should not expect the humanities to affect us the way that sciences and technologies do. Apples and oranges and bananas are nutritionally good for us, but if what we need in our diet is a great deal more protein, then we had better look to grains, eggs, dairy products, and meats. A missile carrying a hydrogen bomb is one thing. So is a footprint on the moon. Or an indoor flush toilet.

But a Galilean carpenter, his mind weighted, burdened with an idea of how people ought to act is quite another. So, too, is that fragile gossamer we call imagination which resulted in the dramas of Shakespeare—and the art of Michelangelo—and the vision of the Keplers and the Curies and the Einsteins and the Salks and the Marian Andersons of this world.

But who is willing to say that the former are "real" and therefore important, while the latter are not and therefore aren't?

What I'm going to do is start off inside the Academy, because most "professional" humanists earn their bread working as teachers. Then, I'll work my way back out.

...

During his luncheon talk in Charleston, Steven Weiland, of the Federation for Public Programs in the Humanities, said a number of things about the future of academic careers. Not only did he suggest there would be fewer jobs available, but he also pointed out problems of faculty morale stemming from vocational emphasis in curricula, lack of interest in humanities courses, frozen salaries, and lack of mobility.

> Who would dispute, for instance, Weblin's judgement in *The Higher Learning in America*, which came out just at the end of the First World War, that, as he says, "No one whose energies are not habitually bent on increasing and proving up the domain of learning, belongs legitimately on the university staff"?

> Most humanists have, in fact, remained loyal to traditional standards of teaching and scholarship, like Weblin's, and have declined opportunities through grants and otherwise, to undertake activities only marginal to the basic academic enterprise.
>
> Several factors now suggest, however, that fidelity to traditions of teaching and scholarship may not be enough to maintain the satisfactions of academic careers. The vocational emphasis of the undergraduate curriculum, the decline of student interest in humanities courses, along with the apparently declining capability of many of those who *are* interested, the near frozen salaries and the lack of mobility of those tenured in the profession, and of course the bleak prospects of those trying to get in or stay in—all these conditions mean that there are good reasons to feel frustrated and even angry about their circumstances.

Weiland then talked about how discouraged early Danforth Teaching Fellows were now that they were in mid-career, and he cited a former chairman of an English department in the South as saying that the "Youth"—both literally and figuratively—had gone out of the profession. Weiland continued by quoting further.

> It is in fact the isolation of English and the other disciplines from public life that has made these professions sad and solitary. We are paying, he says, a high price for having encouraged the brightest of the last generation to follow academic pursuits rather than to distribute themselves throughout the larger world that sponsors our centers of learning, creates the need for them, and provides the means. We reap the solitude of our island now, and we do not like the world unto itself that we have helped to make.

After quoting a passage from Erik Erickson's life of Freud (in which Erickson points out that a scholarly researcher's gathered facts eventually become a point of emotional involvement with the thing studied), Weiland concludes by quoting Erickson,

> "An adult studying a child, an anthropologist studying a tribe, or a sociologist studying a riot sooner or later will be confronted with data of decisive importance for the welfare of those whom he is studying. While the strings of his own motivation will be touched, sometimes above and sometimes well below the threshold of awareness, he will not be able for long to escape the necessary conflict between his emotional participation in the observed events, and the methodological rigor required to advance his field and human welfare.
>
> "Thus his studies will demand in the long run that he develop the ability to include in his observational field [this is what Erickson took to be the structure of Freud's career] his human obligations, his methodological responsibilities, and his own motivations. In doing so, he will in his own way repeat the step in scientific conscience which Freud dared to make."
>
> Well, if we are to proceed in our professions with a fully developed humanistic conscience, then we will see our studies in the same way as the subject of a social contract that makes their use and enjoyment a matter of public record.

Professor Edward Tucker, then head of the English department at East Tennessee State University, addressed the question of language and the necessity for *all* professionals to be able to understand the special intellectual contributions of other kinds of professionals. He spoke of the pitfalls awaiting those who grow further away from each other because they do not see the connection—the nexus," as he put it—between language and ideas, which should draw us closer together.

> Today, after decades of computer-assisted knowledge explosions in all fields, ultra-specialization within the professions, the enormous growth of bureaucracies which threaten to control if not overwhelm professional authority, these

divergent roads seem so far removed from each other that meaningful communication is virtually impossible.

Furthermore, if we do contribute a modicum of usefulness in this world, the sphere of usefulness begins to shrink to much narrower dimensions, and we discover severe limitations on our ability to discourse with the world at large about our achievements. As we progress, we gradually find ourselves locked into the prisons of our own expertise.

I would propose that the chief difficulty confronting us is a problem of communication.

The finer problem which so many professionals seem not to see is that a clear nexus exists between language and the ability to conceptualize, to the very nature of thought itself. An inability to discuss common human experience com-prehensively betrays a limitation on the individual's understanding of the realities he lives. And this incompetency beyond one's own sphere of discourse inevitably cuts the professional person off from his ability to share and participate in these experiences. It is insufficient to promote the study of language solely for its occupational benefits, because the unilateral flow of communication can only limit or dam the exercise of creative genius.

William Tribby, a dramatist and director of General Studies at the North Carolina School of the Arts, related his experiences working with the Tri-State Planning Conference which met in November of 1980. That conference came into being because a number of humanities teachers realized that they spent most of their classroom time teaching students who had virtually no prior interest in or plans to major in any subject of the humanities. More or less independently, they concluded that teachers needed to be more concerned about developing curricula, and faculty more closely attuned to the various professions that their individual schools were serving. Tribby spoke of their elation at realizing that each of them was not alone.

> What remains, persists, is an excitement born of discovering and sharing similar dreams and frustrations, of realizing that although each of us serves widely different publics, we are all working to integrate the humanities and humanists with the particular needs of a profession and its people. We are in unique environments which pay at least public allegiance to the essential importance of the humanities in the education of the young professional, that it is the implementation of this philosophy which truly tests and defines this allegiance. Most of all, we have realized that we can't remember having felt quite so excited at a gathering of fellow professionals.

Tribby then proceeded to list a number of central recommendations that grew out of the conference, ideas which marked the growing sense among many humanists that the humanities and the non-humanities need desperately to be recognized both by humanists and non-humanists alike as being part and parcel of each other.

> Provide strong, continuous humanities education to students preparing to enter professional/technical fields (whether these students are in medicine, law, engineering, the arts; whether they are being trained in high school, undergraduate, or graduate environments.)

> Exchange ideas regarding innovative curricula among the more traditional high schools, liberal arts colleges, and universities, and the professional/technical schools. (The last group has much to contribute to the others, especially considering the increased career orientation among "traditional" students.) Provide additional ways in which connections can be made between a variety of learners—public school children through adults.

John C. Guilds, then dean of the College of Humanities at the University of Arkansas, moved a little further in a similar direction when he quoted Robert Hutchens, the late president of the University of Chicago.

> "Thus, though the liberally educated person may be a specialist, he is at home in the world of ideas and in the world of practical affairs, too, because he understands the relation of the two."

It is precisely that relation between the two worlds, the one of ideas and the other of practical affairs that drew James Abbott, professor of Philosophy at the College of Charleston, into a project called Trident 2000. "The major focus of the academic humanist," said Abbott, "is in identifying the values issues and considering the fundamental concerns which arise when private rights and public needs are brought together, and when one considers the whole issue of growth in a community."

Abbott outlined the details of the Trident program which ultimately involved not only academic humanists, but city planners, health officials, and other "practical" people, including lawmakers.

> The major thrust of this project is to promote the direct interaction of all the various participant groups; to create dialogue among academicians, elected officials, residents in particular communities and subdivisions, administrative staffs of public offices, and representatives of private enterprise, and also other special interest groups.

Abbott then reported some of the hard questions that were and had to be asked.

> What sort of a community do we want to live in? What sort of a community ought we to have? How ought we to be involved in the affairs of what goes on? Ought the decisions that are made about land use, about growth, about progress: Ought these things be left up only to the elected officials and the policy makers? Ought it not to be the case that humanists themselves have something that they can say, and something that they ought to say, and something that they ought to have a chance to say?

Abbot concluded by asserting that humanists ought to leave their journals and library stacks now and again in order to bring their expertise to bear on those matters which directly affect human beings.

One who had done just that was Robert Watts, a humanities scholar with the Georgia State Legislature. He was part of a program designed to attach humanists to legislative staffs to help them deal with questions that are primarily values-oriented.

> Our training enables us to see connections between problems, and moves us to leap beyond the fragmentation inherent in the legislative process.
>
> Our training often tempts us to think that we can or should inject values into other realms. Such condescension will result in rude disappointment. We would do a much more important service by explicating and analyzing the values that already permeate that other realm.

Watts reminded us that to the classical mind politics was essentially a humanistic activity and that the framers of our own Constitution considered a humanist education to be proper preparation for public life.

> Placing humanities-trained people in a political environment is not so much an idea whose time has come, as it is one whose time has come again, a recovery of an older notion of politics.

Voicing that idea even more sternly was Robert Vaughan of the Virginia Foundation for the Humanities.

> We should not be asking whether the humanities have a contribution to make to the determination of public policy, but why—given 2500 years of tradition and experience—we should now consider the contribution faddishly innovative and at worst narrowly political and ideological.

...

For the most part, so far, I have cited humanists speaking to other humanists, saying what they are doing, what they're concerned about, and what more needs to be done.

But I want to turn now to people from outside—those non-"professional" humanists—to see what they say about being educated in the humanities.

Because the Southern Humanities Conference was held at the Medical University of South Carolina in 1981, it would be appropriate to hear from some medical people.

Dr. William Kniseley, then-president of the Medical University, in his welcoming remarks quoted from a statement which had originally been read at the opening of the third session of the Medical College of the State of South Carolina in 1826. The opening address that year was given by Dr. Stephen Elliot, a Broad Street banker in Columbia, South Carolina, who was the only non-physician on the original faculty. Though botany was only what might be called his hobby, Dr. Elliot had written a two volume, definitive study of the plants of South Carolina and Georgia. Dr. Kniseley quoted Dr. Elliot.

> It is to students that these observations are directed. The human frame, its structure and the derangement of that structure, its organs and the functions of those organs, will be your particular study.
>
> But man is not an isolated animal. He must be examined in relation to other beings and to the great system of nature. He is not only a physical, but a moral, an intellectual being, and his passions and his understanding as well as his muscles and nerves and bones must be the object of your investigations.
>
> In all of his dependencies, in his connection with material or immaterial systems, his affinities should be traced, and the more extended shall be your views, the broader and deeper your generalizations, the more profound and accurate and the more worthy of confidence will be your conclusions.

Dr. Kniseley concluded, "Now isn't that a remarkable statement?"

Also at the conference was Dr. William H. Hunter, a practicing physician and a member of the Hegel Society of America. Long interested in matters beyond the examining rooms of his private practice, Dr. Hunter often has been asked to serve, by interviewing applicants to the Medical University. Though he noted that these potential future doctors had higher and higher scores on their SAT and MCAT tests, he still had grave fears—not about the future of medical science, but about its practitioners.

> I think that professionals that are being turned out, that can be turned out under the circumstances that we talk about, are dangerous. They are not well educated people, these brilliant people. And what are we doing? We are taking the best and the brightest of a generation coming along every year. We're taking a big hunk of them in medicine and we're educating them *only* in the physical sciences. Only. These people, I say, are dangerous in the long run.

Echoing a similar concern was Teresa E. Christy, professor of nursing at the University of Iowa. Taking the position that the nurse should be an advocate for the patient, MS Christy elaborated on a hypothetical situation. She stated that she had a very fine speaking voice, and as a teacher used it to great effect in the classroom. "Suppose," she suggested, "that I should be diagnosed as having cancer of the larynx."

> I would refuse to have an operation that would make me voiceless. I would rather die. I would rather live for six months using my voice, than lose it to live longer. Teaching is my life. You're going to give me another twenty years and take away what is my life? I've never been dependent on anybody in my entire lifetime. I've done everything.
>
> But a physician would not understand all that. I ask my students, "Would you fight for my right to do that?"
>
> "Well," they'd all say. "We can learn so much from you. You can still write. You write so well."
>
> I don't want that. What I'm trying to illustrate is that there are times when a patient makes a decision based on something that is more important than living.

MS Christy asserted that nurses—in order to be patient advocates—needed more training in the humanities. To quote her again,

> The questions that are coming up today in medicine and nursing are ethical ones. Because the physician has greater knowledge in diagnosis and cure, does that also mean that he has concomitantly more knowledge on the ethical issues?

At the Shenandoah College and Conservatory of Music in Winchester, Virginia, there is a program designed by the nursing faculty to do just what Ms Christy was talking about. The aim was to do considerably more than merely add humanities hours to the nursing students' courseload. The object was *not* to lay on a thick gloss of culture. The nursing faculty itself insisted that there be at least one inter-disciplinary course.

Dr. Bruce Souder, at the time professor of humanities and chairman of the Arts and Sciences faculty, outlined the curriculum required, the nature of the course offerings, and the results.

A portion of the official aim of the course was to "include a seminar format establishing a milieu in which students, faculty-facilitators, and guests from other disciplines will be able to discuss broad topics of social, political, ethical, spiritual, psychological, and biological issues as related to the humanistic view of man and the health care delivery system."

> I can also say that, despite the fear often expressed by other humanists that cooperation with career fields will lead to "watered down" courses in literature for nurses or literature for businessmen, I have found that our students have developed a new interest in literature and philosophy.
>
> Finally, as a humanist among the nurses, I was not as much the fifth wheel on a four-wheel cart as I thought I might be. If there ever was any question in the minds of the students about my presence in their midst, they never openly expressed it. From the beginning there was free exchange among us. As a matter of fact, after the first class meeting, one of the students remarked, "I have a feeling we are going to understand one another as humans better than as professionals."

In addition to the medical profession, the world of business and that world which includes others professions as well, has been raising some concerns of its own. Professor Steve Goodman, of Boston University, has spent considerable time as a humanist with the business world.

> Let me now focus on whether it has been or should be suggested that business programs restructure the curriculum to include more coverage of liberal studies.
>
> The Rockefeller Commission's Report makes a comment that joint conferences be convened to discuss the kinds of preparation in the humanities that professional schools should have. I should note that one of the groups mentioned in the Report is the American Assembly of Collegiate Schools of Business, which is the subject-accrediting group in the field of business.
>
> Also, a recent report by the Association of American Law Schools concerning pre-law preparation, something that Association has never prescribed, indicated that "because of a general decline in the undergraduate degree requirements since the statement was made in 1953, law schools could no longer assume that students were getting adequate exposure to high quality liberal arts courses."
>
> Some people might argue that these recommendations for the restructuring of the curriculum came from academia and that business is holding everyone back. A recent survey of chief executives who are members of a group called The Committee for the Support of Private Universities indicated that more than three-fourths of them agree that corporate support should be given without interference in academic matters, "without strings attached."
>
> In addition, a recent *Business Week* article about the new crop of MBAs revealed that business finds graduates lacking in basic exposure including communications skills.

> Why does one have to wait to become a chief executive of a major corporation to attend liberal arts seminars at Dartmouth or Aspen or other places?

...

It would be appropriate at this time to hear from another group of humanists. I have cited teachers and people from the medical world and the business community. But humanism also includes the arts, and it should be interesting to hear what some more concerns of the humanists are.

Communication is clearly an important aspect of humanistic concerns: the ability of people in different fields of interest to be able to speak with each other and to understand what others are doing. But the late Ben Shahn—painter, print maker, muralist, mosaicist, and highly articulate spokesman for art—had a word of warning. In a speech delivered to the annual meeting of the American Society for Esthetics in November of 1953, he said,

> Communication, which has, no doubt, been the chief instrument of civilization, has also…become its curse. Some 20-30 years ago our great captains of communication discovered a certain hypothetical fourteen-year-old mentality that was supposed to be the norm of the public mind, and they have been assiduously addressing it ever since.
>
> This ideal individual is without moral conviction, without taste, without any critical capacity. Thus, presumably, any matter that is outside or above his intellectual level would be controversial and that might end in some major sales disaster.
>
> But in their earnest search for an ever and ever more common denominator, the wonderful communication systems have gone far toward *creating* just such a public as the one that they assume. And I think that one might deduce from that situation that *communication cannot be held as an ideal in itself.* There is always the *stature* of the thing communicated.

> The artist must operate on the assumption that the public consists in the highest order of individual; that he is civilized, cultured, and highly sensitive both to emotional and intellectual contexts. And while the whole public most certainly does not consist in that sort of individual, still, the tendency of art is to create such a public—to lift the level of perceptivity, to increase and enrich the average individual's store of values.
>
> Whether there exists some outside hierarchy of values in the light of which those of any given time, or of a nation, or of individuals could be judged true or false must, I suppose, always remain a moot question. But if there should be such a hierarchy of values, I believe that they could be (or have been) achieved only through an earnest search for truth—truth in the zone of politics; or of justice; in the realms of interplanetary space, or planetary affairs—truths of poetic perception; of spiritual matters; of art.
>
> Of course these truths themselves must alter with each new era of under-standing. But I believe that it is in a certain *devotion to concepts of truth* that we discover values.

In a similar vein, the late novelist Susan Sontag expressed her concern about what she called the "deterioration of literacy" in America. "People are constantly reducing literacy to communication and information," she told a group of educators meeting at Bard College in New York.

> The main tool of civilization is language. It is through language that we evaluate reality. As language becomes poorer and as people's ability to use language becomes poorer, we are simply in touch with less and less reality. We become literally less intelligent.
>
> This is the ultimate justification for anything we can do as educators to try to roll back all the forces that conspire to reduce literacy. Literacy has essentially and profoundly to do with the transmission of culture. Our sense of what

literacy is has been eroded because we are also losing our sense of culture.

In his book *The Zen of Seeing*, artist Frederick Franck moves toward another facet of the humanities. Franck had been feverishly preparing for a drawing workshop. Early in his relationship with his class, he had them sit on the ground and pick out something to stare at. The class ranged in age and experience from young to elderly, and from absolute novice to an experienced winner of local juried competitions.

He told them to find an object in nature and stare at it until, as he put it, "You are alone on earth with it." Then he told them to close their eyes for a few minutes, open them again, look back at their original subject, and draw it.

He wandered around making some quiet observations, then sat down to do some drawing himself.

> For a while I forgot about them, for I discovered a marvelously hairy caterpillar on a leaf. I could not resist it. At lunch my workshop decided unanimously to continue until dinner time.
>
> "Wonderful," I said. "And then let's have an exhibition tonight: but one that is strictly anonymous. Don't sign your drawings. You'll recognize your own and that is all that is necessary. No prizes, no honorable mentions! Arrange your drawings...then I'll go around and tell you what I see in them, then we'll have a general discussion about the experiment."
>
> A young woman asked, "Why am I so scared?"
>
> "Maybe you're afraid you're making a fool of yourself and that all the others are so much better! Or maybe it frightens you to be all on your own, without radio or TV, without talking. Alone in the world with your eyes..."

The humanities—at their best—help people be able "to be alone in the world with their eyes," as Franck put it. As others might put it, be alone in the world with themselves.

After relating the experiences of three prisoners of war—including Bruno Betelheim—and how they managed to survive with their sanity intact, Professor Malinda Snow, of Georgia State University, concluded her paper at the Southern Humanities Conference with,

> The humanities nurture the imagination and allow individuals to preserve themselves free and whole. As examples, I have considered the experiences of three prisoners, not because we or our students are likely to be prisoners, but because the lessons of the prison are valid for us, faced by lesser threats, depri-vations, and indignities.

Betelheim concludes,

> There is thus good reason to be concerned with what could be done to make it possible for all people to achieve autonomy through self-respect, inner integration, and a rich mental life, and the ability to form meaningful relationships. It is not because they might need all these desperately should they ever find themselves in an extreme situation, but because they need them all their lives. The resources we need in extremes are those we cannot afford to discard.

...

I started out with the suggestion that people in the humanities may well have been turning their backs on the rest of society and creating a kind of wonderful world of isolation for themselves. Such hermetic, totally self-contained worlds may exist with flawless perfection in mathematics, but not in the messy, day-to-day world of human beings dealing with human problems.

Then I related—in their own words, for the most part—how some humanists, disturbed by the image of splendid isolation, have attempted to re-think their own attitudes toward *their* own work so that it might more persuasively affect the work of other people's worlds. And I have cited people outside the humanities who honestly apprehend the need for humanists and non-humanists to recognize each others' interdependence and worth.

Still, to a very large extent that initial gasp of recognition of the force of the humanities is in those close, personal spaces of one's Self, where we must find our own ways before we can toss our nets out effectively into the wider, public world. But like bread cast upon the water, we always find that it has come back, is there at our centers, waiting.

While delivering a paper at an honors colloquium at Clemson University, Dr. Claire Gaudiani, then professor of French Literature and a fellow at the Humanities Research Center in North Carolina, related an incident involving her brother Vincent, a heart transplant surgeon. Professor Gaudiani's paper dealt with the need for what she termed "dual literacy"—the need for people to be able to understand both languages: that of the humanist and that of the scientist.

> Vincent is a person who has the kind of dual literacy I want to talk to you about…He's able to move easily from one kind of very specific science work he's doing and move back toward Yeats.
>
> When [my husband and our children] were there, (we spent last Christmas with them)…Vincent lost a patient Christmas morning. He came back from the hospital very sad. She was a very elderly lady. She was not a heart transplant patient, but a by-pass patient. It was just an unfortunate thing, but he lost her and he was very touched. And when he came back, he went into his study and closed the door, and was in there about an hour and a half.
>
> Then one of the children knocked and went in to get a toy, which distract-ed him. So he got up and went into the kitchen for something to eat, and I went into the room because we were sleeping in that room, and on his desk was an open copy of Yeats.
>
> When his scientific background, and all the know-how, and all the wonderful machines, and one of the most terrific installations in acute cardiac care had failed him, he had somewhere to go.

He was literate in another area that could bring him something else and make it better. And I think that is very important in maintaining our humanity.

...

When I was very young one of my favorite books was *Mother West Wind "Why" Stories,* by Thornton Burgess. In those stories old Grandfather Frog, who sat like a garrulous Buddha chug-a-rumphing on a lily pad in the pond, was the source of information about all the creatures in the forest. Peter Rabbit, a winsome if insatiably curious little fellow, was always hopping to the pond to seek out Grandfather Frog to get an explanation of the wonders and mysteries of the world such as, How the Chipmunk Got His Stripes, Why Peter Rabbit Couldn't Fold His Hands, Why Unc' Billy Possum Plays Dead, Why Mr. Snake Can't Wink, and so on.

Those stories—like Kipling's *Just So Stories,* which I also loved to read—were much alike in their format: a novitiate or Innocent of some sort, comes to a source of information to find out about the world. I seldom remembered any of the individual stories particularly. (Didn't the elephant get his trunk by misbehaving? Wasn't he warned *not* to go near the river because the crocodile might grab him and hurt him? But he did, and it did, by latching onto his nose and pulling and pulling until it was the great long thing we know today?)

What did come through to me was that all the people (or creatures) who wanted to learn went to the story teller, who was not only the poet, the bard spinning out the yarn, but also an old person—*Grandfather* Frog—who remembered the history of the creatures, and whose stories took an ethical, if not always quite philosophical, point of view.

That's how we learned what the world was all about and how we would be well advised to act in it: what was safe, what dangerous; what mean, what generous. It is the basic form of the Biblical parables, and it is the basic form used so often by Joseph Conrad, as Marlowe spun his stories through the dark nights.

In our own time, the storyteller—whether it is Grandfather Frog on his lily pad or a hissing snake in a cave or a bearded prophet in the desert or a hermit on top of a mountain—the story-teller, the humanist, is no longer

On Breaking One's Pencil

who we go to, to find out about things. The scientist or technologist, I suppose, now squats on the lily pad.

He looks vaguely familiar, but most of us have no idea what he's saying no matter how urgently he blinks and bloops and bleeps and blips at us. The problem, we sense, is not just that R2D2 has shoved Grandfather Frog off his pad, but that R2D2 still needs to be interpreted. Much as we may admire the fact of the little robot's existence, we should pay some heed to John Guilds who said, "Too much emphasis has been placed for too much time by too many people on the technology of how to do it and the well-intentioned belief that how to do it is more relevant to the needs of our society than understanding what should be done and why."

I like to think that the creatures of the forest are starting to rustle and stir about: that the creatures of the forest are starting to realize again that Grandfather Frog needs to be allowed back on his lily pad. It may well be that the creatures of the forest have needed—and *still* need R2D2 to tell them facts, to provide data—how Johnny Chipmunk *really* got his stripes.

But they also need Grandfather Frog to help them understand wherein those facts alone don't necessarily mean a thing until touched by the value and the quality of human experience—like Michelangelo's vibrant God in the Sistine Chapel, stretching himself toward the reclining, passive Adam to charge him into life with the awesome shock of humanity.

SOME THOUGHTS ON THE GEE AFFAIR

Revisiting a Recollection with Hopes For Something Approaching Tranquility

WHEN I WAS A TEACHER, I found myself avoiding department heads as much as possible, and certainly deans and presidents. Department heads looked at me either like I was getting ready to foment an insurrection of some sort (they may have had accurate intuitions along those lines) or that I was ripe for getting appointed to some dreary departmental task or other because they saw me before I could duck down some murky hallway to avoid them. Deans I saw seldom, because they were always busy doing their dean-y work, whatever that was. Presidents, though, lived almost completely in worlds of their own, coming out only for obligatory faculty/staff meetings and Homecoming Parades at football games or whatever.

A flap of a couple of years back, as presented by the *Wall Street Journal* in an article about E. Gordon Gee, therefore, left me more curious than outraged—either at his presumed perfidy or at the *Journal*'s presumed "hatchet job." I found out about the article in the first place from a long-time friend and fellow Vanderbilt University alumnus. He clearly was *not* a Gee fan (for reasons he did not elaborate on) but let that be known quickly, though with such pained nostalgia that I felt compelled to revisit the matter, wondering if others had been moved in that direction as well.

First, I'm thinking a little history here, and I may not have the details quite right any more, memory always being suspect. Around the early '60s when my wife and I left Nashville for our two years at the University of

On Breaking One's Pencil

Iowa, it seems to me that the organizational structure of the university had been changed. Harvey Branscomb was still chancellor, I think, but the role of president had been instituted. This was done because the work of governing such an institution had grown too heavy for a single person to bear. (I noted that Gee was referred to as "Chancellor," so I assumed he was not "President." That made me wonder if both positions still existed.)

In any event, it was done for a division of labor. The purpose was to have one person be responsible for the academic side of the University, while the other person was to be the "point man": the glad-hander, the back-slapper. The fund raiser, in short. That gave the University what can be thought of as an inside man and an outside man. So organizationally the Academic head ran all things relating to faculty, staff, departments, colleges, schools, hiring, firing, promotions, etc.—and probably the public relations/news and information division.

That left the outside man to raise the money needed to pay for all the good stuff the inside man wanted to do. So he doubtless also had the Development Office directly under his wing along with a PR staff of his own, which would have to include a heavy, heavy presence of publications folks. Clearly this is a beautiful idea. Clearly it ought to work like a charm. "He works his work," Tennyson has Ulysses say of his son Telemachus, "I mine."

All the same, it seemed to me that there was essentially a built-in conflict in that kind of organization. As an old bromide has it, "When two men ride the same mule at the same time, only one of them can sit in front." So is that going to be the inside man or the outside man?

Even 'way back when I worked for the Development Office, there was considerable friction between the Main Man there and the Main Man in the Information and Publications Office. Some of it may have been personalities (one the handsome, well-proportioned, elegant, pipe-smoking, tweed jacket-wearing, conservative-appearing fellow; the other a big ole Arkansas country boy who didn't try to camouflage his twang or his rough hide or how his clothes looked sort of thrown on). Some of it may have been the insider versus the outsider. I also finally suspected that a lot of it was that they had totally different attitudes toward the means used to foster, develop, and nourish an incipient "Great University."

For example: In 1978 the Information and Publications Office developed—at some expense, I imagine—a pretty nice hard-bound book entitled

The Vanderbilt Campus: A Pictorial History. It was a lovely and interesting piece, mailed out to nearly all alumni, I think, many of whom, I expect, delighted in it and still have it out on a coffee table somewhere in a basement game room or whatever. But a legitimate question was, "What was it for?" If it was "to do something nice for our alumni," I expect it was a success, but if it was to raise money, I expect it was a bust. As I recall, there wasn't even a return envelope inside with a request for an additional donation to what was then called the Living Endowment.

The Development Office sent out direct requests for money, with cunning and beautifully written pamphlets, etc., setting out the "Vanderbilt urgently needs..." pieces (many of which I worked on.) Here, happily, I must say that I greatly admired and learned much from **both** men.

In short, there's room for a lot of bad feelings when a new kid barrels into town, sets up shop, makes a lot of demands (as well as making "important" friends), gets what he wants, then—seemingly to rub salt into the gashes he's opened up—gets the job done because he's just plain old damn good at knowing how to do it. And smiling all the way, of course. Amusing folks by making his bow tie wiggle? No matter. One just does have to admit that adding one BILLION dollars to the coffers over a six-year period has to be considered a pretty successful piece of work for a fund raiser. That's one hundred sixty-six and two/thirds MILLION dollars a year for each of six years.

That's one way of looking at this.

...

Now, here I would like to include "**Sorrelli's**" **Personal—Though Not *Totally* Private—Rant,** having mainly to do with higher education in these here United States mostly during the Sixties and Seventies, some of the results having been relevant in my own mind to the topic of Mr. Gee.

However, I've reduced it extensively, limiting myself to my conclusions without much in the way of my supporting reasons,

...

More and more, "education" has come to mean technical training. Not only that, but the new absolutes in attitudes created a new dichotomy: school was either boring or entertaining (the logical error of the occluded middle is too often present in public discourse.) So the teacher's primary job was to make learning "fun."

The idea that you had to **know** certain things now before you could **do** certain things later, and that everything would be a chaos of mystery until you got to that point is a concept apparently lost to educational pedagogy. In my field, what that meant was that language would always be a stumbling block to most young people, but never a building block.

The attitude I saw so much, was the sense so many students impart that they *deserve* something simply because it's there. I see it as a TV issue: They've been raised on ads that say they *deserve* that fancy car; they *deserve* that trip to Hawaii; they *deserve* that six-pack of beer. So now they *deserve* an A or a B because they've bothered to sign up for the class.

Some of this came about during the '70s when colleges had to start hustling to get stu-dents: Severe economic downturns forced many parents to start looking at Duke instead of Harvard, Furman instead of Duke, Clemson instead of Furman, the University of Iowa instead of Coe, Rochester Community College instead of Winona State, etc. The result was that colleges with huge bills (faculty retirements as well as salaries, mortgages, and dangerously long-deferred maintenance and upkeep on vast physical plants—not to mention skyrocketing line item costs for campus security—etc.) called in market people who began their standard processes of research which included targeting potential markets (formerly called students), in order to "sell" the college, and all the rest. Much of that resulted in college administrators who forgot what the academic missions of their schools were, forgot that "selling" education was not a business in the same way that selling cars, RVs, PCs, and municipal bonds was. The marketing terms seemed to fit, but administrators then confused the metaphors *consumer* and *product* with the real thing: students and education—the seekers and the knowledge they were presumably seeking.

Novelist Susan Sontag once talked about her concern for what she called the "deterioration of literacy" in America. "People are constantly reducing literacy to communication and information," she said. "As language becomes poorer and as people's ability to use language becomes poorer, we are simply in touch with less and less reality. We become literally less intelligent."

Much of this winter of my own discontent, certainly, is the realization that time has passed or is passing me by in certain regards. That's not a happy thought. But it's not only that. Yeats's question from his poem "The Second Coming" haunts me more and more: "And what rough beast, its hour come round at last,/ Slouches towards Bethlehem to be born?" Scarily, I'm afraid that rough beast has long-since arrived.

...

Which gets me back to Gordon Gee and the *WSJ* article.

Gee was a fund raiser. More and more, the nation's academic fund raisers are vitally important to their colleges and universities. Part of this has to do with the loss of Federal and other types of funding. Grant money has tended to dry up—NIH, NSF, NHA, NEA—the whole panoply of alphabet organizations that came into being after WW II and during the ensuing Cold War.

College presidents have always been in the position of having to get money for their schools. Even the presidents of state colleges and universities have to go to their state legislatures (hats in hand) to beg, borrow, or steal additional funds, and the issue comes up every election time. To fund or not to fund? To increase funding here and cut it there, or vice versa? The tales about Vanderbilt's Chancellor Kirkland abound—about how he would go a-visiting to whatever neighborhood was appropriate and pound on the door of some deceased department head's poor widow and demand she give him a thousand dollars for Vanderbilt University. And though Harvey Branscomb deservedly had the reputation of not being able to remember any-body's name, he **did** manage to remember the names of the folks who were responsible for dispensing the Ford Foundation's largesse.

Well, it's become more sophisticated these days, of course. It was sophisticated enough back during the $30,000,000 Capital Gifts Campaign that I worked on in the very early Sixties. But the amount of money being gone after now is astounding—to me, at least.

So, a question: How much should a chancellor or president make when he's dealing with such vast sums? Lots of profit-making companies are trying to get a handle on that these days, too. Common sense might suggest a percentage of gross sales. I don't know, because I don't think in businessmen's terms. But what is a reasonable income for the chancellor of Vanderbilt University, which has no gross sales? And if there are no gross sales because there is no "product," and it was true that he was getting an annual bonus, what's that bonus based on? What else can it be based on and paid from other than the amount of money he's brought in?

After going back over the *WSJ* article some more, it struck me that putting Gee in a big house with lots of party space made sense. I assumed that in all of the five schools he had previously headed, the schools maintained ownership of the properties he was housed in. If so, then Gee made nothing on the real estate deals—except, of course, that he was never out any money in an initial property purchase and didn't have to worry himself about re-sale when he left town.

As for being on the boards of five corporations? That could suggest he had a lot of time to spare, and that he might have spent it more fruitfully for Vanderbilt than he had—but then I have to go back to that billion-dollars-in-six-years figure and assume that some or even many of his contacts from those other boards ended up making donations to VU in one way or another.

Then, what has he done with those donations? I don't know, but from what I had read he's done well with Women's Studies, Black Studies, Blair School of Music, interdisciplinary research, etc. Not to mention that he did whatever he could to rein in the athletics by insisting they be part of the University, too. Also, about that same time, I saw that Peabody got a $10,000,000 grant to study the effectiveness of various teaching programs. I also saw that a member of the faculty got a MacArthur "genius" award for whatever he was working on.

But a lot of the *WSJ* article seemed to be questioning Gee's "flair," I guess you could say. Seemed to be suggesting that he was really pushing the envelope of what was "appropriate" behavior and what was not. I personally wouldn't know what to do with a private chef, but it does sound like fun having one around—as long as I don't have to clean up the kitchen after him. And his wife's lowering the flag to half-mast when Bush was re-elected was an act that many of us felt right at home with, though the complaints about it sound more like catty neighborhood gossip sort of stuff than anything else.

However, if the state of Tennessee had outlawed the use of pot—even for legitimate medicinal purposes—then she shouldn't have used it. "Caesar's wife must avoid even the *appearance* of wrongdoing," or however Shakespeare phrased it.

So a lot of what's been going on in a how-the-money-has-been-spent kind of way, looks to me like the VU Board ought to have been taking more hits than the Chancellor in that it wasn't doing what it ought to have been doing all along. I've been on a board before (nothing so posh or elegant as the VU Board, of course) so I'm aware that they can be organized in various ways. Some run the whole show (even down to arguing about what kind of soup should be served in the dining hall on Thursdays—[honest!]). Others understand that what you need to do first is to decide what kind of person you want to run the place, and what you want him to do; then get yourself the best such person available; then stand back and let him run the show. If you can't or don't trust him to do that, then you ought not to have hired him to start with.

That means to me that the VU Board really needed to get to work looking at how it might need or want to revise its own by-laws. But that's pretty tricky, too. You really *don't* want to get into micro-management. On the other hand, if people are elected to the Board pretty much solely on the basis of how much money they can (or are expected) to give the University, then there's a real problem. I gathered that way too many of the Board members didn't have a clue as to how much money was being committed to whom and to what and for how long.

Also, it seemed to me that having forty-four board members for an entity no bigger than Vanderbilt University is a good way to get into trouble—that kind of trouble—because I would wonder what the specific duties are for each of the members. If the members don't have particular areas of expertise or concern or responsibility, then why are they there? Sounds like fund raising again.

All of which suggested to me that if there were an "image" problem in all of this, it belonged to the Board's failure to perform what typically is a board's oversight responsibilities, at least as much (if not more) as it belonged to the Chancellor's penchant for living a high-on-the-hog life-style. After all, I expect that if most of us asked for the moon we'd take it if tendered, as long as we convinced ourselves it was legal to do so.

Unconscionable is another matter, of course, but what's unconscionable to one can be totally conscionable to another. "Pornography is a matter of geography," many of us loved to point out in our randier days, but why should a significant income and lots of the perquisites of the good life **ex**clude

On Breaking One's Pencil

academicians (and ministers who don't make out on TV) and **in**clude only doctors, lawyers, merchants, and chiefs?

On the other hand, it is always prudent to remember and ever note that Money and Power waddle and grunt their ways along Life's Path snout by snout: Power attracts Money; Money buys Power. A sweet merry-go-round. In recent times we need only remember the names of Abramoff, DeLay, Enron, Madoff, etc. So the beat goes on…and on and on.

I did quote Yeats earlier, and it is certainly possible that Gee and people like him are indeed the "rough beasts." If there has come to be no difference intellectually, ethically, aesthetically, or spiritually between *student* and *consumer*, *learning* and *product*, *sage* and *fool*, then my highly redacted rant in the section before this one may have cut pretty close to the bone, come pretty close to the heart of "the Gee Affair."

...

I don't know that any of this has dealt at all with the concerns my friend had about "the directions [in which Gee] is taking the school," because I didn't know what he saw those directions to be or how he would have redirected things. Further, I was unsure about his plaint that "the character of the school that we knew" was changing. It was always changing. Just a list of some very *minor* matters: We went from a quarter to a semester system; we went from fall rush in the freshman year to a sophomore rush period; fraternities and sororities were once very popular and powerful, now less so; we went from only one major and one minor to split majors and minors; we saw new classroom and dormitory buildings, new dormitories filled; stiffer entrance requirements; we bought Peabody; we got Blair; the Art Department became pretty good, with art holdings that were also okay.

In the same vein, my first teaching job was at Murray State College, which had begun life as Murray State Normal School, and now has become Murray State University. Clemson University started out as Clemson Agricultural College, South Carolina's land-grant college and a military academy just like Texas A&M or VPI used to be, and now proudly points to its new Phi Beta Kappa chapter. Memphis State College morphed into Memphis State University, and now into the University of Memphis. Change is endemic to life. In that regard, I have had my own Vandy devils to deal with.

But I'll close by sharing a little incident that happened to me during our second go-around in Clemson.

We were living in a vermiculite house ("wave of the future" construction) which I had not-so-lovingly (but pretty accurately) nicknamed the Roach House. It was owned by a retired mechanical engineering professor at Clemson. He was there one day checking out the thermostat/furnace, etc. We were chatting about one thing and another and during the conversation he mentioned that some friends of theirs who had lived in his same neighborhood years earlier had returned to Clemson to retire. After they had been back for a while, the woman noticed that their house in the old neighborhood where all their children had played and grown up together was on the market and she was begging her husband to please *Please!* buy it for her, that she was so homesick for that house.

"I told him," my landlord said to me, "don't you dare buy her that house. She isn't *home* sick. She's *time* sick. And those times can never come back."

Selah!

BOB DOLE AND THE MARCH OF TIME

A Reflection
"What's Past is Prologue"

I READ AN ITEM IN the Minneapolis *Star Tribune*, just less than a week before the 1996 presidential election. It quoted from a *Newsweek* article about Don Sipple who had been Bob Dole's media strategist before getting canned during the closing weeks of that campaign. *News-week* apparently quoted Sipple as saying, "[Dole] is a very good, very decent man. Noble. But my inescapable conclusion is that his clock stopped in the late 1950s, or early 1960s."

The *Star Tribune* article went on to quote Sipple: "[Dole] thought the presidency was a reward system and he was next in line for the ring."

And still further on, in connection with Sipple's view that Dole probably wouldn't have been a very good president, he mentioned Dole's "obsession with self-reliance."

I'm a Democrat myself, born a month and a half before Roosevelt was elected to his first term; born in the heart of the Great Depression (though our family wasn't directly affected by it); born into a newspaper family with a goodly couple of lawyer/judges in it; born nonetheless, apparently, an elitist Populist. I don't have much truck, in other words, with Republicans, as a general rule, though most of my friends from years ago at college and at least half my family helped swell their ranks. Also, what I remembered about Bob Dole was that for many years he seemed to be mainly a party hack willing to be the hatchet man for those who really ran things on his side of the Senate aisle. He was no Joe McCarthy, to be sure, but I always sensed either that he didn't have the imagination or that he didn't have the stomach for the kind of random, loose-cannon carnage McCarthy created, though he might not have been all that squeamish about the results.

Still, one thing early in Dole's '96 campaign struck a terribly sensitive node in me, and that was when he said, "My generation has one more mission before we're through."

It was a reference to the Second World War, of course, a war I claim even though the one I was drafted to fight in was the Korean "Police Action," as the euphemism of the time had it. Even though I served during the Korean War (luckily for me not *in* it)—got drafted out of college for it—I was still more influenced, I think, by the other one. My oldest brother was a lieutenant, a paratrooper in the 82nd Airborne, was under fire in Italy, was jumped into combat in southern France on D-Day, and later was hustled into the breach as a reserve for duty during the Bulge, etc. My brother-in-law, also a soldier, a PFC, though probably mustered out a corporal, saw combat on Okinawa among other blooded dots in the South Pacific. With two wartime marriages in our family, then, plus a father who probably shortened his life with a stint in Washington organizing the press division of the Office of Censorship, all that was war enough to last me a lifetime.

So when Dole spoke of his generation and one more mission, I responded with a peculiar emotion.

...

Bob Dole, as we all know, served honorably as an officer during the Second World War, was terribly mangled by enemy fire, and essentially given up for dead. Rescued at the eleventh hour, he underwent operations, physical therapy, and all the rest, living the remainder of his life clutching a pencil or a rolled piece of paper in his maimed right hand so people wouldn't try to shake it, shaking hands being a hallmark—if not an intolerable habit—of politicians and lawyers.

One more mission. It would be hard for someone with a well-honed sense of duty, someone who had spent much of his life as a "good soldier" doing what had to be done even if it meant effacing himself, taking himself away from his own desires and needs, to fault Bob Dole in that direction, the direction of one who puts himself into the breach yet one more time.

On Breaking One's Pencil

Still, a military mission usually is devised by people other than those who rise up from their foxholes with their M-1s (or M-16s) at the ready to charge with fixed bayonets across the fields, up the hills, over the waters as they face the fire of the enemy. An old Army field manual—FM 22-5, as I recall: *Leadership, Courtesy, and Exercise of Command*—said the mission of the United States Army was "to seek out and destroy the enemy."

Second lieutenants don't devise such missions. Second lieutenants don't even get consulted about such missions. Such missions are too big, too grand, too sweeping and all-inclusive. What second lieutenants do is pretty much what PFCs do—obey orders. Granted they get to give some, too, but never on the grand scale. So who does? The answer is deceptively simple, I'm afraid. The citizens who vote administrations into office do.

The real question to me is who gives a man a mission to run for the presidency of the United States? Senator Dole took it upon himself to become president. He devised the idea of mission for himself, attributing it to his entire generation as though that generation had, in effect, been commanded by a Greatly Superior Authority to do its bidding. And what was that bidding? What was Bob Dole, senator (or former senator) from Kansas, bidden to do? To seek out and destroy an enemy? If so, who was that enemy? And, if named, how were they to be destroyed?

What a horrible image, yet how reminiscent of president Nixon with his Enemy's List. Nixon was always a man who saw enemies to be destroyed rather than opponents to be out-researched, out-argued, out-thought, out-voted, or even out-conscienced. What a terrible thing it is to see your countrymen as people who must be destroyed because they disagree with your vision of the world.

Don Sipple suggested another interesting military comparison, though. Dole would have been a good, old-fashioned (1920s, 1930s) peacetime officer. Advancement was slow, requiring you to wait your turn. Because troop strength stayed at a pretty constant level, virtually no one was promoted until someone of higher rank had retired or died. Then, according to your date of commission (among some other things), it was your turn to move up the ladder a bump—not ignoring, either, that military promotion could be highly political, as in the natural attraction of political parties to media-hyped war heroes, or as in whether you got your commission from West Point or from the ROTC unit at some East Jesus Tech.

(It's impossible not to wander into this mine field of military imagery, because so much of it was continued from the '92 election by Dole himself as well as by other of the more hard-nosed rightists who insisted on taking umbrage at President Clinton because he never fought in a war and thus, presumably, never killed anyone [along with Dan Quayle and numerous other young men of that period who figured they had too much at stake in their lives to risk getting splattered into the jungle muck from combat in Viet Nam fighting a war that not only most in this country never understood, but one the South Vietnamese themselves seemed morally underwhelmed by, and one which nearly tore our own nation to shreds.] Think about the entire drug culture, for instance. That war, as the Korean War before it started to become, was like most wars, as the old bromide has it: a rich man's war and a poor man's fight. Much also was made of the fact that Clinton had to take lessons on how to salute properly, and once, I heard, someone was reduced to the desperately snide remark that Dole, at least, had *earned* the salutes he got from the attending Marine escorts or whomever.)

In any event, Sipple's remark about Dole's thinking it was simply his turn now—that he had put in his time and had all the credentials you were supposed to need and certainly all any-body else had ever had, not to mention all the political (not military) favors done that should be getting called in—may have something to do with his suggestion that Dole had gotten "stuck" in time, that something serious had happened to him somewhere along the line.

It's a sad thing, and it happens to many of us. It isn't always that people get stuck in time, though. Often, perhaps, it's a matter of time having sped up in such geometric ratios that we simply *can't* keep up with it. It passes us by. We are out of time, and, like a soldier at close-order drill who is out of step, we trip and stumble, our feet getting in each others' ways, our legs splaying awkwardly, and there seems to be nothing in the world we can do to get back in step. Perhaps our timing wasn't really good in the first place. Perhaps there were other matters we paid more attention to. Perhaps we were outstanding on the firing range. But there at parade, passing in review, we were so out of step that everyone could see how spastic we seemed, how removed from what everyone else apparently understood so well how to do.

"[H]is clock stopped in the late 1950s or early 1960s."

On Breaking One's Pencil

What was going on those days? Male college students had a reputation for wearing buttoned-down collars a neck below their buttoned-up minds. Campuses had lots of panty raids. Young ladies then wore fluffy sweaters, loafers, white socks, and pearl necklaces. Senator Joe McCarthy was proclaiming over and over and over that he had a list of hundreds of names of communists who were in the state department, (yet how many were ever brought to trial and convicted?) And no one, apparently, ever saw the list on the scrap of paper he kept waving around. The House Committee on Un-American Activities (HUAC) held hearings all across the country accusing (though almost never charging) all kinds of people with being Com-Symps, Fellow Travelers, Communists, anti-American, and on and on, convicting no one of anything illegal within their major charges, but nonetheless ruining reputations by what came to be known as "guilt by association," until one elfin-looking lawyer at a Senate Committee meeting investigating some of these issues finally asked the senator from Wisconsin, "Senator, have you no shame?" And with that, the name of Joseph P. Welch was praised after which Joseph McCarthy more or less soon died, after having asked, apparently with sincerely innocent confusion, "What have I done? What have I done?" like a twelve-year old boy who has been found out to have thrown rocks through numerous windows on numerous occasions of numerous people's homes, churches, and places of business.

What else?

Particularly during the early Fifties, colleges were still filled with returned veterans, re-shaping educational attitudes about classroom protocol and values in a way no one had ever done, an attitude, it seems to me, which later—during the Viet Nam era—was debauched into a brutal and mindless parody of itself that flipped education into a maelstrom from which it had just barely begun starting to recover.

Otherwise, people who could never have thought about the possibility before were going to college; Americans were still filled with the euphoria of having won another World War; we were clearly the most militarily powerful nation that had ever been; there was a sense that with the Marshall Plan, NATO, and all the rest, there was nothing we couldn't do if we simply wanted to; that what we wanted to do was what ought to be done because, well, we could do it. Life was pretty good, in short . . .

...until the clouds of the '20s and '30s proved they hadn't blown away at all, that after a war is done, the old horrors—needing always an enemy, a "them" to blame for everything that might go wrong—come back: commies, niggers, kikes, (now joined by Muslims and Mexicans), and other sorts of troublemakers who want a piece of the pie. Oh my, they hadn't been vanquished at all, and then it was time to get back to the real business of the country—making it safe for all the people it had always been safe for.

Spoiled by victory and softened by wealth, America became politically stunted as well by focusing for forty some odd years on one thing—an anticommunism foreign policy that effec- tively prevented us from having a foreign policy at all. It forced us into supporting some of the cruelest, most vicious and brutal tyrants of the 20th Century (some now still in power) in the name of this anti-communism; it required that we see any kind of diversion from a given line of thought as anti-American; it slam-dunked a generation of Americans through a hoop of single-issue mentality; it resulted in refusing to understand that keeping a Mississippi "nigger" from voting was a threat to the rights of every person of color in the nation; and it allowed a generation of politicians and highest level law enforcement officers like J. Edgar Hoover to proclaim that anyone who wasn't born in a certain place but who disagreed with how things were being done—a person born in Philadelphia, Pennsylvania, say, who went to Philadelphia, Mississippi, on a bus—was nothing but a lawless outside agitator.

Was Bob Dole stuck in the late fifties? Probably, or at least quite likely—even in the late forties. He seemed stuck in something during the '96 campaign: stuck in the Second World War, stuck in the horror of his life there, stuck in his recovery, stuck in the power as well as in the glory, trying his best, perhaps, to Take America Back—always *Back*, it seems, always away from the less innocent cares of adulthood, *Back* to the more innocent remembrances of youth.

Taking America Back is a double entendre, of course: Take It Back *from* those who, Dole might have perceived, had taken it away; and Take *it* Back *to* an earlier time.

Those times were filled with hate, fear, and arrogance—as in the question, "Who Lost China?" as though China had been ours to lose. That whole era was interesting, too, because it was a classic example of slaying the bearer of bad news, in that case the "China Experts" who told our government that Chaing was going to get his ass wiped out by the communists. They were right, of course, but there had to be a devil, (not to forget Reagan's Evil Empire, certainly, as well as the second Bush's Axis of Evil), had to be someone at fault. There had to be someone to blame. It wasn't good enough to consider the possibility that the times they were a-changing, and to try to get on top of the times. It was a time when—in a very real sense—all our clocks stopped ticking for about forty or so years—until the Berlin Wall fell apart in as beautiful an objective correlative or symbol as any T. S. Eliot or aspiring English-Studies graduate student could ever have imagined for the world.

...

Hillary Clinton is probably as socially, politically, and professionally ambitious a climber as anyone who has ever bothered to stalk the corridors of power or rub up against it any time they had a chance. But during the '96 campaign or thereabouts, she came out with a book entitled *It Takes a Village*, the point of which dealt, as best I remember from reading at a couple of reviews, with the nature of community and how children become socialized by societies.

I can't speak to the virtues of the writing or the impact or freshness of the book's vision because I have never read it—as I suspect Mr. Dole had never read it, either, when he excoriated it at the Republican convention by saying, "It doesn't take a village to raise a child. It takes a *family!*" At that buzzword, which trivialized the whole concept of *family* as we have come to know it (as buzzwords always trivialize what they purport to uphold and promulgate), the convention cheered roundly and soundly with a vigor born not only of desperation but of a smallness of understanding, as well as a meanness of spirit.

What the Republicans were attempting to do, of course, was to retain their appropriation of the term *family*, as though they had invented the concept and structure themselves, which, patently, they had not. Never mind that the family as we know it is historically a fairly recent development, just as the idea of children being children rather than small adults is pretty new, too. What they wanted (and what the Democrats to their disgrace kept aping) was the idea of Family Values.

Family Values quickly became another buzz phrase used mainly as a concept to oppose the idea that homosexuals, as one example, were real human beings whose identities were not totally driven by their sexual "orientation" any more than were their wants, interests, hopes, aspirations, and talents, not to mention their political preferences.

The whole nasty idea of appropriating concepts such as Family, God, Americanism, Love of Country, Desire for Personal or Spiritual Growth, etc., so that if one simply doesn't believe the way some politician believes (or says he believes, depending on how deep the pockets of his supporters and how deep his belief in the national clout of those particular supporters) then you are ipso facto *anti*-family, *anti*-American, *anti*-Country-God-Decency, and all the rest. This is the ploy of a spoiled child ("Gimme what I want or I'll know you don't love me and I'll hate you,") or of a rotten man, ("If you really loved me you'd *do* it!") which, sadly, seems to work over and over no matter whether the source is Republican, Democratic, Ross Perotistic, or what. It has been around, I suspect, for as long as there have been rulers (leaders don't need to be nearly so blatant) who have had to depend on the good will of a constituency, even if that constituency didn't have any votes in the matter. (An angry enough populace armed with pitchforks, scythes, and their pressed mass flowing toward the royal palace like a wild Vesuvian stream quickly constitutes a formidable body of opinion.)

...

I want to get back to the business of villages raising a child, for a minute.

The old word is *Community*. People lived in communities. In many cases they lived in close proximity for safety. Then there was a collective work force involved, too: Many hands make for light work, or whatever. Also, someone has to raise the children, whether it's the 1990s or the 9990s BCE. The females, being the ones who bore the fetus as well as the ones who lactated, tended to be around the small ones more than the bigger men who, being stronger if not wiser or particularly more enduring, tended to see to the foraging for food, the defense of the compound, or the raids against others' compounds to drag back some additional women to jack up the local gene pool.

We know all this. We know this about the hunter-gatherers—that they needed to cooperate with each other to help themselves live. We know this, and we know it was going on in various forms ages and ages before people developed agricultural societal models. We know all this.

Closer to our own times a community was a whole set of communities all of them touching, abutting, crossing areas with many of the rest. A family was one community; it existed in an area (on a street) with other families; they, in turn, lived in a larger area we'd call a neighborhood with a number of streets; and they, with other neighborhoods, in an even larger grouping called a section of town; and so on until there even came to be nations that seemed to have some sense of community—in language, religion, race, and in all sorts of ways—so that it was possible to draw them all together, more or less, in times of large urgent needs like wars, floods, or huge financial depressions.

And again, we know all this. With all the programs from the federal government down, or from local street-wise initiatives up by black or Hispanic mothers who've had it with drive-by shootings and drugs and all the rest, we know that unless the children are tended to by the genetic family *and* the extended family *and* the neighborhood adults they get into trouble. Bad trouble. We know this. Not only is it common sense, but there are still some places where it works, where a child is openly reprimanded by an adult if that adult sees that child involved in some in-appropriate or unacceptable activity. There was a time when a parent would tell a child that if he got into trouble at school that would be just the beginning of the trouble he'd get into at home because of it.

Community. People in life together. People cooperating to help each other so they them-selves are better off. Remarking on the bromide that charity begins at home, Aesop is supposed to have said, "Most people are kind to their neighbors for their own sakes." That's what we call enlightened self-interest. So? Why not?

There's nothing new there. We know all this already, so what was Bob Dole's point? What was the point of the Republicans' nastiness about the village raising children?

What it had to do with was a lack of vision, not just on Dole's part, but on the part of this entire nation, I'm afraid. Politics has always managed to bring out the worst in people—we all know this, too. At election time those who are *In* want to *Stay In* (even those who rant about term limits want to stay, though surely just long enough to make certain some sort of term limit—other than elections, of course—is made law), and those who are *Out* want to *Get In*. The result is partisanism at its purest. That wouldn't be so bad if it were all done in good fun—playing the game and all that. But when people take these non-issues so seriously, then great damage can be done.

The rise of the one-issue candidate, for example, is probably the greatest and most dangerous manifestation of a lack of community this country has seen in ages. It is a manifestation that says, "Only I am right, and if you don't agree with me, then I will do my utmost to destroy you or at least to keep you from getting much of *any*thing you might want." It refuses to accept that there are good people, intelligent people, who have deep and abiding commitments to ideas which happen to be different from our own; that refuses to accept the need to talk to those peo-ple so they can understand each other—really and truly know what those who disagree with us *are* saying, rather than what we *assume* they are saying (or *say* what they are saying). It is an unwillingness to cede anything, an unwillingness to accept our differences so we can commune and, in the best sense, communicate with each other. It is a matter of an unwillingness to place ourselves into a larger frame, an unwillingness to see that we most likely are not *the* focus of the picture; an inability, perhaps, to understand that there is always a larger framework, one that compels us now and again to give up something of ourselves for the benefit of—here we are again—the community.

...

Stuck in the '50s. The presidency as a reward system for hanging around long enough. What else did Sipple get quoted as saying? An "obsession with self-reliance."

That's a tough one because so many of us are or want to be self-reliant, or believe in self-reliance as a major virtue, a value issue. This will take some time.

There grew up in America a Wild West mentality, never mind that the Wild West as immortalized (and mainly fictionalized) by Zane Gray, John Wayne, and seemingly zillions of other pulp writers and actors, lasted about fifteen years at best. The image of the rugged cowboy (the morphing of Barry Goldwater and the Marlboro Man among them) became one of the standard features of the American Ideal: Man against the elements; man against the savages "mak[ing] mild,"/ as Tennyson's Ulysses says of his son Telemachus, "making mild a rugged people" to help "Subdue them to the useful and the good."

The rugged individualist, the rough-hewn man beholden only to his own powers of observation, his own penchant for back-breaking sweat labor as he cleared the land, fought the Indians, "rassled" bears, built cabins, married and protected his women, raised his male cubs to be independent and strong in the belief of his rightness, asking no quarter against evil and certainly giving none whether the evil was the British Crown, the Mexican Bandito, the war-pathing Indians, the rustlers, the cattlemen (if they were sheep herders) or the sheep herders (if they were cattlemen), etc.

This was not just the Wild West, either. Ole Rolvaag's prairie settlers did the same, though apparently with less gunplay involved.

It's a haunting image, and a believable one—especially for those who've seen the prairie, the desert, the brush, the big sky and the tall mountains; the unfordable rivers; the virtually impenetrable forests of Mississippi's delta wilds.

It's understandable when you remember that the road up the Boston Mountains from near Fort Smith, Arkansas, to Fayetteville was barely paved until the First but even more the Second World War; that it was not until those wars that people were moved in massive numbers from their Ozark and Appalachian hollows to places around the world; that urban ghetto kids still thought somewhere six blocks away was virtually another country. The isolation was enormous.

After a fashion and in its own way, though. It was by no means total. Indian trails, as it turns out, had been major trade routes across this country long before the coming of the independent buckeroo or frontiersman. What we did was pick up on the most romantic aspects of life—the self-reliant individualist whose isolation made him *have* to stand alone against all possible depredations of man, nature, and his own madness. While there surely were those who picked up and moved as soon as they saw the smoke of another cabin within ten miles, there were vastly more who built towns, schools *in* those town, railroads *to* those towns—why else were the railroad barons so anxious to get government rights of way, and local towns so anxious to get those railroads to come through their towns? They not only wanted to make a bunch of bucks, but they didn't want to be isolated, either. They didn't want to be alone out there on the desert or the prairie. They didn't want to have to do it all themselves. They wanted to *settle* a continent, not retire to one. And the railroad bigwigs certainly did NOT want the government "off their backs" when it came time to carve up the public lands for rights of way.

Still, the image of the free individual, unencumbered by any allegiance to a "gummint," goes a long way back in this country—starting, I suppose, with our own revolution from a government far distant and in whose governance we had no clear hand.

Then there was the "Whiskey Rebellion" in 1794 during Washington's tour of duty as President. Alexander Hamilton, Secretary of the Treasury, had gotten an excise tax levied on distilled spirits in 1791, but three years later some good folks in western Pennsylvania kicked up a fair ruckus about the government taking away their rights to sell as well as to consume the products of their labor etc. etc. etc.

There was some pretty solid intellectual background, too. Ralph Waldo Emerson's 1841 essay *Self Reliance* may have been more misunderstood than read (then as now), but people certainly remembered the title—*Self Reliance*—and took it quite to heart. Following in 1849 was Henry David Thoreau's essay, familiarly known as "Civil Disobedience," in which he railed against slavery mainly, but saw the Mexican-American War as a ploy designed to extend slavery, and said, "I quarrel not with far-off foes," while demanding that if government wasn't decent enough to cease its existence, it ought at least to become better. And he asked, "Must the citizen ever for a moment, or in the least degree, resign his conscience to the legislator? Why has every man a conscience, then?"

Even later, folks during Lincoln's administration rioted against conscription laws to fight an increasingly unpopular war, and certainly in our own time the likes of Ghandi and Martin Luther King, Jr. harked back to Thoreau.

So the more current crop of rugged individualists has a long history in this country: Robert Welch, founder of the John Birch Society, from whose mouth *Conspiracy* flowed like wine and to whom Dwight David Eisenhower was a Com-Symp (a portmanteau abbreviation standing for Communist Sympathizer); The Branch Davidians at Waco, Texas, and what many would consider their paranoid fears of the government; the folks at Ruby Ridge, Idaho; the Una-bomber, Theodore Kaczynski, whose isolation and extreme Ludditeism certainly qualified him as a type; and Timothy McVeigh, found guilty of murdering some 168 people when he blew up the Murrah federal office building in Oklahoma City; plus all the paramilitary, camouflage-dependent militia types with their visions of black helicopters, conspiracies, and all the rest.

An "obsession with self-reliance."

It seems a true virtue has gone sour with all this. There seems to have grown up a sense that the government will not, cannot, and should not do anything for the common good, for the community. This has taken certainly two paths: the violence of paranoid bombers and the attitudes of some conservatives that *any*thing a government tries to do to help people become a part of the mainstream is suspect at best, dangerous at worst, and—to that particular breed of conservatives—dangerous seems always to come out meaning anti-American.

So it returns to the shibboleths, the easy definitions, the turning away from what *is* to a remembrance—romanticized more often than not—of what *was*, some golden Good Old Days when things were all Hunkey Dorey.

I suspect, thinking of my own reminiscences, that what we have here is what a friend of mine some years ago referred to as time sickness. He was telling me about a friend of his whose wife had seen a house for sale that had belonged to them years earlier when they were young professors with young children playing in the neighborhood. That other couple had moved away, then much later returned. That's when she saw the house and begged her husband to buy it for her, that she was so homesick for it. My friend, he related to me, told his friend, "Don't you dare buy her that house. She isn't *home*sick, she's *time* sick," by which he meant she didn't want the *house* again, so much as she wanted those *times* again when she was young and life was still opening out for her and her family and all their friends.

...

"One more mission before we're through." That still resonates with me, but largely, I think, because it summons up a time when we were more willing than not to join hands to accomplish a common job, a time when people seemed to understand community more than now. An article I've long-since misplaced, by someone whose name I can't recall, quoted Saul Bellow speaking about his immigrant forbears in Chicago around the turn of the previous century. "The country took us over," Bellow said. "It was a country then, not a collection of cultures."

He may have been right. Of course he may also have been romanticizing. The point is that Bob Dole in waiting his turn to be president had nothing to offer—Bush One's "vision thing" again, or lack of it; the point is that Bob Dole—"stuck in the fifties"—brought none of the virtues of the fifties with him; the point is that a fierce independence and an extreme self-reliance—*rootless* more than *ruggedly individualistic*—breaks us apart, fragments us, at a time when we desperately need to look at what *Is*, not at what once may have been. It is a time when we need to "look shining," as Auden said in his poem "Petition," "look shining at/ New styles of architecture, a change of heart."

Of course, I doubt that Bob Dole ever began his day reading poetry. His credit card advertisements on TV—not to mention the puff for Viagra—didn't suggest he did. Still, he looked happier in those ads than he ever did while in Washington.

"It doth make a difference," Saint Augustine has been quoted as saying, "whence cometh a man's happiness."

It does indeed.

...

I chose to subtitle this piece, "What's Past is Prologue," from Shakespeare's *The Tempest*, but it could as well have been Santayana's, "Those who cannot remember the past are doomed to repeat it," from his *The Life of Reason*. Either way, the Bush/Cheney administration, as it harked back to the Nixon administration's life of sequestered paranoia, raised the level of manipulating the public through inducing fear and terror in the hearts of the people in order to construct an unbelievably effective firewall against being questioned, disagreed with, or chal-lenged in any way. Yet again, free speech belonged only to those in power. Where, one must ask, where oh where had the Congress been?

If Bob Dole was stuck in the Fifties, John McCain appeared to be stuck in the Vietnam war. The terrifying horrors of his captivity, the beatings, the cages, the barbarity of that impris-onment did indeed make him a hero, but it did not "*therefore*" make him right about all things political.

And now the TEA Party has joined us—a new low in education, a sadly dangerous vision of the Public Good, a frightening scorn for all the "others" in our land. But it seems that perhaps the TEA Party folks have already found themselves on that downward slope most third parties have lost their footing on in our history.

Personally, I hope so—but stay tuned. As the old feller said to his antsy grandson, "Set still, Boy. The Opry ain't over till the fat lady sings."

ONCE MORE INTO THE BREECH

(On again considering something about what Art is in response to various e-mails from an old friend whose life had been devoted to it, and to see if there might still be something I have to say about it after many years of silence on the matter).

I'VE BEEN MULLING OVER YOUR letter spurred by your friend's letter to you—all about art, or as Yeats had it, "...we descant and yet again descant/ Upon the supreme theme of Art and Song[.]"

I have to admit I didn't think I had anything further to say about any of this, or that I might even be interested in joining the issue if it were raised in my presence. All that seems so long ago, talk about Art, so infused with late-into-the-night bull sessions, with such passionate intensity, so filled with the seriousness of theory—all the *sturm und drang* of heady under-graduate days and all that. Yet, here I am responding I'm not sure to whom or for whom or for what.

Some things you said in your piece have intrigued me in a positive way, some others less so. But good stuff first.

. First: that Art partakes of the sacred;

. Second: that dialogue is essential between those who have done and those who are about to do art;

. Third: that Art is magic which transforms;

. Fourth: that the "art" of Art is manifested in that moment our imagination says, "Wow!"

That last is likely what actually got me up off my sagging duff, because though I may have thought something of the kind before, I hadn't thought of it *as such*, and it's an intriguing idea. If I understand what you may have meant, it's something to the effect that the piece of art—the painting or sculpture or poem or music—is simply a delivery service, and that the "art" itself is in whatever recognition gets zapped into our lives as a result of something in us having been moved to feel, touched to experience, or led to understand.

In the script for a radio program I did about the Humanities, I said at the end, facts alone don't necessarily mean a thing until touched by the value and the quality of human experience—like Michelangelo's vibrant God in the Sistine Chapel, stretching himself toward the reclining, passive Adam to charge him into life with the awesome shock of humanity.

There is your idea, I think, though I hadn't conceived of it in your terms. Of course for a long time (or at least since I.A. Richards) poets and poetry theorists have talked about metaphors in terms of the "tenor" and the "vehicle," the tenor being the thing being compared, the vehicle being the comparison itself: in *La vida es sueno* LIFE is the tenor, but it is THE DREAM—the vehicle—which carries the imagination where the poet wants it to go.

I also thought of what Robert Frost said about translating poetry when I read that. As I recall, he said something to the effect that the "poetry" of a poem is what's left when you're trying to translate it into another language— that which is untranslatable, in other words. My own way of thinking about that has been in the image of the radium stain in the bottom of the Curies' petri dish after they had boiled down tons and tons of pitchblende.

Still, though excited about that concept—that the "art" of Art resides in the moment of its effect on a given person rather than in anything intrinsic to the thing itself—there still remain gradations of competence in creating art. While it is surely true that not all people will get their jollies looking at a Hopper or a Rodin or a Picasso; or reading a Faulkner or a Mann or a Shakespeare; or listening to a Yo Yo Ma playing Bach's suites for solo cello or a Glenn Gould's pedal-less *Well-Tempered Clavier*, there has to be something in the thing itself that *can* spark a powerful and meaningful response in someone.

Another image, this from my past as a radioman in the Army during the Korean War (which, mercifully, I fought in Salzburg, Austria), might make sense here. If you're going to get a message from here to there, you've got to have **both** a transmitter and a receiver, which means both the radios as hardware have to be in good working order, and the radiomen as users of the hardware have to have good fists to send and good ears to receive, have to know the Morse code, the correct radio procedures, how to operate the M-209 Converter for coding/decoding, etc. This of course does not suggest that there is no serendipity: We sometimes were helped—or hindered by—atmospheric conditions over which we had no control at all.

From that, in any event, I conclude Henry James was right: There is good writing and there is bad writing. The obvious corollary: There are *good* readers and there are *bad* readers. A good reader may well get something fine from a bad book, but a bad reader will never get any-thing fine from a good one (your Platonic cave, fire, and shadows image again). However, I also suspect that what good a good reader gets from a bad book will be an instructive lesson rather than a jump-started imagination, but like everything else we can say, that's moot.

Still on this business of where the art resides, I have to suggest what might be a demurrer, though it just as well might not be.

I am basically an institutionalist (which isn't really off the subject at hand but fits me into a syndrome of sorts), and as such I am one who likes process, order, and intent. This you doubt-less remember from other pieces, so it shouldn't surprise you here.

I sensed a suggestion in something you said—just a hint, I think—that Art (as we're using the term) is a swinging, freeform sort of thing without obligations to the past or concern for the future. I know you haven't said that, and I'm not trying to invent a straw man, so this is mainly just a furtherance of what I'm thinking, an extension of this whole messy subject.

I think back to classes I've taught and remember loving to teach Dylan Thomas's "Do Not Go Gentle" because it's so wild and swinging and free—yet a villanelle, for all that. So I always loved to talk about form and how even the most seemingly restrictive forms still could carry the burden of passion and the sense of breaking out. Or Browning's *Fra Lippo Lippi*, that dramatic monologue you can be half way through before it hits you that it's written in those terribly restrictive rhymed couplets, but his use of run-on lines hides that. Or closer, perhaps, to your artistic home, Michelangelo's bodies, such as the Young Slave, I think it is, breaking away from the clutch of marble slabs.

Well, all that requires an artist to have an understanding of form; a willingness to use it; the whimsy to see how far it can be bent (like a blues guitarist bending a note to get the crying *wah-wah-wah* he wants); the discipline to work it and work it until it comes as close as he'll ever get it to what he sees so clearly in his head; and the intelligence to know when he's on to something worth the effort—and when he's not.

...

How about my second point next: the dialogue business? I've also written about this in a SAMLA piece: Faulkner and Phil Stone; the Fugitive poets' meetings; Plato and Socrates; Ben Jonson and everybody else around at the time; Hemingway and Stein and Fitzgerald; students and teachers in formal classroom settings.

To that you can add Henry James's prefaces to his novels; E.M. Forster's *Aspects of the Novel*; T.S. Eliot's *On Poetry and Poets*; Paul Engle's *On Creative Writing*, a collection of essays by various poets and writers; R.V. Cassill's *In an Iron Time*; John Gardner's *The Art of Fiction*; even Wayne Booth's *The Rhetoric of Fiction*; Rilke's *Letters To a Young Poet*, many of Donald Hall's books. There's seemingly no end to such a list, and all of the books mentioned here are "conversations" by writers (Booth, perhaps, the wonderfully notable exception) with other writers or wannabes.

Thinking back to my own times of intense conversational discourse with other writers, I don't know that I was ever convinced, particularly, of the especial efficacy of their "arguments," but as with any such meetings what was sharpened was my own ideas about whatever specifics we happened to be dealing with on any given occasion.

So often, then, what writers—or any artists—are doing when they talk to each other is justifying through argumentation their own activities. We tend, it seems to me, to use whatever hold on logic and persuasion we may have to justify how we're spending our time. Our fellows, in turn, invariably point out—just as logically and with as much rhetorical persuasion—how we're wasting our time in following old worn-out paths, persisting in passé media, bothering still with dated forms or stale theories or long-ago disproved (or merely dismissed) assumptions.

Interestingly, we all tend to be right quite as much as we tend to be wrong.

This "conversation" business easily slides into other realms, I find—though that's the nature of conversation, too—and where it's sliding right now is into the danger of spending too much time with the "cutting edge" folks, those who always know the latest trend, the most recent fad, the most brilliant up-and-coming genius, the presumably obvious direction things are heading, and so on. "Beee-ware, Oh take care," as the song has it. Beware, oh take care lest we lose that most essential spark of ourselves and spend our lives always chasing the next chimera someone *else* has convinced us is the way to go.

"Art," Picasso often gets quoted as saying, "is a lie that tells the truth." I love that, but Picasso's truth doesn't have to be John Acorn's truth. Segovia's truth doesn't have to be Mark Regnier's truth. R.V. Cassill's truth doesn't have to be Bob Sorrells's truth. So what the learner writer, poet, painter, print maker, potter has to learn from those older and more experienced heads is not What To Do, and certainly not, Do as I Do, but, Listen To Yourself. Hemingway talked about his built-in shit detector: Listen to your own. Faulkner talked about the old verities of the human heart. Listen to that, too. Pope wrote, "Fool, look into thy heart and write." And Rilke, well, Rilke is worth quoting at even greater length: "Go into yourself," he said.

> Find out the reason that commands you to write. This most of all: ask yourself in the most silent hour of your night: *must* I write? Then, as if no one had ever tried before, try to say what you see and feel and love and lose.

Lose. We pay not only for our failures, but also for our successes.

...

"But leave the art to what happens/ when scales fall and ears open/ and the magic of the words transforms," you wrote.

I think this "say[s] more with less," quite well, and it comes in the context of gathering and collecting art, or in the context of not being able to gather and collect art. Not truly.

So we're now into the magic that transforms. *Magic* is an interesting word to use, too, because it takes on the mien of trickery: of pulling rabbits out of a hat, of sawing people in half only to have them reappear whole, of knowing exactly which card you have pulled from the deck, of making someone disappear in a **Whooof** of smoke—before your very eyes!

Magic.

But magic is always explainable, and there were folks on TV some time back who made their livings by showing us how the magic is done, how the **trick** is done. It was a wonderful show, and as far as I'm concerned it didn't take anything at all away from the "magic" of the magic, but made it even more amazing when I saw how adept the magicians were at performing, and how cunning at being able to think up such complex deceptions.

In all our conversations, as I was suggesting above, what could we expect to learn from Picasso about drawing? He might as well say, echoing US Army field manuals, "Grasp the charcoal with your right thumb and forefinger, and with a smart snap of your wrist strike the charcoal's flat edge across the face of the already prepared newsprint..."

He would be telling us something, all right, something useful, in fact—we do need folks to tell us *How To Do Things*—but would it be what we were asking about? At one point in Dylan Thomas's *A Child's Christmas in Wales*, the narrator is cataloging his presents—at that point the "Useful Presents"—among them being a book "that told me everything about the wasp, except why." (Parenthetically, and interestingly, he's telling a younger child about Christmases of the past.)

And there's the magic of transformation, when it comes. Something happens to us, and there's no accounting for why it happens. I always think it must be because we are ready to be "happened to," so to speak. We are—for whatever reasons—finely tuned or attuned receivers not only soaking up all the signals floating through the ethers of the universe, but understanding them as well.

But as soon as I say that, I take it back, because there are also times when we know that *some*thing has broadsided us, but we haven't a clue what in hell (or heaven) it is. All we know is that we are changed, that some new standard, perhaps, has been set for us; that we can't ever see the world (or at least portions of it) in quite the same way again; that we have been touched by the ineffable and now know something so mysterious we don't even know what it is we know.

Sometimes it isn't even a complete "work" such as a Brahms symphony or a novel by Tolstoy. It may be simply a brief phrase from a piece of music or an image from a poem or some quick stab of insight that may flit away as quickly as it came. And even if we forget what it was we knew, we still retain the knowledge of our having known it for even so teasingly and maddeningly finite a time. Camus, I think it was, has been quoted as saying,

> On certain mornings, as we turn a corner, an exquisite dew falls on our heart and then vanishes. But the freshness lingers, and this, always, is what the heart needs.

A stain in the bottom of a petri dish.

I can only give examples. When I rounded a corner of the MOMA and suddenly saw Hopper's painting *Gas* I was stunned. Was it the red pumps so blatant against the dark green of the trees behind? Sudden, unrooted, nonspecic memories from my childhood reacting to the flying horse logo of Mobilgas? I have no idea.

And also Hopper's *Nighthawks*: I knew those people in that cafe in the middle of the night, taking their coffee together or apart, lonely and alone, no matter.

And Andrew Wyeth's *Christina's World*. Same thing. I knew those pathetic arms and legs, that awkward dragging of one's self across and up fields to the equally stark world of whatever was in that house, itself equally as stark, as set apart, as raked by the wind as the field, and of necessity, I should think, as wracked as the souls of the people who lived around there.

And there's no end to the music, either: virtually any version of "Amazing Grace"; virtually any form of Barber's "Adagio"; the final duet of Aida and Radames; much of Arvo Pärt; and certainly including Vernon Dalhart singing "The Prisoner's Song," Hank Williams and "I'm So Lonesome I Could Cry," Willie Nelson and "Blue Eyes Crying in the Rain," and of course nearly anybody on "Will That Circle Be Unbroken."

Magic. In a panel discussion in September of 1999, E.L. Doctorow said,

The point about any art, I feel, where my own sentimentality comes in, is that it's made out of nothing. I don't know, some paints in a tube, a few reams of paper, a kid with a guitar, or a piece of stone.

And on it goes.

...

"Made out of nothing."

A couple of paragraphs back I used the word *mysterious*. I like your word *magic*, but I also respond to mystery, and certainly it works here as a pretty neat segue into my first point (yours, actually), Art as partaking of the sacred.

You disassociate Art from art forms where you talk about this, and I still wonder how to do that, still hear Yeats asking, "How can we know the dancer from the dance?" A little more context might help there: "Oh chestnut tree, great rooted blossomer,/ Are you the leaf, the blossom or the bole?/ O body swayed to music, O brightening glance,/ How can we know the dancer from the dance?"

Does a tree make any noise when it falls in a remote forest if there's nobody around to hear it? Or, as a current wag has it, "If a man says something in a remote forest is it still wrong even if his wife's not around to hear it?" These Koan-like questions are intended to be futile, I think, except that they may indicate the limitations of logic while expanding the possibilities of responses and connections.

Now having said this, I can talk more directly about mystery and the sacred. In "Among School Children," Yeats is getting around to the question of ultimate reality and all that: Do we experience life through *action*, or through *being*? Or is it in both? Or is it whatever?

In the penultimate stanza to "Among School Children," Yeats draws a parallel between nuns and mothers who worship images, but how those images are different, the nuns' "keep[ing] a marble or a bronze repose," as distinguished from the mothers' "reveries." But both, he says, "break hearts."

For most people, that which is sacred is that which we worship, but in conventional attitudes toward The Sacred, it would be considered idolatrous to worship something other than a (or The) god. So how literal can we get in this sort of discussion? With you—and perhaps with your young friend as well—it likely would be assumed that there is in no way a need to equate The Sacred with Religion. A religion is an institution designed to provide a place (physical or otherwise) for those to whom specific forms, procedures, or habits of worship are encouraged and promulgated.

As for myself, I seem to be drawn toward mystics of various sorts, and though I have hardly spent a lifetime in deep study, still what I have read leads me to conclude that in many ways they tend to be saying much the same thing: Find God. Wonderfully enough, they all seem to agree (more or less) that there is no single path to that fulfillment. One way or another they all seem to be saying that the Ways are many and that we must all find—and then follow—that way or that path which leads *Us* to God, that Mystery known only when known, the great I Am. Christian, Buddhist, and Hindu mystics would seem to have more in common with each other than Presbyterian, Methodist, and Baptist mainliners have with each other.

And you speak of Art as illumination, "a kind of revelation, if you please." When I read that I thought again about Browning and his *Fra Lippo Lippi* where the good friar tells the nightwatch, "we're made so that we love/ First when we see them painted, things we have passed/ Perhaps a hundred times nor cared to see." Right after, he continues, "Art was given for that;/ God uses us [painters] to help each other so,/ Lending our minds out."

Maybe that's what artists are for—to lend their minds out. And if they do it well enough and if we allow them those roles as teacher, interpreter, sage, visionary by paying attention to their work, then perhaps they are functioning as Messengers of God and are as worthy to be heeded as any other kind, for I do believe that "In my father's house are many mansions," as John reports the words of Jesus.

But back to worship, which may or may not involve a religion. I may be more comfortable talking about worshipfulness, since I'm not yet ready to say that I **worship** anything or anyone. I hope that lets me pass into the realm of spirituality, because I want to be a spiritual person, and think I am one, or at least have a spiritual sensibility. About Jesus, for instance: Some four hundred years ago one of our religious forebears in Transylvania, Francis David who remained a *uni*tarian rather than a *trini*tarian, held to this about Jesus: *Serviam, non adoramus*: Serve (or follow), but do not adore (or worship). That makes sense to me: Jesus as spiritual director or leader or teacher; one through whom God may well speak, but not himself God.

The business of spirituality these days gets pretty clouded in a number of directions. First, my own Unitarian Universalist denomination was long dominated and still is strongly influenced by the precepts of what's usually called secular humanism, an attitude with some roots in the Renaissance ideas of Humans as the center of things, with nothing but themselves to rely on (akin to "God helps those who help themselves," though without the God part); and by a rational approach to the world in general, leading to a belief (never mind the irony there) in science or at least in the scientific method, as the true path to understanding all that needs understanding, etc. Secondly, there probably is a holdover of confusion of spirituality with the late Nineteenth Century Spiritualists with their panoply of table tapping, voices from "beyond," automatic writing, and all the rest—bad magic, as it were. Third, there is the New Age spirituality with its warm fuzzies and soft center, its dearth of intellectual rigor, and its lack of any real cohesion— its basic structural anarchy. I've thought the New Age stuff was essentially harmless, though back in the nineteen-seventies there was a soft porn queen named Emmanuelle, as I recall, whose philosophy of life was (or so it was bruited about by press agents and such), "If it feels good, do it." Apparently the two—New Age spirituality and Emmanuelle—have stayed glued together in my own head.

Closer to my own nature is the kind of stuff Margaret Fuller and Ralph Waldo Emerson talked and corresponded about for so long. Apparently Fuller kept leaning against Emerson to move him away from the abstract and theoretical idealism he felt comfortable with (I'm paraphrasing a lot of things here from a sermon my wife delivered once) toward "biographical ideal-ism" which involved an "idealism that is concerned with ideas only as they can be lived, with laws only as they can be seen in events, with the word only when it becomes flesh, with the spirit only as it animates the material." Or, to intrude myself into some pretty potent company, in the final lines of a poem I wrote *many* years ago, "To know the timid, lusting flesh of poetry/ Requires the naked entrance of a poem."

Doctorow's art being made out of nothing, your art as "something that illuminates," Fuller's insisting that idealism is pointless without some form of action to manifest it: All this along with Emerson's, "Man is the point wherein matter and spirit meet and marry" all come together in a wonderously mad jumble in my head. Can't we say that Art *Becomes* when the idea and its realization meet in a person's head or heart or spirit or whatever?

Barry Moser was an engraver who did scenes from the Bible. (I read this in an interview in the April 2000 *AARP Bulletin*.) He said he wasn't a religious man in an institutional sense, but clearly he understands something about good and evil, mystery and agony. "Religion and art," he said, "seek to make some sort of order out of chaos." Then he said he realized "[his] work was [his] prayer."

That falling away of the scales you talk about is the same as the epiphanal gasp when one realizes that he *Believes*.

What I felt when I saw the Hoppers or heard the Samuel Barber, or felt Rodolfo's wrenching loss of Mimi at the end of *La Bohème*, crying out her name in helpless desperation, was essentially the same as what I felt once after reading a passage from a speech by Robert Bellah—a sense of understanding what Christianity was really all about, and nearly converting on the spot myself—because I understood something more about what love was, or at least how it could be perceived.

You said to me once that you didn't know anything about God. I allowed as how no one did, but in a traditional plainchant, there is the line *Ubi caritas et amor, Deus ibi est*: Where there is charity and love, God is there.

It's the same about Art, for me. My responses tend to be much the same. As The Sacred requires that which *is* Sacred, Art requires that which *is* Art. That is, we know God by that "knowledge carried to the heart," as Allen Tate put it, when we are in the Sacred Presence. We know Art the same way: when we know we are in its presence. In both cases not only are we transfixed, staring in believing disbelief, but—like a maiden who is struck suddenly by the purity of her felt lust when she is in the presence of the one who, she knows, will be the one to teach her what human love is, and feels the need to look away at least for a moment until she can compose herself—so we must adjust ourselves, ready ourselves for that power which has possessed us. There is a moment—psychological, physiological, emotional, actual, it doesn't matter—there is a moment of absolute quiet, a stillness, a stasis during which our hearts, our minds, our souls, our most fleshly bodies are at one with everything, when all mysteries are understood even if only for a nanosecond.

I think it's why God invented the word *ineffable*. It is all the mystery of that which must be experienced more than understood.

I'll give the final word here to ole Emerson. "Trust yourself," he said. "Trust the instinct to the end, though you cannot tell why or see why."

-30-

I NEVER HEARD MY FATHER SING

WHEN I WAS PUSHING 60, I found out something strange about my father: He never owned but one house in his life. As an adult he had lived in his home town of Pine Bluff, Arkansas; in Oklahoma City, Cleveland, Memphis, Fort Worth, New York City (Tudor City section); then to Westchester County in Chappaqua, Scarsdale, and Pelham Manor; then back into the City (West 9th Street in the Village). The only house he ever owned was in Pelham. My oldest brother told me that, and I had trouble believing it.

I never knew my father very well. He died in February of the year I was sixteen. He lacked five weeks of being fifty-two. That's young.

But when I say I never knew him, what I mean is not that he wasn't around much, but that I never knew him the way you can come to know a parent as you yourself grow into an adult. I was always a child around him, or a boy.

I'm not quite sure why that bit of information about the house surprised me so much. I suppose I always assumed Dad did lots of things the way everybody else did: buy a house, have a mortgage, develop equity in the property so you can get something out of it later—usually when you move—which, of course, you use to put into another house, or, as Kurt Vonnegut had one of his characters say, "and so it goes."

Sometime later, though, I remembered something Dad had written. He had been talking about how he and my mother, after they got married, had started off from Pine Bluff to work their way around the world. They only got as far as Cleveland, Ohio, I gather, when Mom got pregnant with their first child, John, my oldest sibling. So much for seeing the World.

Then something else eased into my head, and that was the Pack Trip. It was the Pack Trip that became the focus of much of my attention while I lived in Pelham, and for me it was a matter of living the Trip in my imagination: cinching the saddles to the saw horses, mounting the sturdy steeds on whose sure feet and good tempers my life would depend for the next however many weeks or months (hours?) I would be aboard, and all the rest.

Aiding and abetting my own imagination and desires, of course, was Holling C. Holling's *The Book of Cowboys*, a gift to me from my Dad on Monday, June 21, 1943. After reading it straight through (I was laid up in bed with a pretty rotten cold) I wrote on the page before the frontispiece, "Dad bought this book for me,/ and I shall keep it all of my life./ To *me* [underlined] it will be *priceless* [underlined twice]. Bob Sorrells [underlined] June 21 1943 (Monday)."

But I now wonder what it meant to my father. If he never bought a house until eight years before he died, and if he was willing to spend a lot of good money on western saddles, bridles, saddle blankets, rifle scabbards, and Lord knows what else, then it must have been a knot of some sort in his planning, because—intuitive as he was and much as he trusted his intuitions—Dad was an organized man, or he never could have filled the jobs he had.

And there was one other thing. He bought a farm outside of Memphis one time. Or was going to. I think he actually did, though I can't imagine what my mother thought about that. They had few public discussions about their disagreements when we children were present.

But I think that he did finally buy the farm. I never saw it. I don't think Mother ever went to it. I remember watching my oldest brother read the realtor's prospectus about it and marveling. As I recall, he was still in uniform after getting back from the War. Or maybe it was while we were still in Washington before he went overseas. But that seems less likely. Or maybe...Well, whenever. I do remember my brother looking up and saying, "This guy's sure no piker." But I don't think Dad ever went there to see it for himself. He could have, though, because he had to make trips to Memphis as part of his job. I simply don't know. I do remember that the resident foreman wrote that one of the cows had calved twins, but they didn't survive. That saddened me, for some reason. Probably because I wanted to be a rancher. I wanted to help create a strain of Palominos. At that time in my life, I think Palominos weren't an actual breed. (Are they now?) As I recall, you had to play hit-or-miss to get one. But please remember I was only ten.

On Breaking One's Pencil

Also, when I was a few years older, I used to go down to the Split Rock Riding Academy and help by mucking out stalls, leading folks out to the main trail, helping the regulars curry the horses, watering them down, and mostly trying to be helpful while staying out of the way of the "real" guys.

Well, if you put all that together—wanting to work his way around the world, never buying but one house in his life (and that because a good friend and colleague finally *begged* him to buy it from him), buying expensive stuff for a pack trip he surely knew he would never take, and buying a farm in Tennessee while he lived in New York City, knowing the while that he was not in good health—then what is there to make of that?

What I make of it is that my father was a man who always needed to have an escape route planned out. In the Old West he would be the hombre who never sat with his back to the door or window in the saloon, would always have had a *compadre* who looked out for back shooters, would always have had a horse stashed out with saddlebags packed and ready to go in case things got tight. Or, to change the scene, as an officer in an infantry line company, he would always have known who was on his flanks, where there was another trail "out" in case he had to go "in," etc. In short, Dad was a man who needed to know he could get away if he really had to, who could pack late and leave early in case something came up that whispered across the ear of his soul with far greater urgency than anything else had.

He never did leave home.

He was a man with a weighty sense of responsibility and duty. Still . . .

Still, he must have wanted to leave home now and again. Not out of pique or lust or any of those things, but just to be away for a while. The Pack Trip, for instance. As I recall, he really did have it planned out, though I can't remember any of the details or even his talking about the details. It would be Out West, on horses, and for an indeterminate period. Other than that, it was an energy mainly of excitement—and that, I suspect, mainly my own.

...

Because my father died so young, I've had to piece a lot of things together about him from my oldest brother, my sister, newspaper clippings, a bunch of columns, editorials, and other pieces he wrote as a newspaperman. It's a strange thing, this someone's dying when you're still young. There's always—at least with me there's always—the temptation I too easily fall into of thinking about what my life would have been like if Dad had lived until I was twenty-five, or he was sixty eight, or whatever.

Also, when you're the youngest of four you're that much farther from your parents than the older children. The result with me is both a fantasizing of reality and a kind of researching of the ascertainable facts of the past as well as possible. It's pretty much like a lot of fiction writing, come to think of it: a blend of rampant invention and judicious ferreting out of demonstrable detail. One path into all that, of course, is my parents' hometown of Pine Bluff, Arkansas.

I have fond memories of Pine Bluff, but they are a boy's memories: two days here, a week there in the occasional summer. They weren't even the romanticized "to grandmother's house we go" sort of thing. There was a grandmother and grandfather, all right, but Mother's, not Dad's. His parents had died within ten minutes of each other four months before I was born.

Still, on Linden Street there was heat lightening; as well as the house my mother grew up in; there was the icehouse down town somewhere; there were honeydew, cantaloupe, and water-melon balls in the great tureen on the dining room table at mealtime; there was the lovely smell of Lifebuoy soap. Lovely to me, at least.

But "home" can be a boy's childish games. When my father became a man he put them all away. He left them to busy himself with his present and with his future that was spinning out of his increasing past. When he looked back, it was to take a sighting, a sort of back-azimuth to make sure where he'd been, to help correct, if necessary, his bearing on the future.

That's what I say, at least. That is what I say when I think of my father as the man who wrote an article in praise of Rotary and all the twiddle-twaddle approved of by all the Babbitts of the world. But my father was a bad Rotarian. He was a bad joiner, a bad club man, a bad follower (though a very good team player). Gregarious and outgoing as hell, he nevertheless was a stand-offish person, intensely private, tremendously internalized. Or as he put it, he played his cards close to his vest.

Dad likely would never have approved of what I just said. Closer to the mark, I think, is to say *not* that my father left Pine Bluff because he matured into a man and understood both intellectually and emotionally that the hometown syndrome was mostly crap; *not* because home towns are real only in the sentimental nostalgia of middle-aged failure, *but* that he left because he did. Not arrant nonsense or mere playing with words at all. He left because the Scripps Howard Newspaper chain had no use for a man in Pine Bluff, Arkansas. How could the managing editor of the *Cleveland Press* live there? Or the editor of the *Fort Worth Press*? None could, naturally. They could only have come from there. He did what he did because he was what he was, and he was strong enough and sure enough of himself to take the risks of leaving the known, the easy, and by stepping outside the perimeter of the soft and familiar, risk it all on the outside. And it is a risk.

The whole business of my traveling must have started with my mother and father. They left Pine Bluff, Arkansas, to work their way around the world, but got only as far as Oklahoma City when their plan—vague at best—was overtaken by nature. Four more pregnancies and three more children put an end to those original plans, such as they were, and resulted in responsibilities, permanent jobs, and respectability.

So Dad left the home of his birthing and growing up; the town where he'd run the ends and hit the deep flies to center field; where he'd coached the football boys, worked, fallen in love, married; where his folks died within five minutes of each other three months before I was born. He left. His brother stayed. Both died young.

...

My father died about five weeks before his fifty-second birthday. At the time, we were living in New York City. That is, my parents were. I was the youngest of four children; fifteen; and, with my older brother, Bill, in a military prep-school in Virginia.

In spite of its rampant self-absorption, crudities, cynicisms, vulgarities, and erupting juices of sexuality, fifteen is a tender age. Maybe vulnerable is more accurate. In any event, it's an age when a boy—even a boy/man—really needs his father. It's a fragile time, because the boy coming into manhood is coming into a period when he's just about ready to start knowing his father as another man, as a person, as a human being, as a wonderfully imperfect critter he can love in a way that transcends the lad/dad relationship.

It's always going to be father/son, but when the two are adults, that relationship changes, deepens, transforms. At least, that's what I've seen and heard from those who got to go through it, and as I've experienced it from the father's side with my own son.

But I was suddenly and unexpectedly cut off from that chance. One night my father was alive, sitting at a card table in the living room reading—likely a mystery novel, as I recall my mother telling it—in their small apartment in New York. My mother had retired to their bedroom where, I think, she might have been reading as well. They had entertained a long-time friend of ours from Memphis who was visiting the City for a few days, and after they got her to the railroad station that night to head back South, they returned to the apartment. That's when Dad got bushwhacked by a massive heart attack.

From the bedroom, mother said she heard something fall. Hurrying out to see what had happened, she found Dad on the floor. She knelt by him and said he kept looking up at her asking, "What's wrong? What's wrong?" as though something had happened to her. Within five minutes he was dead.

These days, what might be called "a lack of closure" absolutely overwhelmed me, and one way or another I have been looking for my father ever since. One way or another his wrenching disappearance has informed virtually everything I myself have ever written.

...

Dad was a newspaperman with the Scripps Howard newspapers, serving, among other jobs, as managing editor of the *Cleveland Press*, managing editor of the newly merged *Memphis News Scimitar* and *The Press* into *The Memphis Press Scimitar*, editor of the *Fort Worth Press*, his short life ending while Executive Editor of the entire chain. In Fort Worth, he wrote a daily column, "As Uncle Panther Sees It," and as executive editor in New York City, he wrote many editorials representing the chain's position on various national issues. The editorial he wrote on the occasion of the death of Harry Truman's mother, for instance, was nominated for a Pulitzer Prize—which I had never known about until I was in my sixties.

During World War II, my father was asked by Byron Price, then-Executive News Editor of the Associated Press and newly-appointed Director of the Office of Censorship, to come to Washington, D.C., to organize the Division of Press Censorship. He did, then stayed on as its director, and within six months was named deputy director of the entire Office.

While editor of the *Fort Worth Press* (his appointment in 1927 apparently made him the youngest editor of a major daily newspaper in the country) he wrote a style book entitled *The Working Press*. Later, while Executive Editor in

On Breaking One's Pencil

New York and shortly before his death, he completed *A Handbook of Scripps Howard*, a brief history of the chain with biographical sketches of the papers, editors, and top brass—including himself. He also wrote about his family history; his hometown; letters to his brother (himself editor of the local Pine Bluff newspaper) about matters such as Roosevelt, communism, Russia, etc.

In those manuscripts that Dad wrote about his hometown or family, he quickly came back to one subject: his grandmother who clearly had a profound influence on his life, and who truly must have been a remarkable woman. But something tells me that the land was filled with such women: strong, hard-working, dedicated: achievers who helped do everything there was to be done—not because they were particularly driven, not because they were particularly ambitious, not because they were particularly "good," or "moral" or "virtuous," but because that's what you did if you were going to survive. You had to. Life was hard, but that was simply the way life was. There didn't seem to be a whole lot else to compare yourself to, except those who drifted down into various sloughs of despond after "The [Civil] War," or those who just never had the pride to try to amount to anything.

The people in Pine Bluff are just people, the place just another place. Yet we have undergone so many wrenching changes in our lives since the end of the Second World War that whatever roots we have, seem to have receded with such terrible speed that we forget—quite literally—who we are. In that sense reading about Dad's recollections was incredible to me: My father—my very own father—was raised largely by a woman, his grandmother, who was born "some dozen-odd years" *before* the Mexican-American War. That would be about 1836; whose grandfather raised a troop to fight in the Civil War; my father, himself born in 1896, who didn't live in a house with electricity or an indoor privy until he was a boy of about eight or nine.

Pine Bluff was never my own home, so in most ways I wasn't reading about "my" place at all. But the pictures my father draws of his Pine Bluff are pictures that could be drawn of many places that are now big towns or small cities, places that not very long ago were truly frontier settlements. We are still a very young people.

...

While my father was editor of *The Fort Worth Press*, he wrote a daily, by-lined column he called "As Uncle Panther Sees It." I think he started the *Press's* tradition of a front page column from the editor, and those who have never had to write such a thing about five days every week have no idea of what that can be like. Teachers who have to prepare lectures every day understand something of it, as do ministers who have to have sermons ready every week.

But exposing yourself every day to thousands of readers and having to be smart or clever or interesting or, at the least, simply not awful every day is a real challenge.

In reading the sixty or so of those columns that I have had access to—I don't know how many there were all told—I was surprised to find that my father was really a businessman as much as a writer; a booster; and strangely anti-intellectual. I suppose much of that comes with the turf: Newspapers have to make money to stay afloat, and they can't make money if they exist in communities that don't have a viable, if not thriving, economy. We all ignore economic im-peratives at our peril.

Still, it seemed to me that he let his Booster's cap slip pretty far down over his critical writer's eye when it came to dealing with academicians in general sorts of ways, and writers such as Sinclair Lewis and Eugene O'Neill in rather specific ways. In short, "intellectuals" bothered him, though he was more inclined to talk about "stuffed shirts," pomposity, and pretense. It may be they were just different channels in the same river to him.

If so, that may have been one reason he never went back to Washington and Lee University after the First World War to finish his final year of college.

Instead, he went back to Pine Bluff, started working again as a reporter on the *Graphic* where he had worked summers and as a high school stringer, and in 1921 or 1922 became its editor. Then began what I think of as his Wandering in the Wilderness years.

In 1923 he left Pine Bluff for Oklahoma City and a job on the *Daily Oklahoman*, where he moved from copyreader to make-up editor to news editor in a very short time. (One source said he spent time in Indianapolis, where there was a Scripps Howard newspaper, but I don't think he ever worked on it if, in fact, he ever went there at all during that time.) In any event, he went back to Pine Bluff after not too long, apparently, writing copy for the Arkansas Light and Power Co., then down to Fort Worth for a short stint with the *Record*, a Hearst paper; then back to Oklahoma City on the *Daily Oklahoman* as news editor until September 1925 when he joined

Scripps Howard as news editor of the *Cleveland Press*. In June 1926 he was named managing editor, but stayed in Cleveland only until that November.

Then Scripps Howard sent him to Memphis, Tennessee, to help "expert," as he put it, the merger of two papers—the *Press*, founded as a Scripps Howard paper, and the recently purchased *News Scimitar*—into the *Memphis Press Scimitar*.

It was in the spring of 1927, while he was the managing editor of the new paper, that he organized the newsgathering of the great flood of the lower Mississippi. Because of the vast sweep of damage, the Army Corps of Engineers—hard pressed to deal with the flood itself—apparently tried to put a lid of denial on news coverage. In the February 1, 1930, issue of *Editor and Publisher*, an article about Dad said, in part:

> Memphis was in the center of the worst of [the flood], and the only [United Press] center outside of St. Louis and New Orleans in the [Mississippi] valley. Sorrells personally took charge of the story and covered the valley from St. Louis to the Gulf, without aid from any news service until after the waters had started to recede.
>
> He commandeered airplanes, radio broadcasting stations, long distance telephone lines and ran up an expense account that made the editorial budget look like a French franc. But he covered the story. It was during this flood that news-papers, it is believed, were first delivered in any quantity by airplane. Sorrells did it.
>
> When the levee at New Orleans was blasted to save that city, he hired a plane and rushed a photographer to the scene to get exclusive air pictures that the Press-Scimitar used the next day.

That June he was sent to Fort Worth as editor of the *Press*, which had been established in 1921 after the owner of the Fort Worth *Star-Telegram*, Amon Carter, had refused to sell his paper to Hearst in 1918 or to Roy Howard in 1920. Dad stayed there until 1930 when he moved to New York City, the editorial headquarters of the chain, as executive editor of Scripps Howard newspapers.

So those "Uncle Panther" columns were written between 1927-1930. In spite of some stylistic conventions of the times that might now leave us sighing if not gently smirking, and what I consider some of his blind spots as an observer of and player in the human comedy, there keeps surfacing a power and a strength that showed him to be a journalistic innovator. Coupled with that there emerges the drive and energy that made him the youngest editor of a major daily newspaper in the country when he was sent to Fort Worth at age 31, and helped explain why after only about eleven years as a full-time, working news man he was promoted, at age 34, to the position he held until his sudden and early death.

The likelihood, it seems to me, is that this sort of rise was part of the Twenties, when this country was growing and opening up in incredible ways. After World War I we seemed to feel ourselves without limit as to what we could accomplish.

It was a time when everything was expanding. The Scripps Howard chain, as one example, added eighteen papers in the '20s, only three in the '30s.

The heyday of the afternoon newspaper likely got much of its impetus because of the First World War. London, Paris, and Berlin were five-to-eight hours ahead of New York, Chicago, and San Francisco, which meant that reports filed from Europe during the day were getting to America in the morning—perfect for afternoon papers whose first and second editions, typically, were starting their press runs by mid-morning.

Today's computer and allied electronic industries may be the only ones comparable to businesses in the '20s as far as being wide open for expansion, and in which a person could make his mark without any especial regard to age or seniority.

The Uncle Panther of the title of his columns probably came from Fort Worth's calling itself Panther City. It seems that in 1873 the Texas and Pacific Railway Company ran out of steam—not to mention money—about 26 miles outside the city, and the population dropped from 4,000 to 1,000. A Dallas paper, ever ready to smirk a smirk toward its western neighbor even back then, said that Fort Worth was so dead a panther had actually been seen sleeping in the middle of Main Street at high noon. Panther City it was, and "As Uncle Panther Sees It" it became.

Amon Carter, by the way, who takes a drubbing in at least one of my father's columns, apparently was instrumental in encouraging Fort Worth businesses to advertise with the *Press*, feeling that a one-paper city posed a serious threat because it subjected its population to only one interpretation of events. He also seemed to be very fond of my father and sent him (as well, no doubt, as hundreds of others) a smoked turkey every year at Christmas, from his turkey farm. This continued well into the 40's after we had long-since moved to New York. I can remember that annual turkey being put in a large, old-fashioned ice box off our back porch in Pelham, one you could reach from both inside and outside the house.

. . .

When I was a boy I never had a very clear idea of what my father *did*. He knew what *his* father did: *His* father was on the action side of the courtroom railing at the lawyers' table often enough watching him. But having a father who practiced law in the local courthouse of a smallish town, with offices right down there near the depot, the saloons, the prostitutes, and the hotels, was very different from having a father whose office in a New York City skyscraper was a thirty-two minute commuter train ride from Pelham, New York, the six-year home of my youth from third through eighth grades. There just wasn't much chance to casually drop in after school. Besides, we all more or less know what lawyers do, but what does an executive editor of nineteen newspapers do? Mainly I remember that I didn't know how to spell *executive*. It always came out *exutive*.

In any event, Dad was not a "Casey, Crime Photographer"; nor did editorials for the chain carry by-lines; and he was never featured—much to my boyishly shameless desire to have a famous father—on the old radio program "The Big Story," (I think its name was), a show that dramatized great scoops by newspaper reporters.

On my own hook I've come to learn a fair amount about the process that begins with an idea or event and culminates in a piece of printed matter—the same basic procedure as putting a newspaper together.

What my father "did," I slowly came to understand, was to know the newspaper business, perhaps better than any other working journalist of his era. He allowed (with some possibly ironic hint of humility) that he was pretty good at organization. No doubt that was his forte: That's why Scripps Howard sent him to Memphis in 1926 for the merger of the *Press* and the *News Scimitar*; possibly why they sent him to Fort Worth as editor in 1927, when the *Press* was only about six years old; likely why they wanted him in New York where he could lay his hands on the entire operation (his first assignment, according to my oldest brother, was to figure out which papers weren't paying for themselves and sell them off or otherwise get rid of them); and very probably why they named him president of the Memphis Publishing Company in 1936 when they bought the *Commercial Appeal*—a paper with an established and respected 96-year old reputation in a town that had already had a Scripps Howard paper for thirty years. How were the two separate entities going to get along with the *Commercial* retaining its own visual identity so it didn't look like other Scripps Howard papers? How was it going to maintain itself as a Scripps Howard paper while having the editorial freedom to disagree locally with its "in-house" competitor/brother—not to mention the various logistics of sharing the same physical plant and business offices? Certainly at the time those were not altogether simple problems to be solved.

I don't doubt that Dad could have been successful in any number of kinds of businesses, but it wasn't simply his ability to organize that made him so valuable to Scripps Howard. If his genius was organization, it was a genius absolutely bonded to making newspapers, and not just as a product, some "anything" that could be packaged and marketed with no questions about values or ethics or an importance larger than itself, but a product that bespoke a man's pride in what he was doing.

...

In *Jefferson Davis Gets His Citizenship Back*, Robert Penn Warren, in a section about the ephemeral nature of words, says, ". . . being truly adult is largely the effort to make the lying words stand for the old living truth." This particular will-o'-the-wisp chase of mine—trying as best I could to get to know my father—has little to support it now *but* words, so I have to dig into my father's bin of them up to my wrists—my elbows, even—to feel them, smell them, listen to them, sneeze at the dust I've raised from them. I garner what I can of him: reap, sift, fill in, assume, question. How do his words lie, if they do at all? What was the living truth about him? And, thinking of Yeats among his school children, "How can we know the dancer from the dance?" Well.

...

The Second World War was the last one in which this entire nation went to war: Everybody was subject to conscription: The sons of newspaper editors, U.S. Senators, and U.S. presidents were there right along with the sons of laborers, bus drivers, head waiters, and ice-men; sugar was rationed, along with gasoline, tires, butter, meat, tobacco, and other products; families had ration books; school children knitted little squares which presumably were to be made into afghans for the boys overseas; billboards and the sides of buildings were plastered and painted with war slogans and cautions of the "Loose Lips Sink Ships" and "You Can't Spell Victory with an Absen*T*" variety; Rosie the Riveter came into existence; there were air raid drills—taken pretty seriously in coastal places like the New York City area, where I was a boy at the time, though people in Caruthersville, Missouri, or Bemidji, Minnesota, may have had a harder time believing that German or Japanese bombers might actually be near at hand; older men joined the Civilian Defense Corps, donned World War I helmets, and made their rounds during nighttime air raid alerts to pound on people's doors if they spotted an errant light peeping from behind the blackout curtains; the sirens howled—and the dogs right along with them.

No American—even those not involved directly in the war effort in some way—was able to ignore what was going on.

My father was called on the phone the day after Christmas, 1941, by Byron Price, a newspaperman who had been in Washington for twenty years, eventually becoming Executive News Editor and Acting General Manager of the Associated Press. Price was named Director of Censorship by President Roosevelt, and immediately started assembling his team. He wanted my father to come to Washington to organize the press division. Dad agreed, and officially became the first Assistant Director of the Press Division on December 26, 1941. On July 1, 1942, he was named Deputy Director, second in command of the entire Office of Censorship.

We lived in Washington as a family for about a year, first, as I recall, in the old Shore-ham Hotel where my older brother and I had fun running around the spacious grounds, playing Yankees and Rebels. Later, we moved to an apartment where we took a trolley every day to a tutor named, interestingly, Mrs. Teachout, who lived way out who knows where.

But on January 1, 1943, Dad withdrew from active duty to return to Scripps Howard, and became the Deputy Director on leave without pay. On January 31, 1944, it became clear he wouldn't be able to return to Washington, so he resigned, leaving the Office of Censorship completely.

...

His concerns about press censorship were considerable. As free enterprisers and dealers of ideas through words from way back, most U.S. newsmen found the idea of censorship abhorrent. At the same time, people realized that intelligence gathering was a matter of putting lots and lots and lots of tiny pieces of information together in hopes of constructing a meaningful pattern from them.

What my father wanted was a maximum of voluntary regulation by the papers. To that end it was his position that if the editors and publishers of our papers understood the urgency of the need for extreme caution about the possible usefulness to the enemy of military—or even potentially military—information they came across, they would do the job themselves and all the Office of Censorship would have to do would be to provide clear, precise guidelines and be available to help interpret the *Code of Wartime Practices (For the American Press)* which Dad had largely written.

Censorship was nothing especially new to the country. Dating from World War I there were a number of acts that were relevant: the *Espionage Act* of June 1917, the *Trading with the Enemy Act* of October 1917, and the *Sedition Act* of May 1918. So with some of that still fresh enough in people's minds, in addition to feeling queasy about the possibility of a layer of war-time laws getting set in place that might later be seen as some sort of precedent for peace-time, the press censorship people—my father, I gather, leading the charge—wanted to give voluntarism every possible chance. Apparently the voluntarism did work.

...

In an obituary of my father, one of the Scripps Howard senior executives noted that newsmen tend to be people who want to write, but that when they become editors they become executives, and executives "don't have time to write."

So I was stunned when I realized the mass of writing Dad did while he was Executive Editor of Scripps Howard. I don't know how he did it and still tended to his duties that involved "budget control, labor contracts, personnel and staff organization, news handling, promotion, and other odds and ends of editorial administration," as he put it himself, for a chain of nineteen papers from New York City to San Francisco. And, usually, two budget trips a year (by train) visiting every paper on the circuit—not to mention at least a full year off during the war while he did his duty in Washington with the Office of Censorship.

A lot of it had to be the times, I'd guess. Just think what was going on from 1930-1948: probably the worst depression this country had ever had, with one-third of the work force without work; the perfectly legal but unprecedented—and, therefore, to many, unspeakably frightening—prospect of a presidential third term; a truly global world war that not only finished off what was started in the First World War—the toppling of the old monarchies and alliances, and with them the collapse of the already sagging underpinnings of a way of life, which meant assumptions about how to live and how to act and what to expect from life—but also gave rise to the reincarnation of the Phoenix of nationalism from what might seem to be a Pandora's box of tribal and clan animosities, the horrors of the holocaust, and the mushroom cloud blowing us into an entirely new age the limits of which we are just now barely beginning to understand the import of; a fourth presidential term—even more frightening than the third one; and a Cold War. Any one of those was cataclysm enough in the history of this country, each a major shifting of the plate tectonics of the geo-political world, with its vast complex of aftershocks. But to have all of them on your watch was pretty overwhelming. In short, there was a lot to write about.

But there was also the man. I knew he was a writer, of course, but growing up, I seldom saw Dad writing. I think I remember a typewriter, possibly the sound of the keys clacking away at night. But that's a stretch. I do remember my own little typewriter at Christmas when we lived in Scarsdale, New York. I would have to have been under eight when I got it, and probably closer to six. I do remember him always with a book in his hands, whether it was in the evening after he had come home from work, or at night after dinner, or on a hot, summer Saturday afternoon sitting out in our back yard on a recliner, in a bathing suit in Pelham Manor, New York, tanning himself into the semblance of good health. Reading, reading, reading. History books, mostly. "Who-dunnits." Never a "literary" novel. I've still got some of them with his virtually illegible marginal notes, written always with the newspaperman's grease pencil: You didn't sharpen those pencils. You pulled a string down the side and unpeeled a little more of the black paper wrapping around the writing part—it wasn't lead—and the writing was thick, the mark greasy to the touch. They were like thin, black crayons.

Aside from the workaholic, there was the writer who must have made a hell of a lot of time for himself. And there was the Patriot, the Free-Enterprise-System man, the American-Way-of-Life man. I'd never seen or heard that from him, and I wondered where he'd been living.

The Free Enterprise System entered his Scripps Howard editorials a lot, yet the tone of some of those seemed—if not more strident—then at least more duty-bound than he sounded in some of his letters, with less a difference of thought or belief or sense of principle than of emphasis. Tolerance, maybe. He profoundly and morally detested the way people in Com-munist nations (Russia) lived, but as for Commun*ism* he simply had no respect for it as an economic way of life. It just didn't seem to work without the massive trappings of a crushingly tyrannical state making sure everyone pulled in but one direction—an image of Volga River laborers, leaning into their ropes to haul the creaking old Ship of State upstream always came into my mind.

What appears over and over are continuations of his conversation with himself about the dichotomy between "security" and individual initiative which, to him, appears to be the same as "free enterprise."

What also shows up again and again is the word *spiritual*. My father was not a religious man in a go-to-church way (he always said he lived by the code of a gentleman), but he had a highly developed sense of duty and responsibility. *Noblesse oblige* was not a quaint concept to him. It was a way of life that balanced privilege with debt. If a system was good to you, you owed it something. If it wasn't good to you, then you needed at least to consider that you might have expected too much of *it* and demanded too little of *yourself.* If the system was really closing down people's chances, their opportunities to make something of themselves, then it needed fixing. Straight away. But that didn't mean you had to throw out the whole system.

Still, having the chance to succeed also clearly meant, to Dad, having the chance to fail. He seemed suspicious of governmental safety nets. What he was sure about was that if you bought a glass of beer for a quarter, you were spending the head along with the tail when you slid the coin across the bar. Spirituality somehow subsumed some of that idea, I think, yet more, as well, and he may simply not have gotten around to figuring that out himself. If he had, he would have written something about it, and I haven't ever seen that. Still, from what there is, *Spirituality*, to him, seemed a matter of committing yourself willingly and fully to something of value that was, finally, in the service of others.

...

I don't know how newspapermen do it now, with the use of computers for writing as well as layout, makeup, and all the rest, but in the old days when a reporter was writing a story, at the bottom of each page he more often than not would type *(more)*, which, simply, indicated there was more copy coming in on that story. (Stories couldn't always be handed in all at once.)

But at the bottom of the final page he would type *—30—*. That told the typesetter there was no more copy coming in on that piece. It was finished. Done. Over.

So I'm thinking of that old newsman's rubric to mark the end of this piece with two obituaries.

The first was what Dad wrote when my Uncle Walter died in the fall of 1946. I'm reproducing it in exactly the way it appeared in the Pine Bluff *Commercial*, including the head note.

The second is a Scripps Howard editorial Dad wrote on the occasion of the death of President Harry Truman's mother and which was published July 28, 1947. That editorial earned him a nomination for a Pulitzer Prize, though he was not awarded one.

Both, I think, speak for themselves.

WHAT DO YOU THINK?

For 17 years Walter B. Sorrells Jr. was editor of The Commercial. His daily column, "What Do You Think?" was a fixture of the newspaper and of the community. When he died—October 16, 1946—among those attending the funeral was his brother John, then executive editor of the Scripps Howard newspaper chain. Unannounced, John Sorrells came to the office the day his brother was to be buried, October 18, 1946, and wrote the following tribute to his brother:

THIS IS WALTER SORRELLS'S LAST column. I'm writing it for him because Walter couldn't find his pencil. He lost it during the slow-wheeling hours of that last long night, a night in which he tried valiantly to find his way through a fog of delirium in a crossing other than Charon's.

All day, in his poor tortured mind, he had been editing the paper. But as night came on his spirit became troubled: He couldn't find his pencil. Those of us who kept the vigil with him would pretend to hand it to him, and with the trustful amiability which characterized him always, he would accept our assurances and proceed industriously with his work… until he lost his pencil again.

He needed rest, and sleep; but driven by a subconscious will to duty, he kept at his chores through the night, and into the slate gray of a drizzling dawn. Editing the paper was the only life he ever really knew; and it was his life, even to his death. It would have been so much easier for him that night if he hadn't kept losing his pencil.

…

On Breaking One's Pencil

The kinship of brothers is a peculiar relationship. It has in it, not merely affection, but comradeship...and other spiritual and emotional equations too subtle and sensitive to define. It is no accident of language that men attempt to describe their highest concept of human relations with the term "brotherhood of man." The word brother has a rich meaning; it has a unique connotation.

A man's brother is what he himself would like to be, because we always think our brothers are better men than we are. And usually they are.

...

None of us can appraise our brothers objectively: We are all subject to a common human frailty in this respect, and it therefore violates no canon of good taste when we speak of our brothers. My brother was a brave and a gentle and a compassionate man. He was kindly. He was genuinely humble. He was the only columnist I ever heard of who could write with a lower case "i."

Walter was not a nationally famous journalist. He was not a great journalist, even. But he was a great man in journalism, because as Clyde Martin wrote about him the other day, he could not stand to see anybody pushed around. Shrewd men can make money in journalism; quick and clever men can make reputations. But the freedom of our institutions are guaranteed only by those great men in journalism, who...though neither shrewd nor quick nor clever...still cannot stand to see other men pushed around.

Walter touched up a lot of people in his sixteen years as editor of The Commercial. Most of them became—or remained—his friends. That was because he wrote without malice. He simply felt that something ought to be said about a situation, and that it was his duty to say it. And so he said it, but not meanly, because there wasn't a mean bone in his body.

...

Walter didn't accumulate anything. He spent his sweaty wages, and his health and his life with the prodigal hand of a man who was big and generous in all the things that he did. Yet I believe he was the most successful man of my acquaintance. He was successful because he won the respect and the regard of everyone who knew him, in a small community, and that's doing it the hard way, because in a small community one cannot hide his deficiencies by remoteness. There is nothing as shrewdly and knowingly and as justly critical in its judgements as a small community. A phoney cannot pass for the real thing. One's fellows know him for what he is.

...

Walter was a man without pretensions, and without pretense. He was what he was; and he never stooped to the slightest device to make himself appear any different.

In that great story of Rudyard Kipling's, "The Man Who Would Be King," there is a one-line preface which reads, "Brother To a Prince and Fellow To a Beggar. If He Be Found Worthy." Walter adhered to that stern law of life; he could walk with the great, and give them whatever due was theirs, nor yet lose the genuine feeling of comradeship which he had for his fellow men.

I think the great tragedy of Walter's life was that he never knew...he did not realize...he was too genuinely humble and modest to understand what a great success his life was. He was truly a worthy man. What do you think?

YOU WERE NOT TOO LATE, MR. TRUMAN

IN THE SHY AND SENSITIVE years of boyhood, a son is rarely able to reveal in spoken words the love he holds for his mother. His tongue will not utter the tenderness and adoration which swells his heart. Nor can he tell her of his great dreams for her—of the comforts he will bring her—of the triumphs which some day he will lay at her feet.

It is the tragedy of many a man that when a measure of success has come—when maturity has unlocked his tongue—death will have deprived him of the opportunity to say to her how great was his love, how deep was his understanding and appreciation of her; he is cheated of the chance to share with her what degree of fortune and success he has attained.

Harry Truman was privileged beyond many men, for while he arrived too late to be at his mother's bedside before she died, she had lived long enough to know from his lips the depth and fidelity of his love. Her span was sufficient that he was able to share with her some measure of his material estate. She lived to see him occupy the office of highest trust among his fellow Americans. For Mr. Truman, it was not too late.

Mr. Truman was otherwise privileged with respect to his mother. She was of a stock and breed—of a mind and character—which has given him a rich endowment of personal qualities. She was blunt, forthright, courageous. A pioneer woman, she lived in an age and in a land which bred a matriarchal society. With the menfolks often away—riding the circuit, hauling to market, driving stock, or off to the wars—the management of the home and farm devolved on the woman. Circumstances conditioned them to work, to trouble, to responsibility. They were tempered. They had mettle.

Martha Ellen Truman was the daughter of a frontiersman who ran a wagon train, and herded cattle from Independence, Mo., over the Overland Trail as far away as Salt Lake and San Francisco. Sympathetic to the Confederate cause, her family was harassed by the jayhawkers, and finally driven from their home. Her girlhood was spent in the manner of frontier women. Her people were well-to-do, but in that era, land and property meant responsibility as well as physical labor for women.

It was an environment which bred the sort of fortitude which enables people to face their troubles serenely. Martha Ellen Truman was of that breed who had the ability to accept life without asking odds; she had a gay quality which often is blood-sister to gallantry. She was a good horse-woman, she liked to dance. Her sense of humor was active and direct. She once described herself as a "light-footed Baptist."

Her allusions were earthy—"Harry always plowed a straight furrow," she once said; her expressions reflected the talk of her own times and locale—she didn't like "fuss" and when something ruffled her, she would explode, "Oh, fiddlesticks!" She was a spry, and a staunch, and a lovely old lady. She lived to see the fulfillment of some of her dreams; in her son, she looked on her own works and considered them good—"Harry was a good boy."

The life of Martha Ellen Truman was altogether in the American tradition, and the relationship of this son for his mother was also in that tradition. To him, she was always "Mamma."

Vast numbers of men hold political views opposite to those of President Truman; but in the death of his mother, there is a solid kinship. His fellow Americans share his grief. They also share his pride in such a mother, and acknowledge the privilege which has been his—of having his mother live long enough to know from him all the things he felt about her.

...

I'm adding a minor addendum after the Truman piece. The death of a grown man's mother was something Dad had been carrying around with him for a long time—since his own mother died in May 1932—within five minutes of his father. I had always been told her final words, as she climbed onto their bed after the doctor had pronounced that he was gone, were, "I can't stand it, I can't stand it."

In a column dated April 10, 1941, Ernie Pyle, the great World War II columnist who worked for Scripps Howard, wrote a column about the death of his own mother and how that affected him. When Dad read the piece, he was so moved he wrote Pyle a letter, saying,

Only one who has lost his mother after he has reached manhood, and has thus been able truly to appreciate her, can understand clearly what the passing of your mother meant to you. I lost my mother just a few years ago, and only then did I realize the meaning of "too late." In the last years of her life, I tried to do things to add to her comfort, and to her happiness. Possibly I succeeded in both, but it was far too late to do what I fear I never was able to do, much as I wanted to do it—to get over to her how much she meant to me. What a swell audience she had been. What a grand sport. Oh hell—a hundred things that she meant which I never, somehow, could tell her.

Sometimes, the best of a writer is his writing, and I have that, at least, even if I can't ever know my father more, even if I can't summon up memories later than my boyhood. He died so young, and I was still so young, but at least I was spared having to see him deteriorate physically or mentally, wasting away in some urine-stenched nursing home. I *have* to settle for that, of course, but I also hope for such good luck for myself.

My mother used to tell me that when Dad was a younger man he would listen to the radio for amusement, now and again. There was a popular singer of the time (a young fellow—a tenor, at the time, named Bing Crosby) and Mom used to say that Dad would sing along with Crosby on the radio, and, she said, you almost really couldn't tell the difference between them. My mother was a person who said what she thought, was essentially a person who didn't try to gild the lilies of life. So I had to take her at her word.

But I don't *know* that. I never heard my father sing.

BILL

BACK WHEN I WAS A little boy, back before I could read, which seems back almost before time, Bill, my older brother, would read to me.

I have agreed with myself that I would have been five (or maybe four) which would have made him eight (or maybe seven). No matter. I think probably he must have read more than one story to me, but the one I remember most is Kenneth Grahame's *The Wind in the Willows*.

Even now most people still know about Ratty, Mole, Mr. Badger, the stoats and weasels, and of course the irrepressible Mr. Toad, dear old Toady— even if it's remembered because of the animated cartoon movie rather than the book.

Mostly they were the Riverbank animals playing out their days in the predictable ways of rats and moles and toads and in the predictable times of their seasons. There were friends and acquaintances; there were picnics to go on and food to gather; deep sleeps to take, adventures to share, old homes to be found and mourned over; and there were the dangers, most of which lay, for them, in the forest—the Wild Wood—where there were creatures who were, well, all right after their fashion, but the sort that you were better off not being around if you could avoid them.

I remember my brother reading about all those adventures and loyalties, pleasures and melancholies. And when he read to me, I would sit very still on a chair. I see myself yet, hands flat on my thighs (or under them if things got scary and I shivered into myself), my eyes watching my brother's mouth as he read; his eyes, as his reading grew animated; his hair as it fell straight over the pale skin of his forehead.

I would like to think that his reading to me was an act of love. And perhaps it was, but my older brother was a strange person: remote, aloof, seldom able to demonstrate affection, often biting and cynical if affection was offered. We grew up close, but mainly because of our ages. Beyond him was our sister, four years older than he, occupying her own world of pop music and boyfriends, or at least *one* boyfriend. Three years ahead of her was another brother, the eldest of the four of us, and for years a God-like presence to me who later, when I was only fifteen, became my surrogate father after Dad died of a sudden heart attack.

So I doubt that my older brother read *The Wind in the Willows* out of love for me so much as to have an audience while he read. (We both had our own kinds of flair.) But you never know about people: It may be that something in him was offering me what it could in the terms of affection he could deal with. In any case, I was a much read-to child, which meant a much-loved child.

When I had my own children I read to them. There was, of course, Watty Piper's ubiquitous *The Little Engine That Could*, with its incessant "I thought I could, I thought I could, I thought I could." And there was a Mother Goose and a little Grimm, and some wonderful, wonderful others discovered by our children who read them to us in turn: *The Railway Children, The Secret Garden*, and something about *The Lodestone* (or whatever) *of Blasingame*. They were wonderful stories and those were wonderful hours when we were together. Not just in the same room, but *together*.

Eventually the children were older and there was no more of that kind of reading to them—except at Christmas. Then, starting when they were *very* little and going on still (though sadly less often because they're grown and usually not around) there were always the two books I read to them—and to my wife. The first was Dickens' *A Christmas Carol*. It's divided into five staves, so I read a stave a night. My daughter, who was so conscious of the appropriateness of space, would prepare to put on the Christmas music (when the time came), light candles, turn off the floor lamps, and cocoon herself into a knitted afghan. Then when *she* was ready, *we* were allowed to start, and when I read, "Marley was dead. Of that there can be no doubt," our evenings for the next six nights were set.

Then on Christmas Eve I read Dylan Thomas's *A Child's Christmas in Wales*, a wonderful, lyric *piece*. And when I finished with its always evocative ending, ("I crept into bed, turned out the light, said a few words to the close and holy darkness, and slept,") we paid it the greatest of compliments by sitting very quietly, listening to the music of the carols and of ourselves.

My children are grown and usually gone now, but I did make a tape of Scrooge for my daughter when she was away at college. And my brother is dead now, a man who never seemed quite able to fit very comfortably into this world: a newspaper copyboy, something-or-other with an import/export firm, a man puzzling his way to a choice between Conrad or Christ, as he put it, choosing Christ by becoming an Episcopalian, then a priest, recognizing—but likely never quite admitting—what must have been a terribly wrong decision; a man leaving two wives, five children and a "significant other" behind—as well as me, his sister, and our other brother, both now also gone. He was a sad man, my brother Bill, who gave me so great a gift of love so long ago simply by reading me a book.

...

Bill probably was born in Pine Bluff, Arkansas, the home of our parents, though they would have been living in Fort Worth in October 1929. Dad had been editor of the *Fort Worth Press* for about two years by then, and was less than a year away from moving up to New York City as executive editor of the whole Scripps Howard newspaper chain. It was a time when many women still went back to their mommas, when they could, to have their children.

Because I lived in the City for only about nine months after I was born, I don't remember a thing about that double apartment, and all I know of Bill's stay there was through my oldest brother who said he was always wandering off. I gather that even as a baby he had an itchy heel, and when he became a toddler, there wasn't much of a way to hold him close. Let the front door of the apartment stay ajar for just two minutes and *Zoop!* Bill was on his way to wherever he meant to go.

It seems he liked to walk or crawl **Up**, for the most part, unless he was falling out and down. Often when no one had noticed that he didn't seem to be around the apartment, a neighbor would knock at the door to announce that he'd been spotted up on the top floor, or the phone would ring and Mrs. So-and-so would call to say Billy'd come to visit her—*again*—but would someone please come get him.

On Breaking One's Pencil

Even falling out of ground floor windows onto the front sidewalk or onto the garbage cans out back didn't seem to have any discernable affect on him, because that penchant for wandering stayed with him a long time.

I don't really remember that much of him in Chappaqua, where we lived next for three years. It's stuck in my head that we shared the same bedroom, and I remember a few other snippets of him, but in Scarsdale, I remember my brother as a frail child, pale of skin, dark of hair; knobbly kneed; eyes that seemed always to be looking for something that wasn't around. I fancy him with the expression of death camp survivors, though that's pure-D invention on my part. But I easily attach sunken eyes set deep into cross-hatched shadows, and a stare that be-spoke either terrible knowledge or, worse, a glazed and lost yielding up of his spirit to whatever a child could understand of mortal inevitability. I always see that image of him as a charcoal sketch, never in the softening wash of an ink drawing, and certainly not in the colors of pastels or even the rough, textured surfaces possible with oils.

Well, it's invention in-so-far as the discernable facts are concerned, but maybe I saw something there my father never saw. I gather he used to refer to Bill as "My pallid poet," and apparently not in an especially warm and loving way.

We moved to Scarsdale in 1936, so Bill would have been seven that fall, and we stayed there until the summer of 1940 when we moved to Pelham. I stayed a constant three years younger, ages four to eight. Memory can be tricky, of course, but I recall that he had learning problems: special tutors for schoolwork, eye examinations, lots of testing of various sorts. Parents seldom spoke to children in those days about such matters. Certainly no one would have tried to explain to me that my older brother might be suffering from dyslexia or slight retardation; or that he might simply be willfully passive aggressive; or that there might be other mala-dies on the Top Ten Probable Psycho-Socio-Physio-Cause list of the times.

Whatever it was all about, he was a "problem" and a source of woe to our parents. He also maintained a very healthy wanderlust. Running away was his main stock in trade. Once, even, he hooked me into his plot to run off to the City where we would grow up, become rich and famous, and return home to the joy and delight of our folks.

I thank whatever gods there may be that it didn't work out as he had planned it, because on that lovely spring Sunday morning at about 7:30 or so, the station attendant at the New York New Haven and Hartford Railway Station had enough sense not to sell two, one-way tickets into New York City to two little boys, one of whom (me) could barely see over the shelf at the ticket window. As Bill was still trying to talk the agent into a sale, on an impulse I peered out through the doors just in time to see our parents' car pull up, our parents get out, and our parents head right straight toward us. I knew the jig was up, and frankly had never before in my life been so glad to see my parents.

We went home to a wonderful breakfast after which I went back to bed and slept, but had sad dreams featuring my brother's face quivering across the breakfast table from me as he tried not to break down into tears at the failure of his dream to *Go!* Still, there was also set in his face some shade of will that said this was only one try, that he was still very young, and that there was world enough and time for further adventures.

And indeed he made use of them. The one I remember best happened after we had moved to Pelham and he had started in at Staunton Military Academy in Staunton, Virginia. (*Nota bene*: Never mind the spelling, it's pronounced **Stan**ton.)

Staunton was the county seat of Augusta County, and in the original deed, or whatever, it stretched from the Atlantic Ocean west, clear out to wherever someone someday might wander. It was in the Shenandoah Valley, a place shining and fecund with apple orchards in the fall, lush with apple blossoms in the spring, and chock-a-block with the still-echoing hoofbeats of JEB Stuart's cavalry, Stonewall Jackson's stubborn defenses, Lee's amazing maneuvering, Jubal Early's running the Yankees ragged up and down the Valley and everywhere else: Winchester, Port Republic, Sharpsburg, Cross Keys. There seemed no end to the Civil War there. You have to remember that in 1943, the year Bill started at Staunton, "The War" had been over for only 78 years.

I started at SMA in 1946. I was the third of the three of us brothers to go there. The first one, John, went there because he wanted to be a professional soldier. He also wanted to be an officer, which meant he wanted to go to West Point. The best way to prepare himself to go to the Point was to go to a good military prep school. He chose Staunton on his own hook after sending off for and poring over all the brochures and pamphlets he could find. His senior year he was the highest ranking cadet in the Corps of Cadets—First Captain, Cadet Lieutenant Colonel.

Bill went there because he was a mess. He ended up a technical sergeant in the Medical Detachment.

I went there because Bill and John had, and because it was convenient for my parents for me to go. I was the last child and they wanted to get rid of the big house in Pelham so they could move back into town. I ended up as a company commander, a cadet captain.

But Bill's sophomore year he and another cadet ran away. They ended up in Ohio some-where, where the other lad lived. I gather it hadn't been to flee an impossible situation or an oppressive environment or to escape from hellish iniquities or any other such profound reason. It was mainly a caper, I think, and was true to Bill's history of wandering.

They went back to school where they were received with penalties, but also with great sighs of relief. Their elders knew what could happen to sixteen-year-olds loose on the highways of America, Bill's parents knew their son, and the school's administration knew the position it could have been in if anything really bad had happened to the boys.

In the spring of Bill's junior, my freshman, year, he and some friends got caught by the wrong faculty member in the midst of a drinking bout. The man who caught them was a stickler for the rules, a Colonel James, as I recall, the physics teacher and a truly no-nonsense man both academically as well as militarily. They were turned in and dismissed for the remainder of the year.

However, if they had been caught by Captain Lou Onesty, the swimming coach and a hard-nose in his own way, he would have worked their asses off after school hours by having them run laps, do nip ups, wind sprints, and other such blood-purifying exercises, or—what surely would have been worse—might even have turned them over to Colonel Joe Taylor, the boxing coach (when there had been a boxing team), and the man in charge of the mess hall. He more than likely would have put them through some other extra-curricular activities involving his own favorite sport which likely would have included his climbing into the ring with them, never mind his age. He would not have been the boxer at a disadvantage.

There is always more than one way to make a point.

The next year, Bill was back at SMA keeping his nose clean so he could finally graduate. We were rooming together with a fellow in my own class from Miami, Ray Polizzi, when our father died in late February, and Bill, being the older, was called into the commandant's office to be told the news. He came back to our room and told me.

We packed our bags, picked up our tickets which must have been bought for us somehow, and made the journey back to New York, first on the C&O to Washington where we changed to the Pennsy for the rest of the trip. From New York, we traveled with our mother to Memphis on the Southern, and from there to Pine Bluff on the Cotton Belt. That's how I remember it, at least.

But the main thing is that it was my big brother who told me our father was dead, even as he had told me nearly three years earlier when I had come home from school one fine spring afternoon, that our grandfather—up from Pine Bluff with our grandmother visiting us in Pelham—was also suddenly and unexpectedly dead.

And as if that hadn't been enough in a few short years, the next year, his freshman year at college, my junior year at SMA, our first Christmas without our father, he accidentally shot himself at a party. Mother and I had moved down to Memphis because she had no intention of staying in New York and because there were two Scripps Howard papers there with people she and Dad knew well and fondly.

My sister and her family were living in Memphis at the time, too, and I stayed with them while Mother went back to New York to be with Bill during his early recuperation.

That was 1948. In 1951 he was drafted into the Army because of the Korean War, and got married much against the wishes of my mother as well as the young lady's parents' wishes. Seven years later our mother died, and shortly after *that*, Bill started in on his first divorce.

Please understand: This isn't any *Mommy Dearest* dirty linen. It's my older brother. It's the way he was, and it's who he was. He was a very real flesh and blood human being getting through life as well as he could. Some of us may simply have been a little luckier than he was. Or maybe we dared less, or tried for less.

...

On Breaking One's Pencil

I wasn't with Bill when he died, but I had seen him not too many months before.

In 1979 my son was a junior in high school, and as good parents who had read all the articles we were supposed to about college selection, we had taken a long trip to let our son see some places. The trip included a trek up through Virginia with a stop off in Roanoke where Bill was living with a lovely woman who had refused to marry him even though he had asked her to, explaining her decision by reminding him of his two previously failed marriages.

The next year we were making that same trek to take our son to a small, Quaker-founded college in Pennsylvania just outside Philadelphia. On the way, we stopped again to see Bill. In the intervening year he had gotten sick. He went into a hospital on a Monday, and by that Wednesday he was totally paralyzed from his chest down. It was cancer of the lung, but of a sort that typically sweeps around to the spinal column.

By the time we saw him again he was bed-ridden forever in a hospital bed set up for him in their small house on Tennessee Street. He was flat on his back at the mercy of the county medical people and the cancer, and the loving and tender mercies of his final partner.

My wife and daughter and I had found their house without any trouble, and when we saw him he didn't look too bad, considering. He stared at our daughter for a long time, that quirky, inscrutable smile on his face. Then he said, "You look just like Becky," and he nodded his head toward the bureau where a picture of one of his own daughters had pride of place. And they did look alike.

We chatted, the five of us, trying to make the small talk that some people don't under-stand. Sometimes it *is* just filler, but sometimes it seems to be the best way to fill in gaps and learn things at the same time. What did we want to know? Not just the How Are You of casual conversation, but the How Are You **Really**? And we wanted to know what his spirit was, how he felt in himself, as the Brits say.

I stood by his bed while he started fidgeting. He would look around now and then, making sure that Donna, his woman, was still there close.

His woman, I heard myself think. What a terrible expression, yet what else was possible? "Significant Other" rang with the tinkling brass sound of our times when people were so desperately uptight about being "sensitive." But a man can have a woman, it seemed to me. My wife used to call me her good man, and I didn't take it amiss.

He told me about the catheter and the infections. He told me about the visits from the county health people. He told me about the feeble attempts at physical therapy.

"Do you use that thing?" I asked, talking about the metal triangle, suspended over his bed like an infant's mobile, he was supposed to use to help himself shift around. He could use it to do pull-ups to keep at least some upper body strength, help keep his lungs from collecting fluid, give him something three times a day to focus his attention on so he wouldn't brood.

"Not much," he said. "It doesn't do any good."

"I'll bet if you used it regularly it would," I said. "You have to do that stuff regularly."

He never even looked at me for that one, just totally dismissed it.

"Can't they help you do stuff?" I asked, using a vague *They* he pounced on almost before I got it out.

"Who're *they*!" he nearly shouted.

"I don't know, Bill. The physical therapists or whoever."

"They don't really come any more," he said, trying to scrunch around a little, clearly edgy, starting to sweat some.

"Why not?"

It was Donna who answered softly. "There's a time limit on all that kind of service," she said.

"Oh," I said. I was rubbing his arm that he had finally let be still at his side on the sheet.

Then I noticed even more sweat beading up on his forehead, and he started to fidget again.

"Well maybe we should get back to the motel," I said. "We need to clean up some and have supper."

He nodded at that and looked relieved.

"Can we come back for a little while after?" I asked.

Donna said that would be good.

I patted the top of his hand as we left, and on the front stoop Donna said, "He gets awfully tired, and then he's still got a little infection. But he wants to see you all," she said. "He really does." She looked at my wife for a second. "He *needs* to see you all," she finished.

We stepped down to the yard.

"My boy might drop in later, but just come on. He's sometimes here, sometimes not," Donna said.

We waved ourselves away from the house.

Later, after we had all eaten, after we had talked to each other back in the room, after we had started getting used to the idea that my brother wouldn't—couldn't—be alive much longer, we drove back out to their place.

Bill seemed more relaxed and a little more chipper, but just a little. I was less chipper than ever, but it was a good visit with the usual kinds of catching up on things: schools, dates, plans, all the rest of a family's conversational detritus, the stuff that lets us know we're where we ought to be, doing what we ought to be doing, and doing it with the people we ought to be doing it with.

I stood by his bed again, wanting to be close to him, I guess, wanting for once to be really and truly close to this brother of mine.

"If I was here," I said, "I could help you. I could help you work out. I could help you do things and Donna could get more rest. I really could."

It could be he heard the desperation in my voice. Maybe the anger. Maybe the love. The fear. Maybe not.

"It wouldn't make any difference, Bob," he said. His voice sounded neither impatient nor defeated, neither angry nor hopeful, neither cross nor deferential, neither annoyed nor particular-ly concerned. It was so matter-of-factly neutral I knew that when we left that night I would never see him again.

I was very angry about that for a long time. It was a modest bit of hubris, I expect: I the Loyal Little Brother could save the wandering and errant Bigger Brother; *I* the True Believer could save the Broken Priest; *I* the Good Son could salvage the heart and the soul and the spirit of the man. And he? *He* the big brother, *he* the broken priest, *he* the prodigal son, *he* the shepherd wandering in the desert no longer searching for his lost flock much less his own soul: He didn't especially want me to help him, though I expect he probably thought it nice of me to offer.

And then I would see that slight sneer that often appeared—sometimes quite clearly, other times no more than brushing his smile like a caress—and I would feel my old fear: that I was helpless, finally, to love anyone enough to matter when it counted.

...

About a year later word was sent that the University of Virginia School of Medicine was done with him and that his "Cremains" were on their way. My wife and I and my oldest brother and Bill's oldest child whom I hadn't seen since he was three, went to Pine Bluff where the ceremony of interment was performed by my oldest nephew, himself a Presbyterian minister.

It was a cold day, sleeting, dangerous for driving, especially when the semis, their drivers sitting mutely up in their cabs above the frozen, blinding slush they threw against your wind-shield, passed you doing fifty-five and sixty on those long haunting, and for me haunted, stretches of Arkansas highway leading back to Memphis.

...

But I was saying that back in what must have been pre-history there was a time when I couldn't read. Being the fourth of four I was always the smallest, the dumbest, and the most spoiled—at least by my mother—who always read to us. How strange it seems now that it was Bill, the sad man who died far younger than he needed to, who used to read to me most. As I suggested, it wasn't likely an altruistic act. Being closest to me in age, I was *it* during those times he wanted to play with someone, if, of course, he chose to "play" at all. With Bill, *to play* seemed an oxymoron at best.

But he read Grahame's book to me and—knowingly, intentionally, or not, blessed me for-ever. It was probably what made me a writer, one of those blessings that curses, or curses that bless. Whatever, it was my focused introduction to a world of love and companionship, useful labor, straight acting, potential violence, and loss.

One of the most memorable chapters in the book—"Dulce Domum," it's called—is the one in which Moley rediscovers his old home, which he had left on such a whim so long before. But when he came back to it, or it to him, he was overwhelmed by such a sadness he could barely function. So it fell to Ratty, the faithful friend, to save the night, which was, after all, Christmas Eve.

Because Ratty understood his friend's anguish, because Ratty was clear headed in the situation, because Ratty loved his friend, they were able to have their fulsome celebration when all the little animals from the old

On Breaking One's Pencil

neighborhood came a-caroling, not knowing, apparently, of the changes in Moley's life and the fact that he was no longer one of them, quite. Then, the next day, they left the old home again, wending their way to Ratty's River bank which was by then, really, Moley's home, too.

In the book up till then Moley simply longed to be free of the quotidian routine, to escape into the wider world of adventure and new friends. Then came the chance encounter with things past, the coming back into contact with a life gone forever, apparently, and for whatever reasons: whimsy or calculation, chance or bad judgment.

Moley's literal, tactile, and emotional re-establishing of contact with his past was accomplished by an inevitable and ineffably crushing sense of loss. It was like looking at yourself in a mirror one morning and seeing the person you were twenty-five years earlier.

Think about that. Even though that kind of back azimuth may stir some eddies of salvation and renewal, while that kind of encounter may in fact help you transcend the world in some way, still, it also keeps you rooted, possibly even mired in it.

To me there was all of life in that chapter. That's how I *say* it now, but it was that in-tensely felt when I was four or five or six—whenever it was I first heard it from my brother—and it has been confirmed across the years as I have read and re-read the book. Something in me knew that that chapter spoke to my sense of the past as fully as the chapter called "Wayfarers All" spoke to me of the solitariness of The Journey, the restlessness, the rubs of love that tickle and itch us on our ways.

It wasn't, back then, that I had all that much of a past to remember or ponder, of course, but if you are the youngest child in a family and the oldest is nearly a decade older than you, why you have an additional ten years in your own life, because that brother can speak of things that were when he was your age. That meant I was able to encompass the world since 1923, the year my oldest brother was born, rather than just since 1932, my own birth year.

It can skew your perceptions of the world a little, give you a strange sense of being older than you are, larger-in-life than you really are, even wiser than you otherwise might have thought yourself. I was in touch, somehow, with more than myself, and that can be a strange feeling.

...

I haven't really intended to make my brother Bill's life parallel *The Wind in the Willows* at all, but there is something about the book that just does make us see *our* realities in *its* terms. I suppose that's why it's lasted for so long.

The "Wayfarers All," chapter, for instance, in which Ratty gets into a funk because it's time for all the creatures to start their various peregrinations: the field mice move to new digs; the birds ready themselves for flight south. It all leaves Ratty's world discombobulated, and when he himself starts feeling the pull of faraway places, of romantic climes, and all the rest, he's fresh meat for the tales of a passing seafaring rat, a coaster (rather than a trans-oceanic voyager), who's been a place or two in his time, and seen what's what in the world.

I reckon it's the itchy heel syndrome of the seafaring rat that helps me make that kind of connection with Bill. I have the same condition. So did my father, a man with a sizable curiosity bump, who used to tell me that he and Mother had intended to work their ways around the world. They only got about as far as Oklahoma City or Cleveland, though, when she got pregnant the first time.

My oldest brother, John, and I were the two "Southern" children in my family. Bill and my sister, Peg, were the Yankees. Yet Bill finally had left Connecticut and its nearly New England winters to head south again. He got to Roanoke, a place of no particular significance to him except that it's where Donna was living. Yet there he was—back in Virginia, one of the places he had run from so many years earlier; back in the South again, which had always pretty much been our clan's home, a place which had never really been his heart's home. I don't know if he saw any particular ironies in that or not. After all, fairly or not, we can't be held responsible for how other people may interpret our lives.

DEAR MOE AND FAMILY

I'M REALLY SORRY I WASN'T at Peg's memorial service, but at the same time I didn't "need" to be there, either. It was one of those damned if you do/damned if you don't sort of things. Ruth called and tried to talk me into going, and I really wanted to, but I had been up there with y'all last Thanksgiving and had talked to Peg shortly before we left for Florida and the South on the ninth. Still, I wanted to be with the rest of the family too. Janie I haven't seen since 1978, Kathy since she was a child, John only once, and none of the grandchildren for ages—the ones I *have* seen.

Also, I hate to be a bother, and I really would have had to have folks get me from one place to another at appropriate times. So what follows is the result of some months—even years, I guess—of pondering Peg and her RA (rheumatoid arthritis) and her nerve and guts and strengths and foibles and, yes, her mulishness ("True Grit" is not always easy to be around). So this may be my way of sitting at the dinner table with my family at the tag end of a meal and a day, finishing off the wine, summoning up our often faulty memories as we recall and feel again the energy and depth of the life we memorialize by speaking to each other about both her and it, letting the past hold us more gently than not, at such a time, when we recall our people with love. That setting really is an *Occasion*, the sort, as May Sarton put it in one of her many fine poems, when memory "makes kings and queens of us all."

...

Peg was seven years older than I was, so in growing up I wasn't as close to her as I was to Bill—if anyone was ever "close" to Bill. Still, he was nearest me in age, and I've read that a six-year difference is a *lot* of difference in growing up. I always felt close to John, though, an august presence to me, and for many years later I (and then *we*) lived near them after you all went back to New York. Also, Peg was a teenaged girl who liked pop music and was dating you, Moe, virtually the entire time we lived in Pelham. All of which is to say she and I lived in very different worlds. I remember *wanting* to be close to her, but seldom feeling much from her in return on that score. Peg could be pretty icy at times, pretty absolute about things, pretty unbending, pretty opinionated. Our curses and our virtues tend to be cut from the same cloth.

So I was in Tennessee then Kentucky then back to Tennessee; then to Iowa, South Carolina, and Arkansas; then to England and back to South Carolina; then again to Tennessee; and now Minnesota for the past ten years. During most of the "southern" years, I had little contact with Peg. I visited and stayed with you in 1978 when I got the National Endowment grant, but that was after about 20 years—maybe 21or 22.

With all that apartness, though, there was never any estrangement; at least I never felt any. The familial relationship was simply sporadic, tended to in its own way. Yet I never recall feeling *out* of touch with her. My life had taken on the checkerboard of moves and jobs, and her time was certainly spoken for with five chillern to raise and a TV executive to do for.

All of which is to say that our getting back in touch was truly in the nature of a re-discovery as well as a reunion, and a very full rediscovery it was, because it involved re-discovering you and your children and your lives. There's another way of saying that: *my* brother-in-law, *my* nephews and nieces, and *my* grandnephews and nieces.

What a gift I feel that to be.

When I finally got Walter and Patti and Jake up to Pelham the year Walter got the Edgar Award for his third novel, and we were all together for that wonderful evening, he was telling me later how good he had felt about being around all of you, how comfortable he was. From Walter that was quite something. Social ease and acuity is not usually his thing. So he was casting about for some way to say what he had felt, and then—a big grin on his face—he came up with, "We all looked alike."

...

Certain kinds of psychologists talk about "anticipatory grief." It's what we all have surely gone through with Peg over the years: How many more heart attacks, how many more strokes, how many more operations can she survive?

On Breaking One's Pencil

We all knew the odds, we all saw the relentless declines in her health, her body's increasing debility, and all the rest. So when Peg finally died, the fact of her death was met more with sorrow than with shock. I'm speaking for myself, of course, but I assume it was much the same for all of you. Moe, remember how we agreed that she turned loose rather than gave up. She died in a place she loved surrounded by the people she loved most. You of all of us, along with John and other combat veterans, know how lucky she was in that, at least. God knows she had merited that much and more over the years.

But if the shock was slight, the sorrow is profound. Part of it John Donne wrote about in the often quoted section from his *Meditation 17*: "Any man's death diminishes me, because I am involved in mankind; and therefore never send to know for whom the bell tolls; it tolls for thee." That's a broad sweeping view, though, one which says simply that the tolling bell reminds us all of our mortality and thus of our ends.

Closer to home, Peg's death makes me the last of the four Sorrells kids, and that is a very spooky feeling. I can't ask her questions any more. I had meant to ask her whether she was actually born in Pine Bluff. (It was still a time when many women went back home to have their children.) And were they living in Cleveland at the time? That sounds right, but Dad had some wandering years around then and I was never sure. I can't ask anybody those questions now. For the most part, if I don't know the answers, no one does, and the fact that probably no one wants to know the answers to such questions doesn't really matter.

In this case, it's not just watching Peg die, but seeing as well the fading away of a generation, and though I'm not quite of that generation, it's more mine than not. World War II still informs my attitudes and much more than that Korean "Police Action" of the fifties.

I'm sorry if this seems to wander, but as Donne was saying, any one person's death not only yanks us into focusing our attention on the immediate event—Peggy Ann Sorrells Moore has died—but is cosseted about with such layers of associations that we cannot help but incorporate them into a huge ball of so many other deaths and losses: People, times, events, possibilities, chances.

Well, I expect that in future when we think of Peg, we can all cherish Albert Camus' lines:

On certain mornings, as we turn a corner, an exquisite dew falls on our hearts and then vanishes. But the freshness lingers, and this, always, is what the heart needs.

In my own final words to Peg I found I was paraphrasing Shakespeare's famous "Good-night, sweet Prince" lines from *Hamlet*. They're spoken by Horatio at the very end of the play when he sees all the carnage around him, including the dead Hamlet. "Now cracks a noble heart. Good night [my sister],/ And flights of angels sing thee to thy rest."

Stay in touch, one and all. Stay in touch.

With Love,

A GIFT OF UNCLES

FOR SO MANY YEARS IT had been the same. Each Christmas, I came home to Memphis from either the military academy in Staunton, Virginia, where I went to high school, or from Nashville, where I was in college. Each year my mother and I kept Christmas together: got the tree, decorated it, did our shopping, set out our last minute surprises for the next morning, got up with our stockings, ate breakfast, then opened the presents under the tree.

It was all so familiar from my childhood, yet so different with my father dead, my brothers and sisters grown and gone, long since keeping their own Christmases with their own families, growing into their own traditions.

I felt sad when I looked at my mother putting up the good show. It wasn't the smallness of the stacks of gifts, though that was always a reminder of how many fewer people there were in our world now—certainly in her world. But I knew the year would have to come when I'd call her on the phone or write her the letter saying that I wouldn't be home for Christmas that year, either.

The thought of not being home wasn't a particular sadness to me, to my anticipations. When I didn't get back it would be because I needed to be somewhere else. As it turned out, I was in the Army my first Christmas away. Rather, sneaking looks at her as she slowly undid a package, I felt an overwhelming sadness as I pictured her by herself: no husband, no children, few really close friends. Then how long would she keep up the bother of a tree? The music box record we always played? A sad and sterile phone call with everyone sounding too cheery: That's what would be left. It would be cold, no big meal, no energy of bodies to charge the apartment. And even if she spent the rest of the Christmases wherever *we* were, it wouldn't be the same, because it wouldn't be *her* place. She would always be the guest. She would always be somebody's mother-in-law.

But the truly awful part of Christmas always came in the afternoon when we drove—*had* to drive—over to Little Rock to see Mother's mother (Big Momma to all us children) who lived with Mother's sister and her husband. Both of us had come to hate that trip. It had become so obligatory. But there was no way out.

Then I used to wonder: Was it such an awful thing, after all? One night in the year to drive two-and-a-half hours to see the grandmother you virtually never otherwise had to be around, the grandmother who used to make you so mad when you were a small child because she pinched you all the time even when she *knew* you really didn't like it? Was that so awful? At least my mother didn't have to keep her the rest of the year: My aunt, after all, was willing to do that. Was it all that awful to see your aunt and her husband one night a year, even if you had finally come to look on her as tedious more than sad and him as silly more than clever? Was it all that awful? To swap some gifts, to stretch the day's giving and joy out just a little more: Why should that be so awful?"

"Well," Mother would sigh, her gaze lingering on me for just a moment, lingering as she looked past me and out into the living room.

We made certain our brief lists of the presents we had gotten were complete for the thank you notes, gathered the things together, tidied up, finished dressing, got the Little Rock presents all together, looked around our snuggery, and left.

...

That's the way it usually was. But there was another year, the year my mother's brother came up from Louisiana. That was a good Christmas.

...

"I got something for you," he'd told us on the phone, his heavy voice resonant. "Won't send it. Gonna hand it to you. Personal!"

We had actually looked forward to that trip over, and when we got there, saw his trailer parked out on the drive, *Sportsman's Paradise* printed on the license plate, we looked at each other and grinned like children seeing the first Santa Claus of the season.

Inside, it was hugs and kisses, have a beer, fix a drink, swap the presents. With him there, there was always an energy that glowed, beat slowly and heavily like the heart of a long-distance runner at rest. It was always warm where he was. Listening to the conversations—my mother and uncle flirting, my aunt's laugh high and hysterical, her husband telling his long, never-quite-funny stories, I started seeing them all in colors and images and sounds. My uncle was golden, brown, warm, and quiet, with the kind of voice little children can go to sleep to when they're finally put to bed. My aunt, my mother's sister, a sewing machine needle flitting from side to side, *hunning* in a higher and higher-pitched whine—*fiddle-de-dee-dee-dee-dee-dee-dee*—like a mechanical Scarlet O'Hara gone mad. She was electric green, her spaghetti and beer-heavied body pirouetting, still sadly insisting on girlhood. And there was my uncle's wife—a petite frame, always a near smile on her face, almost as kind—and as tough and warm as her hugs

But it was fun that year. The hand-delivered extra was a bottle of wine. Apple wine. Ozark apple wine bought from a good source. A bottle for me, one for my mother, and one for himself.

"C'mere," I heard him say. Nobody else in the room could have heard him. Or understood him if they had. When he talked, he sounded like a man with a deep cold clearing his throat. That's what I had always loved about him: We could sit two feet apart and share secrets without whispering. *What?* Everybody else would always shout at us. *What'd you say?* We would just smile back at them.

After all the noise of our arrival and such had more or less settled down, he led me out to the trailer. I'd never been in one before. But my uncle did all the things an uncle should do, which is simply all those things my parents didn't. He'd lived in a trailer, he'd been a butcher, he'd never made any money; he'd always been responsible, but without ever seeming too settled about it. I knew my mother worried about him.

"Have a glass of wine," he said when we got nestled in the trailer, "and tell me how you're doing."

"What do you want to know?" I asked him importantly, sipping the wine, tasting the sweet ferment of apple in the back in my throat.

"Everything," he told me.

So I told him all about college and fraternities; all about school and loneliness; all about love and fear; all about friends and books; all about Nashville and cold people; all about missing my father and wanting to teach; all about being without a home, about not having a place to call home; a little bit about rankling at my mother, feeling responsible to her and for her and without knowing how to *do* anything about it; all about having to come over there to Little Rock—except when *he* came, my uncle…

"I'll drink to that," he said. My uncle was named Gordon. It was my brother Bill's middle name, my maternal grandmother's maiden name. My older brother and Gordon never got on all that well.

But we drank a glass to all of those topics anyway.

And to several others, too, as I recall: my university's football team, my fraternity's wrestling team, all the girls I was in love with (or wanted to be), all the girls Uncle Gordon had been in love with (or had wanted to be), to morality, to the president ("God bless him"), to *all* the presidents (Uncle Gordon could recite them in order with their dates of office and middle names correct), to each of the forty-eight states (Uncle Gordon could also recite all of them without missing a lick because he knew where in the country they were and recited them by geographical blocs), to my father and all the other noble dead, and to that wonderful Christmas day because it was doing what Christmas is supposed to do: bring our family together and let us see we were—or at best could be, or at the very least at one time had been—friends as well as family, too. And of course we toasted Johnny Appleseed.

Often.

Then it was Uncle Gordon's turn, and the tales that man knew: butchering and sawmills and learning all about Indians in Arizona and teaching himself civil engineering by correspondence and about not being able to be a father and about getting stuck as an engineer with the Louisiana State Department of Highways…

"Because I never went to college and they don't give a poot about what you know or what you've learned to do if you don't have that degree to back it up with…"

…and about hunting and fishing and being a Boy Scout and loving America, and getting so drunk one night that—even with a perfectly clear head—he fell on his ass because his legs wouldn't stand up right.

"Right on my *ass*," he said. "Right there in the parking lot, and I knew what was happening just like I knew my own name. But…"

On Breaking One's Pencil

It had reached my funny bone, that image of my Uncle Gordon, his face probably perfectly straight, sober looking as any judge, but with a slightly confused cast to it as his brain tried to figure out why the legs should behave in such an unseemly and indecorous manner as to let the rest of his body grunt to a jolt there on the tarmac.

Uncle Gordon had a hard time telling the rest of the story because the two of us were laughing so hard we had slid nearly to the floor.

I finally managed to get out, "Did...did...did you ever getbackhome?"

Which Uncle Gordon took to be something like the funniest question he'd heard in a coon's age.

"Naw," he finally managed to answer. "I'm still there."

At which we both slid the rest of the way to the floor of the tiny trailer, each of us begging the other to quit—Please! *Jeeeeesus!* quit—before we got sick from laughing so hard.

At which we laughed all the harder, of course, gasping for air, our rib cages rocked and aching.

Until finally we were aware of a banging at the trailer door, which Uncle Gordon had locked.

"Whooooo whooooo whooooooooo?" I hooted.

Uncle Gordon leaned up from the floor and pulled the door open. He saw his sister, my aunt Zuzu who was called Sookie by my mother and uncle. He pushed the door shut quickly.

She banged again. He opened it a crack and called out softly, "Whoooo gooooooes theeeeere?"

"You should be ashamed," she hollered, just barely avoiding an act of grave bodily harm on him as she smashed the door open the rest of the way. "What in the world do you think you're doing?"

We had managed to recover by then and even had started to answer, when Uncle Gordon picked up the two empty bottles from the floor, held them to his eyes as though they were huge naval binoculars, and slowly swung his head around, scanning a hostile horizon, until he came to rest his gaze, finally, on her. Then he let out a scream as he recoiled in mock terror and took the bottles from his eyes, collapsing again in tears.

"Whoooo, whoooo?" I joined in. "Whoooo, whoooo?" right at her face.

"No," Uncle Gordon choked out, belching at the same time and getting tickled at that, too. "Whaaat *is* it? Whaaat *is* it?"

"You fool!" Zuzu shot out. "What have you done to that boy?"

"Uncle Gordon," I said, my face serious. I reached out and gently took the separated binoculars from my uncle. "Tssk tssk. Oh *durn*! God, Uncle Gordon. I'm sorry. Lookee here. We has done drunk up all of your bottle and all my pore Momma's bottle of apple juice. Mine's the onliest one's left."

Uncle Gordon looked carefully at the two bottles. "Why, boy. I believe you're right. What'll your Momma say?"

"We'll tell her it got broke?"

"Fool!" Zuzu spit out again at Gordon. "Get in the house right now. We've been out of our wits with fright at you. Whyn't you tell us where you were going? We thought you'd gone someplace in a car and had a wreck or something. Uncle Charles was beside himself about you, Bobby. Don't you know it's midnight already? Big Mama's gone to bed hours ago wondering where you were."

I couldn't keep from laughing clear back to the house, especially when Uncle Gordon asked, his head down, his voice petulant like a child's, "Wasn't anybody beside theirselfs with worry about me, too?"

"Oh shut up!" Zuzu snapped again.

I snorted once, which set Uncle Gordon off again in his own series of snorts and *haw haw's*. So we tripped and pretended to fall, hooted, belched, and snickered our weary ways clear back to the house—at least thirty feet.

"Uncle Gordon, when you laugh it comes all the way up from the soles of your feet. Did you know that?" It struck me that that wasn't really quite what I was trying to say. What was whirling through my head was more along the line of *souls*. His laughter always came up from his *soul*, which Uncle Gordon may have understood anyway. But it brought on another peal of *haw's* and *snorts* in any event.

"The very idea. What will our neighbors think? Whatever possessed you to get drunk—and on Christmas day...!"

Fiddle-de-dee-dee-dee-dee-dee-dee-dee-dee, I heard screeching around in my head.

Fiddle-de-dee-dee-dee.

When Aunt Zuzu finally got us herded back inside the house, like two errant geese fled from the gaggle, I looked at my mother and my Aunt Monica, Uncle Gordon's little bird of a wife. They looked officially miffed, but more amused than not.

"Charles was scared out of his wits," Zuzu started in again, when—taken with a fit of gleeful malice—I turned toward her and, 'FIDDLE-DE-DEE-DEE-DEE-DEE-DEE," I bellowed. Then, turning to my uncle, I exclaimed, "Merry Christmas, Uncle Gordon. Merry by-God Christmas."

He *haw-hawed* once, then grabbed me in his rough clutch, that secure and little-child-gruffling hug. Then I was clutching him back, loving him, but knowing it wasn't my father who had given me this precious Christmas.

"Merry by-God Christmas your own durned self," Gordon growled back, himself knowing he wasn't the Father and I wasn't the Son. But in that jointly desperate, crushing embrace, knowing, too, that it was as close as either of us would be able to get—Gordon ever, and me ever again. We knew it would just have to do.

And *Oh!* by God, it did.

THE SINGER

I USED TO HAVE A very nice singing voice. Not really good, but pretty good—good enough to blend with glee clubs or fraternity quartets. I also used to have a very good speaking voice—or so folks said.

It wasn't that it was a *fine* voice, at all, but apparently I could make it do things that others couldn't do with theirs. I wouldn't say, even, that it had "signature," whatever that might encompass. I always thought it was fun just because other people's voices never *sounded* like mine. That is, other people couldn't make their voices do what I could do with mine—either in speaking or singing (or mimicry).

I always wanted to sing.

...

As a matter of fact, in Primary School in Pelham Manor, New York (I would have been in either 4th or 5th grade at the time probably), our class had to sing in the smallish school's auditorium for some occasion or other—a run-up to Christmas would be a likely guess. We were arranged in a semi-circle of probably 20 children, singing songs that the music teacher doubtless had chosen for us.

In any event, I happened to be placed at one end of that line and so stood directly in front of the piano. It was a Baby Grand, and it had been angled so the piano player (maybe one of the teachers) could more easily see the director as she was directing us. I was what you might call one of the two "End Men" (or Girls) of our event.

Whatever, I was standing directly at the curve of the piano's harp.

We sang our songs vigorously, I assume, and—given our voices, attention, and interest—gave out with pretty good flair and even some tone.

On Breaking One's Pencil

After our performance was over and folks had started more or less milling about or looking to see if they could shuffle away without breaking their children's' hearts, I heard the lady who had played the piano, softly call my name. I turned to look at her across the harp of the piano. The lid was down, so we were looking directly at each other. She had a look of awe on her face, and very softly she said, "Bobby, you have a lovely voice."

...

I can't say that her complement was a ground-breaking event in the career of one of the most notable singers of the modern era, seeing as how I have never sung even for a plugged nickel, but it was one of those events I obviously never forgot. Hence, it lay dormant within the realm of my psyche: *I Have a Lovely Voice.*

What I was really interested in, was writing. Why not? My father was a writer. He was a newspaperman with the Scripps Howard newspaper chain (Executive Editor of the whole shebang for the final part of his too-short life); his kid brother was a newspaperman (editor of the *Pine Bluff Commercial* in Pine Bluff, Arkansas); one of Dad's grandfathers had started a newspaper in Pine Bluff years earlier; my oldest brother worked on the *Commercial Appeal* in Memphis for years; after WW II, my brother-in-law worked on newspapers a number of years, then went with ABC News, and I spent the summer after my Freshman year at Vanderbilt University working as a copyboy on the *Knoxville News-Sentinel.*

So what's with singing?

...

During my undergraduate time in Nashville (there was a two-year hiatus in there with the US Army during the Korean War which, mercifully, I spent in Salzburg, Austria, operating and repairing radios and hanging out on US Army radio nets), I finished my Bachelor's Degree, stayed at Vanderbilt another year, earned a Master's Degree in English, then off to teach in Murray State College for two years, then back to Nashville, working at my own writing, then earning a living for a year by working in the Development Office at Vanderbilt University writing brochures for a $30,000,000 Capital Gifts Campaign ("Vanderbilt University urgently needs…"), then back to my own writing. Then marriage, then to the University of Iowa's Creative Writing program to earn the MFA, then to Clemson University for five years teaching in the English Department, followed by a year at the University of Arkansas as a Visiting Associate Professor teaching in their MFA Creative Writing Program, then a self-granted, nearyear sabbatical with the family in England...

...then back to Clemson, South Carolina (where I had taught for five years, remember)—but this time it was odd jobs which involved writing: three, six-months stints at the Publications and Graphics division at Clemson University; writing a commissioned history of Clemson University's Experimental Forest; and radio work on the Clemson/South Carolina NPR station I had begun that included readings—which, of course, required a good voice...

In a way, I had been in seventh heaven—writing and speaking. I was happier, just about, than I had ever been in my life.

...

All the while, I was still writing my short stories, re-working them, and doing all the things that fill up your time when you need to look busy—sending stories out to wonderful magazines that would never buy them because they didn't come from an agent, spending money to enter prize-winning award competitions that would show the world that "You, **Too**, Can Make Big Bucks" as a writer, and so forth.

A heady life. A heady, heady life.

And the only thing about such a heady life is that it's close to being the only thing you really want to do. The only thing that lets you understand that you are still a writer—samples on demand.

...

But I was talking about singing.

I began this piece with song, and will end it with song—Christmas Songs. Carols. Harking Angels. Good Kings. Feasting. Beloved New-born Babes in Cribs...

At some time after I had returned to school from my Army service—probably after I had graduated with the BA, likely after I had returned, even,

On Breaking One's Pencil

when my two years at Murray State College were done with, and perhaps after my self-granted sabbatical had ended with my joining the Development Office job—there was the annual Christmas concert in Neely Auditorium on the University campus. When The University choir and perhaps some other groups—quartets, male-female ensembles or whatever—had finished with their programs, the ritual was for the audience to leave that beautiful chapel-auditorium to do a sing-along in a fairly generous space outside the front doors.

It was night. It was chilly. Christmassy.

Usually, for those of us who hadn't quite gotten our fill of music inside, several of the lead singers of the choirs would lead in a sing-along of some Pop Christmas songs but mostly the standard carols and hymns. There were almost always a goodly number of such folks, and it was not only a lot of fun, but was an extension of the spell for almost all of us in the run-up to Christmas.

I was with a long-time friend—a fraternity brother—who was always *en courrant* about things. We were getting in to the play of the event—singing with a will, mellowing in the moment, awash with the wonder of beautiful music…

For some reason, there were two groups of people, a happenstance sort of thing, and my friend and I were in what could be called the front row of the rear group. Toward the back "row" of the front group I happened to notice a young woman who periodically would turn around about half way now and again, as though looking for someone. Our singing continued, and she kept looking behind her now and again as though searching for someone in particular.

At last we came to the inevitable and haunting wonder of "Silent Night"—*Stille Nacht, Heilige Nacht/ Alles schlaft/ einsam wacht…*

As the members of the crowd slowly fell apart with the inevitable calls to all for a Merry Christmas, chatting each other up or to go their own ways into the evening, the woman I had seen, turned and headed right toward my friend and me.

"That was *you* I heard singing," she said in a voice nearly accusatory.

"Well, I was certainly singing," I said, wondering where she was going with this.

"You have a beautiful voice," she replied. "Do you sing?"

"Wellll…," I smiled, assuming she knew she hadn't stated things quite the way she meant.

"Do you sing *professionally*, I mean," she amended almost curtly.

"Oh no, I answered," as flattered as I had ever been in my life. Flattered and mildly awed. Flattered and mildly frightened.

"You *should*," she said, her voice firm and assured of what she was saying. "You should really take voice lessons from a really good teacher. **Really!**"

And with that, she was gone.

My friend—who understood protocol and enuendo to a fare-thee-well and who always knew who *important* people were—looked at me quietly and with awe.

"You know who *that* was, don't you?" he muttered in his finest way of knowing who Everyone of Importance was.

"No," I said quiely, still under the spell of whatever it was. "No, I don't."

…

I was plagued for a long time after that event, wondering whether I should begin to start the search for a teacher. I knew of one in Nashville—a young lady, a local—who had already gained a fine reputation as an operatic/concert singer and eventually sang lead rolls in European companies, but I never started looking seriously, never made even a first call. At all. I can think of reasons why—even pretty good reasons. But it nagged at me for a long time. Why didn't I bite the bullet and at least get in touch with the person I knew of? She knew and was friends of many people in Nashville I also knew. The worst she could say was she didn't have the time, or she already had as many students as she could handle, or she didn't take beginners, or…

…

So that was the end of that—a "road not taken," as Brother Frost had it: "how way leads on to way…"

And even though a regret still lingers, I had, apparently, made my choice. After all, there's no reason I should or would or could have been more adept at voice than at words.

Nota Bene

I had always thought of the phrase "breaking his own pencil" as coming from the jargon of newspaper newsrooms, in which case it would suggest that someone was retiring.

But later, I realized that it also applied to writers of novels or poetry or history or dramas. In those cases, it usually meant the writer had no more to write—or saw no reason to continue...

"No, 'tis not so deep as a well
Nor so wide as a church door,
But 'tis enough,
'twill serve."
Romeo and Juliet

William Shakespeare

Photo of the author

By
Bonita